PREJUDICES

ROBERT NISBET

PREJUDICES

A PHILOSOPHICAL DICTIONARY

HARVARD UNIVERSITY PRESS
CAMBRIDGE, MASSACHUSETTS, AND LONDON, ENGLAND 1982

LIBRARY OF CONGRESS CATALOGING IN PUBLICATION DATA

Nisbet, Robert A.
    Prejudices: a philosophical dictionary.

    1. Social sciences—Philosophy—Dictionaries.   2. Civilization,
Modern—20th century—Dictionaries.   3. Philosophy—Diction-
aries.   I. Title.
H41.N57 1982   103   82-6157
ISBN 0-674-70065-1

MANY OF OUR MEN OF SPECULATION, instead of exploding general prejudices, employ their sagacity to discover the latent wisdom which prevails in them. If they find what they seek, and they seldom fail, they think it more wise to continue the prejudice, with the reason involved, than to cast away the coat of prejudice, and to leave nothing but the naked reason; because prejudice, with its reason, has a motive to give action to that reason, and an affection which will give it permanence. Prejudice is of ready application in the emergency; it previously engages the mind in a steady course of wisdom and virtue, and does not leave the man hesitating in the moment of decision, skeptical, puzzled and unresolved.

—EDMUND BURKE, 1790

PREFACE

I TAKE PLEASURE in thanking Harvard University Press for the invitation to undertake this book. I was asked for something along the line of Voltaire's *Philosophical Dictionary*, directed to my own age and furnished by my personal observations, likes, and animadversions. Whatever initial diffidence on my part there may have been was dispelled by reflection that for four centuries thousands of people have been writing pieces along the line of Montaigne's *Essais* and thousands of others along the line of Defoe's *Moll Flanders*. In any event, titles notwithstanding, more than a few others have been writing "philosophical dictionaries" these many years. It is a literary form we were given by Voltaire, not a sacred text.

As readers of Voltaire's classic know, that book is neither philosophical nor a dictionary. Neither is this book. It is a miscellany of around seventy topics, choice of which has been mine alone, though not without fertile suggestion from others. The topics range from the historical to the current, the didactic to the whimsical, and the personal to the abstract. That all of the topics reflect the author's prejudices—more in Burke's than in Mencken's sense—goes without saying. My hosts predicted that I would find pleasure in the writing of the book, and I have. If only a small amount of that pleasure is transmitted to the reader, I shall be satisfied.

There are some individuals I must thank with fullest appreciation: Michael Aronson, General Editor of Harvard University Press; Joseph Epstein, Editor of *The American Scholar*; Nathan Glazer, Professor of Education and Social Structure at Harvard University; William Goodman, formerly General Editor at Harvard; and Virginia LaPlante, Senior Editor at Harvard and companion in the preparation of the manuscript for publication. From all five I have had interest, suggestion, and valuable criticism. I am much in their debt. Finally, I acknowledge once again with deepest gratitude what my wife has given to this and other books.

CONTENTS

A BORTION

IT IS A reasonable supposition that the first abortion in the human species took place sometime after a natural miscarriage was recognized for what it was. Primitive woman may not have known the cause of pregnancy, but she knew what to do about it if she was so disposed. Or if the kinship community was opposed to yet another mouth to feed. By the same power that the community could encourage reproduction through appropriate obeisances to the spirits, it could discourage reproduction by termination of fetal life or, when necessary, infanticide. The needs and desires of the kinship group were sovereign.

One thing is certain. Sentimentality about fetal life was absent, as, for that matter, it was absent about the freshly born infant. The physical act of birth gave no sanctity. True birth was a ritual admission to the kinship community, and this never occurred until a period of time had passed during which the decision could be made as to acceptance or rejection. The physical and mental condition of the infant was taken into consideration, as was the ratio of males to females and the balance between population and potential food supply. If the decision was affirmative, the infant received a name and for the first time membership in the clan and household. If it was negative, the child was put to death.

Those who today oppose abortion on the ground that it is destructive of the family have a difficult time supporting their case through history and tradition. No kinship system has ever been stronger and more central in the social order than was the Roman family, especially during the Republic. The sacred *patria potestas* gave the house father authority over fetuses as it did over the lives of members of the family. In the contemporary world it would be hard to find a family system more honored and more important in its authority than that of Japan. But abortion there has for long been easily available. The essential point is that physical birth and also blood relationship have never counted for much in reckoning true kinship, which is social and determined by custom, tradition, and law.

It has been said that every abortion is the murder of an innocent human life. But if this is so, it is odd that there is no record of any religion, including Christianity, ever pronouncing an accidental miscarriage as a death to be commemorated in prayer and ritual. Given the rising intensity of the antiabortion cause, it is entirely possible that such funeral services will begin, but if so, they will not have the sanction of history.

The ancient religions are almost silent on the subject of abortion. In the Bible, there is a detailed listing (Exodus 21–23) of the strict injunctions that God, through Moses, imposed upon the Children of Israel. There is no prohibition of abortion. Indeed the only reference to miscarriage reads: "When men strive together, and hurt a woman with child, so that there is a miscarriage, and yet no harm follows, the one who hurt her shall be fined, according as the woman's husband shall lay upon him; and he shall pay as the judges determine. If any harm follows, then you shall give life for life, eye for eye, tooth for tooth, hand for hand, foot for foot, burn for burn, wound for wound, stripe for stripe." True, there is Jeremiah 1:5 which quotes the Lord: "Before I formed you in the womb I knew you, and before you were born I consecrated you; I appointed you a prophet to the nations." But the words are directed to Jeremiah alone. There is not the hint of generic reference.

Both Plato and Aristotle approved of abortion, the former in the interests of wise population policy, the latter chiefly on the ground that it was an element of the family's proper freedom in the state. Hippocrates' words on the subject are, in the original Greek, somewhat less blunt and categorical than modern takers of the Hippocratic Oath have sometimes suggested. All Hippocrates says is: "I will not give to a woman a pessary to produce abortion." There were other means of abortion known to the Greeks, none of which Hippocrates abjures. In sum, while the ancient world doubtless had its categorical opponents of abortion, one is hard put to find much against the act among the Greek and Roman philosophers.

Abortion was declared a sin by the early Christians, and sin it remained thenceforth in Christianity. But as a sin, it received no special emphasis, falling among the sins of sex outside marriage, adultery, birth outside wedlock, wife abuse, gluttony, pride, and a good many other lapses. It is unlikely that abortion was dealt with in practice by the church differently from the varied other sins which communicants took to confession. After all, though a canon against marriage by priests had existed from the beginning, it was not until the eleventh century that the church began to take steps toward mandatory celibacy. Illegitimacy, contraception, abortion—whatever may be their status as sins, venial or cardinal—have tended to be widely indulged by ecclesiastical and civil governments in Western history, and on the ground generally of the autonomy of the family.

Laws against abortion have been strictest and harshest in the despotisms of history, presumably because of the desire for military recruits, though desire also to weaken the hold of the family over its own should not be discounted. Czarist Russia had very severe laws against abortion. With the Bolshevik Revolution there was a temporary abrogation of the laws, but as the real militarism of the Soviet Union became ever more manifest and the Stalinist dictatorship more oppressive, abortions were once again discouraged and made difficult of attainment, though not actually prohibited by law. Nazi Germany and Fascist Italy both had laws and also incentives designed to increase population and naturally to discourage contraception and abortion. The surest sign of despotism in history is the state's supersession of the family's authority over its own. Often such supersession is justified in the name of conscience or individual welfare.

The contemporary preoccupation with abortion has its roots in the late nineteenth century, a period of many moral preoccupations and of causes to advance them. Although abortion had been a sin in the Christian church from early on, it had taken its place with a large number of other sins. Now, however, abortion became the centerpiece of a moralistic crusade. So did a good many other matters, including alcohol, tobacco, premarital sex, masturbation, meat eating, narcotics, Sunday saloon openings, and Sunday baseball. Contraception, pro and con, was also the subject of moral crusading. Never have so many laws been passed, first by the states, then the federal government, prohibiting so many actions which for thousands of years had generally been held to fall under family authority. It can be fairly argued that the present infirm state of the family in Western society is the consequence as much of moralistic laws assertedly designed to protect individual members of the family from one evil or another as it is of anything else. Current efforts to prohibit abortion categorically and absolutely might be viewed in this light. It is not so much the "woman's right to choose" that is being assaulted as it is the ethic of family and its legitimate domain.

The nineteenth century also generated the romance and sentimentality of children, especially small ones. Before that century, children had been seen pretty much as immature or incipient adults, scarcely as treasures in and for themselves. From their romanticization it was only a short step to romanticizing pregnancy and therewith the fetus. Certain religions, notably but by no means exclusively Roman Catholicism, commenced crusades among their respective memberships against contraception and also forced miscarriage. More and more states and communities passed laws making it illegal to induce miscarriage in a pregnant woman, and abortion mills acquired the ill fame they continue to carry. But all such attention by law and religion has to be seen in the context of the considerable number of actions along the same line—against alcohol, tobacco, prostitution, sex for pleasure, profanity, and others, all novel utilizations of the law and religion which would have been deemed egregious by earlier generations. The Victorian age on both sides of the Atlantic was, from one point of view, a gigantic crusade by the middle class against the mores and folkways of the other classes, upper included. The use of the sovereign powers of the states to achieve success in this crusade was manifest in the epidemic of so-called Blue Laws in America.

Abortion existed in a kind of twilight zone until 1973 when the Supreme Court thrust itself and the authority of the central government into abortion. Prior to that act of nationalization, abortion, though indulged in, was almost universally considered unattractive morally, if not quite as flagrant as birth out of wedlock. Laws, customs, and mores varied widely among the fifty states; in most there were laws forbidding abortion, but the wording differed substantially from state to state, as did the temper of prosecution for violation of such laws. Physicians found guilty of performing abortions were disgraced, but given the simplicity of abortion within the first month of fetal life and the social and economic pressures which play upon all professions—pressures of political influence, friendship, compassion, and the like—it may be assumed that abortions in otherwise morally immaculate physicians' offices were not unknown. The multiplicity of attitudes, the plurality of practices, the diversity of laws and customs in the states, all constituted a twilight area, one in which history— Hegel's "cunning of reason"—might well have disposed of the issue of abortion, as in the past history has disposed of other moral issues thought to be insoluble by reason and law. History disposes as well as proposes, and its capacity for making a burning issue simply irrelevant in due time should never be underestimated.

But any such possibility was destroyed by a majority of the Supreme Court in 1973, in *Roe* v. *Wade*. In that decision the Court summarily wiped out the laws, mores, and customs of fifty states by declaring abortion to be constitutional and legal throughout the nation. At a stroke, abortion was lifted from the twilight zone of pluralism, compromise, and conflicting dogma in which it had lain for millennia and was made the subject of centralized, national mandate. Possibly not since the Dred Scott decision of the Supreme Court in 1857, which marked the Court's arbitrary preemption of another agonizing issue, has a Court decision generated passions of such intensity. If a single cause of the Civil War exists, it must be the Dred Scott decision, which also lifted an issue barely controlled—but controlled nonetheless—by the usual constraints of twilight zones into one that thenceforth moved America inexorably into the bloody and devastating Civil War.

In the present day too, as a consequence of a Supreme Court decision, crusades for and against abortion have reached passionate intensity. Forces of total good are arrayed against total evil, the sure sign of a dogma encased in the struggle for absolute power. On both sides what once existed in the shadows of convention and ordinary adjustment is now bathed in the pitiless glare of the apocalytic. Tragically, some who defend the woman's right to abortion now declare the act of abortion desirable merely as a symbol of woman's escape at last from the tyranny of family role. Abort at will, is the thrust of this misguided propaganda, for only thus can a woman assert her final independence. Zeal in behalf of killing one's own fetus leads the militant abortionists to march happily with lesbians, homosexuals, and others whose interest in freedom is matched by a desire to vent punitive fury upon the family. Thus, ironically, the act of abortion is given, in many circles, the same sacred significance once given to birth alone.

But repugnant as this whole spectacle is, it does not present the danger to the social fabric and to individual liberty that is posed by the ranks of the aggressive antiabortionists. In denying the right of the woman or of her family to terminate pregnancy, these soldiers of righteousness strike at the very heart of both family and individual rights. The effort to pass a law or enact a constitutional amendment abolishing abortion puts this act on precisely the same level of illegality as murder of the most vicious kind or any other felony. To declare the patently inhuman fetus of four weeks "an innocent little baby" is as preposterous as so declaring the sperm and egg at the split second they have united, which is exactly what the more zealous of the antiabortionists desire to be brought about by constitutional amendment. When Mother Teresa leaves her indescribably squalid slums in Calcutta and comes to America to say that "abortion is the greatest poverty a nation can experience," dogmatism triumphs over saintliness. Abortion is indeed regrettable in most circumstances, but by no means in all. It takes inquisitorial cruelty to reach the decision that the fertilized egg must be protected even when it is the result of rape or of a father's systematic sexual abuse of his teenage daughter. No spirit in any way related to the divinity can justify programing the minds of boys and girls to repeat: "I love my mother, but if the choice is between preservation of her life and that of the embryo, I want my mother to die so the innocent baby can live." The moralizing and sentimentalizing about embryo and infant has reached its highest point of intensity in human history in the United States, and there is no sign that its ravaging of the social bond and its wanton commitment of the issue to the centralized state will abate.

Zeal and passion feed on themselves in political-moral causes, as in revolutions.

Such sentiments represent the dissolution of reason, proportion, human experience, and even sound and humane theology. When it is said that all life is sacred and that therefore the life of the fetus may not be terminated under any circumstances whatever—rape, incest, health of mother, economic condition of family—one of the oldest of mankind's perspectives is being violated, that of the scale or chain of being. Doubtless it would not occur to the most fanatical of pro-lifers to declare the existence of a fly the moral equal of the life of a horse or a cow, though it would so occur to the mystics of many faiths in the world, especially in the Orient. Then it should be similarly unconscionable, in the scale of being, in the chain of life that has been cherished in the West since Plato and Aristotle, which is the very spinal column of Christian theology, to declare the barely formed fetus the equal, even the superior in moral status, of the mother or, for that matter, of the lives of other members of the family. Yes, all life is sacred; it has been in one or other perspective for close to as long as man has existed; but from this it does not follow that all life, or even all human life, is equally sacred. And the "innocent" that invariably accompanies reference to the unborn babies comports strangely in a theology that has original sin as one of its foundations.

Still another quintessentially Christian principle of morality which is pertinent to abortion is the principle of development, central in Christian theology from Saint Augustine to Teilhard de Chardin. This too is a borrowing from the Greeks, who almost without exception saw reality in terms of growth and becoming. Goodness, like any other element of reality, must be seen in terms of its achievement, of its realization in time through the actualization of the potential. The true value of the undeveloped, the merely latent or potential, lies in its prospect of becoming developed or fulfilled. The seed is vital of course, or the tender young shoot which promises the grain, but what alone is blessed is the full-grown, fully realized plant or organism.

So with respect to human life. The seed is important, as is the fetus. But the importance of both lies solely within the perspective of development, which does not become real until its *telos*, its end or purpose, is realized. Thus to refer to a first-trimester fetus as "an innocent baby" makes no more sense than to refer to an acorn as an oak tree.

But as far as human freedom is concerned, the most menacing of the proposals made by those who describe themselves as pro-life is that which would define by congressional statute or constitutional amendment the origin of human life in the mother's body. To this end, the antiabortionists declare that soul begins with the union of sperm and egg, thus arrogating to themselves as a special interest political group a judgment that has eluded or troubled some of the greatest prophets and theologians in human history. The pro-lifers' dogmatic insistence upon the sanctity of any and all fetuses is clearly at odds with Pauline Christianity. For the only sexual relation between man and woman that is declared good and holy is that between man and wife, duly solemnized by sacrament. This in turn confers special status or legitimacy upon the issue of such God-made unions. What, however, is to be made of sexual relations between father and daughter, brother and sister, rapist and victim, participants in pornographic spectacles? Are these somehow invested by God with sufficient sanctity to extend this sanctity to the fetus that may be the result of such odious liaisons? In the entire Christian Bible, in the works of the Church Fathers, indeed in the pronouncements and works of any known religion, it is impossible to discover such sanctification.

Rousseau, true founder of totalitarian political theory, asserted: "The most absolute authority is that which penetrates into a man's inmost being, and concerns itself no less with his will than with his actions." In Rousseau's proposed commonwealth all who enter must abandon their native rights and freedoms of any kind, individual or communal, in the interest of the closest and most direct possible relation between the state and the most intimate recesses of the individual spirit. Nothing less than this abhorrent Rousseauian power lies potentially at least in the antiabortionist proposal that the origin of life be made a matter of political or constitutional law. The "power which penetrates into one's inmost being" penetrates into the very womb, fragmenting in the process the moral authority that properly belongs to the family. Define life as the second in which sperm and egg unite, thus making abortion automatically a murder under the Fourteenth Amendment, and heretofore private natural miscarriages will become overnight subject to innuendo, suspicion, perhaps outright arraignment. Rarely has sheer zeal overtaken a moral question in the measure that is found on both sides of the abortion question. What is badly needed at this juncture is a liberal infusion of expediency in Edmund Burke's noble sense of that word.

Hegel noted that the greatest crises of history are not those of right versus wrong, but of right versus right. Who was right and who was wrong in the Reformation? Who, by their own lights at least, was right and who was wrong in the American Civil War, given all the issues attending it—the rights of the states, as well as the abolition of slaves? Who is right and who is wrong with respect to alcohol and tobacco and the abolition of each? Without doubt, impressive cases have been made for the deleterious, often fatal, effects these substances have upon their users and, it is increasingly argued, upon others around the users. From the zealous vegetarian's point of view, the eating of any meat verges upon human cannibalism, just as the killing of any insect is, for the member of certain Buddhist sects, tantamount to the taking of human life, the web of life being seamless.

These are matters to be decided, not by coercive law of the states, but by Burke's "expediency," meaning respectful recognition of the powerful and necessary role in human existence of privacy, use and wont, tradition, and practicality, not to forget larger or long-range consequences. Burke argued that "very plausible schemes, with very pleasing commencements, have often shameful and lamentable conclusions." He added: "Is, then, no improvement to be brought into society? Undoubtedly; but not by compulsion—but by encouragement, by countenance, favor, privileges, which are powerful and lawful instruments. The coercive authority of the state is limited to what is necessary for its citizens."

So much is true and was once descriptive of the situation which existed with respect to abortion. But it appears now that, unless some extraordinary event or change intervenes, passion and zeal and sheer hatred have reached an elevation, a plateau, on which only continuing, worsening war is possible.

ALIENATION

IT SHOULD BE at least a misdemeanor to be found using this word without immediate and explicit referent. Alienation? Of and from what? Even when that question has been answered, though it rarely is, one should remain wary, for on the evidence of much twentieth century writing, the referent is all too often some boneless abstraction or empty generalization. These specimens give one pause: "Anxiety is the natural state of twentieth century man" intones a leading novelist; "crime is caused by alienation" concludes a committee of clerics and others innocent of any knowledge of crime; "America suffers from a spiritual malaise" declares a recent President for want of anything to say on revitalization of the economy; "alienation is the chief cause of revolutions" concludes the editor of a two-volume work on the idea; "the human spirit is alienated by technology from its roots in nature" is said *ad nauseam*. Such declarations give cant a bad name.

Sadly, alienation, anxiety, *angst*, all can be and are learned in the schools. It is a rare course in literature or philosophy that is not anchored in alienation consciousness under whatever actual label. Modern youth is pronounced alienated by its teachers, with the result that youth knows nothing else to do but try to live up to its labeling. Alienation is taught from high school through college as the Gospel once was, chiefly in letters and arts. If there is one thing that has given twentieth century literature and philosophy increasing monotony, it is its combination of subjectivism and the recurrent image of alienation.

Ideally, the word should be confined to the legal context it had for so long. It was clear enough when reference was simply to alienation of property. Nor can one quarrel with the word when used to express the loss of a spouse, though given the current state of morality, it is not likely that many cases will appear in the courts having to do with the alienation of affections, once fairly common.

Law is not, however, the oldest context of the word. That appears to be theology. Wyclif wrote in 1388 of the widespread sloth among clergy as a manifestation of the "alienation of God." By the seventeenth century, the word had acquired political meaning, and Robert Burton noted Alexander the Great's sorrowful recognition of "an alienation in his subjects' hearts." Still later Burke remarked of the American colonists that "they grow every day into alienation from this country." Such uses are unequivocal, direct, and free of sponginess. There would be no reason for eschewing the word today if the simple theological, legal, and political referents were still the standard of usage.

But they are not, and the reason lies squarely in German philosophical thought in the nineteenth century with its limitless capacity to blow up the concrete into the cosmic and the abstract. Borrowing from Protestant theology, Hegel wrote of the self as being endowed with *Entäusserung*, literally "self alienation." It is the nature of the human mind to be alienated, Hegel observed, for there is conflict between the "I" as actor and the "I" or "me" as object. By virtue of the gift of soul or self-consciousness, man is condemned in effect to being an "alienated spirit."

Matters become a good deal worse in the writings of the young Hegelians. Among them is Feuerbach, who announced that all supernatural religion is a reflection of man's alienation or estrangement (*Entfremdung*) from himself. Religion *is* alienation, declared Feuerbach.

Because of some primordial disintegration of the self, man projects into the skies an essential part of his self and calls it God. Thus, what Christian Platonists had centuries earlier perceived as an alienation of man's spirit from God, necessitating man's constant effort to restore, through prayer and meditation, his natural unity with God, becomes, in Feuerbach's treatment, mere anthropology. Man is estranged from himself, which is demonstrated by the existence of supernatural religion. Only the abolition of supernatural religion will rescue man from his alienation.

Marx's reaction to Feuerbach was harshly negative. While agreeing that man's alienation is merely historic, not timeless or rooted in the nature of the human mind, Marx, in a radical break with Hegelianism, took alienation out of a religious context altogether, insisting that it is economic at root: "The positive abolition of private property as the appropriation of human life, is thus the positive abolition of all alienation, and thus the return of man . . . to his human, that is, social life." In sum, this is one more of the numerous secularizations of religious concepts which fill nineteenth century thought. That Marx's theory has elements of the mythic and mystical, despite its resounding emphasis on private property as the sole cause, and that it is as unverified and unverifiable empirically as most of Marx's key concepts, does not lessen its mesmeric appeal. More than a billion people on earth today live in societies whose ruling governments are strongly influenced by Marxian dogmas. And among these dogmas, that of the necessity of worker alienation under capitalism stands high.

However mystical the Marxian concept of alienation might seem, it does have a reasonably explicit and concrete referent: work done in economies based upon private property. The same cannot be said for many of the more popular and seductive theories of alienation in the twentieth century, those, say, of Marcuse and Sartre, into whose initial devotion to Marx have crept alien strains of thought. The present-day view of alienation is a compound of Hegelian ontology, Kierkegaardian existentialism, Freudian struggle between the pleasure and reality principles, Husserlian phenomenology, and the elements of the pathological memorialized in Eriksen's identity crisis and in Laing's studies of the schizophrenic mind. Almost certainly this mélange will take its place in history's dustbin. So will Sartre's once-hypnotic statement of alienation as man's ineradicable picture of the world as meaningless and absurd.

Room is left in serious, rigorous thought for the idea of alienation, but only when it has been thoroughly purged of all such elements of pseudo-philosophy. What is crucial is linkage of the concept with the specific and concrete. There is, beyond question, an alienation from politics, in any and all forms, among rising numbers of citizens in modern times. An alienation from work, irrespective of the kind of economy, capitalist or communist, may well be a growing phenomenon in the twentieth century, what with the decline in importance of such dogmas as progress and the so-called Protestant ethic. An alienation is spreading in Western, perhaps chiefly American, society from certain historic values, such as marriage, family, property, and established religions. Quite possibly the number increases of people who believe themselves to be powerless or who are chronically and irremediably bored with, cynical about, or uninterested in anything beyond their immediate selves and the instant gratification of whatever narcissistic, hedonistic, and solipsistic needs arise in their selves. In sum, when the idea of alienation has been freed from cant, and when it has been given a reasonably precise referent or orientation and made to signify some visible, verifiable form of estrangement or separation of the individual from manifest values and relationships in the social order, the concept can be a useful basis of the study of man, society, and history.

ANOMIE

THE OED pronounces this word obsolete, but that judgment must have been reached quite some time ago, for the word has shown a good deal of life in the twentieth century, and with excellent cause. It is close to indispensable in proper summation of the dislocations and estrangements of life in a century that has seen the disintegration of so many tribalisms, kindreds, villages, neighborhoods, and other social structures which are the common carriers of custom, convention, tradition, and morality. *Anomie* comes from the Greek, from the privative *a*, meaning "without," and *nomos*, meaning the large body of laws, traditions, and mores which people inherit from the past and which provide the norms, values, incentives and constraints in their lives. Gilbert Murray, borrowing from geology, referred to *nomos* as "the great Inherited Conglomerate," drawing attention to the processes of accretion and cumulation by which both the earth's crust and the *nomos* are historically evolved. In ancient Greece, *nomos* had become by the Enlightenment of the sixth century B.C. the preferred word for what earlier had been epitomized by *themis* and *dike*, each flavored with a personality and directness of authority that is not to be found in *nomos*.

Every individual and people possessed a *nomos*, an identifying corpus of custom and convention. Anyone separated from his *nomos* was to be pitied and also feared, as the "lawless" or "masterless" person was pitied and feared in the Middle Ages. Greek drama is rich in the crises of the individual's relationship to family, genealogy, and *nomos*. *Anomia* was the dread state of the conventionless, amoral being.

Although the precise word *nomos* is apparently not found in Homer, the meaning assuredly is. When Homer described the primitive Cyclopes, he did so in the terms that an anthropologist might use to describe a primitive people. The Cyclopes, in Homer's report, are as all mankind once was long ago: without true society, without language, weapons, implements, houses, or cooking—without, in a word, civilization. "They have no gatherings where they deliberate nor any *themistes* (laws, customs), but each one sets his own *themistes* for his womenfolk and his children, and they have no regard for one another." All in all, repugnance, even a certain horror, is the reaction of Odysseus and his men to these savage people devoid utterly of the elements of law, morality, and culture.

In the fifth century B.C., a fascinating concept- and word-drama began, in which the antagonists were *nomos* and *physis*, the latter probably best translated as "nature," meaning not the great outdoors but rather those qualities of human behavior which are inborn, which do not depend for their existence upon conventionalization or socialization through education. The drama began with the Sophists, generally thought to be deeply experienced from their diverse travels in the *nomos* of dozens of societies and therefore relativists when it came to the morally good and right. A Sophist, when asked, "What is right?" could shrug and simply say: "It is one thing here in Athens, something else in Sparta, something else again in Boeotia and Syracuse. Take your choice."

But what began as a kind of skeptical, cynical relativism with respect to *nomos* became the basis for a positive philosophy of *physis* among many of the Sophists and also the artists, dramatists, and political figures whom the Sophists influenced. Far more important than *nomos*, this philosopy declared, is *physis*, that is, the inherent, innate, natural faculties of human beings. Convention and other inherited rules of behavior have their place, but what is most important and what is most to be encouraged is nature and the natural. A distinct cult of the natural sprang up, and it became fashionable to sniff at *nomos*—the conventional morality and social disciplines—and to declare the great superiority of being utterly natural. The classicist E. R. Dodds gave some choice examples: "Be natural," says the Unjust Cause in the *Clouds;* "kick up your heels, laugh at the world, take no shame in anything." "Nature willed it," says an erring daughter, "and nature pays no heed to rules: we women were made for this." "I don't need your advice," says a homosexual; "I can see for myself; nature constrains me." Even incest is dismissed as an offense against the *nomos:* "There's nothing shameful but thinking makes it so."

These quotations are chiefly from Euripides, who probably did not share the anomic views of his characters, and from Aristophanes, who most certainly did not. What was taking place in Athens was the transition from a "shame culture" to, first, a "shameless" culture and then a "guilt" culture, the last two being far more egocentric things than a shame culture, which rests upon the powerful coercions implicit in a society's expressed disapproval of what an individual might errantly do. To be criticized in such a culture is to be shamed and driven to a humiliated resolve never to do that act again. The impact of the Sophists and of their even more extreme philosophical spawn, the Cynics and certain Epicureans, on Athenian shame culture is evident in much written at the end of the fifth century and during the century following, when Plato and Aristotle wrote their great works. Plato, in the eighth book of *The Republic* and in *The Laws* and other dialogues, gives a vivid picture of a shame culture becoming a shameless culture, the latter poised, as it were, for decline into an egocentric, narcissistic, guilt culture. These passages convey a portrait of the anomic individual, one who either has been stripped of the disciplines and guideposts of *nomos* or else has eroded them through uninhibited self-indulgence.

Anomie has ever since been a highly pertinent word to describe certain conditions in a culture or certain types of behavior in an individual. The seventeenth century moralist Lambarde remarked, "That were to set an Anomy and to bring disorder, doubt and uncertainty upon all." About the same time, Hooker wrote of "Men's lusts, animosities, enormities and Anomies." The word seems never to have disappeared in subsequent writing, and in the nineteenth century, especially in France, *anomie* is found more and more often in literature. To be rendered anomic was to be cut off for one reason or other from any "Inherited Conglomerate" of beacon lights and guideposts in culture and thrown back, often in anguish and despair, upon one's own individual resources. Lamennais, the defrocked priest who, for all of his biting social criticism and his active engagement in politics, never got over the loss of the church he had been so intimately and powerfully involved in for close to three decades, once wrote: "As man moves away from order, anguish presses around him. He is the king of his own misery, a degraded sovereign in revolt against himself, without duties, without bonds, without society. Alone, in the midst of the universe, he runs or seeks to run, into nothingness."

At the end of the century, the French sociologist Durkheim made anomie one of the two predominant causes or conditions of the escalating suicide rates in the Western world, the other condition being egoism. Durkheim thought that the psychological affliction of anomie was built into modernity, for the effect of a rising standard of living, of broadened educational opportunities, and of the whole Faustian spirit characterizing modern Western Europe was to stimulate ever new ambitions, desires, and worst of all, expectations. What has been called the revolution of rising expectations cannot help but spread widely the conditions of anomie. To rise suddenly from poverty to wealth, to move from a devout Christianity to a life without any faith whatever, to see one's whole economic world destroyed through depression and bankruptcy, to be ethnically marginal to two or more groups, in but not of each—all this forms the environment for individual anomie. It is not poverty, Durkheim emphasized, that leads to anomie, for the true culture of poverty is one without expectations to be blasted by reality. Thus, there is not only far less anomie among the chronically impoverished but also almost no suicide and a minimum of unhappiness. Anomie is the direct result of changes of economic, social, and religious conditions which in turn lead to changes of self-identification, changes fraught with disorientation and disorder.

Any loss of devout faith can induce anomie. Richard Crossman records testaments of the kind of anomie that was suffered by such intellectuals as Silone and Koestler when, at the end of the 1930s, they found belief in communism and Marxism no longer possible. The old philosophy could no longer merit faith, but there was nevertheless torment in having wrenched oneself from the securities and ties of faith.

In so many places, contexts, and ways anomie rages through the whole twentieth century. The relentless spread of egoism, egocentricity, narcissism, and subjectivism in Western culture has taken a heavy toll from *nomos*, and it is doubtful that any age in history—not in Hellenistic Greece, or in imperial Rome, or in the European Renaissance, so called—can equal the amount and diversity of anomie in the twentieth century West. The anomic individual is seen everywhere: in the schools perhaps most crucially, where under the stimulus of "progressivism" and overall permissiveness the educational

nomos has largely disappeared, leaving hordes of youthful anomics.
The breakdown of family, neighborhood, local community, parish,
and other traditional reservoirs of *nomos* has inevitably meant the pullulation of youths whose anomie ranges from boredom and apathy to
destruction, through chronic violence, crime, and suicide. The death
rate for the young has gone up steadily since 1968, and the reason is
not far to seek, given the proneness of the young toward violence.
Western art, literature, architecture, and other areas of culture all reveal in diverse and fascinating ways anomie—the separation of the
artist and writer, usually by choice, by a kind of craving, from any
nomos. In this respect contemporary artists, novelists, and poets differ
radically from the Melvilles, Hawthornes, and even the Faulkners and
Hemingways of the past who, however bold and original, still had
ties with *nomos* or a *nomos.* Western culture, like that of post-Pelopon-
nesian Athens, has passed from shame to shamelessness and now, increasingly, to guilt. This last stage, on the evidence of public behavior, is still some way off. A more shameless culture though would be
hard to find—in religion, politics, business and finance, education—
everywhere.

Anomie, however, can be, under certain circumstances, tonic
rather than toxic. To a degree, all creative work has implicit a measure of anomie, for the essence of creativity is that the creator move
far enough away from one orthodoxy or conventionality, perhaps in
conscious approach to another, to have the feeling "I am I" more
strongly than he would were he still closely bound to *nomos.* Creation,
like liberty—in contrast to license and anarchy—exists within the interstices of a culture or a "conglomerate." The great difference between the truly creative and the merely nihilistic and rebellious lies
no doubt in the presence among the first group of some degree of the
discipline and guidance of *nomos* while they are making their way toward new mansions in *nomos,* whereas the latter group—so appall-
ingly prolific today—are content with the anomie of isolation from
nomos and with literature and art which are no more than self-
projection or, oftener, self-abuse.

By all odds, the most pernicious form of anomie is that which expresses itself in the philosophy of the goodness of natural man and
the tyrannical effect of all disciplines, coercions, and institutions.
Burckhardt in the late nineteenth century expressed the conviction
that the unqualified belief in the intrinsic goodness of natural man,
the cult of the noble savage, would in the long run lead to a future in
which the savage, with no nobility whatever about him, would triumph. Burckhardt has not been proved wrong. Uncountable savage-
ries have been perpetrated in the twentieth century, commencing

with World War I and the rise of Communist Russia by what Burck-hardt presciently called "booted commandoes," at work creating a social order that would for the first time in history be proper habitat for man—born free and good, but everywhere in chains. The mind boggles at the thought of chains, tortures, terror, murders, exiles, faceless imprisonments, and genocidal slaughters which all have their origin in the fanatical effort to make the world safe for the noble sav-age of Rousseauian delusion. In the revolution of nihilism that is the totalitarian state in this century, anomie and the anomic man are legion.

ATHEISM

ATHEISM IS commonly thought of as the very opposite of religion, and the word's Greek etymology gives justification for this because it means literally "without god or gods." Atheism is therefore held to be the sworn enemy, the potential destroyer, of religion. But this is not so. Chesterton, writing on that dedicated modern atheist Joseph McCabe, bitter renegade Roman Catholic priest and author of count-less learned assaults on all religions, remarked in praise of McCabe that it is not atheism which kills religion, but indifference. And, the Catholic Chesterton concluded, much is owed to McCabe and all other atheists for keeping people from being complacent and then in-different about their religious beliefs.

This function of atheism corresponds to the function that Durk-heim gave to crime in the social order. Vital to the social bond, ar-gued Durkheim, is the individual's sense of commitment to the fun-damental values of a civilized society—such as respect for life and property. If it were not for the occasional act of deviance from these values, as in murder or theft, and the ensuing punishment of the de-viant by the forces representing society, the individual's commitment to the social bond would be weak, wavering, and anemic. Sheer so-cial death would be the ultimate consequence. People are never so re-minded of their devotion to any moral value as when they see it flouted or assailed.

Much more dangerous than atheism to religion are the erosions of devotion to God and his works which are so manifest in many of the mainstream churches today, the Presbyterian, Methodist, Episcopal, and other. Memberships in these churches have been declining spectacularly all the while memberships have been increasing impressively in the evangelical and fundamentalist religions. It is reasonably clear from the contrasting statistics of membership that more and more people have come to feel rebuffed in some of the mainstream churches, rebuffed in their quest for what is essential to religion by ecclesiastical fare that is more often political or sociological than theological. A religion that is not spiritually exacting and directed at the communicant's faith in God and sense of grace is not at bottom a religion at all. It invites the indifference that kills, whereas atheism cannot fail to stimulate faith in considerable degree simply by virtue of the challenge it mounts.

But the paradox of atheism lies in the fact that, its annihilative intent notwithstanding, it becomes itself, willy-nilly, a body of creed, practice, and faith that has conspicuous religious characteristics. The essence of any religion, Durkheim taught, is the sense of the sacred coupled with the community or cult within which this sense of the sacred is held and transmitted to others. Theoretically, as Durkheim observed, anything can become sacred and thus invested with religious potentialities. "God does not exist," stated sufficiently often in meetings of the converted, is bound in time to engender feelings which are no different from some of those described in William James's *Varieties of Religious Experience.* Marx described religion as "the opium of the people." He went on, "Religion is the sigh of the oppressed creature, the heart of a heartless world, just as it is the spirit of an unspiritual situation." But there are millions of people in the world whose relationship to the essential principles of Marxism—the proletariat, the dialectic, class conflict, the socialist millennium—and to the major figures in this philosophy—Marx, Engels, and Lenin—is scarcely less than religious, in the ordinary sense. Marxism owes much to Augustinian Christianity with its Manichean residue of conflict between the City of Man and the City of God, which is to culminate in time in first a thousand years of happiness on earth, then eternal bliss.

Freudianism is much more nearly a religion than a science, inasmuch as the relation between analyst and patient has a great deal in common with that between priest and communicant at confessional, and such ideas as the Oedipus complex, the superego, the libido, and the id exert an effect upon the converted which is almost identical with what flows to the devout Christian from godhead, trinity, grace, and immortality. The religion known as Christian Science is not the less a religion because it believes that all of its constitutive principles are the scientific findings of Mary Baker Eddy. The origin of the word *religion* is to be found in the Latin *religare*, which means "to bind together." Community is the ultimate essence of religion, and that is why such philosophies as Marxism, Freudianism, and atheism are bound to become fresh forms of religion as time passes.

AUTHORITARIANISM

By AUTHORITARIAN SOCIETY is meant one in which governmental repressiveness is habitual, the role of the military is commonly great, and use is made of such practices as torture, imprisonment without due process, and summary, anonymous execution. But at the same time, government in authoritarian as opposed to totalitarian societies is naturally checked in its powers by the continued existence of largely free institutions—family, clan and kindred, church, social class, village and town, cooperative and confederation, all claiming and in large measure receiving corporate rights of autonomy. The values of tradition tend to be very strong in authoritarian societies, particularly the values of kinship, religion, and regional culture. Spain under Franco, Portugal under Salazar, Argentina under Peron, and Saudi Arabia are all examples of authoritarian states in the twentieth century.

But this kind of state has to be seen in historical terms, for the fact is that all modern European democracies are simply developments of what were, down through the eighteenth century in most cases, out-and-out authoritarianisms, in the contemporary sense of the word. England, mother of democracies, was assuredly an authoritarian state under the Tudors. The king ruled by divine right, summary execution was common, star chamber proceedings were equally common, torture was frequently utilized, and the most drastic of punishments—flaying, drawing and quartering, mutilation, solitary confinement in dungeons, hanging, and beheading—were well known under the Tudors and indeed later in English history. Yet the strength of social class, kinship, church, guild, and the like are no more to be underestimated in Tudor England than they are in contemporary Argentina or South Korea, for it was precisely such intermediate institutions which limited the institutional power of the state and made possible the gradual appearance of largely democratic states in the late eighteenth and nineteenth centuries. Tocqueville, Taine, von Gierke, Acton, and Weber are only a few of the historians and sociologists who have shown how these intermediate institutions operated in the historical transition from authoritarianism to modern democracy. Given their long existence, their deep influence in people's lives, and their sheer roles of competitors to the political state, these institutions were bound to apply significant checks to even the most theoretically despotic of early modern European states.

It is possible for a society to be authoritarian and at the same time relatively free of speech and, more important, high in intellectual and cultural creativity. Elizabethan England is surely one of the more spectacular golden ages in the history of culture, and there was a veritable obsession with authority in that age—in considerable but not entire degree the result of England's fear of Spain and its agents and also of Jesuits, so many of whom served as agents of espionage. Even Shakespeare, in his lines which begin, "Take but degree away, Untune that string," makes clear that, for all his occasional need to slip by the pestiferous censor, authority is the absolute condition of any culture. Fiction has often soared in authoritarian societies, for one way to beat the government is by disguising a message in the plot and action of a novel, play, or short story. The Russia of the late nineteenth century was by all odds authoritarian in nature, what with its hereditary monarchy claiming absolute power, its aristocracy, its established church, villages, and strong kinship ties. Such an authoritarian character did not prevent an impressive age of literature, music, and science from materializing. Censors often abound in authoritarian states, but the greatest artists and philosophers have on the whole found little difficulty in circumventing them. In Franco's Spain the word *possibilismo* was a kind of code for the art of getting away with everything possible, through subtlety, wile, arcane specialization, massive erudition, or satire, all calculated to disarm or neutralize the public censor. One does not have to argue for a system of censorship to recognize that in authoritarian contexts it has frequently had a fertilizing influence upon the nuances of language.

Very different are the totalitarian states, peculiarly creations of the twentieth century. Here the state is all-in-all, by its very design a kind of permanent revolution against competing forms of association. Whereas in authoritarian society everything is permitted that is not explicitly forbidden, nothing is permitted in totalitarian society that is not explicitly authorized. The animating objective of the totalitarian state is the obliteration of all forms of association, culture, morality, and convention which are legacies of the past, which lie by their historic nature outside the boundaries of the political, and which, by mere virtue of their existence, represent constant threats to the ideal of monolithic unity in the state. Nothing outside the state, all within the state, and nothing against the state is the way totalitarianism was defined by Italian Fascism in the early 1920s, although if only because of the presence of the powerful Roman Catholic Church and of the sovereign Vatican within the Italian state, Fascism in Italy never became as stringently all-encompassing as did Nazism in Germany or Communism in, first Russia, then a gradually enlarging number of areas—Albania, Bulgaria, China, North Vietnam, North Korea, Cambodia.

Much of the essence but also the fragility of totalitarianism lies in its determination to create totally new values, forms of association, norms of culture, and even individual consciousnesses. Totalitarianism springs directly out of the millennialist, eschatological, and profoundly revolutionary utopianism of the nineteenth century in Europe. Rousseau had given to the legitimate state the primary duty of making citizens, that is, transforming social and cultural man into perfect political man. He followed up with the vision of a political community where the condition of membership was the absolute renunciation of all rights, liberties, and freedoms by individuals, and he charged his paradigmatic or metaphoric legislator with taking from man all of his natural or conventional ideas and dispositions and replacing these with ones that were totally compatible with the general will.

The Jacobin measures in the French Revolution seemed often no more than practical efforts to realize the Rousseauian dream, and it was indeed the effort by the Jacobins to extend their people's state, as they saw their creation, into the minds and hearts of all citizens that gave the French Revolution its totalitarian character. The makers of the American Revolution had been quite content to work with man as he is, shaped by traditional kinship, local, and religious institutions. For the Jacobins, however, nothing would do but the remaking of man through the power of the state. Hence the abolition, commencing in 1790, of the ancient estates, the monarchy, the aristocracy, the communes and provinces, the patriarchal family, the guild, the school and university, and any other structures which, by their long existence, might interfere with the state's work of remaking human consciousness. Within three years France went from an authoritarian society to a form of government in which at least the dream of totalitarianism existed.

But this was no simple development of authoritarianism into totalitarianism; it never is, for the two are diametrically different. In France, as has been the case everywhere else, the revolutionary destruction of authoritarian society was what laid the groundwork for the rise of totalitarianism—everything within the state, nothing outside the state, and nothing against the state. The authoritarian society is distinguished by its tolerance of, even outright support for, nonpolitical, independent institutions. It is this pluralism that makes possible, even under a Franco or a Russian czar, a degree of culture, a level of art and literature, unthinkable in a totalitarian state. There is, after all, a genuine literature in Argentina, Brazil, and South Africa. The Soviet Union, Maoist China, Albania, and a dozen or more other totalitarianisms of the twentieth century are horrifying examples of the near obliteration of any literature, art, and science that is not either created by the state or tolerated by the state for political ends.

This distinction between authoritarianism and totalitarianism throws light upon the degradation of liberalism in the West in the twentieth century, when liberalism began to change from an ideology based in the main upon the ideas of Tocqueville, Mill, and Spencer— ideas that pivoted upon freedom—to an ideology based more and more upon the goals of equality, redistribution, and social reconstruction. Rousseau and in some degree Marx are the patron saints of the new liberalism. This above all is the reason that liberals have such an equivocal attitude toward political power in the modern age. There is enough Mill left in them to endorse such things as the First Amendment, but enough Rousseau and Marx have also crept in to give them dreams of just the right kind of power that would not need any checks whatever upon it. Moreover, from the Enlightenment on, European liberalism has had a vital strain of animosity toward the traditional, toward strong kinship systems, religion, social class, and the like. This explains the current distaste, even repugnance, among liberals for the distinction between authoritarian and totalitarian. It is not that they like or endorse the realities of a North Vietnam or a Soviet Union; it is rather that they instinctively detest more the authoritarian state's retention of social class, private sector economy, religion, and patriarchalism. No matter how many times the phenomenon of a Soviet Russia is repeated by history—quick transition from an early and brief-lived libertarianism to an all-out despotism far severer than what preceded it—liberals live in hope that *this* time—in Nicaragua, El Salvador, even the Cambodia of Pol Pot—it will all be different. The main thrust of the liberal mind in the twentieth century has been in the direction of the totalitarian rather than the authoritarian. Liberal hatred of Maoist China or Stalinist Russia— each with its unequaled record of torture, exile, secret imprisonment, commitment to work-death camps, and genocide—has never come even close to that expended on Franco's Spain, South Korea, or South Vietnam under Diem.

Nothing seems to be more necessary to the future of freedom

than preservation of the sharp distinction between the authoritarian and the totalitarian states, but nothing seems more likely at the present moment than the continued erosion of this distinction. When the point has been reached where the two are declared equal in their despotism, then the way will be opened wide for the triumph of the latter, not only over the former, but over liberal democracy as well. Authoritarianism even at its worst is limited, by the very traditions that it tolerates, and by the inefficiencies which so often attend governments obliged to respect, if not like, powerful kinship, ethnic, and religious institutions.

Yet in the long run, authoritarian states are more stable than are totalitarian orders, for the latter are made inherently fragile by their design: the remaking of human personality. On the natural infinity of individual characteristics the totalitarian government seeks to impose a uniformity born of the totalitarian mystique of a Rousseau or a Lenin. Regardless of what the mystique is called—communism, fascism, whatever—given its mission of the obliteration of human differentiation and the instituting of a general will or some other form of collectivism, it cannot hope to survive very long in history. Such will surely be the case in the current totalitarian states—the Soviet Union, the People's Republic of China, Vietnam. Already the stresses and the resulting compromises are evident. The Soviet's failure to implant the Leninist-Stalinist nightmare in Poland, Hungary, and other nations in Eastern Europe is only too evident. For a short time the absolute terror of Stalinism can bend and break its victims, but in due course it goes beyond the capacities of those, whether in the Politburo or in the guardhouses of the Gulag Archipelago, who must sustain it. And as for the victims, their final power lies in the fact that each new generation is born genetically, evolutionarily, resistant to the imposition of an artificial homogeneity upon it.

BOREDOM

AMONG THE FORCES that have shaped human behavior, boredom is one of the most insistent and universal. Although scarcely as measurable a factor in history as war, disease, economic depression, famine, and revolution, it is far from invisible in either the present or the past. A stream of chronicles, diaries, memoirs, and biographies yields much information on attacks of boredom and their consequences as well as on antidotes or preventives. Suetonius, Petronius Arbiter, Robert Burton, Saint-Simon at the Court of of Louis XIV, and the Marquis de Sade are among those who left observations, reflections, and analyses of boredom. The range of cures or terminations of boredom is a wide one: migration, desertion, war, revolution, murder, calculated cruelty to others, suicide, pornography, alcohol, narcotics. Whether it is Tiberius relishing those he tortured, or Sherlock Holmes taking to the needle, the pains and the results of boredom are everywhere to be seen, and nowhere more epidemically than in Western society at the present time.

Man is apparently unique in his capacity of boredom. We share with all forms of life periodic apathy, but apathy and boredom are different. Apathy is a depressed immobility that can come upon the organism, whether amoeba or man, when the environment can no longer be adequately assimilated by the nervous system, when the normal signals are either too faint or too conflicting. It is a kind of withdrawal from consciousness. Once sunk in apathy, the organism is inert and remains so until external stimulus jars it loose or else death ensues.

Boredom is much farther up the scale of afflictions than is apathy, and it is probable that only a nervous system as highly developed as man's is even capable of boredom. And within the human species, a level of mentality at least "normal" appears to be a requirement. The moron may know apathy but not boredom. Work of the mindlessly repetitive kind, which is perfectly acceptable to the moron, all else being equal, quickly induces boredom in the normally intelligent worker.

Work, more or less properly attuned to the worker's aptitudes, is undoubtedly the best defense against boredom. As Denis Gabor emphasized, work is the only visible activity to which man may be safely left. Keynes observed: "If the economic problem is solved, mankind will be deprived of its traditional purpose. Will this be a benefit? If one believes at all in the real values of life, the prospect at least opens up the possibility of benefit. Yet I think with dread of the readjustment of habits and instincts of the ordinary man, bred into him for countless generations, which he may be asked to discard within a few decades."

There have been workless strata before in the history of society. Think only of the half-million in imperial Rome on the dole and circuses out of a total of two million people. The results were unsalutary, to say the least, and Toynbee gave this "internal proletariat," with its bored restlessness, its unproductivity, and its rising resentment of the government that fed it, credit for being, along with the "external proletariat" or invading barbarians, one of the two key causes of the eventual collapse of the Western Roman Empire. In the modern day, chronic joblessness, especially among youth but in other strata as well, not overlooking the retired elderly, produces its baneful results, ranging from the mindless violence of youth on the streets to the millions of elderly who, jobless and also functionless, lapse into boredom which all too often becomes apathy and depression.

As Gabor further observed, man's central nervous system evolved over millions of years, during which alertness, vigilance, and aggressiveness were necessary to survival. Being necessary, these traits were bound to enter the very essence of man's nervous system. If, as is widely assumed by biologists, few if any significant organic changes have taken place during the past five thousand years, there is certain to be something of a traumatic effect on most people from enforced idleness, unwonted leisure, security from predators, or relative abundance of food. Boredom is in sum a response of the human brain to conditions alien to its long formation.

Satiety is doubtless a key element in boredom. Someone has written that the only thing worse in life than not getting any of what one has struggled for is to get all of it. Boredom is almost certainly the secret canker in utopias, as Schopenhauer warned. B. F. Skinner seemed to think that positive reinforcement would ward off all social ills, but he forgot about boredom with perfect freedom and virtue. Orwell did not forget, and his proles stay content and passive only through endless gin. Huxley, for all his utopians' built-in, genetically formed safeguards, nevertheless provided them with abundant supplies of the drug Soma to raise the spirits of the depressed or bored. In sum, utopians too can lead "lives of quiet desperation."

Boredom resembles authority in one respect. The closer and more confined the setting, the greater the pain to the victim. The worst of tyrannies exist within the intimacies of life, and the same holds for life's boredoms. The very closeness of the relationship gives added poignancy to the individual sentiments or emotions aroused. If one had to choose between absolute despotism in a large country or a small, the former is to be preferred. Its very size makes possible interstices in the net of power which are unlikely in a small tyranny. Similarly, nothing bores like the small group, the intimate relation from which one has become in some degree estranged yet to which one is still bound and confined. There is a large literature on the intolerable boredom generated by small towns where public opinion has a thousand eyes and ears, or by jobs whose monotony leads to mental breakdown, drugs, and drunkenness. One shudders at the thought of the boredom induced on the farms of America in the nineteenth century, especially on the endless flat plains of the Middle West. Cabin fever, as boredom is known colloquially, comes from being pent up for long winters without recreation or even work.

Of all the primary relationships, marriage is probably the most fertile in its yield of boredom, to wife perhaps more than to husband if only because, prior to recent times, her opportunities to forestall or relieve boredom were fewer. There is another side to this, however, and the recent evolution of the Western family is pertinent. In very large degree, as a result of the industrial revolution and the transfer of economic functions once embedded in the family alone to other institutions, the family has largely ceased to be the micro-economy it once was, with each member holding occupational as well as kinship role. By loss of its ancient economic foundations the family has become almost entirely a purely personal relationship. In marriage, this can and does make for closer, more intimate personal relationships of love than were perhaps possible in a domestic economy. But such intimacy of personal relationship, unrelieved by economic functions, by prescribed and necessary roles of provider and homemaker, can also—and it plainly does—multiply the sources of tension, of conflict, and of the onset of paralyzing boredom of mate with mate. Again, work or division of work, mandatory work, can be salutary when personal bliss has been succeeded by personal tension and ennui. Quite possibly God expelled Adam and Eve from the Garden and into the perilous unknown as a way of warding off the boredom that might have come with marriage-in-utopia and perhaps fruitlessness.

Being educated, being an intellectual, does not insulate one from feelings of monotony, tedium, and satiety. Doubtless Hamlet, "sicklied o'er by the pale cast of thought" and finding "weary, stale, flat and unprofitable . . . all the uses of the world," is the heroic example of this. The Marquis de Sade considered himself an intellectual, a *philosophe* committed to revolution, and he has left some respectable writings on political and social matters. But he is nevertheless the source of the word *sadism,* and his vignettes of the exercise of sustained torment and cruelty, saturated by sexual perversion, are unmatched in modern times. Those vignettes are his recipes for release from satiety and the torment of tedium.

Boredom may well have played a part in the tragic death by killing of a young and promising actor in New York in 1981. A famous novelist, known for a long series of bizarre escapes from routine, received some letters from a convicted killer, an inmate of a Midwestern prison. Titillated by the Genet-like celebrations of raw violence and murder in the letters, the famous novelist enlisted the efforts of a famous publisher and famous book review editor in having a book done by or for the pathological inmate. Compliant book reviewers quickly endowed it with the essences of Genet and even Dostoevsky, and a best-seller was formed. Life must have become sweeter for the literary triumvirate. Heady with success, they aided in the release on parole of the inmate-author and brought him to New York for a little lionizing by other literary celebrities and all-round celebrating for the best-selling author that he assuredly was. Whether the literary community wearied of the psychopath-autodidact, as could so easily have happened, is not known for sure. What is known is that the paroled literary celebrity, one early morning in uncontrollable rage, stabbed to death through the back the young actor who served in the coffee shop where the psychopath-celebrity had gone for breakfast. Famous author, publisher, and book review editor were all sorry, as became them, and the matter was generally considered settled and over.

Although the net effects of boredom in history are probably malign, good has also been served by this state of mind. Many an evil dogma, doctrine, or other intellectual continuity has in the end been undone, not by assault, but by boredom on the part of its victims. A secret weapon against the Soviet Union and the Marx-Leninist creed is the stupefying boredom that this creed induces in the minds of the second and third generations brought up under it. In all probability boredom was what ended the dreadful witchcraft craze in the seventeenth century. Certainly the leading lights of the day, most of whom believed as ardently as any peasant in the witches and in the necessity of their destruction, did little if anything to stop the practice. It was not, in short, legal, moral, or religious argument but sheer boredom with the spectacle that won out. "When you've seen one burn, you've seen them all" might well have become in time the saving thought. It is boredom above anything else that brings literary continuities to a welcome end. The public is grateful for Milton, but deplores the Miltonians. So it is with the ascendancy of political parties: the more powerful a party-in-office becomes, the greater the boredom it produces in the public mind.

The sense of emptiness of life is pronounced in almost any onset of boredom. Samuel Johnson, for all his prodigious expenditures of energy, was in almost constant dread of what he called the "vacuity of life." Second only to his fear of the disease of envy was his fear of the psychic affliction under which one sees everything as meaningless, futile, or superfluous. In *Rasselas* the pyramids of Egypt are described as monuments of royal boredom, constructed from the torment of thousands of workers over protracted periods for the purpose of relieving the pharaonic burden of satiety.

Enforced separation from a cherished vocation is a sure recipe for boredom. Much damage was done upon the public weal in ancient Rome when the legionaries were temporarily out of war, chafing to get back to work, making the civil population feel their enforced idleness cum boredom. The knights of the Middle Ages were more dangerous to society when they were not in combat, for the onset of boredom at home could be formidable, its toll commencing with the knight's own wife and children. Ghastly though the American Civil War became in its unending slaughter and epidemic disease, there was no end to the lines of young men fleeing the deadly monotony of farm and village for enlistment under one banner or the other. Boredom even within combat circumstances can drive field soldiers as well as officers into tactics or individual acts bound to yield a heavy harvest of fatalities. Stupidity should not be taken away from the generals of World War I, on both sides, for their appalling movements of vast armies over a few hundred yards of terrain; but neither should one forget the inevitable, galling tedium of trench existence. In sum, war can engender as well as give release from boredom.

There is a history as well as a sociology of boredom. It must surely have been first felt by man when he made the transition some twenty thousand years ago from a hunting or pastoral existence to village life and the tyrannies of soil and season. It is one thing to be mobile, in constant search for security and food. It was something else to face the sheer drudgery of tilling and harvesting and the monotony of life in the village. The word *paradise* comes from the Persian, where originally it meant "wilderness," and there is no doubt a lesson there.

Very probably play came into existence as an anodyne to the tedium of life. *Homo ludens* spelled off *homo faber*. The principal function of ritual in primitive society, it has been suggested by anthropologists, is to prevent boredom. Ritual punctuates the long and dreary sameness of life. Calendars began indeed in the listing and timing of rites and feast-days. Through history and among all peoples religion generally has been a major antidote to what would otherwise be the sense of world-weariness, of passive indifference to life, in a great many minds. The religious "awakenings" which fill the history of religion in the West since the late Middle Ages have their roots, in some degree at least, in the desire for ecstatic release from tedium. Life on the agricultural frontier in the United States could be grim indeed in its relentless tedium, and along with religious enthusiasm, a desperate desire to escape this tedium lay behind the innumerable revivalist camp meetings of the nineteenth and early twentieth centuries. Some of these meetings could be orgiastic on occasion, and a special kind of forgiveness went to those in the backwoods and on the prairies whose occasional evangelical writhings sometimes included unpremeditated copulation in the environs of the revival tent. The very word *revival* suggests that psychological as well as religious inspiration was sought and given.

As for the future of boredom, Harlow Shapley ranked boredom third in a list of possible causes of the destruction of civilization, a list that included nuclear war, natural catastrophe, and pandemic disease. Bertrand Russell concluded: "If life is to be saved from boredom, relieved only by disaster, means must be found of restoring individual initiative not only in things that are trivial but in the things that really matter." One may agree with Russell, but without real hope that such restoration is likely in contemporary society. The modern state through its centralization of power has destroyed or eroded away too many of the historic social contexts of initiative in "things that really matter." Modern technology and industry, for all their benefits to mankind, by their very nature leave more and more people as spectators and mere consumers. Even the demographic foundations of America promise an increase in boredom, for the aging of the population is, short of catastrophe, assured for a long time to come, and old age is a natural prey of boredom, all the folksy retirement centers and organized tours notwithstanding. Durkheim, Freud, and a few others in the late nineteenth century saw unhappiness as positively correlated with the advance of civilization, and their visions of the future were generally pessimistic. Boredom may become Western man's greatest source of unhappiness. Catastrophe alone would appear to be the surest and, in today's world, the most likely of liberations from boredom. If catastrophe has a runner-up in the probability tables, it is a religious awakening of vast proportions throughout the world. Faint signs of this exist at the present moment.

BUREAUCRACY

THIS IS THE new despotism. In America, bureaucracy has become the fourth branch of government, threatening to emasculate each of the other three—executive, legislative, and judicial—the while it lies like a heavy blanket over society, suffocating more and more of the freedoms and rights the Constitution was framed to protect.

A century ago Bryce observed that the major problem of modern democracy is that although societies are increasingly democratized, governments are not. The democratic-egalitarian ethos suffuses the social order—family, church, class, school, and profession—leaving individuals ever more rootless and insecure in their widening separation from institutional authorities and protections. But political government, far from manifesting any of the "tyranny of the majority" that Tocqueville, Mill, and Maine so feared when democracy was beginning to reach its full stride in the nineteenth century, seems to become weaker and more confused. This is the consequence in part of the ravages of special interest groups—the tyranny of the minority— but in far larger part of the octopus-like bureaucracy that now reaches into the most intimate recesses of human lives from the cradle to the grave.

It is no wonder that Parkinson's Law has attained its magisterial position in Western thought. Parkinson, a British historian, discovered by chance that as the British navy steadily declined in size, the number of officials in the Admiralty increased. Ships became fewer and fewer, but the Admiralty bureaucracy prospered. Whereas in 1914 a mere 4366 officials could administer the largest navy in the world, in 1967 there were 33,000 officials to administer "the navy we no longer possess." This phenomenon, by no means limited to the British Admiralty, Parkinson epitomized in the law: "work expands so as to fill the time available for its completion." Protective coloration naturally develops with the organism. Bureaucrats, Parkinson concluded, "seem to have studied the habits of the cuttlefish, which confused its pursuers by the ejection of ink." But the real secret of bureaucracy lies in the "esoterrorism" it produces: "the babble of consultants and the jargon of the London School of Economics." Or Harvard, Yale, and the Brookings Institution, if Americans prefer.

Awareness of the danger posed by national bureaucracy goes back to the middle of the nineteenth century. Mill wrote of the "dominant bureaucracy." Slightly later Carlyle spoke of "the Continental nuisance called 'Bureaucracy.' " American concern with bureaucracy was manifest well before the end of the nineteenth century. In Harper's Magazine there was a hostile reference to "a great centralizer and bureaucrat," and Populist animadversion extended to the government's growing number of unelected, paid officials in Washington. Such awareness and concern in America did not, however, reach the height and intensity of European expressions. After all, until well after World War I, there was a substantial difference in both sizes and proportions.

In America through the early twentieth century the tradition of self-help—individual, state, and local—and of free enterprise was strong enough to render suspect even small increases in the numbers of appointed, paid officials. Not until the administration of Buchanan did the Presidency itself receive from Congress the funds sufficient to support a tiny staff: one full-time clerk and two half-time assistants. How far the country has come is illustrated by the present size of the White House staff, sufficient to congest two large wings of the White House and an entire architectural monster, the Executive Office Building, but never large enough and constantly added to by Republican and Democratic Presidents alike.

By the end of the nineteenth century there were only 100,000 civil servants in the federal government, and these included the military, postal workers, and the staffs provided the several cabinets. Irrespective of relative size and proportion, the President, Congress, and the Cabinet secretaries were never in any doubt of who gave the crucial orders and who obeyed and followed them. Matters were no different in the states and municipalities. Teachers in the public schools, police, and firemen constituted the overwhelming majority of public sector employees, and any thought then that such workers would ever organize for bargaining purposes and actually strike against the public would have been deemed insane. In those years something akin to the feudal ethic of service prevailed, perhaps best symbolized by the respected postal system.

World War I changed much of that. Rarely has the historic affinity between war and bureaucracy been so dramatically illustrated as in the United States commencing in the spring of 1917 when at President Wilson's behest, Congress declared war on Germany and its allies. Wilson's passion to enter that war following his reelection in 1916 was equaled by his passion to wage the war with every possible resource on the home front. To the mobilization of millions of recruits for the armed services was added the almost total mobilization of the economy and of substantial sectors of the social and cultural realms. The result was and had to be an immense enlargement of the numbers in the bureaucracy in order to supervise the war state. Those numbers diminished considerably once the war had been won, but they did not return by any means to their prewar level. Nor was America ever again, after its massive mobilization for the war, the land of localism, regionalism, and decentralization it had been down to 1914.

Second only to war as the breeder of political bureaucracy is economic depression. Even in Tudor times, institution of poor laws led to a rise in the royal bureaucracy that closely followed the rises consequent upon war. In America, shortly before 1930 the concept of the provider-state came into being, and with it an enlarged bureaucracy, which President Hoover, in his desperate efforts to meet the Great Depression, created a significant number of federal agencies and enlarged others.

Ironically, Franklin D. Roosevelt made Hoover's enlargement of the federal bureaucracy one of his primary targets during the campaign of 1932. There must be, Roosevelt declared, an immediate 25 percent cut in the federal budget and in the size of the civil service. But by early 1934, President Roosevelt was well on his way with the New Deal and with it to the largest bureaucracy in American history. The New Deal did little to meet the ravages of unemployment and productivity, but along with instilling hope in many American hearts, through Roosevelt's magnetic personal leadership, it substantially enlarged the federal bureaucracy.

What ended the depression in the United States was World War II. Once again war proved, as it has so many times in history, to be the saving, restoring force when economic fortunes are low. And once again war showed, commencing in 1941, its unfailing power to swell the ranks of bureaucrats. No European power, neither totalitarian Russia nor totalitarian Germany, exceeded the United States in the sheer number of those on the nonmilitary federal payroll. When the war ended this time, there was a conspicuous preservation of bureaucratic agencies which had been brought into being for purely wartime reasons. This or that bureau was occasionally abolished after the war, but much commoner was the practice of relabeling it in accord with whatever new function could somehow be found.

A great catalyst in this process of the bureaucratization of America was the intellectual, particularly the academic class. Once intellectuals had held themselves aloof from bureaucrats, no doubt relishing the old aphorism, "There is more difference between two intellectuals, one of whom is a manager, than between two managers, one of whom is an intellectual." But not during and after World War II. The proudest boast of one of today's social scientists is that he helped run a federal agency in World War II that had 39,000 employees. The fusion that underlay the hydrogen bomb in the late 1940s was no more epochal in the long run than the fusion of intellectual and bureaucrat. Aiding this fusion was the tidal change that took place in the American university, with the absolute and proportionate size of administration rising exponentially for two decades. To manage a school, college, division, or above all an institute or center became the standard faculty dream across the country. Exceedingly helpful to the fusion were the vast federal sums poured into universities. Nothing helps a marriage like property, and indeed there was much property to exchange between the two partners, government and university. The marriage proved fertile, and today a new class, a hybrid of academic and bureaucrat, is everywhere.

Bureaucracy neither dies nor fades away. It is said that Plato's Academy was still in existence, albeit in greatly altered substance and form, a thousand years after his death, in Byzantium. If this is true, one thing is certain: the Academy became, early on, a part of the bureaucracy, ultimately the Byzantine bureaucracy, maze-like in its complexity, rock-like in its durability, but primitive by comparison with the federal bureaucracy in the modern United States.

Once firmly established, bureaucracy can blunt the swords of the most despotic of rulers. Napoleon was responsible for large increases in the French bureaucracy, but more than a few orders and decrees emanating from him as emperor and first soldier in Europe languished or died once they had entered the corridors of bureaucracy. Albert Speer, Nazi intimate of Adolf Hitler, reported that through much of World War II Hitler—Reichsfuhrer, absolute ruler of the state that was to last a thousand years—tried, without success, to have his World War I pension increased by the office of pensions in Germany to the level he believed he had earned as a combat soldier wounded in action in that war. For good or bad, many a despot has undergone a like experience. So have a good many nondespotic presidents and prime ministers of the twentieth century. Roosevelt, Truman, Eisenhower, Kennedy, Johnson, and Nixon—all are on record for the sense of frustrate fury that comes when the constitutional chief of government is unable to realize a legitimate objective because of the obtuseness of a bureaucracy that is more loyal to its channels and hierarchic levels than to the elected President of the United States. The very essence of bureaucracy is to say no—in a hundred different ways.

The relationship between democracy and bureaucracy is paradoxical, as Burke, Tocqueville, and Weber all recognized. The expansion of the corps of paid functionaries in Europe and their gradual replacement of those who, in the feudal tradition of service, were unpaid, living by the dogma of *noblesse oblige*, took place among the same historical currents as did the rise of democracy. Burke, in commenting on the French Revolution, pointed to the almost instantaneous swelling of the ranks of bureaucrats, placing them among the "sophisters" and "new dealers" he so despised. He caught also the full significance of the Jacobins' strategic obliteration of the old centers of patriotism in France, the communes and the provinces, and their ingenious establishment of new ones, such as cantons and departments. Long before Orwell, Burke knew that the aims of despotism can best be furthered by wiping out memory of the past and that this means the creation of new contexts of memory. But he also saw the inherent weakness of the new contexts. "No man was ever attached by a sense of pride, partiality, or real affection to a description of square measurement. He will never glory in belonging to District 71 or to any other badge ticket." And so it has turned out in the subsequent history of bureaucratic rationalization.

Tocqueville was profoundly aware of the historical affinity between democracy and its combined centralizing and leveling tendencies and the spread of bureaucracy which served both tendencies. It is possible, Tocqueville wrote, to measure the advance of democracy by the increase in number of paid servants of the state over the unpaid. Every fresh upsurge of democracy is followed immediately by an upsurge of bureaucracy. But the most powerful of Tocqueville's strictures on bureaucracy came when he described the kind of despotism that democracy has most reason to fear: "Above [the people] stands an immense and tutelary power, which takes upon itself alone to secure their gratifications and to watch over their fate. That power is absolute, minute, regular, provident and mild. It would be like the authority of a parent if, like that authority, its object was to prepare men for manhood; but it seeks, on the contrary, to keep them in perpetual childhood: it is well content that the people should rejoice, provided they think of nothing but rejoicing. For their happiness such a government willingly labors, but it chooses to be the sole agent and the only arbiter of that happiness; it provides for their security, foresees and supplies their necessities, facilitates their pleasures, manages their principal concerns, directs their industry, regulates the descent of property, and subdivides their inheritances: what remains but to spare them all the care of thinking and all the trouble of living . . .

"After having thus successively taken each member of the community in its powerful grasp and fashioned him at will, the supreme power then extends its arm over the whole community. It covers the surface of society with a network of small complicated rules, minute and uniform, through which the most original minds and the most energetic characters cannot penetrate, to rise above the crowd. The will of man is not shattered but softened, bent and guided; men are seldom forced by it to act, but they are constantly restrained from acting. Such a power does not destroy, but it prevents existence; it does not tyrannize, but it compresses, enervates, extinguishes, and stupefies a people, till each nation is reduced to nothing better than a flock of timid and industrious animals, of which the government is the shepherd."

It is almost certain that Max Weber, the most systematic and

learned of students of bureaucracy, was well acquainted with both
Burke and Tocqueville. Certainly their insights are to be seen in
Weber's "principle of rationalization" in modern European history.
Rationalization is the historical process that involves "the disenchantment of the world," the loss of the traditional, the personal, the charismatic, and the purely human, and the substitution for these of the
rationalized—whether in politics, education, the military, or the economic realm. Bureaucracy, for Weber, is simply the infusion of this
larger rationalization in the political process, an infusion that destroys
or cripples the traditional and the charismatic in politics. Weber detested most of what he saw in the way of the bureaucratization of society. Everywhere, in government, schools, churches, and business
firms, Weber saw only functionaries, bureaucrats. "It is horrible," he
wrote, "to think that the world will one day be filled with nothing
but those little cogs, little men clinging to little jobs and striving to-
wards bigger ones . . . This passion for bureaucracy . . . is enough to
drive one to despair."

With every reason Weber despaired. It is unlikely that anything
short of catastrophe—of the kind perhaps that destroyed the Roman
imperial bureaucracy in the sixth and seventh centuries, namely the
barbarian invasions, which laid the foundations for the feudal system
with its almost total absence of bureaucracy—will do what is necessary. There is so much in contemporary society that not only invites
bureaucracy but is ultimately dependent upon it. Big business, public
education, medical care, social welfare and security in all its forms,
are only a few of the institutions in American life which have by now
become utterly enmeshed in governmental regulation. The single
most popular ideology in the United States, on the evidence of the
last half-century, is liberalism, and this creed, far from being what
Mill lauded, is little less today than a vast celebration of bureaucracy,
or at least of the governmental interventions in society which automatically bring with them a network of bureaucrats. Liberalism has
its own distinctive affinity with war and the social opportunities
created by war. Were von Clausewitz alive today, he might emend
his "War is the continuation of foreign policy by other means" to
"War is the continuation of social policy by other means." Even conservatism, however, seems far more interested today in capturing Leviathan for its own uses than in freeing human beings from it.

Chesterton once said that the bureaucrat is like an inverted Mi-
cawber, always waiting for something to turn down. But today's bureaucrat, nurtured by the vitamins of progressive liberalism throughout his life, is equally pleased to turn up, turn out, turn over, turn in,
and of course turn on. The greatest problem that is presented in this

whole sphere of government is the fact that the children of the bureaucratic welfare state, the countless recipients of bureaucratic aid,
have come, in true Freudian fashion, to hate their father. How that
love-hate relation will be resolved is one of the more interesting
prospects of the next half-century.

CHAIN OF BEING

THIS IDEA ILLUSTRATES as well as any the kind of power that can
be exerted by a metaphysical concept for twenty-five hundred years
upon the human senses, and more, upon the sciences, natural and social, lasting well into the nineteenth century. The idea of the universe
constituting a chain of being goes back to Plato, who arrived at it, as
he arrived at most of his ideas, through intuition and contemplation
of the requisites for perfect being. Everything in a perfect universe
must constitute a continuous, ascending series of things or beings,
rising from the smallest bit of matter on earth all the way through
the organic kingdom and to the great universe over which a perfect
God presides, while also completing the chain. Such a chain, Plato
concluded, has to express the "reign of a rational divine power in all
that exists and all that comes to pass in the world." The reference to
the future highlights the fact that, contrary to the common view
about Plato's inability to see more than a fixed world of fully
achieved perfection, he could see his chain of being in dynamic as
well as static terms. There is more than a hint of Aristotle in these
words.

Aristotle's *scala naturae* is no more than a revision of Plato's chain
of being, but it was the first instance of the triumph of a metaphysical assumption over perceived reality in respect to the chain of being.
For Aristotle was a professional naturalist who spent much of his and
his students' time in collecting specimens from far-flung places. As a
naturalist, he knew that, from the evidence at least, there is no chain
of being, no perfect continuity of either inorganic or organic being.
On the contrary, what is revealed is discontinuity, substantial breaks
and gaps in the *scala naturae*. Nevertheless, Aristotle wrote: "Nature
proceeds little by little from things lifeless to animal life in such a
way that it is impossible to determine the exact line of demarcation
nor on which side thereof an intermediate form should lie." More
than anyone else, Aristotle communicated the idea of a chain of

being to natural philosophers and scientists from Lucretius to Darwin.

One other idea, equally metaphysical, equally based upon intuition and imagination rather than observation, is pertinent in this context: the idea of plenitude. This too is a creation of Plato and accords with his philosophy of perfection. Everything that can be in the universe, wrote Plato, is. Whatever the rational mind is able to conceive in the imagination as necessary to plenitude and perfection has already been created, even though it may not be seen. A perfect intelligence could only have created a perfect world and universe. No gaps, no omissions, exist; there is fullness, plenitude. Aristotle accepted this view, adding only that many of the substances may have come into and already gone out of existence, or even that many may not yet have come into existence. But of the plenitude of things, Aristotle had no question or reservation.

The concepts of both a chain of being and plenitude were resplendently existent in Roman thought, especially in Lucretius, Seneca, and Pliny, and also in the writings of the Church Fathers. Belief in the chain of being grew steadily in the Middle Ages, nowhere more lushly than in Aquinas, and was among the many ideas to be conveyed directly from the medieval to the modern world. At no time in its history did the chain of being enjoy greater popularity than in the philosophy, science, and poetry of the seventeenth and eighteenth centuries.

The most influential expositor by far of the idea in the modern world was Leibniz, who built his whole system of thought around the two ideas of the chain of being and of plenitude. He related them to the march of evolution or history: "And to the possible objection that, if this were so, the world ought long ago to have become a paradise, there is a ready answer. Although many substances have already attained a perfection, yet on account of the infinite divisibility of the continuous, there always remain in the abyss of things slumbering parts which have yet to be awakened, to grow in size and worth, and in a word, to advance to more perfect state. And hence no end of progress is ever reached." Equally pertinent is Leibniz's "law of continuity," epitomized in his phrase *Natura non facit saltum* (Nature never makes leaps): "Everything goes by degrees in nature and nothing by leaps, and this rule as regards change is part of my law of continuity . . . Accordingly men are linked with animals, these with plants, and these again with fossils, which in their turn are connected with those bodies which sense and imagination represent to us as completely dead and inorganic."

No one expressed more charmingly the idea of the chain of being than did Alexander Pope:

Vast chain of being; which from God began,
Natures aetherial, human, angel, man,
Beast, bird, fish, insect, what no eye can see,
No glass can reach, from Infinite to thee . . .
Where, one step broken the great scale's destroy'd;
From Nature's chain whatever link you strike,
Tenth, or ten thousandth, breaks the chain alike.

The brilliant young Turgot in 1750 first placed the idea squarely and almost irremovably in the social sciences. Turgot, explaining the successive advances of the human mind, rested his case essentially upon the chain of being: "All the ages are linked together by a chain of causes and effects which unite the existing state of the world with all that has gone before . . . [and] the existing state of the universe, in presenting at once in the earth every shade of barbarism and refinement, shows us in a manner at a single glance the monuments, the vestiges, of every step taken by the human mind, the likeness of every stage through which it has passed, the history of all ages."

Down through the present century, the effect of this chain-like representation of human cultures and societies on earth has been profound. The vaunted "comparative method" of sociologists and anthropologists in the nineteenth century was hardly comparative in any proper sense of the word. The early eminences in the social sciences conceived of mankind as a single, ascending, chain of cultures and civilizations, commencing with, say, the Australian Aborigines and reaching, link by link, a final height in, naturally, Europe. The influence of the Leibnizian metaphysical pronouncement on continuity, "Nature never makes leaps," was deep and almost universal. "From the wretched inhabitants of Tierra del Fuego to the most advanced nations of western Europe," declared the founder of modern sociology, Auguste Comte, "there is no social grade which is not extant in some points of the globe, and usually in localities which are clearly apart."

The passages from both Leibniz and Turgot are unambiguous statements of development or evolution. What distinguishes the eighteenth century's expressions of the chain of being from those before is their "temporalizing" of the chain, to use Arthur Lovejoy's apt word. There is the chain of being, but more important, there is the development that mankind has undergone through ages precisely in accord with the chain, in step-by-step fashion. Comte based his whole perspective of social dynamics on this temporalizing: "The true general spirit of social dynamics consists in conceiving of each of these consecutive social states as the necessary result of the proceeding, and the indispensable mover of the following, according to the axiom of Leibniz—*the present is big with the future.* In this view, the object of science is to discover the laws which govern this continuity, and the aggregate of which determines the course of human development." Literally no important figure in the study of social change and development, not even the revolutionists such as Marx and Proudhon, deviated significantly from Comte's statement of the developmental chain of being in society.

In the biological sciences also in the eighteenth century the ideas of the chain of being and plenitude prospered. In the writings of such notable biologists as Buffon, Cuvier, Maupertuis, Bonnet, and Erasmus Darwin, grandfather of Charles, the theory of biological evolution was first set forth lucidly and comprehensively. Although some held firmly to the separation of the species, envisaging evolution in the Aristotelian terms of intraspecies, others anticipated Charles Darwin in stressing the linkage of the species in time through the emergence of one from the other. The Platonic vision of perfect, uninterrupted, absolutely continuous nature and of plenitudinous nature reigned widely, though it is doubtful that any of the evolutionists had the remotest notion of the origin of their visions of the past and present. Breaks in the chain were as obvious to the naturalists of the eighteenth century as they had been to Aristotle, but this merely intensified the search for "missing links."

Erasmus Darwin chose to put his theory of organic evolution, complete with the concept of natural selection, into poetic form:

Organic life beneath the shoreless waves
Was born and nurs'd in ocean's pearly caves;
First forms minute, unseen by spheric glass,
Move on the mud, pierce the watery mass;
These, as successive generations bloom,
New Powers acquire and larger limbs assume;
Whence countless forms of vegetation spring,
And breathing realms of fin and feet and wing.

It was in the eighteenth century that Linnaeus brought Aristotle up to date with his own vastly more comprehensive classification of an immense diversity of life. Like Aristotle and everyone else, Linnaeus found no perfect chain of being in fact, but this did not prevent him from conceptualizing the chain and from assuming, as Leibniz had, that if the full record of past as well as present could be known, it would reveal a perfectly continuous chain. Linnaeus had a very clear idea of the evolution in time of what he classified: "All the species of one genus constituted at first one species . . . they were subsequently multiplied by hybrid generation, that is, by intercrossing with other species."

Lamarck, who has been called the most important interpreter of the biological world between Aristotle and Charles Darwin, accepted fully the implications of the chain of being and of plenitude, and he knew, moreover, that both ideas had come from the Greeks: "In considering the natural order of animals, the very positive *gradation* which exists in the increasing complexity of their organization, and in the number as well as perfection of their faculties, is very far removed from being a new truth, because the Greeks themselves fully perceived it; but they were unable to expose the principles and the proofs, because they lacked the knowledge necessary to publish it."

Lamarck recognized that the vast majority of those who had seen organic nature in terms of a perfect scale of being, commencing with Plato himself, believed this scale or chain to be the result of the infinite imagination of the Creator, one that foresaw all possible species. But Lamarck disagreed: "My *personal conclusion:* nature, in producing successively all the species of animals, and commencing by the most imperfect or the most simple to conclude its labor in the most perfect, has gradually completed their organization; and of these animals, while spreading generally in all the habitable regions of the globe, each species has received, under the influence of environment which it has encountered, the habits which we recognize and the modifications in its parts which observation reveals in it."

The conception of a perfect chain of being and of plenitude dominated the mind of Charles Darwin just as much as it had his grandfather and the other evolutionists of the eighteenth century. Darwin frequently cited the Leibnizian *Natura non facit saltum* in the *Origin of Species,* often using it in almost incantatory fashion when the evidence did not support his theory. The most striking instance of the hold of the chain of being on Darwin's mind occurred in his discussion of the bearing of paleontological and geological evidence upon his theory of gradual and continuous evolution. He would not have known, he admitted, how "imperfect" this evidence was had it not run so diametrically counter to the maxim "Nature never makes leaps." Equally potent on Darwin's mind was the doctrine of plenitude.

Two minds in the eighteenth century, however, were not captured by Plato's seductive metaphysics of the chain of being: Dr. Johnson and Voltaire. Thus Johnson wrote: "This Scale of Being, I have demonstrated to be raised by presumptuous Imagination, to rest on Nothing at the Bottom, to lean on Nothing at the Top, and to have vacuities from step to step through which any order of Being may sink to Nihility, without any inconvenience, so as we can Judge, to

the next Rank above or below it . . . It appears how little Reason
those who repose their Reason upon the Scale of Being have to triumph over them who recur to any other Expedient of Solution, and
what difficulties arise on every Side to repress the Rebellions of presumptuous Decision."

Voltaire had this to say in rebuff of the concept of a chain of
being: "At first imagination delights to see the imperceptible transition from brute matter to organized matter, from plants to zoophytes,
from these zoophytes to animals, from these to man . . . and finally to
a thousand different orders of these substances which, through degrees of beauty and perfection, ascend up to God himself . . .

"[But] this chain, this so-called gradation, no more exists among
vegetables than it does among animals. The proof of this is that there
are species of plants and animals which have been utterly destroyed
. . . And then, how could you have, in the great empty spaces, a chain
that linked everything? If there is one, it is surely the one that Newton discovered; the one that makes all the globes of the planetary
world gravitate toward one another in the immense void.

"O, much admired Plato! You have told nothing but fables."

Bravo! But for every Johnson and Voltaire, there are, even today,
thousands for whom any questioning of either the chain of being or
plenitude smacks of heresy in the dread form of creationism. Not for
them any nonsense about the evidence. With Robespierre they are
able to say, "Perish the colonies rather than a principle." And of
them may be said what a Victorian wit said of Herbert Spencer: "His
idea of a tragedy is a beautiful theory ravished by a gang of brutal
facts."

CHRISTIANITY

THERE IS A striking paradox in this world religion, one present almost from the beginning of its history. The precepts and admonitions
on which Christian faith is founded are overwhelmingly directed toward heavenly things and toward man's hope of departing this world
in order to reach the next. Yet the original success of Christianity in
first and second century Rome, and its continuing success through all
subsequent ages in the West, are results, not of doctrinal emphasis
upon heaven, but of Christianity's supervening attention to the

worldly—to the physical, historical, and social challenges of this world. Three crucially important attributes of Christianity, not one of which is heavenly in content or thrust, are, first, the religion's early and persisting concern with the social, more specifically with *organization;* second, its early and lasting philosophy of history, deeply rooted in and overwhelmingly concerned with life on this earth; and third, its unambiguous stand, unique in world religions, on the obligation to govern, develop, exploit if necessary, the earth and life upon it.

All three of these attributes draw, not from the basic teachings of Jesus, but from ideas and practices acquired by early Roman Christians from Judaism and Greco-Roman culture. Had the fate of Christianity depended solely upon, say, the Sermon on the Mount, it is unlikely in the extreme that the Christians would have defeated their formidable religious rivals in early imperial Rome.

First in significance is the profoundly social character of Christianity, a character reflected in theology in impressive measure, as in the Communion of Saints, the hierarchy of angels, and the City of God, but far more significantly, in the actual social structure of the religion on earth. The communal foundations were established early on: the multiplicity of small, cohesive, family-like communities within which the Good News was assimilated and passed on to succeeding generations. As a number of historians of Christianity— Taine, Murray, and Latourette among them—have stressed, the only proper way to see primitive Christianity is not as a church, least of all as a unified, organized church, but rather as a congeries of tiny communities, each autonomous, scattered through Roman civilization, all having in common a few beliefs about Jesus, his redemption of man, and his assurance of heavenly bliss for the faithful, for those who would prepare for salvation.

What is important about these communities is somewhat less their beliefs than their social structure. Judaic precedent was crucial here. The Essenes and other ascetic Jewish communities were founded not only on worship of the Law and on belief in immortality but also on the very practical ethic of cooperation, brotherhood, and even common ownership of property. Such communities had existed for a century or two prior to the appearance of Jesus, and it is probable that from the very beginning those Jews who chose to follow and to revere Jesus and the God he was descended from organized themselves into communities very much like the one described in the Dead Sea Scrolls. The communal essence of apostolic Christianity is in every important respect a borrowing from Judaism.

The appeal that these small Christian communities had in the Roman Empire, especially in its cities and towns, was as much social and this-worldly in character as it was spiritual. The promise of heaven for the saved was attractive enough, but there were many religions in Rome which had heaven and salvation to offer. What Christianity had to give in addition to the imminent security of heaven was the more immediate security of life, mind, and fellowship on this earth. Most if not all of these communities were burial societies, important enough in itself but also important as a means of neutralizing official Rome's suspicion of all intermediate groups and associations. But certainty of proper burial was only one of the kinds of security that a Christian community could give to its converts, so many of whom were from the ranks of the rootless, the alienated, and the disinherited in Roman society. Mutual aid in economic as well as religious matters was important. Though it is unlikely that all Christian communities were built upon common ownership, the letter of Pliny the Younger to the emperor on these communities, which Pliny had been asked to investigate for potential subversive nature, shows that some of them were communistic as well as communal. Not least in importance was the social and psychological security that came from the fact of membership, close association with others, and the whole sense of extended family.

The last cannot be overestimated in importance in Rome. Throughout the history of the Roman Republic the family, based upon the *patria potestas*, was the pivotal unit of Roman life. And although this family system was beginning to weaken in structure and appeal as the result of legal invasions of family autonomy by the Caesars—bent upon the centralization of society as well as state and upon the removal or weakening of all associations, family included, which challenged or threatened this centralization—it remained a luminous model. From earliest times apparently the nomenclature of kinship was adopted by the Christians in their small societies, for the terms *mother, father, brother,* and *sister* had become important and fully accepted by Christians in their relationships with one another when in the third century Christianity took on a more or less unified and organized form.

A conflict must have existed between these novel, Christian, family-like communities and the actual families in Rome. Just as the twentieth century has seen the rise of religious organizations which in effect seek to take, through conversion, children from their parents, and which on occasion are bitterly resisted by the parents of the children, so must such conflicts have existed during the early phases of Christianity. Not every *pater familias* could have taken lightly—even after his traditional authority had been diminished by the Roman state—to the loss of son or, more often, daughter or even wife to a

Christian commune. The conflict between Christianity and Roman family was a suitable and perhaps evocative context for the adjurations of Jesus himself on religion and family. In Matthew 10:34–39 Jesus insists that "he who loves father or mother more than me is not worthy of me." In Mark 3:31–35, after being informed that his mother and brothers are seeking him, Jesus says, "Who are my mother and brothers"? Then, looking out to his congregation, he concludes: "Here are my mother and my brothers! Whoever does the will of God is my brother, and sister, and mother." Jesus could wax militant, as in Luke 14:25–26: "If anyone comes to me and does not hate his own father and mother and wife and children and brothers and sisters, yes, and even his own life, cannot be my disciple." How far these are accurately related declarations of Jesus, and how far they are later declarations by the authors of the synoptic gospels in their war with the Roman family, which was a form not only of kinship but also of religion and thus inevitably an obstacle to Christian proselytization, is difficult to say. But the very intensity of the assault upon traditional kinship is a strong indication of the familial character of the Christian community.

By the third and fourth centuries in Rome much of this early communal character of Christianity was gone, succeeded by an ever more organized, rationalized system of government that drew a good deal from the Greco-Roman political tradition, especially the Roman, with its centralization and departmentalization of function and authority. Bishops appeared all over, in many instances with authorities reminiscent of those enjoyed by earlier Roman custodians of the public rites. Just as the Sacred City was the center of the Empire, so it, through the bishop of Rome, became the center of Christianity. What the early Christian communities had begun was continued, *mutatis mutandis*, by the constantly growing bureaucracy of the church, which provided firm structure and authority to protect faith and to repulse error and heresy.

But important as the official organization of the Christian religion became, lasting to the present day, even more important was the continuation of the communal ethic that had come into being so concretely in the cities of the Roman Empire. The tiny communities disappeared for the most part, but their pristine existence survived in church lore to serve as a model for many an eruption in the social history of Christianity. The whole monastic tradition that began with Saint Benedict and perpetuated through all succeeding centuries the ideal of communality, the numerous communal sects spawned by the Reformation, the rise in the nineteenth century of Catholic guilds, cooperatives, and trade unions in Europe—all of this and more must be seen as in lineal descent from early Christian communalism. If, as is often claimed, Western socialism really began in More's *Utopia*, then it began in monastic communalism in substantial degree, for More's veneration of the monastic ideal lay behind a good deal of the communal form of society in which he placed his utopians.

Second only to the ethic and spirit of community in the history of Christianity's early triumph and lasting authority in the world is the philosophy of history that the early Church Fathers, Saint Augustine foremost among them, gave to Christianity. This force too is Judaic in origin, deriving from the sacred history set down by the Jews in the old Testament. History was sacred because every element— every thought, act, movement, birth, marriage, death—in the life of mankind on earth was declared, first by Jews, then by Christians, to be the work of an all-powerful, omniscient, and omnipresent God.

But what appears in the Old Testament is history rather than a philosophy of history. Moreover, it is an account of the Jews alone, or of those peoples who come into the history by virtue of Jewish contact with them. In the works of Tertullian, Eusebius, and most effectively, Augustine there appear the real beginnings of both universal history and, within this, philosophy of history. Borrowing heavily from Greek philosophical thought, Augustine fused with Judaic sacred history the Greek metaphysical elements of teleological unfolding in time, naturalness of all growth, necessity of all growth, a design embedded in the very origin of the whole process, and a fixed, predetermined succession of stages of mankind's historical development.

There was practical and worldly genius in the fashioning of world history that Augustine laid out in his *The City of God*. It was not enough simply to declare the goodness and truth of Christianity before pagans. The religion must be presented in the garments of not just truth but a truth that can be put in the form of historical necessity. The ultimate goal of Christians was ascent to eternal heaven, and such ascent was to be the reward of all who believed in the Christian God. But what Augustine did was to put this next-worldly existence as the final stage of a developmental series of epochs that had begun with the Creation, that is, on earth, in this world. Moreover, the protagonist was not a single chosen people but all mankind, this irrefragable unity the consequence of all mankind's descent from Adam, "a solitary," whose own singleness of being must lead to a singleness of the human race. Mankind, Augustine maintained, has gone through five necessary, sequential stages and is now in its sixth. This stage will terminate sometime, though wisely he avoided precise forecast, to be followed by a seventh stage, still on this earth, within which the good and the just will live a spiritual and tranquil exis-

tence for an untold, unknowable period of time. After this millen-
nium-like stage has reached an end, the eighth and eternal stage will
commence, characterized by the ascent of the blessed and thereafter
by the destruction once and for all of the earth and everything left on
it.

Thus the worldly is made to serve the next-worldly. By demonstrating that the history of mankind on earth can be seen in terms of
five already completed and absolutely necessary stages, by promising
an end to the sixth stage in which all peoples now live and the advent of a seventh and final earthly stage, Augustine was able to put
heaven, the eighth and final stage of history, in the realm of histori-
cal-developmental necessity rather than of hope alone. A millennium
and a half later Marx, who must be regarded as a heretic in but still a
part of the Judeo-Christian tradition, lifted his own brand of utopianism above the brands of his competitors by putting the socialist millennium into a philosophy of the history of mankind that is no less
deterministic than Augustine's. It is religion, and perhaps above all
Christianity, that has made clear even to secularist nonbelievers the
winning superiority of a faith or doctrine that goes beyond the
merely desirable and wished-for to the realm of the inexorable. It is
so much easier to make sacrifices for a promised land that has been
declared inevitable.

The third and final worldly penchant of Christianity is the insistence upon seeing nature as something not only totally separate from
man but, infinitely more important, subject to man's complete domination. Here too the Judaic contribution is crucial, for this view of
man's relation to the physical world goes back to the passage in
Genesis 1:28: "Be fruitful, and multiply, and replenish the earth, and
subdue it; and have dominion over the fish of the sea, and over the
fowl of the air, and over every living thing that moveth upon the
earth."

That theme has been an integral part of the mainstream of Christianity. Only in occasional heresies or near heresies has there been
anything in Christianity suggestive of the numberless cults and faiths
in the world in which man and nature are deemed a single reality, in
which the kinship of man and nature—in the sense of the earth's
crust and all that lives on it—is pronounced so close, so continuous,
that man dare not exploit nature lest he be exploiting himself. One
such case is that of Saint Francis, who has been called the "greatest
spiritual revolutionary in Western history" because he denied man's
dominion over nature and sought to establish the doctrine of total
equality between man and all forms of organic life. Only by a hair's
breadth did this extraordinary man escape the heretic's death that a

good many of his followers did not escape. Had the Franciscan heresy somehow succeeded in taking over the Christian religion, not only would Christianity have been transformed, but so would Western and also world history.

The mainstream of Christian doctrine and practice has been inseparable from the Old Testament injunction to "subdue" the earth and to "have dominion" over all its resources, inorganic and organic. Such a relationship to this world was bound to lead to unremitting effort not only to develop and exploit the riches of the earth but also to understand, through science, the whole of nature. The West is uniquely the civilization of science and technology, all Chinese and other non-Western contributions notwithstanding. Western genius in these areas has not been innately superior to that of China, say, but none of the religious, ethical, and cultural barriers to the development of science and technology which characterized China in its great period of achievement existed in the West.

Secularists since the eighteenth century have emphasized the conflict between Christianity and science, but in truth such elements of conflict as have manifested themselves are vastly outweighed by the affinities between Christian faith and the scientific temper. The origins of modern science lie, not in the Renaissance, as once believed, but in the heart of the Middle Ages. The same basic impulse that led Aquinas to interpret Aristotle and other classical philosophers led such thinkers as Bacon, Grosseteste, and Theodoric of Freiburg to build through experiment and logic upon classical works of science. The twelfth and thirteenth centuries, far from showing hostility or indifference to science and technology, were a period of extraordinary cultivation of these areas of thought. This affinity between Christianity and science persisted in succeeding centuries. The founders of modern science—Copernicus, Newton, Boyle, and Harvey among them—were profoundly religious, and without exception they saw their scientific discoveries as revelations of the divine order. So close was the scientific temper to religious faith among the fundamentalist Puritans in the seventeenth century that they universally believed the successful prosecution of science would actually hasten the millennium. The millennium itself, they believed, would be an epoch, under Christ's governance, of boundless scientific and technological invention, all by way of preparing mankind for heaven.

The victory of Christianity over paganism has been said to be the greatest psychic revolution in the history of Western culture. But the implications of this psychic revolution go well beyond the cultivation of science in the West and also the whole philosophy of domination of nature of which science is only a part. For had this revolution never occurred, had the Christians been defeated by indigenous Greco-Roman gods, by gods imported from the East, or by both, the West would have known only a fraction of the social, economic, cultural, and intellectual history that has been a continuous flow from the earliest centuries of Christianity. Neither the powerful strain of active, advancing organization that is manifest in all areas of life and thought, nor the progressive philosophy of history that has endowed life with such a richly optimistic flavor through two millennia, would have been possible apart from the victory of Christianity. Indeed, the pristine salvational teachings of the founder of Christianity himself would never have won out had it not been for their nonsalvational, nonheavenly strains of thought and polity.

COMFORT

CLIVE BELL NOTED a half-century ago that comfort has never ranked high among the values of great civilizations. Brooks Adams, in his "law of civilization and decay," declared that cycles of history move from pristine vigor, with minimal regard for sensual pleasures, to ages of decadence in which there is regard for almost nothing but sensual pleasures, with animal comfort foremost. These observations have special pertinence to the United States, for on the testimony of a stream of foreign visitors that began with Tocqueville, Americans have special fondness for comfort, and at the expense of values which are indispensable to progress. Tocqueville observed: "In America the passion for physical well-being is not always exclusive, but it is general; and if all do not feel it in the same manner, yet it is felt by all . . . The passion for physical comforts is essentially a passion of the middle class; with those classes it grows and spreads, with them it is preponderant. From them it mounts into the higher orders of society and descends to the mass of the people."

Tocqueville contrasted the middle class's passion for the little conveniences of life with the old aristocracy's contempt for them. All the revolutions, he argued, "which have ever shaken or destroyed aristocracies have shown how easily men accustomed to the luxuries can do without the necessaries of life; whereas men who have toiled to acquire a competency can hardly live after they have lost it."

A craving for comfort may seem timeless and universal in man's history. But this is not so. People have sought subsistence, shelter, and physical security since the origin of man, indeed of life. As civilization gradually developed and expanded, as the possibility of a leisure class was formed, individuals came into existence who coveted power, wealth, status, and in time diversion. Once the ancient instinct for self-preservation was satisfied, a new impulse arose, that of exploitation of others. But neither in the long history of the common man nor in that of the military-begotten aristocracy has there been much concern with the simple ease, physical well-being, and ordinary contentment that is called comfort.

Despite the middle class's familiarity with it, comfort is not easily defined, and it can be elusive for those who seek it. Luxury, power, and status are objectively attainable by those able or lucky enough to win them. Oftentimes they do yield comfort to those who have won them, but more often they do not, if only because comfort is not even a tangible consideration in the mind of the achiever. It has been said that comfort is the hardest thing in the world to supply someone else. The spurned wife of a literary notable explained, "I could provide him with everything he wanted except comfort."

One may easily imagine, without personal experience of it, the blight that sudden poverty can cast upon comfort, among other states of mind. But one is less likely to think of the agonies of discomfort which can be produced by a sudden lift into company and circumstances for which nothing in life has prepared one, where everything is a potential trap, a source of possible humiliation, an occasion for ignorance of the vital nuances of language, and willy-nilly, a constant proving ground. Some of the most pathetic individuals in the army in World War II were the career corporals and sergeants, long used to the class division between noncommissioned and commissioned ranks, who under pressures of the demand for officers were catapulted upward to rank and associates which left them with chronic feelings of unease and sheer discomfort. Literature, from Aristophanes on, is rich in portraits of the *nouveau riche* avid for the company of the high-born but repeatedly made uncomfortable by the psychological price that had to be paid.

Rare is the comfortable middle-class individual who upon first seeing the castles and suits of armor in Europe does not wonder instantly how people could possibly have been comfortable in such abodes and habiliments. The same holds true when looking at an exhibit of eighteenth century dress for high-born women, so unlike the simple gowns today that one can simply slip into or out of and be comfortable. But the answer is, comfort was no more a criterion of the upper classes than of the lower. For the one class, the criterion was display of rank at whatever cost to creature comfort; for the other, it was survival for one's self and family and one's progeny. Had our ancestors been universally oriented toward comfort, there would today be wretchedly little to see in Europe of the castles, great estates, fine furniture, and works of art. It was not comfort but a host of other values, ranging from conspicuous consumption and lust for status or power all the way to *noblesse oblige*, that ignited the desire to possess, to have and to hold.

What is true of Europe's aristocracy is true in large measure of the titans of finance and business in the nineteenth and early twentieth centuries in America. Had the Rockefellers and Guggenheims been interested chiefly in personal comfort, they would hardly have gone much beyond a million or so dollars in their quest for wealth. But *mutatis mutandis*, they were actuated by the same motives which lay in the hearts of the first European barons, earls, and lords: conquest for its own sake, rank, authority, influence, and no doubt sheer covetousness. Neither in the thirteenth century nor in the nineteenth could it have been a lust for animal comfort that led the robber barons to amass great estates, for while there may have been much satisfaction in presenting to the world thousands of owned acres and retinues of servants numbering in the hundreds, along with the other marks of upper-class status, there could have been little sheer personal comfort—assuming that the word was even in their vocabularies—of the kind known by billionaires today in their Park Avenue apartments, their luxurious resorts, and their cruisers, so modest by comparison with J. P. Morgan's yacht. It is the kind of wealth that is crucial. If one was a billionaire in earlier centuries, that fact had to be demonstrated—by time-taking landed estates and the large corps of servants and other attendants who were of necessity required for the care of these estates. Certainly there were immense ego gratifications in these possessions, very probably greater even than those available to the successors of these billionaires in our guilt-drenched modern age. But the desire for mere comfort was not one of them.

The supremacy of comfort among the motivations to achievement is bound to have impact in the long run upon ambition, the desire to achieve and to rise in the world. Capitalism is the result in large degree of essentially feudal ambitions transferred to the marketplace. The celerity with which the newly rich in the eighteenth and nineteenth centuries moved to ape the hereditary aristocracy in landed estate, in dress, and in general style of life is some indication of that fact. The notion of economic man driven solely by desire for financial success is in large part superstition. As Schumpeter observed, to find the springs of ambition in the early capitalist entrepreneur, it is best to forget economic man and to think instead in terms of family, future as well as present, and the often uneconomic marks of status. For the most part in history, money and social status have gone together, so there is no way to tell which is the primal ambition. All that is known is that among the comic and pathetic figures in the history of literature and art, the man of wealth who has somehow not achieved social status is in the first rank. Rarely has the impoverished individual been the butt of satire and humor, but the Trimalchios have often.

Tocqueville thought that one of the effects of democracy and equality upon society would be the lowering of heights of ambition: "The first thing that strikes a traveller in the United States is the innumerable multitude of those who seek to emerge from their original condition; and second is the rarity of lofty ambition to be observed in the midst of the universally ambitious stir of society." There are several causes of this decline of great ambition, but high among them is the lure of physical gratifications of low order, the irresistible appeal of comfort of body and mind. From such appeal, Tocqueville thought, "a kind of virtuous materialism may ultimately be established in the world, which would not corrupt, but enervate, the soul and noiselessly unbend its springs of action."

There are signs of a diminished regard for ambition of any kind or degree in the present age—ambition, that is, in the sense of unremitting desire to achieve or accomplish. The word itself has taken on slightly pejorative implications. To say "he is ambitious" is as often as not a reproach today. There are several causes of this change in national temper, but one of them surely is the ever greater passion for simple comfort.

COMMUNITY

DURING A SINGLE WEEK in the 1960s one hundred thousand young people congregated in open fields near Woodstock, New York. Their professed reasons for coming together were opposition both to America's military presence in Vietnam and to the establishment as a whole, enjoyment of rock music, and freedom to indulge in marijuana and certain kinds of drugs. Afterward, a major newspaper asked a cross-section of those who had been present at Woodstock what was their deepest reaction to that week. Almost without exception the answer was memory of the community, the "togetherness" that had been formed temporarily, allowing escape from the icy waters of ordinary society.

That is one current sense of the word *community*. Another is set forth presciently by Dostoevsky's Grand Inquisitor in *The Brothers Karamazov*, who explains to the returned Jesus the absolute necessity of abandoning the freedom Jesus had brought to his followers: "For these pitiful creatures are concerned not only to find what one or other can worship, but find something that *all* will believe and worship; what is essential is that all may be *together* in it. This craving for community of worship is the chief misery of man individually and of all humanity from the beginning of time."

The combination of a vague but insistent yearning for community and the proffer of community-in-power is a dangerous feature of the contemporary West. The search for community in some form has been a notable aspect of the philosophy, theology, social sciences, and a great deal of the literature of the twentieth century. Nor is the quest limited to these areas. In the formation of close to fifteen thousand communes, rural and urban, in the United States during the last three decades a considerable segment, mostly young, made clear what it thought of ordinary society. Much of the passion for encounter and related groups is at bottom a seizing upon community in whatever form it may appear. The feeling of community lost and community needed is powerful. One indicator of the actual loss of community in America is the exploding rate of crime. It is not poverty but the breakdown of the social bond in family, neighborhood, parish, and local community that leads directly to crime, as an escape from boredom with the void.

Behind the contemporary crisis of community lies a long history of the slow but inexorable destruction of the traditional communities in the West. Much of social history for the past four centuries has consisted of the displacement of kinship, locality, and church as centers of community. Medieval society was rich in concrete communities, and the reason for this bears directly upon the present problem of community. Central power was weak during the medieval period, with the result that human desires and needs had to be fulfilled through cooperation and mutual aid. The idea of a provider-state would have been incomprehensible to medieval man. There had been such a state—imperial Rome—but in the West it finally collapsed after several centuries of erosion and assault from the outside. The history of the Middle Ages is one of the creation of groups to meet the needs left precarious by the fall of Rome. Patriarchal family, kindred, village community, walled town, guild, monastery, these are the relationships which had become strong in man's life by the time medieval Europe was at its zenith. That there was no conscious problem of community in medieval thought was simply because of the sheer abundance of *communitatem* in the age.

It has taken a long time to destroy the social heritage of the Middle Ages, but success has been effected in this century. The process of destruction commenced with the rise of the centralized nation-state. In the act of consolidating its sovereign power over subjects, the state deprived the traditional communities of their historic authorities. Village communities were ruthlessly invaded by the state through what were called enclosure acts; arable land that had been the villagers' for centuries was, by political act, given to favored nobles to enclose for sheep-raising, thus driving the villagers from their communities to the city where they formed the basis of the load of beggars and criminals that Sir Thomas More wrote of in *Utopia*. But the disintegration of other groups proceeded apace, and it did not matter whether the political power was wielded by king or parliament, the effect over the centuries was the dissolution of the communities which lay intermediate to individual and state. The government during the French Revolution was more relentless in its insistence that such intermediate communities be dissolved than any monarchy had ever been. The argument of the revolutionary leaders was that these communities constituted tyrannies in the lives of individuals and moreover threatened to challenge the people's power as represented by the national assemblies and conventions—then by first the Committee of Public Safety and second the Directory.

Capitalism has more often than not been declared the culprit in this historical destruction of communities. Marx and Engels gave that supposition dogmatic status, and others, including so conservative a thinker as Schumpeter, have followed, seeing in capitalism a process of continuing destruction of its social foundations in kinship and locality. But the truth is, the political state, by its incessant centralization and bureaucratization of power, has done far more than capitalism to effect this destruction. The social order in Japan has suffered little during the past century in which capitalism has burgeoned and prospered. The government in Japan has generally acted toward the preservation of family and neighborhood, and the great industries have taken their cue from this. Japan has, even in its cities, low rates of social disorganization, and the consequence is to be seen not least in its low rates of crime.

Democracy, tragically, has seen accelerations in the West of the process of social destruction. The democratic state is inherently more powerful than its predemocratic predecessors simply by virtue of the myth that it is of the people, by the people, and for the people. Rousseau is probably most responsible for the terrible superstition that a people governing itself cannot therefore tyrannize itself. Tocqueville, who had a far more realistic view, correctly saw that democracy, through its intrinsic collectivism and its worship of equality, produced a centralization of political power that no divine right king had been able to bring about. Under the democratic myth, the state's power over its citizens has increased exponentially in the twentieth century, always with the mesmerizing assurance that since the state is the people and works only for the people, it cannot become despotic.

The totalitarian state is a decidedly illiberal corruption of democracy. Whether it is communist or fascist makes not the slightest difference, except that communist states have been more successful in effecting total domination of their citizens. Lenin and Hitler alike saw their regimes, or pretended to see them, as the triumph of the people's power over all alien influences. Democracy has brought the people into prominence politically, and men such as Lenin, Stalin, Hitler, and Mao have merely exploited that prominence.

The danger of totalitarianism is that it can come to seem to its subjects compensation for the loss of traditional community. The Leninist-Stalinist state came into being at a time of widespread social and economic desolation, the result of World War I. Much of Hitler's appeal to Germans in 1932 sprang from their disillusionment with the decadence of the Weimar Republic, with what they perceived as social disintegration fused with lax morality. Hitler worked tirelessly at the creation of new communities in Germany, but one and all they were only extensions of the state in the lives of the citizens. Many Germans were only too happy to escape the freedom of a society in which community was or seemed to be lost and accept the sense of political community that Hitler proffered. The total state is new in human history, but it is only an intensification and corruption of the state that rose on the ashes of medieval society.

The problem in the democracies is that while the appeal of community has risen steadily during this century, the ordinary means of gratifying the need for community have been weakened, largely by the invasion of political power. Once the states, the cities and towns, and the neighborhoods in America provided, along with schools and churches, all the community that the citizen desired. Locality has always been the chief base of community, with village and town its characteristic manifestation. But the ever greater centralization and nationalization of America has inevitably weakened, often displaced, the localities and regions which formed the substance of community.

The federal bulldozer has destroyed, in the name of public housing, countless neighborhoods, that is, communities. The ghetto may have been bad, but it possessed community in a degree that the great public housing complexes do not and will not.

Because state power has enfeebled, even killed community in the historic sense of the word, there is no place for those seeking community to go but to the Woodstocks, or to the often bizarre communes, or to the numberless cults in American life. The spread of movements like the Unification Church and the Hare Krishna may be expected to continue, and it is a delusion to think that many of the young people belonging to these required brainwashing. These groups demand complete surrender of individual freedom of thought, but after all, Rousseau declared the perfect community to be one in which the condition of membership is the total surrender by the individual of all his rights.

This is the terrible power of community in modern times and a full illustration of the fact that community is not a sufficient end in itself. What it is a community *of* is what matters. The Manson family was a community possessed of all the authority and more that used to inhere in local communities and neighborhoods. It was a perversion of community, to be sure, but community all the same.

The real problem of community is that more and more people find themselves in that state of being Dostoevsky described as dominated by a "craving for community." More and more people, especially the young and aged, are pulled inexorably toward such communities as they can find, irrespective of their functional or ideological base. Thus the nation in prospect is one filled with Moonies and their analogues, encounter groups, gangs, clubs, and cults which have at least the veneer of community, which promise relief for their members' craving.

But such an assemblage of so-called communities is inherently unstable and hardly calculated to satisfy for long the demand for "something that *all* will believe and worship." Far more likely in the long run is the kind of community that Rousseau and his descendants have promised: the total political community in which a general will, a collective political consciousness, becomes the haven for those tormented by misery of being alone.

CONSERVATISM

THE ESSENCE OF this body of ideas is the protection of the social order—family, neighborhood, local community, and region foremost—from the ravishments of the centralized political state. It is in the interests of the social order that conservative theories of the state have invariably stressed decentralization, pluralism, and a maximum of individual and social autonomy. Freedom is seen by the conservative in the light of freedom of community and of association as well as of the individual. The problem of freedom is to protect the social ties intermediate to the individual and the state as buffers against the spreading power of governmental bureaucracy.

There have been two significant eruptions of conservative ideology in modern Western thought: first in 1790–1810, in Western Europe chiefly but to some degree in the United States; and then in 1950–1970, largely in America. Each eruption came in response to the same basic challenge, that of a political order extending itself ever more rapaciously into traditional society.

Burke was the author of the first eruption, and it was in substantial degree a revival of the study of Burke in the mid-twentieth century that furnished the stuff of the second eruption. Burke did not consider himself conservative. He worshiped at the shrine of the Glorious Revolution of 1688; he gave full support to the American colonists in their struggle against the British Crown; he sided with the people of India, extolling their morality and social order, against the British East India Company; and his sympathies were almost entirely with Ireland, where he had been born, in its tragic struggles with the English. He was Whig, not Tory, and as much as Dr. Johnson, the quintessential Tory, loved Burke, he grieved occasionally at Burke's political views. But all this notwithstanding, Burke is the fountainhead of philosophical and political conservatism in the West.

There is a continuity running throughout Burke's thought. Hostility to what he called "arbitrary power" asserted by the Crown was the keystone of his defense of the Indians, the American colonists, and the Irish. His attack upon the Jacobins across the Channel proceeded from exactly the same basis. He found the Jacobins, through legislation as early as 1789–1790, guilty of exercising arbitrary power over their own countrymen and of riding roughshod over the traditions, ranks, communities, and ideas which had been the very framework of French society for centuries.

Most of what continues today to be regarded as philosophical conservatism derives directly from the principles and values which

Burke espoused so eloquently in his assault on the French Revolution. These principles and values come down essentially to localism and regionalism, based on the intermediate groups such as family, parish, local community, guild, social class, and church. Burke was therefore bound to condemn political centralization and the collectivization of power. Tradition was for Burke absolutely vital to both social order and freedom. No true government is a contrivance; it is the work of history, inseparable from the organic articulation of traditions.

Burke detested the French Revolution's combination of extreme centralization of power and displacement of the old institutions which had provided cohesion and prevented society from becoming "an uncivil consociation of atoms." He thought the new divisions and departments of France which Jacobin faith in geometrical rationalism had inaugurated absurd: "It is boasted that the geometrical polity has been adopted, that all local ideas should be sunk, and that people should no longer be Gascons, Picards, Bretons, Normans, but Frenchmen, with one country, one heart, one assembly. But instead of being all Frenchmen, the greater likelihood is that the inhabitants of that region will shortly have no country . . . We begin our public affections in our families. No cold relation is a zealous citizen. We pass on to our neighborhoods and our habitual provincial connections. These are our inns and resting places . . . The love to the whole is not extinguished by this subordinate partiality."

Burke saw the fateful affinity that lies between revolution and militarism. The one breeds the other. The more the revolutionary government pulverizes the traditional bases of authority and community, the greater the need for sheer force to hold together the unstable aggregate of atoms that results. In a short time use of the military is unavoidable. To the French leaders Burke wrote: "Everything depends upon the army in such a government as yours; for you have industriously destroyed all the opinions and prejudices, and, as far as in you lay, all the instincts which support government. Therefore the moment any difference arises between your national assembly and any part of the nation, you must have recourse to force. Nothing else is left to you; or rather you have left nothing else to yourselves . . . You lay down metaphysical propositions which imply universal consequences, and then you attempt to limit logic by despotism." Correctly did Burke predict the inauguration by the Jacobins of universal military conscription; the dissolution of the patriarchal family, the guilds, and the provinces; and the laws which sought to de-Christianize France in favor of a religion based solely upon worship of the civil state, in the name of virtue.

All those who during the years 1790–1810 were part of the
Counter-Enlightenment, as the conservative movement came to be
called, had been inspired by Burke, and in one way or another all
gave their support to his central tenets. They included Bonald and
Maistre in France, Coleridge and Southey in England, Savigny and
Hegel in Germany, Haller in Switzerland, and Balmes and Donoso y
Cortes in Spain. These minds formed the top rank of the first wave
of conservatism in the West, though only Hegel proved to have as
long and wide an influence as Burke did. The impact of this efflorescence of conservatism upon the European mind was substantial.
Saint-Simon, Comte, Tocqueville, Le Play, Taine, Mill, Disraeli, and
Maine were among those whose thinking was profoundly touched.

Such intellectual influence did not, however, appreciably affect
the course of Western polity during the nineteenth and first half of
the twentieth century. Liberalism, democracy, populism, and even socialism—all negations in one or other degree of the central propositions of conservatism—played a much greater role in the formation
of Western countries than did Burke's conservative tenets, however
much Burke might be admired simply as a mind. To survey Western
countries as they had evolved by 1950 is to realize that almost everything which Burke and other conservatives stood for early in the
nineteenth century had been vanquished by liberalism and radicalism, by principles of government in which nationalism, centralized
administration, central planning, and mass welfare take precedence. It
took longer in America than in Europe to override the values which
the Federalist Papers—so like in substance to Burke's philosophy—
had perceived as essential in the Constitution, but by 1950 these
values had been largely retired to the shades.

Then occurred the second appreciable eruption of conservatism,
that of 1950–1970. This eruption did not produce a Burke or a Hegel,
but it has led to a major change in national temper in the United
States and has had a highly visible influence upon the intellectual
class. The standard-bearers in the 1950s were Mises and Hayek,
though they eschewed "conservative" as a label, Russell Kirk, Richard Weaver, and William F. Buckley, Jr., among others. The mainstream of American thought was not yet affected, as those who styled
themselves conservatives were regarded as a coterie built around a
conscious, even self-conscious revival of certain nineteenth century
values. They nevertheless won for themselves a surprising degree of
attention, considering the extent to which liberalism cum radicalism
dominated the mind of the intellectual class. The new conservatives
saw themselves in much the same historical position that Burke and
his fellow conservatives had been in at the end of the eighteenth cen-

tury as a result of the Enlightenment and the *philosophes*. Ever since the New Deal, American thought had been governed in extraordinary measure by the gods of political centralization, collectivism, central planning, and devotion to national state over traditional society. Like Burke, the new conservatives called attention to the values of localism and regionalism, religion, patriotism, and political decentralization.

Then came, in the 1960s, America's approximation of the French Revolution, which though different in scale was hardly different in social and intellectual content or in impact upon the national consensus. There were demonstrations and riots from one coast to the other, stormings of everything from college administration buildings to the Pentagon, gunfire, bombings, and a general spirit of social and cultural anarchy. That the American people were troubled, even frightened, is evidenced by the large number of executive decrees and legislative enactments directly responsive to the revolutionary new left.

Side by side with the anarchy developed the Great Society program of President Johnson. Augmented by the American war in Vietnam, one of the greatest explosions of governmental centralization and bureaucratization in American history took place in the decade of the sixties. The American people experienced, in such huge federal ventures as the war against poverty and the model cities program, depredations upon the society and its neighborhoods and localities without precedent in American history.

In such circumstances—a cultural and social anarchy stimulated by the new left on the one hand and an octopus-like seizure of the social order by the already swollen federal bureaucracy on the other—the germs planted by the new conservatives began suddenly to burgeon and to produce ideological consequences that, both in substance and in expanse, had never been seen before in America. Overnight, it seemed, liberals became conservatives first by the hundreds, then by the thousands; such was the middle-class reaction to the new left violence, and such also, though more slowly, was its gathering reaction to the Big Society programs under Johnson. The American intellectual community was deeply affected, especially by the assaults of the new left on academic institutions, and the community divided into partisans of the new left and those who detested it. The latter group furnished the political scene with a new breed, the neo-conservatives, who have been defined as liberals who were mugged by reality. The development of neo-conservatism is one of the two or three most important episodes in twentieth century political thought. Irving Kristol, Daniel Patrick Moynihan, and Nathan

Glazer are key individuals involved in this variant of conservatism.

On the whole, there is more in common between neo-conservatism and the conservatism that stretches from Burke to its renascence in the 1950s than there is difference. The two groups share an antagonism to heavy bureaucracy, national centralization, and collectivism; they share also a recognition of the values of localism, states rights, and a strong private sector. The difference is largely one of degree in these matters, save with respect to religious and moral issues, the conservatives generally being more apt to make these key issues in American life, as with respect to abortion, school prayers, and creationism, than are the neo-conservatives, who are commonly more secular in outlook.

Another spectacular new component of the conservative movement at the present time is evangelical Christianity. *Conservative*, in the Burkean sense, is hardly the word to apply to the millions who form this religious eruption. Burke had no use for enthusiasm in either religion or politics, and enthusiasm is what these evangelicals exude. But of their devotion to religion, family, and traditional morality there can be no doubt, and though their opposition to centralized government and bureaucracy rests more upon religious and moral grounds, such as opposition to abortion and support for school prayers, than upon the neo-conservatives' political and legal grounds, there is still an affinity between the two flanks.

What is the future of conservatism in the United States? Not bright, I think. True, this ideology has recently elected a President and a score of new legislators. Without question it is at the moment the strongest force that liberalism and radicalism have met since the 1930s. There is nevertheless a fragility about conservatism that can only become more apparent with time. There is already clear evidence of fissure and fragmentation. What Burke spoke of as "the dissidence of dissent" is only too apparent at present in the conservative movement. As in all instances of enthusiasm, there is an incessant desire to prove to others the exclusive truth of a single way of life or thought. Thus, within less than a year of the conservatives' election of their cherished candidate for the Presidency, the skies darkened by cries of betrayal, and hotel lobbies filled with caterwauling epigones.

The sole object of the conservative tradition that began with Burke, that continued through Coleridge, Hegel, Tocqueville, Burckhardt, Taine, and many others down to the renascence of the 1950s and 1960s, is the protection of the social order and its constitutive groups from the enveloping bureaucracy of the national state. But at the present moment this historic objective is far from the desires of many self-styled conservatives who are more interested in capturing the state, or a part of it at least, as the means of imposing a given moral value upon the entire nation. There is a growing spirit of nationalism from the right, one that, while decrying the social and economic provider-state, seeks instead a moral provider-state. These preachers with and without pulpits are not agreed or even certain in their own minds just where in the national state they want moral authority to lie, but in their obsession with the perceived evils of the free market—intellectual and moral as well as economic—they do not care very much.

This is anything but conservatism as it has existed in Western thought for two centuries. Burke yielded to no one in his cherishment of Christian morality and religion, but his indictment of the leaders of the French Revolution for their limitless use of the political state to establish "the reign of virtue" doubtless covered some of his own countrymen and doubtless covers a great many now in the Moral Majority. Between morality in the ordinary, historical sense and the sovereign political state there is an inherent and ineradicable conflict.

Adding to the woes of present-day conservatism is the rising spirit of militarism in America. There is no mystery nor necessary vice in this spirit, for it is evoked by the vast and aggressive power of the Soviet Union in the world. This spirit is vital to the American nation at the present time. But it is absurd to frost this military spirit with the ideology of conservatism. They have nothing in common. Burke saw the picture clearly. War, at least the kind of ideological war he saw forming in Europe, can only enhance the nation *une et indivisible* at the expense of the "smaller patriotisms" and the "subordinate loyalties" which are the indispensable molecules of the social order. Between what Burke called "military democracy" and the conservation of these unities there is and can be only deep-seated conflict. As Lenin realized shrewdly, war and war preparation have much the same effect upon the social structure that revolution does, when sufficiently prolonged. In the long run, centralization of power stifles the natural social order. Tocqueville observed that men with a genius for centralization love war, just as men with a genius for war love centralization.

The final reason why conservatism, in any concrete historical sense of the word, which may or may not include those who choose the political right over the left, is not destined for a long life lies in the sheer mass of the liberal provider-state. It has been building, with only rare and brief halts, for close to two centuries in Europe and one century in the United States. Almost everything favors this kind of state, from war to ordinary day-in, day-out civil life, for people at all levels have interests and desires, and there is no surer way of gratifying these than through the provider-state. Current efforts to reduce this state are like nothing so much as chipmunks trying to bring down a giant redwood.

CORRUPTION

THE RECENT HISTORY of this word provides one more instance of the power of political ideology to diminish, deform, and yes, corrupt language. Rarely today is the word, whether as noun, verb, or adjective, applied to anything outside the realm of politics, and even here its use is overwhelmingly confined to a certain type of politics, that of the right wing. In its literal sense the word refers to decay, decomposition, and disintegration. Its original referent was the human flesh after death. In the late Middle Ages there was widespread preoccupation with the corruption of the human body following death, and in a great many churches at the present time in Europe there are still sculptural evidences of this preoccupation: representations of the body in a coffin as it was imagined to be after becoming half-decayed through natural processes and the ravages of worms.

But the word *corruption* had more general and diverse use even during the Middle Ages. Not only human flesh but organic life in general, language, study of the classics, morality, conduct in diplomacy and commerce, art, and though infrequently, political rule could all serve as referents for the word. Very often during the Renaissance and after were references to the earth itself, widely believed to be undergoing gradual decay and disintegration, with its eventual cracking-up and disappearance a matter of certain foreknowledge. From the time of the word's appearance in the English language in roughly the fourteenth century, down through the nineteenth century, all branches of literature and art were rich in diverse applications of it. Although from about the sixteenth century on uses of a political nature became commoner as a result of the increasing prominence of the political state in Western life, such uses in no way interfered with or cut down on applications of the word to the host of nonpolitical referents.

Very different is the case today, especially in the United States.

For every use of the word in a nonpolitical or noneconomic context there are hundreds, perhaps thousands, of uses of monotonously political character. So impoverished has the word become that it is actually startling to see it used in any of its old connections. That there can be, and frequently is, a degeneration or decay of teaching and scholarship in the universities should be a mere truism, but one will search today's journalism and social criticism in vain for any references to corrupt professors or faculties.

Only one significant change has taken place in the twentieth century with respect to the word: its general movement from the political-economic to the political sphere alone and, within this sphere, to government of a highly specialized and less and less common type. At the beginning of the century in America, ascriptions of corruption to businessmen, notably those involved in relationships with boards of aldermen and state legislatures, were frequent, the very staple of, say, the Hearst newspapers or the Munsey publications. The journalism of a Steffens or Tarbell in the period leading up to World War I was largely founded upon what Theodore Roosevelt angrily called "muckraking," essentially the dissemination of news of financial corruption in relation to agencies of government.

"Corrupt political machine" was probably the transitional phrase leading the word from its first exclusive association with business to what would be its ever wider use with respect to politics. By definition, all political machines and all political bosses were, at least by the 1920s, corrupt. Only rarely if at all was this ancient and once-diversely employed word used in other than political ways. Today *corruption* is the first word that springs to the average American liberal's tongue when traditional-authoritarian states are referred to. Almost compulsive is the description of the governments of South Vietnam, Taiwan, Argentina, Chile, Batista's Cuba, and the like as "corrupt." Never, though, is the word used in application to the Soviet Union, North Vietnam, Castro's Cuba, or China. Presumably they are, no matter what other vices may afflict them, immune to the corruption that identifies governments resting on capitalism in one or other of its forms. Deep in contemporary liberal-radical thought is the premise that corruption is possible only where private property is the base of the economic order.

But this is absurd. Lord Acton remarked: "Power tends to corrupt, and absolute power corrupts absolutely." The single most spectacular phenomenon of corruption in the twentieth century is the debasement, the decomposition, of the ideal of socialism that is observed with relentless regularity whenever a self-styled socialist party comes to power through revolution. What began under Lenin and

Stalin has become a hallmark of each and every regime founded upon revolution from the left: the corruption of the ideals which had been held up to the people before the revolution. Nor is this the only manifestation of corruption that is induced by the possession of absolute power. Merely to contrast the style of living of each member of the Politburo, the highest levels of the bureaucracy, and the command levels of the military with the styles of living imposed upon the mass of citizens in the USSR is to see how easily corruption proceeds in matters of entitlements, services, perquisites, rewards, and privileges in a country that has officially renounced all private property and profit. And scarcely a week goes by without reports, released by the governments themselves, of property and monetary embezzlements, of illicit trafficking in commodities ranging from grain to narcotics. So much for the hoary myth that economic corruption is impossible where private property has been abolished.

Absolute power does indeed corrupt absolutely. This fact, though, will in no way diminish the number of curtsies by liberals when Fidel Castro pays his next visit to New York City.

COVETOUSNESS

"THE EYE IS NOT satisfied with the seeing, nor the ear with the hearing." Thus Ecclesiastes on covetousness, an evil that falls only just below envy and malice in the hierarchy of sin. Although the word is occasionally used in an innocent context, as in the friendly compliment, "I covet your experience in the matter" or "Your style is much to be coveted," this is but wordplay. The ancient and lasting meaning of the word is deadly, a corruption of ambition, a sickness of the instinct for preservation. Covetousness is the degeneration of the acquisitive faculty. It is normal to seek to acquire, which is premised on work. But the premise of covetousness is insatiability. Dr. Johnson remarked, "The natural flights of the human mind are not from pleasure to pleasure but from hope to hope." Johnson was as well aware of the necessity for ethical limits upon hope as upon ambition: lack of such limits generates covetousness in the first case and envy in the second. Correctly did Johnson point to imagination as the great nurturing element of covetousness. No matter what one has or manages to acquire in time, imagination increases it a thousandfold, thus torturing the mind, depriving it of power to please and satisfy. Bacon observed that covetousness of money is the root of all evil, but Shakespeare saw farther: "When the Workmen strive to do better than well, They do confound their skill in covetousness."

Covetousness thrives in many areas of society today where one might not ordinarily expect to find it, evidence that money and material delights are not the only nurturing circumstances of this sin. One of the more luxuriant growths of covetousness is in the academic world at the present time, hardly something that our austere professorial ancestors could have foreseen.

It appears in the epidemic of titled chairs in academia. Once the rise to simple unadorned professor was sufficient to satisfy all ambition. It no longer is. What the Constitution forbids, the university world glories in: titles. Such titles, it has been said, are sandwich boards worn alike by donor and recipient. Covetousness strikes at both ends of endowment. Thus when Professor Smith becomes the LuluBelle Fitzmeister Professor of Wildlife Management, something has been gained by both Professor Smith and Ms. Fitzmeister. He has acquired plumage and she has acquired membership, so to speak, on the faculty. One wonders what real satisfaction—apart from salary increase, which is by no means certain—is gained by an already renowned scholar when he takes on the name of some affluent unknown.

The all-time high in academic titles was surely set by a political scientist a decade or so ago. His double blockbusters (he taught at two universities) went something like this: Allison W. Scott Distinguished Service Research Professor and Director of the Miriam Angston Butler Institute for Political Analysis at the University of Renown *and* Elmer Crittenden Distinguished Professor and Director of the Mark J. Smith Center for the Study of Political Dynamics at Urban University Graduate Center. In time, retiring from both universities, "Emeritus" was added to each, but that proved insufficient, for he accepted a post at still another university, it too furnishing him with titled chair and institute directorship. It is said that editors and typesetters cringed when articles were submitted by this political scientist, for he was meticulous about title and did not take kindly to omission of a word.

Institutes, centers, and bureaus have also been the objects of academic covetousness. The prestige given them by the physical sciences in World War II and immediately after aroused the jealousy of first the social sciences and then the humanities. Of a sudden, campuses were dotted with institutes of studies of almost anything one could think of, ranging from econometrics to Renaissance history. It has never been clear, especially in the humanities, how such organizations advance scholarship, but they make a lovely light. The desire to have one's own institute or center can be obsessing. Well do I recall a colleague who, despite fame and salary, went into a state of melancholy that was not terminated until he at last received a foundation grant to establish his own institute on the campus. A reasonable estimate is that two-thirds of all institutes in the humanities and social sciences on American campuses are at bottom ego pacifiers.

Desire for honorary degrees is more and more intense on today's campus—degrees from other universities and colleges than one's own, of course. Since at almost every university a faculty committee recommends—often having virtual authority over—honorary degrees, it is not difficult for anyone worth his salt gradually to get his name before the committee. To be sure, there is the nagging question of the prestige of the institution granting the honorary degree. However much one may covet an LL.D., how far down the ratings of universities can one afford to go? The balance of covetousness can be delicate in these circumstances, somewhat like the balance of marriage calculations in India when the bride comes from a lower caste. E. M. Forster steadily refused all offers of honorary degree, even from the greatest universities, Oxford and Cambridge included. But this is said to have sprung from Forster's unalterable conviction that no honorary degree was sufficient recognition and tribute.

Favorable book reviews are cherished, and many are the lengths to which even the well established will go to make certain that a forthcoming book's merits are heralded. The record in this respect is doubtless held by a diplomat-historian of great fame. With the help of a generous foundation grant, he organized a conference in a luxurious inn to which he invited two dozen ranking historians in the national area of his interest, each to receive a handsome honorarium. In the invitation, the subject of the conference was simply the name of the country concerned. Imagine, then, the surprise of those attending to discover that the total agenda consisted of chapters of the host's forthcoming book. In three days of discussion all virtues and faults were uncovered, and two dozen potential reviewers had been either charmed or else neutralized. Not many academics can afford that route to an assured review, but there are other routes which require only time and postage. Edmund Wilson told late in life that he had gotten in the habit of spending his early mornings rereading old reviews of his books. He differed from university faculty only in being candid about the practice.

Covetousness is wildly manifest in science departments for priority of publication. Originality has come to matter more than perfection, and the lust for it is boundless. To be first: that is the thing. Watson's book on the race between himself and Crick on the one hand and Linus Pauling on the other is likely to be the classic for a long time on how fevered the competition for priority of publication can be. Haste still makes waste, alas, and one hears much talk about this or that mathematician's or chemist's slovenliness of preparation and clumsiness of proof. Even worse is the apparent increase of academic crime—falsification of evidence, pilfering from the works of subordinates, and other forms of embezzlement. Fortunately district attorneys never indict for intellectual embezzlement.

The rage to be honored has become boundless. It makes one think respectfully of the Englishman who was appointed by the Queen to some hoary order and who said, "The best thing about it is there is no damn nonsense about merit." Pursuit of degrees, membership in special societies, awards of distinction, prizes, and fellowships is frantic, and naturally the supply of these keeps up with the demand. The heroic dish is the Nobel Prize. Once it seemed so Olympian that competition for it would have been thought impious or absurd. Not today. There are so many living scientists who are Nobel laureates that, covetousness being what it is in a largely egalitarian society, strenuous competition for the prize is all but inevitable. Indeed the competition is already under way. Thus it is common knowledge that many young scientists are assessing shrewdly the history of the prize—the specific format of contributions with the highest probability of success, the specialized fields which, on the basis of recent throws of the dice, appear to be likeliest to yield winners, the advantages and disadvantages of collaboration, and with whom, and far from least, the individuals abroad and at home whose opinions are apt to be crucial. It will be God's good will that saves the Nobel Prize from descending to the level of a Pulitzer.

The Framers did their best to curb covetousness by forbidding titles of state and the formation of an aristocracy. So did the good citizens who opposed the Order of the Cincinnati. What none of them could have foreseen is that an aristocracy would emerge in time and that it would come from the ranks of teachers and scholars, manifest in their luxuriant titles and degrees. Far better in retrospect to have allowed for the craving for title. One could then prefix the single word "Sir" to the professor's name instead of something like "Albert Thomas Distinguished University Research Professor."

CREATIONISM

IN THE STRICT SENSE, the word means belief in a literal understanding of Genesis 1–2 in the Old Testament. The earth and everything on it were created by God in six days—each of them of twenty-four hours' duration. The redoubtable Archbishop Ussher, by meticulous reading of all the begats and other events in the Old Testament, calculated that God had created the world in 4004 B.C., assigning even the day of the week and the hour that Adam and Eve departed the Garden.

Creationists in this strict and literal sense of the word have few supporters outside their own ranks. It is easy to make them the butt of the kind of humor Darrow indulged himself in at the Scopes Trial. For such literalism cannot be entertained seriously by any but dolts, it would seem, given the ineradicable evidences on earth of the passage of very long periods of time and, in the present day, tests which date almost to the year fossils and other paleological or geological entities found in numerous parts of the earth.

These literalists are well advised in their own interest to go to *Omphalos,* written by Philip Gosse and published in 1857, just two years before Darwin's *Origin* appeared. Gosse was one of the most respected naturalists in England, and without doubt he knew the evolutionary views of his naturalist contemporaries, who did not need the Darwinian afflatus to learn about evolution as a natural process of nature, the works of biologists, botanists, and others of the preceding century having taken care of that. But Gosse saw that, from the point of view of strict logic, the creationists could not be summarily obliterated in their arguments by the kind of evidence that naturalists of the time utilized, to wit, the signs of age in the geological record. The reason, Gosse argued, is that a genuine God, one omnipotent, omniscient, and omnipresent as a genuine God must be, would not for a moment have created the world and its species without creating at the same time the geological and embryological evidences of a long past. After all, in creating man, God created a being with a unique time-binding capacity, with a sense of the past as well as the present and future. Given this sense of past in *Homo sapiens,* God could not but have endowed his creation with an ingrained past. Eric Korn put this view into sharper focus: "The argument is not that fossils were put into rocks to make the world seem older, to confuse geologists or to test people's faith; merely that if the world was created by divine fiat, it could only be created as a going concern, with a created (not faked) past." And as for deriving proof of the actual antiquity of earth and man from the geological record alone, without prior assumption or prejudgment, Korn wrote: "The geological evidence could no more tell you when the world was created than the age of a character could tell you how long a play had continued since the rise of the curtain."

True, all true. The geological record, like tree rings, means absolutely nothing as indicator of the past apart from an antecedent faith in that past. Only in minds already prepared, minds possessed of belief in a law of historical motion, of development, of advancement, can the strata of fossils in this or that part of the earth convey the sense of a long, evolving past. In the history of mankind's consciousness of the past, man did not acquire his conviction of evolution from fossils. On the contrary, man acquired respect for fossils as evidence for an evolution already believed in in some form, divine or natural, slow or speedy, continuous or discontinuous.

Gosse, to the consternation of his fellow naturalists and then to their virtual ostracism of him, saw all of this and more. As is so often the case, what the evidence was said to teach had in fact been learned prior to any evidence whatever, and man then set about, over a period of two or three thousand years, "proving" through evidence what had already been learned from or been suggested by the sages of antiquity. In terms of strict logic, Gosse is irrefutable.

Even so, it is unlikely that the ranks of the literal creationists will swell to much larger number. From whatever source, for whatever reason, most people in Western society have the unalterable conviction of a very long period of time in the history of the earth and of a rather slow evolution of its mantle of life. The Western mind, from its Greek roots in fascination with growth, with seeing the world and everything in it against the metaphors of development and teleological fulfillment, takes to the basic idea of evolution rather easily. The brain acquires, if it does not possess innately, certain ideas very early in life; such ideas are like constitutive tissues of the mind. Evolution, as an idea or perspective, is implicit in one degree or other in the Greco-Roman and also in the Christian tradition, and it has been a staple of the modern mind since the eighteenth century, Darwin's alleged revelation of 1859 notwithstanding.

It is in this light that creationism in the looser sense, as opposed to literal creationism, must be assessed. Nothing can be done for or to the literalists by biologists; they can take care of themselves. But the overwhelming majority of self-styled creationists today are a different breed. They accept the reality of a long evolution of earth and life. But explicitly or implicitly they argue that, such reality accepted, current naturalist hypotheses and theories have proved inadequate and insufficient to explain the astonishing things disclosed in recent years by scientists themselves. These mainstream creationists accept without serious question the spectacle of an evolutionary differentiation of species going back great distances of time. What, however, is not acceptable is a theory that posits only the laws of chance, only an irrational, blind, mechanistic process of selection which is the sole and exclusive causal agent in this whole complex and intricate process of evolution. Sophisticated creationists are as well aware of the current *lacunae* in the purely naturalist theory of geological and biological evolution, of the conundrums and enigmas which virtually scream for recognition, as are sophisticated biologists and geologists.

Such creationists have no objection whatever to a planet of evolving life over four and a half billion years. After all, the principle of development, of fulfillment, of progress is intrinsic to Christianity, to be found all the way from Saint Augustine to Cardinal Newman in the nineteenth century, who used Christian developmentalism to throw light upon doctrinal issues. Moreover, creationists are well aware that not to this moment has any scientist come even close to the manufacture of life in the laboratory out of prebiotic substances. The origin of life is as much a mystery today as it was when Darwin carefully avoided the subject, referring merely, in the *Origin*, to the "Creator." Given such massive, long-lasting ignorance, creationists ask what is wrong with doing just what Darwin did, accepting the existence of a Creator and never pretending that principles set forth to account for the development of the species are sufficient to explain the actual origin of life. Modern biologists are really not much farther along, at least in laboratory results, with the problem of life and its initial appearance than Darwin and his contemporaries were. The question, then, is why the drum beaters for the "church of science" incessantly belabor the public with homiletics to the opposite effect.

If the answer is that they seek to prevent the church of God from strangling the scientific enterprise, it can only cause bewilderment. The close linkage of Western religion and science goes back at least to Grosseteste and Bacon in the Middle Ages. Apart from the desire to explain and illuminate divine laws, the works of Copernicus, Newton, Priestley, and Maxwell are incomprehensible. Newton declared that his entire purpose in writing the *Principia* was from the beginning the explication and clarification of the divine order. From boyhood Newton had been deeply devout in his Christianity, a believer indeed in the imminent millennium. The majority of the geniuses of modern times have had a firm belief that ranged from ordinary piety to evangelical commitment. The idea that there is a conflict between religious belief and scientific conclusion would have seemed absurd to these men. To suppose that any one of them would have considered the exclusion of religion in all its forms from the schools, indeed from the scientific classroom, a salutary, to-be-hoped-for eventuality is to suppose nonsense. They believed they knew the limits of purely logical, rationalist, experimentalist science, and they were perfectly willing to deed over to the divine what lay beyond these limits. Even Spencer, more nearly philosopher of science perhaps than scientist, expressed his contempt for atheists and his confidence in what he called the Unknown and First Principles. In the present day there are scientists who not only are willing to hypothesize the divine but see no real alternative, given the sheer complexity of the world and universe turned up by earth science and astronomy. But their voices are not easily heard in the din created by the fundamentalists of science and their allies in the media and the humanities.

But there is every likelihood of a sharp change in this dominance of pure secularism. The reason, quite apart from the religious efflorescence taking place, is the uncomfortable yield of the sciences concerned most closely with the nature of the universe and man. This yield—scarcely older than three decades—has thrown into question many of the premises and assumptions of the rigorously anticreationist mentality of modern times. It is now known that our own universe, far from being a timeless complex of planets and stars, is finite in age, in existence for only the last ten to twenty billion years, and is very probably the outcome of a primal event, the "big bang." This notion has every bit of the flavor of "creationism," for out of that single event emerged a universe so delicately articulated, so harmonious in the motions of its component bodies, and so marvelously suspended in space as to deserve in and for itself the label of divinity. As an astronomer recently observed: "With every fresh penetration of our universe through space craft tens of millions of miles away from the earth, the suspicion grows that the theologian got there first."

The sciences have also revealed some hard truths about the earth which are *prima facie* much more congruent with the creationist than with the conventional secular view of the earth's age and relation to other planets in the universe. It is now known that the earth itself is only four and a half billion years old, that it too, like its environing universe, is finite, not ageless and eternal as was thought until recently, and that it too has been subjected to great convulsive events which play havoc with suppositions based upon the idea of timeless, uniform, and observable processes. More important perhaps is the dawning knowledge, drawn from the adventures in space of Mariner and other craft, that the earth is, after all, just as the theologians have said for millennia, unique in its possession not only of man but of life. Add to the stupendous improbability of a universe such as ours an earth such as ours, apparently alone in its mantle of organic life, and we become humble.

Add also the stupendous improbability of the origin through purely natural, secular processes of man, indeed of the whole complex and intricate web of life. That purely natural processes of development and differentiation exist is not to be doubted. And among these is natural selection. But the biomathematical improbability of all this emerging solely through one simple process is so immense, given the finite age of the earth, as to invite ridicule and to give impetus to creationist philosophy. A near infinity of noughts is required in the natural selection probabilities for so much as a fruit fly to emerge through natural selection alone. As for the wonder that is man's mind and nervous system, the physiologist Eccles, noted for his discoveries in the transmission of electric impulses of the brain, remarked that only something that is supernatural to the same degree as creationism can even begin to explain man's unique mental faculties. Lovelock's Gaia theory opens up the existence of a biosphere so infinitely complex in its homeostatic mechanisms as to make seriously suspect, irrespective of whether one "believes in God," most of the processes currently adduced by scientists in explanation of these exquisitely interconnected mechanisms. The scenario of homeostasis presented by the organism man is extraordinary enough as a super-Everest to climb, but it is almost as nothing compared with the terrestrial homeostatic processes.

Creationists of the educated, common-sense, rational type are not asking for illustrations in school textbooks of a bearded Olympian to be called God and hailed for having, out of one mind, devised it all, either over six days or over six hundred million years. They could, if they wanted to, appeal to the physicist Bohr and his idea of complementarity. Bohr used this term to characterize situations in man's attempt to understand the universe where there are several mutually exclusive but legitimate approaches to reality. Such situations, as the physical scientist Weiskopf more recently noted, exist throughout science, including physics with its complementary aspects of the atom— quantum state and location. Divergent though the two states of vision are, each is necessary to a full understanding of the atom.

Granted that such a quandary or paradox is a far cry from belief in a divine principle, an aboriginal creative force, but as Weiskopf emphasizes, science has always had its roots outside its own rational mode of thinking. He cites the mathematician Goedel's demonstration that a system of axioms can never be based on itself. To prove the axioms, statements from the outside must be introduced. "Science," noted Weiskopf, "must have a nonscientific base: it is the conviction of every scientist and of society as a whole, that scientific truth is relevant and essential." The physicist Planck, one of the astoundingly creative scientists of the twentieth century and a believer both in the divine and in the service of science to the divine, would have agreed, as he wrote: "Religion and natural science are fighting a joint battle in an incessant, never-relaxing crusade against skepticism and dogmatism, against disbelief and against superstition, and the rallying cry in this crusade has always been, and will always be, 'On to God.' " To paraphrase Chesterton, the time has come when the conflict is no longer between those who believe and those who do not believe, but between those who believe and those who will believe anything. Seek the truth, enjoined Saint Augustine, as if about to find it; find it with the intention of always seeking it. In the present day, that injunction has particular pertinence to the scientists and their camp followers who have so confidently declared God not only dead but never alive.

CRIME AND PUNISHMENT

OF ALL CHANGES in recent American history, the most macabre and chilling is the breakdown of one of mankind's oldest and most salutary communities of will and purpose: that of crime and punishment. Consider. A murder is committed in the village or town. The impact goes far beyond the victim; it goes to family and kindred, indeed to the entire village or town. Tensions compounded of fear, dread, pity, anger, desire for revenge mount quickly and steadily among the inhabitants. A life has been foully taken, a sacred value violated. The tensions become higher as the search takes place, still higher when the murderer is captured and found guilty. Only with his just punishment do the tensions within the locality subside. The stain upon the group has been washed away by the discovery and punishment of the villain. That drama, that pattern or community of elements, is one of the most ancient in the history of human society. It is also one of the most powerful in respect of the development of morality and the preservation of social order.

But this community of crime and punishment is being destroyed today. There are more than 25,000 murders a year in the United States. Each of several cities has an annual rate of murder in excess of that of any other nation in the world. But numbers are not the whole story. The entire ritual of crime and punishment is being lost, the recurrent, stabilizing, and reinforcing drama of crime followed by hue and cry, by search and capture, by trial, judgment of guilt, and then punishment. Once it was possible to find in most murders elements of Raskolnikov's murder in Dostoevsky's *Crime and Punishment*: some kind of rejection of the life process, the triumph of materialistic passion over morality, the surrender to evil means in the accomplishment of some good, the agony of punishment, the presumption of remorse and of transfiguration through suffering. But Dostoevsky would not recognize crime and punishment as he understood them in the Walpurgis Night that has become the American scene in the late twentieth century.

The community of moral and legal elements which once characterized crime and punishment has been fragmented, and in the process the individuality, the distinctiveness of crime, especially murder, has been lost to human contemplation. Memory could hardly persist in a country where 25,000 murders take place each year, a loss of human life greater than that of most wars in history. Not very far back in time, murders and other crimes possessed individuality. Memory is vivid of some of the more celebrated murders of the 1920s and 1930s, including the Judd-Gray murder and execution, the Hall-Mills case, the Hickman kidnap-murder, the Lindbergh kidnap-murder, and the Loeb-Leopold murder. It is no more difficult to recall celebrated murders and trials of earlier vintage—Lizzie Borden with her ax and forty whacks, the Stanford White murder by Harry K. Thaw. These murders all fell into a pattern as old as mankind. They were one and all committed either in the surge of uncontrollable hatred or else with malice aforethought. Within the latter, *cherchez la femme* could be elaborated to include not only the woman but the will, the money, the jewelry, the accomplice. Murder for the most part had a *raison d'être*, however sordid and squalid the reason may have been. It was this that served as the efficient cause of the mobilization of the community of crime and punishment. Few hearing or reading about the murder could remain immune to the tantalizing, even preoccupying questions of motive, opportunity, time. Not only did such a murder, with all that followed, seem like a mystery-detective novel, but the mystery novel drew much of its appeal from its likeness to what could happen in any community in the land.

Fascination with the individuality of murder extended through trial to punishment, usually execution duly reported in full by the press. Many may remember the impact upon the country of the illicit newspaper photograph of the murderess Ruth Judd, taken in the electric chair after the current had hit her, straining cataclysmically against her bonds. Nor was the murder of Bobby Franks much out of the mind of the American people after the story burst from Chicago, its drama not diminished by the presence of Darrow arguing for clemency for the youthful Loeb and Leopold, clemency meaning life imprisonment instead of execution. The country was unequally divided over the true justice of the judge's decision, life imprisonment, with more people favoring execution than imprisonment, because murder was taken very seriously then, as it had been through the whole of human history. But at least no one could reasonably doubt that the judgment would be an unequivocal guilty, with punishment, not psychiatric care, the denouement.

Punishment was as stark and memorable to society as was the crime leading to it. Until recently in the West, especially America, it has always been this way. In the community of crime and punishment there was a functional reciprocity between the deed and the punishment; the first aroused the thrill of horror; the second the thrill of retribution. Payment was made. The community could become dormant once again—until some new murder, robbery, burglary, or other violation of the social contract took place.

Crime fiction followed life with extraordinary fidelity, containing indeed its own community. Typically the murder case—with its murderer-principal, victim, motive, method, trial, conviction, and punishment, just as in actual life—was the substance of the works of Doyle, Sayers, Christie, and the other front-runners in the fictional community of crime and punishment. There was, in novel as in life, little tergiversation about guilt and innocence. The essence of the community was that black and white were the dominant hues, with little if any gray. Often it was assumed that a single murder could, for purposes of the novel, rivet the attention of city and nation. The murders dealt with by Philo Vance in the Van Dine books of the 1920s invariably galvanized the entire city of New York. Nor was fiction much larger than truth. Single murders did rivet public attention until only recently.

The almost epiphenomenal relation that so long was peculiar to the classical murder mystery and to actual life is gone completely now. The ways most murders take place today in life, and the way the guilty party is likely to be treated, if ever captured at all and if ever found guilty of his committed murder, make for an enormous chasm between actuality and the classic mystery novel. No one indeed cares who killed Roger Ackroyd. Edmund Wilson's dismissal of mystery-detective literature many years ago, which outraged so many readers of the genre, has come to possess a significance he did not quite intend. For in the presence of the bizarre mass murders which now befoul the American landscape, no one can much care whether the murderer of one individual is ever found. To read about the sleuth sifting through clues *ad nauseam* merely to arrest, try, and punish some inheritance-grasping relative, while mass murders and atrocities are taking place all over the United States, is an experience in transient schizophrenia.

Howard Unruh is from all accounts a decent young fellow; it is merely that one day on a Camden, New Jersey, street he emptied two Lugers, in the process of which play thirteen people were killed— without reason or motive in any ordinary sense of these words. James Ruppert of a small Ohio town, also a decent fellow by all accounts and "bright" in school, decided one Easter Sunday afternoon, following dinner, that things must change. Within ten minutes he had killed his mother, brother, sister-in-law, and eight children. Gacy of Chicago captured, sodomized, tortured, killed, and then buried under his house some three dozen youths over a period of a year or two. He was preceded in this *modus operandi* by a Texan, with about the same number of scalps, but as that was almost a decade ago, no one can be expected to remember his name or, for that matter, whatever happened to him. Do not forget the "disturbed" student at the University of Texas who, from the top of a tower in the heart of the campus, fired away with high-powered rifles until a dozen or more students lay dead, others badly wounded. Or there is the amiable fat boy in Kansas a few years back, also a "bright student in school," who, suddenly inspired by the thought of leaving home to go to Chicago and become a hired killer, wandered into the living room and shot his father, mother, and sister.

It would be a grievous oversight to neglect two other patterns of murder most foul in the late twentieth century in America. The perpetrator of the first type is epitomized by Russell Baker as "the Cleaver, the Slasher, the Machete Hacker and the Crazed Motorist." The enlarging number of these people simply dash into a subway car long enough to kill and mutilate with a cleaver, randomly slash throats in doorways, playfully apply machetes to any who may be available on the street, and suddenly turn the automobile on sidewalk pedestrians, accelerating furiously and usually getting a good bag. The second pattern is in many ways the most depressing. It is the murder, with or without loot, of the very elderly—in their houses, in their small rooms, or while shopping on the street.

The present world of murder and crime makes a community of

crime and punishment no longer possible. This form of community has suffered the same demise that so many other forms have in the twentieth century. No kind of reaction, after all, no kind of mobilization of emotion and mind, no kind of tension to be eventually relieved by outcome, is possible in such slaughters. It is no more possible to fit the elements of these crimes into a community that dissolves itself when the guilty has been punished than it is to fit the horrors of Dachau, the Gulag, and Cambodia into anything resembling the community of war.

The community of crime and punishment will be missed. It has been a building block of society. Durkheim referred to crime as both necessary and, in proper degree, desirable. Only through an individual's flouting of a sacred value, such as the sanctity of life, can people remind themselves from time to time of the value itself and of its indispensability to the community at large. Crime is inevitable because of the high differentiation of human behavior. It is natural that, just as there are prophets and saints, so there are the villainous, both being deviants from the norm. But so long as crime remains within limits and occurs infrequently, it is salutary, because it reaffirms in the minds of members of the community the social bond. Punishment may be viewed in the same light. The guilty one, according to Durkheim, must be punished if the community is to recover its normal state, for the crime has been one against the community as well as against some discrete individual. And until a catharsis has been effected through trial, through the finding of guilt and then punishment, the community is anxious, fearful, apprehensive, and above all, contaminated.

This view of crime and punishment was once a reasonably apposite picture of the matter in American society down through the 1930s. Perhaps it was the horrifying revelations from Nazi Germany and Stalinist Russia, especially during World War II, that changed the picture. But that still would not explain why things are so different in other countries which also suffered the shock of those revelations. The American people are, on the historical record, as kind, generous, cooperative, gentle, and compassionate as any people ever known to history. Yet America is also the home at present of the largest number of crimes proportionately of any nation on earth, the largest number of murders, and the largest number of brutal or sadistic murders and mass murders. And everything suggests an increase, not decrease, in these numbers.

The reason is not far to seek. In no country of the world has the community of crime and punishment been so badly disintegrated. It is hardly putting too strong a light on the matter to say that America has lost the villain, the evil one, who has now become one of the sick, the disturbed, demanding therapy or at worst incarceration in an asylum, rather than prison or the death house. America also lost the victim, who is more likely to be denigrated for having gotten in the way of the disturbed one than to receive commiseration. America has lost the moral value of guilt, lost it to the sickroom. And finally, America has lost that most vital element, punishment. To punish anyone—child at home, pupil in school, rapist, murderer—embarrasses Americans today. When President Reagan was shot and wounded, even he almost immediately afterward spoke of a "disturbed youth" and commiserated with his parents—which youth, John Hinckley, many months following the indisputable fact of his shooting the bullets, itself the consummation of several weeks of preparation in which above-average acumen, skill, patience, and poise were required, was still undergoing careful examination and reexamination by psychiatrists in a hospital environment to determine whether he could be held responsible and thus guilty. By contrast, in Italy, the would-be assassin of Pope John Paul was in prison, guilty, serving a life sentence, a mere three months after the shooting.

It is no small thing in a social order to erode away the ethic of guilt and replace it by the ethic of nonresponsibility for one's acts in matters of crime. Responsibility lies on the other side of the coin of individual freedom. People are free if they hold themselves responsible for their actions. So thought the Founding Fathers and their European philosopher guides. To press instantly for a therapeutic context in which to examine criminals is to deny them their rights as free citizens.

Not strangely, the Soviet Union, its premise doubtless Marx's contempt for the doctrine of free will, increasingly uses the psychiatric asylum as its means of punishment or exile from society. To be sure, none of this came about in the Soviet Union until well after Stalin had, without any trial at all or with a contrived one at best, sentenced to execution millions of Russians between 1930 and 1941, sending many more to the horrors of the Gulag. They were guilty in Stalin's judgment, not sick and irresponsible as Marxian writ would have it. Were the Soviet Union not so ineradicably bound to its sixty years of horrors, one might find elements of humor in the spectacle furnished. In the beginning, elaborate extenuations were furnished for crimes of property and passion, for such crimes could, by definition, exist only in countries based upon private property and individualism. Foreign visitors and pilgrims were invariably shown hospitals and asylums where the wayward were treated as sick rather than as violators of law. This was in its way a reflection of Samuel Butler's

Erewhon, where those who committed crimes were hospitalized and those who caught pneumonia were given stiff prison sentences. But side by side with the Potemkin's villages that the Soviet leaders offered with respect to property crimes went a harshness for political "crimes," namely dissent or suspected dissent, which became steadily more murderous. Forgiveness or simple therapy for the burglar and murderer, but death, torture, and imprisonment to the ideological dissenter.

Something of this Soviet mentality is to be found in the mind of the Western liberal at the present time, with due allowance for scope and intensity. When it comes to muggings, rapes, burglaries, and murders, the liberal is characteristically so concerned by the injustices—as the liberal sees them—done by society to the wretches responsible that he finds himself poised between sympathy for the criminal and a certain animosity toward the criminal's victim, who the liberal sees as a personification of society-the-offender. It is hard for the liberal to see the mugger as guilty, as a violator of law and morality and therefore deserving of punishment, irrespective of the presumed state of his mental health. Thus the steady decline in the United States during the past half-century of the mentality of crime and punishment and the steady rise and spread of the mentality of sickness and therapy.

But it must not be overlooked that the same liberals who weep for the killer instead of the slain can scarcely control their fury at mention of the "authoritarian" nations and their leaders. In such leaders there is no illness, sickness, or maladjustment—only hard and vicious criminality. Death to all apartheidists, Ku Klux Klanners, Watergate conspirators, makers of nuclear reactors, and their like on the earth; but mercy and therapy for radical terrorists, murderers, rapists, and other takers of life and property. Thus it is that in America at present it is possible for a man found guilty and sentenced to double life imprisonment for having dismembered two women to be given early release, only to murder savagely another woman within the first week of release.

There is little if any community of crime and punishment left in the United States, though the overwhelming majority of Americans, as polls reveal steadily, wish there were. In place of this community there is only the pseudo-community of sickness, victimization by society, and therapy. How that scourge of Victorian society, Samuel Butler, must be laughing from the shades.

DARWINISM

ONCE AGAIN the Darwinian mandarinate is sorely beset. For all its efforts these past few years to assimilate the results of molecular biology, immunology, geology, paleobiology, and astronomy, the fact is too obvious to be overlooked, or to be swept under the rug, that, between the essential principles of evolution which Darwin gave to the world and the principles of evolution which recent research in several areas has yielded, there is nearly total conflict. And although Darwin remains a uniquely hallowed name in Western science, there is mounting evidence of a rising revolt of younger scientists against the once-sovereign Darwinian writ. For a long time the mandarinate was able to protect its sacred heritage; it could successfully identify in the public mind Darwinism and evolutionism, making any criticism of a uniquely Darwinian concept tantamount to selling out to the feared creationists. But this is proving to be less and less possible. And judging from the sheer buoyancy of research in the areas which are closest to the evolutionary process and panorama, the hold of the mandarinate will be as nothing within a few years.

Darwin was one of the greater scientists of his century; he deserves honor. But something less must be said of the Darwinians who became a lobby and special interest group even before Darwin died. Thomas Henry Huxley was probably the key figure in the rise of the mandarinate, though he had associates in England, Germany, and the United States. The mandarinate could then and does now include scientists of individual distinction, and no one can fault it in its respect for a great naturalist. Nor can the Darwinians be faulted for their defense of an evolutionary view of the world in contrast to the literal creationist account in Genesis.

What can be leveled against the mandarinate is the myth that began to form well before Darwin's death, the myth that Darwinism and evolutionism are identical and that any criticism of Darwin is perforce a criticism of evolution and must come from a creationist. Huxley, who had his private doubts about several key elements in Darwinian theory, did a great deal to generate the additional myth that the only real opposition to Darwin's *Origin of Species* was religious in origin. But the criticisms which stung Darwin were those that came, not from the clergy, who were generally respectful to him, but from distinguished fellow-scientists, who made their way almost immediately to some of the logical and evidential difficulties of Darwinian theory, such as Darwin's repudiation of the very geological record he had gone to for verification of his theory and his unsatis-

factory (by Darwin's own admission) account of the nature of variation and its cumulative role in evolutionary progression. These scientists were not critical of the idea of biological evolution, which had
been a very familiar idea since the late eighteenth century; they were
critical of Darwin's special theory of evolution.

The essence of this Darwinian theory is the concept of natural
selection, made by Darwin to support the whole vast, infinitely complex phenomenon of the development and the variegation of the species. Darwin often made the referent of his "my theory" not natural
selection but the whole theory of biological evolution, as though no
one before him had known about or accepted the theory. But in truth
Darwinian theory is no more at bottom than his insistence that the
whole evolutionary procession in time can be explained by "Natural
Selection" (the capitals are his), a process that in Darwin's explication
is exceedingly slow, gradual, and continuous, based upon the infinitesimally small variations which take place from one generation of
an organism to another. The whole of the evolutionary epic can be
explained, Darwin further insisted, by study of contemporaneous
processes in nature, for the processes which were instrumental in the
remote past are said to be still instrumental in the present. Finally,
Darwin was opposed to all suggestions that evolution may operate at
different speeds and be subject to frequent large mutations as well as
tiny variations. This is in essence the special Darwinian theory of
evolution. Darwin himself wondered during his final years whether
he had not overemphasized natural selection, but it is one more sign
of a mandarinate that Darwin's supporters continue to this day to defend the concept on every possible ground and to contemn alternatives.

Darwin's special theory had its critics from the outset at the
highest levels of science. Even his partisans Huxley and Lyell were
troubled by his unyielding insistence on gradualness. Such eminences
as the botanist Gray, the zoologist Agassiz, the astronomer Herschel,
and the physicist Maxwell, who were not in slightest doubt of the
fact of evolution of some kind, were openly skeptical that such vast
developments and differentiations which the evolutionary panorama
revealed can all be explained by a single process of change, one in
which gradualness and strict continuity are the very essence. But
rarely were the doubts and skepticisms of these scientists given their
due by the Darwinian mandarinate. It cultivated sedulously the myth
that criticisms of Darwin were criticisms of the evolutionary view and
that for the most part they came only from the fundamentalists in religion.

The mandarinate had its first serious struggle around 1900 with the opening up to the scientific world of the epochal researches of Mendel. Mendel had done his experiments at about the same time Darwin was finishing the *Origin*. Moreover, he presented the results before the Natural Science Society in 1865, only six years after publication of Darwin's *Origin*, a work that Mendel knew well. Mendel's results were published in detail in 1866, and Mendel even sent a copy of his publication to Darwin. It remained, alas, unread. Had Darwin chosen to open the pages and been up to the mathematics contained there, he would have gotten at a stroke the answer he so desperately needed to the question of the source of variations and the precise mechanisms of inheritance.

Mendel's brilliant and original researches, which first led to the vital distinction between genotype and phenotype, lay largely ignored during the last third of the nineteenth century, in no small measure because of the Darwinians and their consecrated protectiveness of Darwinian writ. The result was that not until the turn of the century were Mendel's discoveries made a part of modern biology, manifest in the new science of genetics. This new breed of geneticists recognized immediately from their experiments that Darwin's theory of minute variations accumulating with infinite gradualness through time simply would not hold up. Their results demonstrated first of all the vital, crucial importance of the genotype in all studies of inheritance and, second, the fact that biological inheritance is replete with mutations and discontinuities, so that Darwin's stubborn insistence upon tiny variations alone could not be sustained.

The result was an embarrassing split in biology, with comparative anatomists, embryologists, and the old-line naturalists on one side, still unyielding in their devotion to Darwin, and on the other side, a significant number of geneticists. For several decades the mandarinate sought to heal the breach, warning that such a breach could only play into the hands of the dreaded creationists. Conferences took place, and there finally emerged the so-called synthetic theory of evolution, highlighted by publication in 1942 of Julian Huxley's *Evolution: The Modern Synthesis*. The "synthesis" was not a true one in the judgment of some scientists, the geneticist Richard Goldschmidt high among them. Tirelessly he pointed out that no synthesis whatever was involved, only a papered-over juxtaposition of Darwinian natural selection and Mendelian principles of inheritance. Goldschmidt was altogether too original and important an experimenter to be ignored, but not enough to be saved from ostracism. To this day, among those who attended the conferences leading to Huxley's book, there is difference of opinion on the degree of unity that was supposedly effected.

There is, however, no difference of opinion on the reality of the present growing assault on Darwinian orthodoxy. Genetics is but one of the sciences that throws doubt on the basic principles of Darwinism. It has been joined by paleontology, geology, immunology and molecular biology. It is a rare meeting of major biological disciplines that does not include a panel or two on the deficiencies of the specifically Darwinian theory of biological evolution. What was but a trickle in Samuel Butler's day, a small stream at the time of DeVries and Bateson, and an unsteady brook when Goldschmidt and Willis were active, has by now become a respectable river. *Mirabile dictu*, it has become possible to criticize Darwin at national meetings and not be ostracized. It is the Darwinian mandarinate that is on the defensive.

To be sure, some of the contemporary rebellion against Darwinian gradualism springs from strange sources. Marx, hardly less a sacred cow than Darwin, is said to be the inspiration for the assault upon the Darwinian emphasis on micromutations at the expense of macromutations. The Marxian concept of revolutionary change is held by these critics to be their model for criticism of Darwinian gradualism. One critic went so far as to argue that Darwin's repudiation of large-scale, "revolutionary" changes was based upon his Victorianism, his preference for the kind of change-mechanism in biology that he saw and felt politically around him in Victorian England. This is absurd. The idea of gradualism in both biological and social realms goes straight back to eighteenth century studies in natural history, an endeavor that included language and morals as well as the earth and its mantle of life. Moreover, some of the most eager Darwinians were inhabitants of countries across the Channel that had had their full share of revolution.

In any event, it is actually comical to present Marx and Darwin as at different poles. Marx had vast admiration for Darwin's *Origin* and compared his own *Capital* to it, down to the very details. Both, Marx thought, had independently discovered the true laws of motion, the one in the organic, the other in the social realm. Marx saw the revolutions of history in much the same way that Darwin saw the emergence of new species: as consequences of slow but insistent changes which accumulate in time. Marx declared his theory of revolution superior to all others around him precisely because, in his view, he had buttressed his view of revolution with his concomitant law of evolution in society. The only striking difference between Marxian and Darwinian conceptions of evolution is that Marx, in respect to social evolution, was very much the preformationist: "higher relations of production never appear before the material conditions of their existence have matured in the womb of the old society." But the reader of *Capital* is bound to agree with Marx that that book is oriented toward the same fundamental principles of change and development which are found in the *Origin*, even to the point of Marxian rejection of "bold leaps."

The contemporary revolt against Darwinism, whether Marxian or non-Marxian in inspiration, rests largely upon the "gradualism" inherent in Darwinian theory. But the rebels fail to see that there is much more than gradualism to be concerned with in any adequate criticism of Darwinism, as Frederick J. Teggart recognized more than a half-century ago. There is, to begin, the whole problem of time. Darwin was not unaware of the difficulty that time presented to his theory of evolution. He cited the skepticism of William Thompson who thought that the earth was probably not old enough to give geological support to a theory of biological change which rested upon the most extreme gradualism. Even Huxley once growled about scientists who "insisted upon a practically unlimited bank of time, ready to discount any amount of hypothetical paper." Maxwell and Herschel were both convinced that there had not been time enough for the spectacle of biological evolution to unfold through the slow accumulation of infinitesimally small variations that Darwin's theory called for. But to all such objections Darwin simply replied that not enough was known about the history of the earth to make possible more than mere speculation on it—true enough in Darwin's day.

The larger point, though, is that Darwin and all the other evolutionists of the eighteenth and nineteenth centuries simply ignored time. Lamarck spoke for them all, Darwin included, when he wrote that "for nature time is nothing. It is never a difficulty; she always has it at her disposal; and it is the means by which she has accomplished the greatest as well as the least of her results."

But one can no longer be indifferent to time and to the compatibility of time and theories of evolution. Time's winged chariot is hurrying near. From discoveries of earth scientists and astronomers has come a budget of time. The earth is known to be four and a half billion years old, in a universe between fifteen and twenty billion years old. Life did not begin on earth prior to about two billion years ago. The more advanced organisms did not make an appearance before a half-billion years ago. These may seem to be large time spans, but they are not, given the boundless complexity of life in its current form, given the immense number of false starts and fixations, and finally, given the exceeding slowness of change posited by the Darwinians.

Events will almost surely have to be taken into consideration if evolutionary change is to be made compatible with the budget of time mankind is obliged to live with. Darwin's world is an eventless one. He wrote: "As natural selection acts solely by accumulating slight, successive, favorable variations, it can produce no great or sudden modifications; it can act only by short and slow steps. Hence the canon of *Natura non facit saltum,* which every fresh addition to our knowledge tends to confirm, is, on this theory, intelligible." But it is not intelligible, not when time is taken into consideration. Again, the shrewd Huxley sensed the problem, writing, "Darwin's position might have been even stronger than it was if he had not embarrassed himself with the aphorism *Natura non facit saltum* which turns up so often in his pages." Darwin's friend Lyell, himself once an ardent gradualist in his geological work, knew that Darwin was only weakening his case for natural selection by rejecting events and insisting upon absolute continuity of micromutations.

Darwin had his reasons—though not, alas, reasons of scientific character—and he was frank in expresssing them. To refute creationists was, he said, one of the prime objects of his book. They tended to identify themselves with the catastrophists of the day, scientists who argued the impossibility of explaining the configuration of the earth's surface except on the hypothesis of primal catastrophic events. To side in any degree with the catastrophists, Darwin said, would be to run the risk of being charged with creationism in some measure. Darwin's apprehensiveness about creationism is perhaps admirable, but such a state of mind is hardly proper basis for a scientific theory. Astronomy and the earth sciences accept the reality of formative events in the past; evolutionary biology can do no less; indeed it already is, *pace* the Darwinian mandarinate, accepting such events both external and internal alike.

The premise of uniformitarianism is yet another flaw in Darwin's theory: the premise that all really significant processes of evolutionary change are uniform through time, and that one need study only what is going on in the present to be informed of what happened in the past. This assumption emerged in the eighteenth century as one of the building blocks of the idea of progress. The Scotch natural philosopher Hutton sought to demonstrate that the history of the entire universe could be reconstructed by study of what is operating in the present. Other natural philosophers used the premise of uniformitarianism to seek to account for the histories of language, social institutions, and other aspects of life. Hutton impressed Lyell, founder of modern geology, and it was from Lyell that Darwin acquired his belief. Darwin, however, was a great deal more fervid in his uniformitarianism than was Lyell, for it was still another means of driving a spike into the creationist coffin. One contemporary Darwinian, Simpson, as faithfully uniformitarian as his master, stated that "changeless immanent forces" which are "inherent in the nature of the cosmos" are all that the student of biological evolution needs to know. Once astronomers, geologists, and also social scientists believed that. They do no longer, though, and uniformitarianism is one more Darwinian idol that needs to be sacrificed in the study of evolution.

Darwin also failed to give proper attention to the fixity, the stagnation, and also the disappearance of species in the past. Natural selection, in Darwin's exposition, calls for unremitting variation from one generation to another. Darwin was adamant in his insistence that such variation leads to change, to gradual development, and to the emergence of new species. Alas, the record is only too clear: there have been and are species which, variation notwithstanding, have persisted for great lengths of time in essentially unchanged condition. Moreover, again attested by the geological record, there have been many species which once existed but then disappeared from the face of the earth.

Darwin was aware of the conflict between his theory of gradual, continuous, and incremental progress in life and what the geological record revealed. Indeed he devoted an entire chapter to the subject; but it is titled, "On the Imperfections of the Geological Record." In it is found the extraordinary statement, "I do not pretend that I should ever have suspected how poor was the record in the best preserved geological sections had not the absence of innumerable transitional links between the species which lived at the commencement and close of each formation pressed so hardly on my theory." Darwin could have paraphrased Robespierre: Perish the record rather than a principle.

Equally suspect in Darwinism is the acceptance—hook, line, and sinker—of the eighteenth century idea of progress. Darwin wrote: "As all living forms of life are the lineal descendants of those which lived long before the Cambrian epoch, we may feel certain that the ordinary succession by generation has never once been broken and that no cataclysm has desolated the whole world. Hence we may look with some confidence to a secure future of great length. And as natural selection works solely by and for the good of each being, all corporeal and mental endowments will progress toward perfection."

It is hard to resist the conclusion that for Darwin belief in progress through natural selection became a kind of surrogate for the belief he had once held in Paley's theory of design. Darwin's voyage on the *Beagle* had convinced him that Paley's God of perfect design could no longer be rationally sustained. That natural selection came to fill much of the gap left by Darwin's lapsed belief in Paley is shown by a passage from the *Origin* which typifies what Ruskin called the "pathetic fallacy," that is, the endowing of human or godly qualities in natural things and processes: "It may be said that natural selection is daily and hourly scrutinizing, throughout the world, the slightest variations; rejecting those that are bad, preserving and adding up all that are good; silently and insensibly working *whenever and wherever opportunity offers*, at the improvement of each organic being in relation to its organic and inorganic conditions of life. We see nothing of these slow changes in progress until the hand of time has marked the lapse of ages."

This was too much even for some of Darwin's most loyal supporters, and he was prevailed upon to add, in subsequent editions, "metaphorically" after the first two words in the paragraph. This was merely cosmetic. For Darwin, natural selection was godlike in its wonders.

Natural selection is far from being one of the more elegant theories in the natural sciences. That the process of natural selection exists and has existed continuously in the past is beyond question; the concept has been known since at least Lucretius. But as a general theory designed to explain the enormously complex phenomenon of evolution, it fails badly. It explains too much and too little. That the whole panorama of evolution from the first manifestation of life to the emergence of *Homo sapiens* can be explained simply by tiny variations proceeding with infinite slowness is not a proposition with intrinsic plausibility. The time given by contemporary earth science to the appearance and differentiation of life is too short. Events, jumps, macromutations, all offensive to Darwin, can be ignored by the mandarinate no longer.

There is an unfortunate self-sealing quality to Darwinian natural selection considered as master theory, a characteristic it shares with Marxism and Freudianism. Whatever is found—red-tailed, black-tailed, or white-tailed birds flying into the red sunset, economic depression or prosperity, compulsive eating or no eating at all—is instantly and unarguably proved by the all-purpose theories of natural selection, the dialectic, and the Oedipus complex. Prediction, in the strictly scientific sense of the word, is utterly absent from the theory of natural selection.

Darwin prided himself on the absence of theory in his *Origin*. He believed he had simply examined the data of life and then drawn directly the conclusions set forth. But in all truth his works are saturated with theory, with metaphysical assumptions indeed, such as his cherished chain of being, plenitude, *Natura non facit saltum*, and progress. It is the old story. An investigator starts or claims to start with his mind emptied of all theory and concept. Only the data will be recognized as source of inference and theory. What invariably happens, though, is that the mind is not emptied—a psychological impossibility in any case—and more often than not the investigator takes as his first axiom something as old as Heraclitean physics and biology. *Natura non facit saltum* is such an axiom in Darwin. But there are others.

Darwin was a great scientist, though all hagiography to one side, he was no greater than some of his contemporaries—Maxwell and Mendel, to name but two. Sadly, a great scientist has been done in by ever-worshipful followers, not content to let him be simply a creative naturalist of the middle nineteenth century with the amount of errors and inadequacies normal to even the greatest of scientists. The shrine that Down has become to all scientists in need of pilgrimage epitomizes the unique position Darwin holds. A laboratory has become a temple and a genius has become a saint.

DEATH

OF THE RECURRING crises of the human condition—birth, marriage, death—the last has drawn the vastly greater part of man's ritual propensity, most of it going to the welfare of the dead in the next world. There seems to be an instinctual disposition to repudiate any thought of death being simply the final stage of the individual life cycle. Even the repugnant spectacle of the human body in process of decomposition has not prevented the almost universal belief that there is some human essence which is destined for survival in the hereafter. Whether one leaves food and clothing in the grave or merely utters prayers, the premise is the same. The community that nourished in life, nourishes also in death. Death as part of the community, death as wound to the community, and death as departure from the community has been for at least fifty thousand years the stated or unstated philosophy of virtually the whole of the human race, the only species to bury its dead.

But in spreading parts of the world, starting with the West and reaching its highest incidence in America, this philosophy is eroding. The socially annihilating individualism—that is, the atomization of society, chiefly by the modern state—that has led to the dismemberment and fragmentation of the traditional forms of community, especially kinship, has removed more and more of the communal properties of death, just as it has of birth and marriage. In modern society people are increasingly baffled and psychologically unprepared for the incidence of death among loved ones. It is not that their grief is greater or that the incomprehensibility of death is increased. The bafflement is in considerable part a result of the smaller size of the family, which gives greater emotional value to each of the members. But even more, it is a result of the decline in significance of the traditional means of ritual completion of the fact of death. Death leaves a kind of moral suspense that is terminated psychologically only with greater and greater difficulty. The social meaning of death has changed with the social position of death.

The social position of death in Western society ranges from a kind of obscenity, whose name is as improper in polite circles as sex was among the Victorians, all the way to a kind of celebrity, receiving immense attention in the form of books, articles, television documentaries, and lectures. With one hand people push death under the carpet, but with the other they reach out almost obsessively for help. "The long habit of living," wrote Thomas Browne, "indisposeth us to dying." But however "indisposed" Paleolithic man and all his successors down to the last century or two may have been, such indisposition could not have been as great where death was just as much a part of family life, of community life, as were birth and marriage. No one was unacquainted with the physical fact of death, directly and personally. It is not entirely that death was earlier and more frequent in human society until recent times; it is rather that death was highly visible to everyone, and in as concrete a way as is possible. Human beings knew death so directly, so recurrently, in the much shorter life cycle, that there was inevitably less of the abstract preoccupation with death known today. In our time an astounding number of people have never seen a dead human body. Our ancestors could, within the house, wash, dress, adorn, and otherwise minister themselves to the corpse in anticipation of burial and mourning. Today people leave that to the mortician and, on a constantly widening scale, avoid even sight of the dead person. Inevitably, cremation and instant dispatch of the ashes crowd out burial. Nor can it be claimed that this behavior is mute recognition of the disappearance of available land for cemeteries, for peoples at other times thought nothing of using and reusing graves, and there were charnel houses for the bones. No, the beginning of the end of funerary and mourning rites in modern society is social, a part of that wider tidal movement of modern history that has destroyed so much which lies intermediate between individual and state.

What has happened to death has happened also to birth, childhood, marriage, and senescence in modern Western society. These
have never before had the same functional role and meaning they
have today. The entire emphasis is now put upon the conjugal couple; the child is idealized and romanticized in a way that would have
been beyond belief before the nineteenth century; and "senior citizens" are venerated once a year as mothers and fathers. But the inescapable fact, despite all of the national holiday devotions and everything that has been done for the welfare of children which exceeds
all other ages put together, is that the true value of these roles has
withered, for they have been extracted from the traditional community, which alone is the source and sustenance of birth, marriage, and
death, and have been located in the individual. In times past, individuals did not have children; the community did in its act of acceptance
through some form of baptism. The physical fact of birth was not
nearly so important as the social fact of birth. In the ancient world no
child was "born" until ten days or say after parturition, when it was
duly and ritually received or, when necessary, rejected. Marriage was
not an affair of two individuals uniting and thus forming a new "family"; marriage was basically a rite of adoption whereby, in strict accord with the bans on incestuous union, the girl from one household
was ritually cleansed of her former family identity, her name altered
so that its new suffix would indicate that fundamentally she was a
daughter in the new family, a possession of husband and house father. Ancient Rome gave the customary and legal base to this sense
of marriage so far as Western society is concerned, but everywhere,
through the greater part of human history, this has been the significance of marriage. There was a conjugal union, to be sure, but its
meaning came from the larger community, starting with kindred.

So long as death was concrete, personally experienced over and
over in life, public rather than hidden or transferred to mortuary
technicians, and above all, familiar ritually in the kinship community,
it was comprehensible and acceptable, at least to a greater degree
than it is now in American society. One thinks of the linguistic
abominations *pass on, pass away,* and *called for,* which so fastidiously
avoid the words *die* and *death,* words as noble as any to be found in
the English language. But all the while people are queasily avoiding
direct personal contact with death, in substance and in name, they
are becoming increasingly obsessed by it in the abstract. No doubt
the current mania about "health"—evidenced in health maintenance
organizations, health clubs, health pursuits of every kind, with jog-
ging the *pièce de résistance*—is but another manifestation of unease
with death. No one knows what health is; sickness, yes; and origi-

nally the treating of sickness, not the maintenance of health, was the sworn responsibility of the physician.

Lewis Thomas reported that in his own experience with the dying, there is, at the very end of life, a detached acceptance of death, a serenity and release from care never known before. Rare indeed is the final struggle, the agony, the unwillingness to die that so many books and television documentaries favor. Thomas cited the physician Osler to the effect that dying is "not such a bad thing to do after all." Osler took a dour view of people who spoke of the pain and grief of death, except in the minds of family, friends, and onlookers. Thomas speculated on whether there may possibly be, as the result of evolutionary adaptation to the inexorability of death, "some protective physiological mechanism, switched on at the verge of death, carrying [the dying] through in a haze of tranquillity." The idea is plausible and certainly agreeable.

But more important than the physical onset of death in the individual is the place of death in the community, or rather in what is left of community in the increasingly anonymous, impersonal Western society. According to the wisdom of the past, death is, first and last, communal, not individual. If death and mourning are contained within the community, seen as wound and remembrance within the community, individuals cannot help but be fortified in the "long habit of life" so far as its eventual and necessary termination is involved. The modern indulgence in individualism has ill prepared people for the very sober responsibilities of the family, of the community in all its manifestations, and indeed of the nation itself. There is nothing extraordinary in the fact that narcissism and egocentricity are the companions of fear of death—or, for that matter, fear of birth, children, and even marriage—for the origins of all these lie basically in the individualism that Comte called "the disease of the Western world." Philippe Aries showed how over the past ten centuries dread, apprehension, and rejection of death have grown in almost precise relation to the growth of individualism and repudiation of community. He distinguished "death tamed," which is what it was in traditional society for thousands of years, from "untamed death," which is what it has become. Possibly the newly oriented medical profession, beginning to be taught how to minister to death as well as to life and disease, will help contemporary man come to grips with death in the way his forefathers did; perhaps the hospice movement will provide surrogate families to give all the sustentive attention that family once did for the dying; perhaps still other adaptations will make their way into currently apprehensive minds and will prove anodyne in the long run. But nothing is likely to matter very much until death, along with birth and marriage, ceases to be regarded as something happening primarily to the individual instead of to the community. Therefore, until somehow the reality and sense of community have been restored to Western society in national, local, and kinship spheres, people will continue to live in the void—ego-gratifying, hedonistic, narcissistic, subjective, and at the same time, timorous, trepidant, fearful of death.

Nothing betokens life in community more than does mourning, with its rites, forbearances, weeds, and wailing. As Burke noted, true society, namely community, is a partnership of the dead and unborn as well as of the living. Death is bound to be a more acceptable, even desirable, fate if it has been known repeatedly in vicarious form through rites of mourning. Above all, there must be a restoration of ritual, of the drama of birth, life, and death. This must be ritual alone, not any of the subjectivisms which the twentieth century has made so corrosive to the social fabric. Of no account in death and mourning is one's actual state of mind and emotion on the occasion of ritual expression. The actor need not feel on any given day every last emotional drive inherent in his lines; he need only act. A New England widow's ritual devotion to her late husband took the form of weeds and withdrawal from society lasting many months. "You are obviously desolated by loss," said one *naif* to the widow. "Don't be ridiculous," she replied. "My husband and I ceased even speaking to one another fifty years ago." More good may have been done the social bond by those weeds and that withdrawal from society than by all the muttered prayers since the beginning of time. The truly strong religions of the world are not those rich simply in the word but, far more important, in the act.

DOGMA

IT HAS BEEN SAID that people will die for a dogma who will not even stir for a conclusion. Such is the tribute reason must pay to faith. As Chesterton remarked, the merely rational man will not marry, and the rational soldier will not fight. The sad state of both marriage and the military in Western society is testimony to the decline of the dogma of patriotism and the dogma of matrimony. But the decline or moribundity of one set of dogmas is invariably accompanied by a surge of faith in others. Think of the dogma of equality which, through law, executive edict, and judicial decision, has destroyed or radically remade the existences of tens of millions of human beings in America. It is dogma, not reason, and least of all common sense, that has school buses crisscrossing the country in pursuit of school attendances which will express in quota fashion the ethnic diversity of American society. It is dogma, not reason, that so inflames the minds of egalitarians that they allow the most ancient of academic traditions—including the corporate right to govern, the power to make curriculum, the freedom to appoint and promote faculty members on merit alone, and the confidentiality of vital records—to be flouted and trampled by the regulations that issue forth from one regulatory bureau after other.

Once it was thought that the decline of traditional religion must be accompanied by the growing appeal of reason, especially political and social reason. The methods of science, including reason, logic, and experiment, would be applied to the social polity. Rationality, utility, majority opinion, and expertise would be the criteria of the good society, and their legacy would be an end for all time to the tyranny of such dogmas as divine right monarchy, hereditary aristocracy, and the sanctified roles of church and family. The individual would be freed of dogmas and allowed to live in the culture of political ideals like liberty, equality, fraternity, and justice. Ideals, not dogmas!

But the human capacity to bend ideals into dogmas is inexhaustible, and there is no comfort in reflecting on the record of the twentieth century in this respect. More lives have been tortured, terrorized, shot, hanged, poisoned, imprisoned, and exiled in the name of one or other of the modern political dogmas of freedom, equality, fraternity, and justice than in all other centuries combined. The dogma of czarist charisma led to a few thousand imprisonments, executions, and exiles in the nineteenth century. The dogma of the workers' state has led to millions of such horrors.

Whether for good or evil, liberating or tyrannizing, dogmas will prevail, and it is absurd to think or hope to the contrary. The word *dogma* comes from the Greek root meaning "seems good," and men will give far more of themselves for ideas or values which have become parts of their very souls, their intellectual tissues, than for ones that have been reached merely through calculated application of reason or through majority will in discussion. Religion and politics are necessarily the realms of life most fertile in dogmas, for only dogmas can ensure that degree of cohesion, of felt community, which is the *sine qua non* of church and state alike.

Descartes urged us to doubt everything and then to readmit beliefs only after they have been subjected to the pitiless light of reason.

Fortunately that Cartesian injunction is psychologically impossible, but if it were, we would be cast into a void. Tocqueville, early in life, wrote, "If I were asked to class human miseries, I would do so in this order: Disease, Death, and Doubt." But according to Morley, "at a later date Tocqueville altered the order, and deliberately declared doubt to be the most insupportable of all evils, worse than death itself." Balzac wrote, "Men have a horror of a spiritual vacuum." And Dos Passos declared: "The mind cannot support moral chaos for long. Men are under as strong a compulsion to invent an ethical setting for their behavior as spiders are to weave webs."

Dogma is as necessary to the individual as it is to the community. For each, it is the steel spring that makes thought and society possible.

EFFRONTERY

THE LATIN ROOT of this word tells something of its current meaning: shameless. Effrontery may not rival any of the seven deadly sins in its pernicious effects upon civility. All the same it can be prodigious in adding to the store of ethical illth in Western society. Effrontery is gall, it is unblushing impudence. It is temerity of the sort that springs from heedlessness, not of danger, but of ordinary decorum. It is chutzpah, but generally without the ingenuity and wit associated with chutzpah. Effrontery is the exhibiting for gain of the unbuttoned ego; it is the hypertrophy of brashness, and the embodiment of insolence. It is invariably associated with an individual's sense of effortless superiority: arrogance at its zenith. Caligula's nomination of his horse to the Roman Senate was effrontery, but so was Uriah Heep's secret ambition under the cloak of "humbleness."

Effrontery must have proper setting, more or less willing victims or audience. No culture that is strong in appreciation of honor, rich in *pietas* and *gravitas*, is likely to experience much effrontery in high places. Retribution would be swift and sure. But in such a political and social order as exists in America at the present time, effrontery is bound to be rife and successful.

Anthropologists tell of "shame cultures," in which a high degree of conformity is induced by fear of shame before one's fellows. If there are shame cultures, then there may also be "shameless cultures," ones so lacking in capacity for shame that effrontery not only ceases to be offensive to a people but becomes actually welcome. Most peoples, certainly all civilized peoples, have known periods of high and low degrees of effrontery. It is bound to have been low in incidence during most of the fifth century B.C. in Athens and high thereafter, for the Peloponnesian war that destroyed Athens' supremacy over Sparta also dissolved a great many of the norms and values of traditional civil life in Athens. Plato is only one of the several guides to the vices, including effrontery, which flourished from the end of that century. Literary evidence similarly suggests that effrontery was mild in scope and intensity during the Republic in Rome, at least until toward its end in the first century B.C. Suetonius, Petronius, and others have set down their records of the high level of effrontery during the Empire.

The United States is without doubt in one of its periods of rampant effrontery in government and society, probably the most fertile period in this respect since Mark Twain's Gilded Age in America in the decades following the Civil War. It becomes steadily more difficult to think of any act or statement from anyone of whatever sphere or status in American society that is sufficiently offensive to taste and morals as to lead to that person's self-removal in shame from the public forum. Even the most egregious acts of license are greeted with bored indifference or else as stepping stones for whatever rehabilitation may prove necessary to get the politically affluent delinquent back in the corridors of power. Mainstream religion is not much better than politics as a haven for the ideologically corrupt and the hypocritical. Elmer Gantry would be a shining light today compared with those who see the pulpit as opportunity for advancing the cause of third world socialism. Of the wealthy television preachers and purported gospel singers, the less said the better. Truly, a needle's eye faces them on their way to heaven.

Effrontery in politics and religion is so blatant that it has received broad attention. In other spheres of life the public gaze has tended to be kinder and more myopic. There is the university president who, having insisted upon a yacht and a private jet or two on top of a lavish salary and expense account, found himself so inept, so impotent before the disasters of the university, which were created largely by his own greed and bottomless effrontery, that he was obliged to flee, from bandoliered blacks, faculty, and students, to the vast relief of all, and who then, with superlative dash, opened offices as a private consultant in—that's right—higher educational administration.

There is the ivy-league professor who became a China expert by virtue of a seven weeks' visit to the People's Republic of China, then

spent the next decade in unrelieved adulation of such Maoist bene-
factions to the Chinese people as sense of community, popular democracy, freedom, justice, and overall liberation from ancient tyrannies, but when revelations from the Chinese themselves filled the air
after Mao's death attesting to genocide, terror, torture, mass exile,
and imprisonment, promptly wrote a "long awaited" book on Mao
that, with consummate impudence, made plain that he had been
aware all along of the atrocities inflicted by Mao on the eight hundred million, indeed had pioneered in so informing the world from
the beginning. Such effrontery was not so much as noticed in the
United States. As Ogden Nash might have written, raping is a crime
unless you rape the readers a million at a time.

There is the industrialist, risen from Whiz Kid of World War II,
known throughout America for having presided over the appearance
of an automobile model that from the beginning became a synonym
for futility and failure, who then, piling Pelion on Ossa, took as his
just reward the secretaryship of the largest and most powerful federal
department, where he commenced a new chapter of success by participating in a Caribbean military venture so patently foolish in conception and so disastrous in consequence that its name too entered
the lexicon of fiasco, who then helped instigate the longest, costliest,
and most unsuccessful war in United States history, winning renown
for his computerized body-counts, for the development of the now
defunct TFX all-purpose, all-service plane, and also for his skill in
being a hawk by day and a dove by night, who successfully escaped
from his own Asian war, after putting more than a half-million
Americans in it, and then managed to rise still farther, this time to
the presidency of a worldwide bank in which, from its luxurious offices in Washington, he could authorize the spending of billions of
the taxpayers' dollars and, without ceasing to be welcome in all of
the world's capitalist offices, could fertilize the growth of socialist
projects in the third world under the gospel of econometric developmentalism. And all of this earned him the plaudits of bankers, generals, industrialists, liberal intellectuals, the media, and large segments
of the citizenry. It is doubtful if any career in Western history has
been as saturated with sheer measureless effrontery as this one.

There is the university professor who, having helped light the
fires of student vandalism on campus, the while assuring the vandals
of their pristine idealism and reassuring the regents of the university
that what was going on in the way of window breaking, library invasion, humiliation of faculty and administration, and public foulness
of speech in the name of radicalism all sprang from existential roots
and, as a revolution, would continue far into the future, then, feeling

the vandalistic flames grow hotter, promptly took to, not the hills, but another academic retreat, where he declared the student revolution now obsolete.

There is the astronomer-impresario who, with the universe itself as protagonist of a television series, did not hesitate to do what God himself would have drawn back from, that is, intrude himself upon every awesome planet, every stunning galaxy, every eye-riveting landscape, and every luminescent sun, his voice in constant incantation of the great god science and in equally constant anathema of all religious impulse. That is effrontery of astronomical magnitude, but the television multitude adored it, and his accompanying book is a best seller. Without doubt, effrontery is a mine of wealth in the United States when properly worked, billions 'n' billions.

One last. There is the White House widow who from effrontery, not grief which is mute ("Light griefs can speak," wrote Seneca, "great ones are dumb"), commanded for her late President-husband, who had been a man of personal charm but little else, a Lincolnesque funeral down to the last detail, the first indeed since Lincoln's own, who also demanded and received a large plot of open earth at the Arlington Cemetery, one that had long been left clear of graves in the interest of beauty and of honoring the dead who lay in Arlington, a plot on which she directed the construction of a large monument highlighted by an eternal flame that would be the beginning of a visual line crossing the tombs of Lincoln and Jefferson, the monument to Washington, and ending grandly in the Capitol, and who then, in effrontery of purest ray serene, had carved just below the haunting words in the Southwest Bedroom beginning, "In this room Abraham Lincoln slept during his occupancy of the White House," the further words that not only had her husband slept there but she had too, and then, as final fillip, ordered the same carving done in the bedroom adjacent. For all of this she was pronounced America's gift to royalty. Verily, the modern age can compete with any in its rich profusion and grateful acceptance of effrontery.

E NTHUSIASM

THIS WORD REFLECTS at least four distinguishable states. The first is the obvious one: the seizure of the mind by a high degree of interest combined with eagerness, loyalty to individual or thing, and visible zeal. Enthusiasm in this sense appears at college football games, political rallies, picnics at their beginning.

Far more interesting and important historically are three other meanings the word has carried. One is its original meaning in the Greek: the seizure and possession of human beings by the divine, the demonic, or the pathologically irrational. In the oldest use in the Greek it meant literally the visitation of the human mind and body by a god. Thus the enthusiast was the cause of quite different emotions in others, depending upon their surmise as to which god or which demon had seized the person. Reactions could range from religious awe of the kind given to demigods and seers to repugnance and fear excited by belief that a wicked spirit had seized and possessed the enthusiast.

The third meaning of the term, which is religious, pertains to the thoughts and actions of those, such as the Anabaptists, Quakers, French Prophets, Levelers, Shakers, and Wesleyans, who in the seventeenth and eighteenth centuries astounded Europe with the manner of their revolt against orthodox and conventional Christianity. This manner of revolt could include human barking and mewing, the gift of tongues, round-the-clock dancing as a form of prayer, the rudest of insults to the high-born or influential, indulgence in gross and promiscuous sexual behavior, chronic states of mind from which external reality was utterly purged, seizures so severe that bodies became deformed, and many other grotesqueries of spirit and flesh.

But to leave religious enthusiasm at this would be ungenerous and inaccurate. For it could also reflect courage in the face of public obloquy and civil penalties including jailing and beating, great learning in Christian theology and history, and sincere belief in God, immortality, and human goodness that was proof against all threat or temptation. Beyond these qualities, enthusiasm could include a perfectly rational, indeed a brilliantly scientific mentality.

This variety of religious enthusiasm has at its core a challenge to the authority of the Roman or the Anglican established religions. The phenomenon is a product of post-Lutheran Europe. Anticipations of religious enthusiasm had appeared among the Corinthians whom Paul addressed, among the Montanists of primitive Christianity, and in certain medieval currents of thought. But these were infrequent, unrepresentative, or minor. Luther stirred up the religious passions of large numbers of Europeans by his revolt against a Catholic Christianity grown decadent and tyrannical in too many parts of the continent. Luther himself became quickly aware of and profoundly alarmed by what he had wrought. Hence his injunction to the civil rulers to put down, however bloodily, all uprisings against church and state which sprang, as did the Anabaptists, from early, revolutionary Lutheranism. For a hundred years the fear of civil repression was great enough to hold back the caged passions—enthusiasms—of Europeans eager to break from the established church in the name of true religion, of true obedience to God's will as known by the individual. Then, as despotism began to wane, as more tolerance and a greater number of individual liberties or at least indulgences accumulated, the dam burst. By the early seventeenth century religious sects, cults, and groups of every kind were seen in most of Europe, all of them, in diverse and exotic ways, attesting to the iniquity of established churches, to the need for not only breaking free of them but also planning for their destruction at whatever cost to civil order and human decency.

At the base of this manifestation of enthusiasm with all its diverse and often repellent symptoms lay one simple conviction: that of the goodness and divine nature of the individual prior to his corruption by the conventionalities of established Christianity. What alone was vital was the nurturing of this goodness and grace, which could be done only by the individual's achievement of direct communication with God, unmediated by sacrament, ritual, liturgy, convention, or law. But in turn, such direct communication was possible only when all these externalities and corruptions of grace and faith were destroyed. Side by side with the belief in effortless grace, to be nourished only by unremitting faith in God, lay the belief in millennium, in the imminent return to earth of Christ and the subsequent commencement of a long period of absolute happiness prior to the eventual ascent to heaven and all eternity.

Enthusiasm can be indistinguishable from revolution. For what it affirms can be made possible or secure only by the annihilation of all the tumors and poisons which have accumulated in the body of the Christian Church since its founding. The armed horsemen who rode their horses into the nave of magnificent Salisbury Cathedral and proceeded to empty the coffins of the bones of the earliest kings of England and then to hurl these bones at the stained glass windows until they had been shattered into slivers and shards were vandals only in a special sense of the word, for they were loyal, devout, and brave Puritan soldiers engaged, under Cromwell, in the necessary work of preparing the earth for Christ's return.

Antinomianism is an almost inevitable accompaniment of religious enthusiasm. The same mind that becomes assured of its attainment of direct and unmediated communication with God is only too likely to come to believe that everything in the mind, every thought and impulse, must be divine in origin and therefore pure. So fortified in spirit, the individual can only believe further that no matter what he does, no matter how heretical, blasphemous, or insubordinate by conventional standards his behavior is, it is nevertheless pure and good, save only in the minds of those who, being wicked, will think all else wicked. The antinomian ingredient in enthusiasm can lead to killings, to burnings, to orgies of sex and gluttony, as well as to the chronically rude and insulting, the habitually insolent manner of the Quaker George Fox whenever he was in the presence of an officer of the government, even the king himself, or a hierarch of the Church of England.

But this bizarre and uncivilized behavior notwithstanding, enthusiasm could also take the notable form of Wesleyanism in England and America. Wesley's was the first real challenge to the Anglican Church since that of Cromwell and the Puritans, yet he himself to his dying day professed loyalty to the Anglican Church, defining himself as one seeking only to restore it to pristine goodness. Wesley believed deeply in the people, in the invisible community of the good, in the religious rights of individuals, in grace, in the sovereignty of the people within their church, in the basic goodness of man, and in a coming millennium in which man's torments and deprivations would be ended forever. In pursuit of converts for these beliefs, Wesley traveled more than 225,000 miles and preached more than 40,000 sermons, often reaching 20,000 people at one time. His success in proselytization was sufficient to rally communicants, a large number simple agriculturalists and millhands, by the hundreds of thousands, alarming church and state in England and leading to the founding of the Methodist Church a few years after Wesley's death. Wesley was a man of prodigious genius, a second Luther in his combination of learning, brilliance of exposition, passion, and sheer charisma. But he was also, first and last, an enthusiast.

The fourth and final form of enthusiasm is political. It is strikingly like religious enthusiasm in its expressions, and it emerges in circumstances very much like those in which the Anabaptists and Quakers made their appearance. The difference between the two lies in the powers appealed to: for the one it is God; for the other, the ideal state. The spectrum is as wide in political as in religious enthusiasm. At one end are minds of the liberal and humane cast of Locke and Jefferson. At the other are Rousseau and his followers or successors, all determined to fashion a new species of man through the uses of absolute political power. Political enthusiasm, like religious, can spawn freedom and rights, but it can also, in its highest intensities, produce terror, inquisition, and mass execution. Political enthusiasm lay behind the Jacobins' inauguration of the Terror, when ten thousand people were beheaded for public edification, and behind their enactment of laws affecting every detail of life. Even prayers and rituals for the new civil religion were composed by the Jacobins.

Whether benign or malign, political enthusiasm in the eighteenth century rests upon pretty much the same spiritual axioms that religious enthusiasm does. There is the same faith in the inherent goodness of man, in his natural freedom and his rights, in the equality of all men, and in the obstacles, barriers, even repressions which are constantly interfering with the individual's quest for the virtuous life. There is the same belief in the existence of a kind of invisible community that, once the external repressions are removed, might come into actuality. There is the same belief in a millennium, with the idea of progress supporting this belief just as it had in the Puritan mind. And there is the same recognition that if progress is to be accelerated, if the millennium is to be realized, destructive work must be done at once, in the form of civil and political revolution.

If the ideas of Locke and Jefferson show political enthusiasm in its benign and ultimately humane form, as do the ideas of Wesley in the religious realm, the philosophy of Rousseau best illustrates in the eighteenth century the kind of enthusiasm that has, when fully developed, wrought such destruction during the past two centuries in the West. From his earliest political writings through the *Social Contract* Rousseau turned his annihilative passions to the social order around him, to family, social class, church, and monarchy. "Man is born free; and is everywhere in chains" epitomized Rousseau's sense of mission. The traditional institutions without exception were the chains Rousseau saw around him, chains placed by an evil social order upon individuals by nature virtuous. His notable treatment of the state of nature was inspired by the same impulses which led religious enthusiasts to sketch the prelapsarian Adam in the state of grace. For Rousseau, the perfect state would be the means of recovering for all men the freedom and virtue they had before the rise of social institutions. But only the most absolute and sweeping of measures will succeed in destroying all that now corrupts and enslaves men: "He who dares to undertake the making of a people's institutions ought to feel himself capable, so to speak, of changing human nature, of transforming each individual . . . into part of the greater whole from which he, in a manner, gets his life and being; of altering man's constitution for the purpose of strengthening it . . . He must in a word take from man his own resources and give him instead new ones alien to him and incapable of being made use of without the help of others. The more completely these inherited resources are annihilated, the greater and more lasting are those which he acquires."

Any of the great religious enthusiasts—the young Luther, John

Rogers, Wesley—might have written those words. Indeed, in one
phrasing or other, they did, and with the same certainty as Rousseau.
Men must be reborn to be made ready for the kingdom of heaven,
and they must be reborn to be made ready for heaven on earth—for
the general will that is Rousseau's ideal government, for socialism as
conceived by Marx and his followers. What Rousseauism, Marxism,
Leninism, and Maoism are about at bottom is nothing less than the
redemption of mankind, his rescue from the toils and torments of existing society, and his secure emplacement in a socialist utopia. And
for this, any extremes of power are justified, however murderous and
devastating. Far more people have gone into paroxysms of behavior
from hearing appeals to the general will or to communism or to national socialism than appeals to Heaven and the inner light. All antinomianism is evil, but as between the religious and political expressions, the latter is infinitely more deadly.

ENVIRONMENTALISM

"FROM THE GOSPEL OF Capitalist Efficiency to the Gospel of Utopianism" would serve very well as subtitle here. It is entirely possible
that when the history of the twentieth century is finally written, the
single most important social movement of the period will be judged
to be environmentalism. Beginning early in the century as an effort
by a few far-seeing individuals in America to bring about the prudent
use of natural resources in the interest of extending economic growth
as far into the future as possible, the environmentalist cause has become today almost a mass movement, its present objective little less
than the transformation of government, economy, and society in the
interest of what can only be properly called the liberation of nature
from human exploitation. Environmentalism is now well on its way
to becoming the third great wave of redemptive struggle in Western
history, the first being Christianity, the second modern socialism. In
its way, the dream of a perfect physical environment has all the revolutionary potential that lay both in the Christian vision of mankind
redeemed by Christ and in the socialist, chiefly Marxian, prophecy of
mankind freed from social injustice.

Contemporary environmentalism is implicitly a revolt against an
ethic of man and nature that goes back to the ancient Jews and the

Greeks. "Be fruitful and multiply, and fill the earth, and subdue it; and have dominion over the fish in the sea, and over the fowl in the air, and over every living thing that moveth upon the earth." Thus Genesis 26, in God's words. The Greeks were equal to the challenge, and terser. Protagoras declared, "Man is the measure of all things." Man!

In the Jewish and Greek respect for the individual human being and for his unique powers of mind lies the beginning of Western civilization and its distinctive contributions to the world. Pagan philosophers and then Christian theologians might glorify the *scala naturae,* the great chain of being, but man was regarded as sovereign; none of that man-abasing, nature-worshiping, pantheistic monism of the East was allowed to creep into Christianity any more than it had into the Jewish religion. The anthropocentrism in the Christian envisagement of the cosmos is receiving more and more confirmation in the twentieth century from discoveries in astronomy. This earth was created, whether by God or the big bang, and it is unique in its occupancy by man.

This anthropocentric and dualistic view of man and nature lies behind the great practical achievements of Western civilization on the one hand, as in the economic and technological conquest of nature, and its great theoretical achievements on the other hand, as in the triumph of science. There were occasional dissenting voices prior to the twentieth century. That of Saint Francis is the most memorable. But his ideas concerning the true relationship of man to earth and its organic mantle—so very different from the Jewish insistence upon subduing the earth and having dominion over all that exists on it, as also from the humanistic, man-ascendant natural philosophy of the Greeks—were regarded by the church in Francis' time as heretical, which indeed they were, and although the founder escaped the heretic's pyre, some of his followers were not so lucky. The saint declared a monistic philosophy of man and nature—and lived exactly as he preached. But from the early Jews and Greeks on, the true, the main, the overriding philosophy of the West has been dualism with respect to man and nature.

The founders of modern American environmentalism—conservation, as it was called in the early part of the twentieth century—were concerned with the prudent use of the earth and its resources solely in behalf of extending the capitalist system of free private enterprise as far into the future as possible. Theodore Roosevelt, Pinchot, and other conservationists repeatedly made evident their consecration to economic growth and progress, in stark contrast to the preservationists of the time, who were interested only in creating national parks and forests which would be off limits to business. Pinchot declared that he took no pleasure in looking at a stand of forest or living in it. What alone was important in its temporary preservation was assurance that posterity would have lumber with which to build houses. "The job was not to stop the ax," he explained years later, "but to regulate its use . . . A nation utterly absorbed in the present had to be brought to consider the future." The conservationists were at bottom simply preachers of the gospel of efficiency, an efficiency that could be inaugurated and maintained only by scientists and technologists serving industry and government. Theirs was an elitist message. Precisely as Taylor and his co-workers sought to achieve time-and-motion efficiency in factory or office through application of the scientific method, Pinchot and his co-workers sought to achieve scientific efficiency in economic production, distribution, and growth.

That dualistic, efficiency-driven view of man's true relation to environment survived in America until about the beginning of the 1960s. Even the preservationists, who had been in existence since the nineteenth century and were responsible for the establishment of Yosemite, Yellowstone, and many other great national parks and wilderness areas to which industrial or technological access was sharply limited when not prohibited altogether, accepted the values and the requirements of the American system of free private enterprise. They asked for and got large expanses of the kind of environment early American explorers and settlers found confronting them, thus keeping intact a precious part of the American past. But not even Muir, for all his almost mystical love of the wilderness, wanted so much of that wilderness preserved that economic malnutrition must strike the nation. The founders of such associations as the Sierra Club and the Audubon Society were concerned with protection of nature strictly in the interest of preserving the American heritage, most certainly not in the interest of redesigning the American economy or of structuring the government at all levels as the means to redesign the economy. In the 1960s, though, all of this changed substantially. The major sources of the change were, first, the environmentalist movement itself and, second, the large and somewhat amorphous group of political and economic radicals.

A number of things happened to conservation during this period. In the first place its numbers began to assume mass proportions; the spirit of proselytization and of conversion was almost religious in quality. Thousands of new environmentalist groups, clubs, and associations, many local but an impressive number national in scope, came into being. From the beginning there was a militancy in these groups that had been lacking in the older conservation and preserva-

tion societies. But even the older organizations were infused by the
new spirit. There was, as is always the case when cult-like groups are
beginning to become mass movements, an enlargement and diversifi-
cation of stated aims. Conservation of resources remained perhaps
the sovereign goal, or stated goal at any rate. But the theme of preservation took on an intensity and scope going far beyond anything
earlier existent in, say, the national park movement. Now preservation referred to creation and protection not simply of parks and wildernesses, but of what became known as ecosystems, however small
or large, however necessary their space might be to the development
of industry or the building of homes for the many rising to middle
class status.

The new preservationism led inexorably to still another theme in
the environmentalalist cause, namely the proper use and control of
energy, so vital to all economic progress. Increasingly the spirit and
aim became that of, not rational conservation of resources in the interest of economic prosperity for the masses, but cutting down on
and even banning indispensable types of energy, with nuclear energy
chief among them. It is the nuclear issue that did the most to transform the old conservationism into the new. All those who, beginning
immediately after World War II, had fought against the use and test-
ing of nuclear weapons in the name of peace but also of environmen-
tal security from radioactivity, now joined the environmentalists in
opposition to the use of nuclear energy in any form whatever, no
matter how carefully the manufacture of this energy was controlled,
no matter how emphatically scientists declared the safety of nuclear
energy in comparison with all other forms, no matter how eloquently
and authoritatively industrial leaders argued its case in the name of
necessary economic productivity. Skillfully and subtly drawing on
the horrifying devastation of Hiroshima and Nagasaki through atomic
bombs, with the aid of an occasional nonlethal accident or breakdown of a nuclear reactor plant, environmentalists were able to persuade millions of Americans that the consequences of such plants
could, and soon would, prove as devastating to American life and
health as the bombings of Japan had been, and on a vastly larger
scale.

This led to still another, increasingly mesmeric theme of the new
environmentalism: the development of new sources of energy guaranteed to be inexhaustible, utterly harmless to earth and life, and ineradicably clean. Almost overnight such anticipated or proposed new
sources were focused in one: solar energy. One of the most ancient
of human religions, sun worship, was of a sudden restored to glory
and power. What a wealthy person might be able to effect in a small

house—nearly exclusive dependence upon solar heating—was immediately declared possible for factories and cities, and possible in a
relatively short time provided the federal government gave it highest
priority in research and development. The combination of nihilistic
assault on nuclear energy and of evangelistic fervor in behalf of solar
power was all that was necessary to put the new preservationism in
the garb and light of an army of righteousness, one dedicated to extermination of everything in any way contaminant of nature and to
achievement of a pure natural environment.

All mass movements must have their sacred texts: the New Testament for Christians, the *Manifesto* or *Capital* for socialists. It is perhaps too early to identify authoritatively the sacred text for all environmentalists in their struggle for the millennium, but at the moment
it would appear to be Rachel Carson's *Silent Spring*, published in 1962.
Carson's prediction of earth's doom unless all chemical fertilizers and
pesticides were banned immediately had, for the preservationists, the
same electric quality given off two thousand years before by Christian preachings and, more than a century before, by Marx's *Manifesto*. It was a short step from Carson's dithyramb of desolation to the
position that what is really corrupting of man and earth is technology
itself, and nowhere more odiously than within the capitalist industrial
system.

The second major source of contemporary environmentalist revolutionary militance was the very substantial number of radicals who
were in dire need of a new faith and ideology. The old socialism had
increasingly come to seem obsolete, even obnoxious, given the presence on earth of such despotisms as the Soviet Union. There were
too many manifest errors or misconceptions in *Capital*; and moreover
it was hard to read and understand by comparison with so transfigur-
ing a text as that written by Carson. Almost overnight the message,
the Good News, spread among radicals, particularly those of the new
left who emerged into national visibility just at the time that Nader,
Commoner, and Brower were developing the new preservationism.
Not a heavenly utopia, not a proletarian utopia, but in historic descent from these, a utopia of nature was their goal. This proved to be
the same kind of holy and golden age, the millennium, that the early
Christians and then the early socialists had yearned and worked for,
albeit in different hues and textures.

As the political left realized by the end of the 1960s, a nature
utopia could enlist a much larger and more diversified following than
could have been reasonably predicted in the first century for the cult
of Christ or in the nineteenth century for a proffered workers' paradise. No one, apart from urbanized cranks, could possibly oppose so

indubitably respectable a cause as rehabilitation and protection of the environment. The middle class could be expected to support in large numbers what it had itself founded at the beginning of the century. Properly envisaged, environmentalism could draw support from the very rich, eager to preserve open spaces around their country estates; from the upper middle class, especially the professional, nonindustrial middle class, intent upon zoning laws that would cut off further entry of people and houses into areas adjacent to those they had once been able to move into themselves; and even from the lower middle class, because abundant national parks and forests meant inexpensive vacations spent camping. Two groups only would resist the lure of the immaculate environment, the owner-manager class in industry and the blue-collar working class. But the managerial group could be consigned to exactly the same conceptual niche it had occupied in socialist legend, that of the exploitative capitalist class indifferent to popular wishes and needs. And the working class group, so unreasonably and anachronistically intent upon jobs and the upbringing of their children, could remain the proletariat, though without historical destiny.

One of the most easily validated generalizations about human history is that successful single-interest movements are inevitably joined in due time by members of or refugees from other single-interest followings. Thus, as Engels himself noted, the socialist, working class movement in his day was already being joined or put in alliance with such motley followings as vegetarians, anti-inoculationists, and nature healers. As Engels further observed, precisely the same had been true of primitive Christianity: "There was no fanaticism, no foolishness, no scheming that did not flock to the young Christian communities." At the present time the same phenomenon is taking place, this time centered upon environmentalism. Pro-abortionists, equal righters, health food addicts, antifluoridationists, and exponents of other forms of "fanaticism," "foolishness," and "scheming," in Engels' words, are beginning to ally themselves politically with the environmentalists. Any given Earth Day's mob is bound to have all these present for worship of the sun, earth, and ecosystem.

Millennialism notwithstanding, each of the three great redemptive movements in Western civilization has its sacred age in the remote past. For Christianity it is the epoch of the prelapsarian Adam. The termination of this epoch through the Fall set in motion the whole epic that would culminate in Jesus and his redemption of the human race. Marxism has its prelapsarian period also, the primitive communism. This period was ended when private property arose, thereby producing an epic human conflict that Marx was the first to understand and explain in order to quicken the historical realization of salvation through socialism. Environmentalism in America possesses a comparable sacred myth, that of the immaculate continent, whose destruction began with the coming of Europeans in the seventeenth century to settle and thus befoul the garden. Without this myth environmentalism would have no more likelihood of success as a mass movement than would have Christianity and Marxism.

There is rich irony in the short history of the environmentalist movement in America. It began as the strategy of an elite group that would, by conservation and prudent replenishment, lead to the reinforcement of capitalism and of all the related forces by which many millions had risen from poverty to middle class affluence. In less than a century, however, environmentalism has become, without losing its eliteness of temper, a mass socialist movement of, not fools, but sun worshipers, macrobiotics, forest druids, and nature freaks generally, committed by course if not yet by fully shared intent to the destruction of capitalism.

Taken over the long run, the sin of environmentalism as we know it so stridently today lies in the created myth that nature has become. We are lulled into the belief that nature is benign, above all innocent. The ridiculous conception of human nature that Rousseau and his descendants advanced is matched by the conception of nature as mild in stream and forest. But one would do better to think of nature as Mount Saint Helens, a raging tornado, an unending drought, an earthquake, incessant visits of locusts, ants, and lice, and regular attacks of everything from famine to smallpox. That is how our forefathers saw nature. Only in an age of high and ubiquitous technology is it possible to think differently.

ENVY

OF THE SEVEN DEADLY SINS, of all states of the human mind indeed, envy is the basest and ugliest. It is also the most corrosive of spiritual and moral fiber in the bearer and the most destructive of the social fabric. Spread widely in a population, envy makes any kind of social concord, any tissue of rights and liberties, any structure of justice utterly impossible. Envy is a compound of covetousness, felt impotence, and nihilistic resentment of anything and everything that is

honored in a culture. The poet Milton did not go beyond the mark
when in *Paradise Lost* he attributed the Fall to the serpent's "guile,
stirred up with envy and revenge." Samuel Johnson, who had known
years of deprivation and poverty amidst the riches of London, so
feared the rise in his own being of the spirit of envy that he deliberately cultivated two other states of mind—pride and charity—whose
presence, he thought, would block the beginnings of envy. And without doubt Johnson was singularly free of envy, something that cannot
always be said of even those who have enjoyed the honor and renown that Johnson did well before his death. Envy, he declared, is of
all the vices the nearest to "pure and unmixed evil," because its aim
is "lessening others though we gain nothing to ourselves."

Emerson wrote that envy "is the tax which all distinction must
pay." There is doubtless some truth in this. It is unlikely that any society or historical epoch has ever been free of envy in at least some
degree. But there are times in which distinction, however based, is
less susceptible to the envy of others than at other times. When
strata of distinction are clearly marked and far apart in a society,
envy from below is less likely than when these strata have become
blurred to vision as the result of pronounced social change, the kind
that carries with it economic mobility and cultural ferment. A degree
of proximity is required between two classes to make possible envy
of the upper by the lower. One cannot envy what one does not know
about, has never seen at close hand, or regards as fixed in a religious
faith accepted by all, as in India. It is inconceivable that a street
sweeper or scavenger would envy Einstein, but it is entirely conceivable that another physicist might, one close enough to know the true
wealth of Einstein's genius and to covet this wealth, but permanently
removed by ingrained inferiority from equaling or exceeding it.

This is why envy proliferates during periods or in societies where
equality has come to dominate other values. If all human beings in a
population either are declared equal in their native strengths and
rights or else are persuaded to believe this, then the eventual realization of the hard truth of the matter—that no amount of redistribution
of wealth and status can ever obliterate inequality in one form or
other—must often take the form of covetousness mixed with resentment: that is, envy. When equality is the goal set for a people, perceptions of inequality, no matter how slight such inequality may be
in fact, are bound to inspire animosity and desire for destruction of
wealth or privilege even when there is no hope of bringing to oneself
any of this wealth or privilege. There are reformers, revolutionists,
and utopians who have made the abolition of the sources of envy
their primary goal, but a more illusory goal is not to be imagined.

Such sources are infinite in potential number and diversity.

Envy can be institutionalized, even nationalized. The number of nations and peoples in the world where envy of the West, particularly of the United States, is a solid fact of life increases constantly. It is not desire to become like, or equal to, Western countries that inspires such peoples and their leaders. Oftentimes indeed there is manifest repugnance for the West's wealth, power, and ways of belief, as is the case among substantial sectors of the population in the Middle East, India, and Southeast Asia. What acquaintance with Western values has generated in such sectors is a rage to destroy, not emulate. There are those who argue that Westerners need only consecrate themselves to equalizing the nations of the world in order to abolish resentment against the West. But it would not be possible to do this in such a way as to repeal Tocqueville's law: "When inequality is the general rule in society, the greatest inequalities attract no attention. When everything is more or less level, the slightest variation is noticed. Hence the more equal men are, the more insatiable will be their longing for equality." And, of course, their envy.

The only remedy for the poisons created by egalitarianism in a society is emphatically not ever-greater dosages of political redistribution of wealth and state, for such dosages worsen the disease, producing fevers of avarice and envy. No, the sole remedy for this pathology is the introduction and diffusion of individual liberty as a sovereign value. Respect for individual liberty makes it possible for human beings to live in and be aware of differentiation—a condition in biology that is recognized for what it is, the basis of progressive evolution, but which in its social manifestation receives no such recognition, because of both the intrinsic inequality in all social differentiation and the ideology of equality that has spread so widely and so devastatingly in the twentieth century. Belief in liberty rather than equality cannot help but make acceptable the differences of strength, talent, and will which are as natural to the social as to the biological order. For as liberty encourages differentiation, so the free flow of differentiation in the social body puts a premium on liberty. But in the present world of equality become religious dogma, of widely escalating expectations, of preoccupation with self and its easy pleasures, and of inflation that more and more appears to be the ineradicable disease of democracies, it is hard to be optimistic about the future of liberty on the one hand and, on the other, the amount of envy in the social sphere.

EPITAPHS

FROM ARTHUR RYDER, Sanscrit scholar:

He succeeded at a great task.
He failed at a great task.
He failed at a small task.
He succeeded at a small task.

Also from Ryder, on a historian and his followers: "A sham giant surrounded by real pygmies."

From Max Beerbohm upon his departure from London as a young man with intent never to write again: "I leave the field to those with months of success ahead."

From William Saroyan three days before his certain death from cancer: "I have always known of course that people died. But I believed that an exception had been made for me. What now?"

From Father Divine upon learning that a judge who had ruled against his church on a zoning matter had thereafter died of a heart attack: "I hated to do it."

Southey, upon hearing of the death of the architect of Blenheim Palace: "Rest heavy on him O earth; he has placed such heavy things on thee."

Hegel, on his deathbed: "You alone have understood me, but you have misinterpreted me."

"Even paranoids have real enemies." Delmore Schwartz.

Justice Potter, in a dissenting opinion: "I don't know how to define pornography, but I know it when I see it."

"Hell is truth seen too late." Hobbes.

FAMILY

IT IS THE NATURE of both family and state to struggle for the exclusive loyalty of their respective, and overlapping, members. A like struggle characterizes the church, as the history of Christianity makes clear. Christianity's earliest institutional struggle was with the Roman family, which tended to resist its proselytizing overtures to women and young people in Roman society, and then with the imperial state, which capitulated in the third century. From the Middle Ages on, struggles for suzerainty among the three institutions dot the historical landscape of Europe. If family is by all odds the weakest today of the three, the church is not far behind. The state is triumphant, for the present at least.

The war between family and state is very old in human history, going back to the primordial moment when wars among once isolated tribes and clans became numerous. The struggle between family and state commenced when the war chief, the prototype of the state, confronted the patriarch, head of the kinship community, over ultimate control of those serving the chief. Throughout history there has been an inversely functional relation between the two institutions. When the family is a powerful allegiance, as in traditional China, the state may reign, but it does not rule; it is relatively weak. Conversely, when the state is powerful, as in the Soviet Union and in lesser degree in the United States and other Western nations, the family tie is weak, loose, and spastic.

Family here does not mean the small household group that is customarily the referent in our time. What is thought of as the family today is no more than a pitiful remnant of a once strong and pervasive kinship community, which counted the unborn and the dead as well as the living, which extended itself into all aspects of individual life—economic, political, legal, cultural, psychological, and biological—and which in political terms was a government itself, monarchy or republic, with no nonsense about equality of membership. Justice, not equality, was the sovereign value of the family. When the word *family* was used until a century or so ago, one instantly thought of, not the nuclear or conjugal group, with husband, wife, and immediate children—a group that today in the United States has shrunk to a pathetic 2.78 average size—but the longitudinal family of generations in time, the family of blood line, of tradition and history, of ancestors and planned-for posterity.

The family had its origin in neither sex nor anything else biological. An apt metaphor for the family's primal origin would be legislator-moralist-sociologist, some primal lawgiver, a prehistoric Lycurgus, Hammurabi, or Confucius, rather than any so-called procreative instinct or sexual urge. The family in the large and historic sense of the word has no more to do with love and romance than do state and church. The fundamental cement of family is duty or obligation, not love. The test of brotherhood or filial virtue is response to duty, not love or even friendship. It has been said that the family is the one group in society that its members do not have to repair to but that has to accept them if they do. The family is the origin, the nidus of society. The power of kinship is reflected in the sheer number of post-kinship groups and associations which adopted without delay the nomenclature of kinship for their own structures.

The family is not, however the origin or nidus of the state. It is rather the sworn enemy of the state, as well it should be. For the state originated in war, specifically in the relation between the primitive war chief and his war band or militia. Inasmuch as the function of the war band was to make successful war, the role criteria for leader and followers were very different from the role criteria for the kinship community, in which age, tradition, exclusivity, blood ties, and ancestral pride were vital. Youth and all its potentially explosive energies were kept in severe check by the old and the wise. Manifestly, no war could be won on these principles, so it is a fair assumption that the war band had its origin in the ashes of defeat of a kinship community that sought to invade or to defend itself in accord with kinship role and rank.

From the beginning, though, conflict between the two entities or principles of organization was inevitable. The patriarch was first challenged not—*pace* Freud—by lustful sons eager to have their mother, but by the youthful, aggressive, and demanding war chief eager for greater liberation from the restraints imposed by ancient kinship values. In Rome the *patria potestas*—the absolute power of family over its members—could only be suspended in degree when war appeared on the horizon. Sons were released from obligation to their patriarch alone and allowed to enter the equally absolute domain of the military *imperium*. So long as war lasted, no external authority could abridge the command of leader over his men. But when war ended, the returning soldiers, during most of the Republic, were obliged to break up outside the city gates and replace military tunic with ordinary dress; upon entering the city, they were automatically once again under the kinship authority, the *patria potestas*.

A great deal of the history of civilization could be written in terms of the breakup of kinship society by the needs and measures of war and then by the establishment of the state. Political sovereignty is no more than the enlargement of the military *imperium* to include all people who live in a given area. Subjecthood and then citizenship has its prototype in the soldier under command. Because the state also requires territory, it is best seen as simply the territorialization of the military. Old forms of kinship society remain and often must be placated and accommodated, but once the state has become securely established, the history of kinship becomes essentially one of decline of structure, and roles. This process occurred in Greece in the late sixth century B.C., in Rome at the end of the first century B.C., and in Western Europe commencing about the seventeenth century. In the first case, the reforms of Cleisthenes, preeminently the abolition of the historic tribes and their component clans and the instituting of the hundred *demes* or territorial units, are perfectly expressive of the transition from kinship to military-political society. In Rome, Octavian's rise to undisputed military master and then to emperor, the first in Roman history, rested from the start upon the army. The *imperium* became *majestas* or sovereignty. Almost immediately changes were made by the government in the role and scope of the family in Roman life. In modern times the history of the rise and expansion of the national state in Europe after the collapse of the medieval system is but the other side of the coin that epitomizes also the decline of the kinship community. After the sixteenth century the clan, kindred, and extended family began to retreat precisely as the aristocracy did. The kind of family known so well today began to emerge in the West, for in its smallness and nuclear character it represents the adaptation of kinship to the needs of the modern state.

All states begin in war. There is no exception in history. The United States, Mexico, Israel, and the Soviet Union are modern analogues to France, England, and Switzerland, which in turn illustrate what earlier happened in Greece and Rome and, before that, in Egypt, Chaldea, India, Persia, and China. Moreover, war is the salvation of the state, just as it is the kinship community's nemesis. State power over society and its members always increases during periods of war.

Once the state assumes command, however, it does not exist permanently in an area. Far from it. A case in point is Europe following the collapse of the Roman Empire in the West. What are called the Dark and the Middle Ages are rich in kinship renascence and in the development of groups such as monasteries, abbeys, guilds, and other communities and associations which mostly took kinship as their models. The political state was only dimly conceived in the medieval epoch.The so-called Holy Roman Empire was at bottom a sham, holy perhaps but hardly Roman and certainly not empire. Kinship and surrogate kinship waxed, the state waned. Characteristically war counted for little in medieval society, at least as compared with the modern world, especially the twentieth century. Knights, vassals, and lords conducted a large number of tiny engagements, but it was an age in which war was limited, technologically, socially, and politically. After all, prior to the rise of mercenaries in the late Middle Ages, vows of military service rarely exceeded two or three months.

The increase of war, commencing with the Hundred Years War,

began the decline of medieval society and its kinship community. Mercenaries, infantry, and gunpowder made their appearance. Those who were most successful in the new warfare became the kings of the burgeoning states, their first duty that of leading their troops. The primary function of the infant national state was military; justice and internal security came later, and later still came the other functions that today are associated with the state.

These recurrences and transitions are not confined to Europe. The history of China in the nineteenth and twentieth century is best read socially as the decline of the Chinese family, a decline generated by increasing warfare and by the invasions of war-minded, exploitative Western states. Maoist Communism is the triumph of the collective state over the family, clan, and village mentalities which had flourished in the vast hinterland for millennia. Since the death of Mao, what is left of the family has struggled to survive and regain a degree of authority over its own.

No greater scene in this respect exists today than the continent of Africa. The Western powers may have taken the model of the national state to Africa, but it required decolonization and the rise of native political rulers significantly to sink the roots of political nationhood in Africa. Even at this moment, states such as Nigeria, Kenya, and Zimbabwe are shot through with the tribalisms and other kinship liaisons which have long been crucial in the daily lives of Africans. Only by the same kind of disintegration of the kinship community that took place in the West during the two or three centuries following the Hundred Years War will the African states become like their Western counterparts.

It is common to refer to "absolute states" as those existing in the age of divine right kings, particularly in the seventeenth century. But in truth such states were not nearly as absolute in their powers over subjects as any modern democracy is. Too many barriers remained to that extension of state power which true absolutism requires. Foremost among these barriers was the kinship community, so hated in its ancient, traditional form by all zealots of the political state. Louis XIV's "L'Etat, c'est moi" is in actuality, if not intent, an expression of weakness. Only when the state becomes a true collectivity, with substantial mass participation in government, does genuine absolutism rise. The French revolutionary state was vastly greater in its powers over the people than the monarchical state had ever been. It is in the twentieth century, the century above all others in the history of mass warfare, that the state in the West has become truly absolute. To compare the powers of the American government today over its citizens, powers reaching every nook and cranny of social and cultural life, with those of Louis XIV or James I is to compare riotous abundance with primitive meagerness.

Similarly, to compare the hold of the state over its citizens with that of the family over its members is to compare Leviathan to near nullity. The current family in the United States, that nuclear household group of 2.78 members, is in no way the enemy of the state or indeed the whole modern temper. Its very feebleness, its anemic structure, and its institutional insignificance make it the perfect handmaiden of the mammoth, intrusive state, as well as a fit receptacle of the narcissisms and hedonistic egoisms of the day. The family will again become strong only if this pathetic end-result of the long decline of kinship authority in the West is replaced by family in the full longitudinal sense, the family of generations, of entail in some form or degree, of recognized authority over its members, and of mutual dignity, respect, and duty rather than mere indulgence of marital passion. Divorce rates do not mark the weakness of the nuclear kinship group, for divorce in considerable measure, not to mention marital hatred and desertion, have accompanied the strongest of family systems. What best measures the sickness of the current family is the collapse of its intergenerational significance, its communal-corporate character, its close alliance with property (social democratic tax policy alone doing the family far more injury than can divorce), and its natural authority over members, especially the young.

Not every family in history is a repository for the good. A depressing case in point is Butler's family as portrayed in *The Way of All Flesh*, or some of the family portraits, especially the Snopes family, that Faulkner drew. The greed, avarice, and hatred which can be compressed into a family line, often for generations, have often been the stuff of tragedy and melodrama. What above all riveted the minds of Athenians in the fifth century B.C. to the plays of Aeschylus and Sophocles was their depiction of lust, incest, and avarice within the institution that Athenians had known longest, that preceded by thousands of years their *polis* or, the whole Greek kinship community, tribe, clan, kindred, and household. After all, these audiences had themselves seen the degradation of kinship as an institutional force in Athens following the Cleisthenean reforms.

The partial decline of the kinship community can be a significant force in the eruption of golden ages in the history of the mind. When the fullness and potential repressiveness of kinship have declined in considerable measure, though not to the point of inanition and chaos, this effects the liberation of individual spirit and the expansion of individual imagination that are cardinal aspects of the great ages of thought and culture. Put differently, the rivalry between state and clan can for a time be creative in cultural terms. This has occurred in all of the great ages of history.

But nothing of the sort exists today. The family, in any and all sense, is fragmented, and the range of its authority is slight. The custom of Mother's Day and Father's Day and such official celebrations as "The Year of the Child" and the White House Conference on the Family may seem to indicate the continuing strength of the kinship tie and its embedded values. On the contrary, however, they are one and all clear evidences of the institutional moribundity of the family. They are like epitaphs. The bloom of the shrub is never so brilliant as when its roots have just been cut. The fact that the political left has in recent years discovered the family and its potential psychological strengths is not likely to affect the matter significantly, for the modern state has, through economic and legal measures, reduced the family's structural importance in the social order to the point where such psychological strengths are largely illusory. The assault by the more militant liberationists, gay and women's, on the family, especially on its historic roles of mother, wife, daughter, and sister, might have been predicted decades ago by anyone familiar with revolutionary movements in history. They are responses to the weakness, not the strength, of what they attack.

The rhythmic alternation of state and family as powers in society will surely continue past the present century. It is likely that something akin to the early medieval renascence of family in the West will take place again. Already there are evidences of the alienation of citizens from the national state and also from the totalitarian state, whose citizens so readily become, on slightest opportunity, boat people, stateless ones, and voluntary exiles. The lure of the political state, so great since the nineteenth century with its evangelical nationalisms and its flowerings of patriotism, has been waning since World War I. Not all Americans look at their country in the way their grandfathers did. It is an open question how many Americans would today, deep in their hearts, prefer to be dead than Red. For all its mammoth bureaucracy, America's currently unchecked invasion of every privacy in the economic, cultural and psychological orders would seem to sit on shifting sand. There is manifestly a turning inward, socially, culturally, and religiously. The ideas of self-help and voluntary mutual aid, refuge in multinational organizations, especially the great multinational corporations, and the whole revival of evangelical religion are warning lights or, from another point of view, beacon lights. Such currents in society invariably contain reviving freshets of kindred and of family in the full institutional sense.

But never in history has the political state been as absolute in its express powers over individuals, as solidly undergirded by military armament, as threaded by espionage and secret police, and as secure in its control of communications and propaganda, as today. Technology, harnessed to the fast-spreading spirit of statism in its several guises, has ensured this fact. Whether democratic, aristocratic, authoritarian, or totalitarian, the state is sovereign in our age. It is also absolute in its law, in its monopoly of military force, in its power to conscript and appropriate, to tax, to license, to define crime and organize police and judiciary, to regulate education and a constantly widening spectrum of personal tastes and habits, to control marriage and family, and in a score of other ways. Such absoluteness is as real in the United States as it is in Argentina and the Soviet Union. There are in America, as there are not in the other two states, persisting claims to rights before the law, rights drawn from the eighteenth century's natural rights, and one of the virtues of the Constitution is that on the whole these rights are respected by the state. But a single amendment could wipe them out, the amendment being no less a part and power of the state over people's lives than are the executive, legislature, and judiciary. The great differences between the Soviet Union and the United States notwithstanding, the truth is that the absoluteness of the state is as real in a democracy as in a monarchy or dictatorship. Triumph of state over family is complete, though no one can be sure that it will last any longer than did that of the Roman state.

FANATICISM

THIS IS TO ZEAL what paranoia is to suspicion. There is no area of human behavior exempt from this affliction. Fanaticism is seen in the lifelong labor of the Baconian, certain each day that the next day will bring the long-awaited proof of the nonexistence of Shakespeare. It is seen in the relentless hatreds of academics convinced they have seen the only true curricular light and feeling betrayed by all who do not see it. And it is to be found in the speculations of "gold bugs" absolute in their faith that only gold will escape the imminent collapse of all equities and securities.

Typical of the fanatic is the boundless certainty of being right, sometimes uniquely right. Reinforcing this certainty is the fanatic's conviction that he has a mission in the world: the insistent broadcasting to all who will listen of the good and the right. Where others see mere problems, the fanatic sees crises, often of cosmic significance, no matter how small and limited in fact the problem or difficulty may be. Such crises, the fanatic knows, can only be resolved by constant vigilance, the aim being the destruction of all opposition. Fanatics can sometimes love individuals, provided those individuals are true believers, but their greater love goes to principle. Perish even friends rather than compromise on principle.

Followers are preferred in any event to friends; thus friendship is possible but only on the basis of total loyalty. Disloyalty, however picayune, is unforgivable to the fanatic. Even the appearance of disloyalty is sufficient for banishment of the offender, no matter how many years of unquestioning devotion have been given; they are as nothing compared to the enormity of the moment. The worst form of treason is inauthenticity or hypocrisy. Those who have, or seem to have, given their support to the good and right and then fall short in some measure are obviously guilty of hypocrisy in the past, of seeming instead of being. The true fanatic will spend everything in the searching out and the punishing of hypocrisy.

As might be imagined, the fanatic has the gift of hate in superlative intensity. Most human beings are unable to sustain hatred for more than a short time; the burden is too great, the temptation to return to normal ultimately irresistible. But the fanatic can hate for a lifetime, if anything increasing the hate as time passes. The fanatic forgets nothing; no detail is too small not to remember for decades and to nourish constantly by the acids of hate.

When it is absolutely necessary, the fanatic sometimes abandons principle in favor of the expedient, but when this happens, it is no longer the expedient but rather a new and higher principle that has been found. In the end, though, it is unwillingness or inability to take the expedient course that brings the fanatic down.

The two great settings of fanaticism are religion and politics. Religion is by far the older of the two; only since the eighteenth century has politics come to rival it as the breeding ground of fanaticism. All of the great founders of religions had, and were obliged to have, strong elements of fanaticism in their beings. How else could they have appeared as authentic to their followers? The prophet must be of unshakable resolve, must have seen the truth and recognized it, must be willing to undergo all the torments of the unseeing and resistant, and must seek constantly to fulfill the mission of bringing the truth to the hungry sheep. One can be as gentle as Buddha or as fierce as Mohammed and still have the common quality of zeal carried to the nth degree. It is customary to think of the religious fanatic in the image of a Saint Simeon Stylites, but religious fanaticism has been far more often that of a Jesus.

The French Revolution gave the modern world political fanaticism. In this respect it differed immensely from the American Revolution a decade earlier. Washington, Jefferson, Adams, and the others who led the Revolution were men of deep faith in what they were doing, but their revolution was finite in goal, limited to separation from Great Britain. There was little evidence of a desire to extend the revolution to all parts of the world, though Adams hoped that what happened in America would be an inspiration to subjugated peoples everywhere. There was nothing, at least among the leaders, of the spirit of fanatical faith, of desire to continue the revolution until all conventions and habits had been changed, until human nature had been transformed, until perfection had been reached at last in the world.

But all of this is seen from 1790 on in France after the revolution had commenced. Robespierre, Marat, Saint-Just, and the others who had controlling force were minds of a different breed from any yielded by the American Revolution. They were engaged, as both Burke and Tocqueville saw, in investing political actions with elements which had previously existed only in religion. It was this that led Burke to write, "All circumstances taken together, the French Revolution is the most astonishing that has hitherto happened in the world." Later Tocqueville added, "The French Revolution's approach to the problems of man's existence on earth was exactly similar to that of the religious revolutions with respect to his afterlife."

Good and evil were seen by Robespierre and his fellow-members of the Committee on Public Safety in exactly the same apocalyptic terms used by Reformation zealots. So were the institutions of French society. Aristocracy, clergy, and nearly all other classes of French society were condemned by law to extinction. Nothing would do but a complete de-Christianization of the French nation. A purely civil religion, as prescribed by their beloved Rousseau, was established by the Committee. Everything from the past must be cleansed if not destroyed, leaving the way open for the new and pure. "The transition of an oppressed nation to democracy," declared the Committee, "is like the effort by which nature arose from nothingness to existence. You must entirely refashion a people you wish to make free, destroy its prejudices, alter its habits, limit its necessities, root up its vices, and purify its desires."

From the French Revolution's furies there is a direct line to those of the Bolshevik, the Nazi, and the Maoist revolutions of the twentieth century. Along the way are zealots of utopianism, socialism, nationalism, and the other variants of political religion in the nineteenth century, those with "fire in their minds," to use Dostoevsky's words. The scene presented by the sixteenth century, occupied by religious fanatics of every kind and degree, is matched by the nineteenth century's setting for political fanatics with heaven on earth in their eyes. Germany and France led the way with their socialists, anarchists, syndicalists, and others, but it was not long before Russia joined the procession with ultimately world-shaking consequences.

No treatment of fanaticism would be complete without mention of the remarkable Jeremy Bentham. As is almost always the case with fanatics, Bentham had a brilliant and wide-ranging mind. No one can take from him his valuable reforms of the common law and his instigation of the public service. There was much in England at the beginning of the nineteenth century that required cleaning out in law and politics. But in time his rationalism overcame him. Everything must be subjected to the test of utilitarianism and to what he called the "hedonistic calculus," the exact measurement of pains and pleasures in order to determine the desirability of an action. His early disapproval of old traditions—inns of court, the universities, trial by jury, the boroughs, even Parliament itself—became a burning hatred, and he sought with every power in his being to have them obliterated. His faith in reason, especially his own, reached the point where he was able to declare that, without leaving his study, he could govern all India. His invention of the Panopticon principle, at first limited to prisons, was followed by frenetic efforts to have that principle adopted for schools, asylums, factories, and other institutions. It was entirely fitting that Bentham should think to have rational-utilitarian use made of his body upon death: seated in full dress and top hat in an anteroom of the University of London, he could serve as an example to posterity.

America began to produce its own political fanatics early in the nineteenth century. Most prominent were the abolitionists. Slavery in their eyes was not simply a grievous political problem, as it had been for the Framers. It represented a crisis of cosmic proportions. John Brown was not alone in his passion, viewing the South as a vast eruption of the Devil's minions, all needing to be slaughtered in ritual sacrifice if America was to be cleansed of its evil. For the true abolitionist, slavery was the touchstone by which friend and enemy could be recognized no matter what the subject under consideration. Abolitionists had their reward in 1860. The Civil War brought one form of fanaticism to an end, but before long a dozen others sprang into existence. It is hard to think of any moral reform movement of the century that did not have its Carrie Nations of both sexes, fanatics one and all in their desire to capture the power of the state and to institute for all people in America a life free of liquor, tobacco, meat, or whatever. Truly, as Charles Kingsley wrote, "the world's work is done by fanatics."

In the two centuries of Presidents of the United States, only one appears to qualify as political fanatic: Woodrow Wilson. "Fanatics have their dreams," observed Keats, "wherewith they weave a paradise for a sect." Wilson had his dreams from boyhood on, and his efforts to weave paradises are the stuff of both bathos and tragedy. Early letters to his adored mother and revered father reveal a mind seized by moralism; everyone, beginning with himself, and everything, government above all, must be tried sternly against perfection of right. During his presidency of Princeton the true believer came dramatically to the fore. The effort to reform the undergraduate eating clubs and the confrontation with Dean West over the location of the graduate school show a mind well on its way to fanaticism, to perception of crises where only problems exist, to invincible belief in his own virtue and unique possession of the truth, to insistence upon total loyalty from followers, and to that amplitude of iron hate which can wipe out friends of a lifetime, leaving a residue of unyielding memory of betrayal. It was at Princeton that Wilson, in a centennial oration, intoned, "I have had a sight of a perfect place for learning in my thought," concluding with, "Who shall show us the way?" Who indeed. One vision after another of "the perfect place" and of his own messianic mission on earth would punctuate the rest of Wilson's life.

His first messianic seizure as President of the United States came early with respect to Mexico. A confrontation involving a small Mexican port and a dozen American sailors quickly blew up in Wilson's mind to a "crisis of the civilized world" and determined him "to teach the South American republics to elect good men." To the shocked bewilderment of European countries, Wilson enlarged with fanatic intensity the tiny incident to a point where American troops were landed at Vera Cruz, with heavy casualties among the Mexican defenders, and, by way of eventually ending the ridiculous tempest, a mediation commission had to be formed of representatives of three nations.

But it was in World War I that all the temper of zealous righteousness in Wilson reached its zenith. In the beginning his policy was neutrality. Whereas other Presidents from Washington through Lincoln to Theodore Roosevelt and Taft would have defended that policy in terms of simple strategy, Wilson was driven to declare neutrality the means whereby America would disseminate its unique goodness to the parties in Europe and indeed to all the world. "Too proud to fight" was his sanctimonious defense of the policy to those who criticized it, and when he was reelected in 1916, it was on the basis of "he kept us out of the war." Only a man who believed that God guided his every decision could have reversed himself as quickly as Wilson did after reelection, and within months he brought America into the war, not for any of the goals recognized by the English and French leaders, but "to make the world safe for democracy." None but a fanatic would have imposed upon the war-weary Allies, their countries drained by three years of the bloodiest fighting in the annals of war, his Fourteen Points, in which ignorance of geopolitical realities was equaled in size only by arrogant pietism. When the war ended, Wilson was irresistibly driven to make his way to Europe in messianic fashion and, in the timeworn fashion of the prophet, to come between the Allied leaders and their peoples.

In the setting of terms of the Armistice, old friends such as Colonel House and Tumulty counseled moderation when Wilson met with Lloyd George, Clemenceau, and others who for four years had fought the Germans, but for such counsel even the oldest and truest of friends were banished from Wilson's life, to be objects of his hatred to his dying day. For the fanatic, no friend can be true who does not follow unquestioningly even to the valley of death. The League of Nations, promised in the Fourteen Points, furnished Wilson with his opportunity for ascent to the highest peak of self-righteousness. Again lifetime friends begged him to compromise on small details with Lodge and others in the Senate, only to suffer the same banishment that so many friends from Princeton on had known at Wilson's hand. In the end, Wilson lost everything and plunged to humiliating defeat, not uncommon in the history of fanaticism. And to his final moment on earth he burned with the acid of felt betrayal by those he had trusted. Only in the history of religious fanaticism does one come across the fusion of furious impotence before the vision of absolute good and of unrelenting hate for the wicked that existed in Wilson after his seizure by stroke while bringing the Good News to the hungry sheep.

There is some humor in the realization that Wilson, his humiliating defeat on the League notwithstanding, joined Lenin in becoming one of the two most revolutionary figures in twentieth century history. Wilson loathed Lenin for his acceptance of German terms at Brest-Litovsk. There was little in their backgrounds besides congenital fanaticism of purpose to link them as human beings. Lenin was the declared world revolutionist against capitalism and its works. Wilson never for a moment considered himself a revolutionist. He was a very pillar of capitalist democracy.

Nevertheless the Wilsonian doctrine of freedom of all nationalties from alien rule, especially imperialist rule, went hand in glove with Lenin's mission of advancing the class struggle throughout the world. It is hard to know which doctrine, Wilsonian nationalism or Leninist class struggle, did the most to bring the old order of nations to an end forever. All one can say is that to this moment, in Africa and Southeast Asia, the revolt against the old order proceeds apace, fueled simultaneously by struggle for national freedom and class revolt.

FATALISM

NEARLY A CENTURY AGO, Bryce wrote of "the fatalism of the multitude." In his view, this fatalism had far more appositeness to American reality than did the more famous reference by Tocqueville to "the tyranny of the majority." Bryce, in his frequent visits to and extensive travels over the American continent, could find little evidence that rule over individuals, in the local community, state, or nation, was other than that of well-placed or zealous minorities. He saw no evidence of individuals cowering before the majority. What Bryce was deeply struck by in America—and to some degree in all democracies—was the kind of mass community that was formed, not by any positive initiative, but by the submission of individuals to their perceptions of amorphous but large and determining forces: "This tendency to acquiescence and submission, this sense of the insignificance of individual effort, this belief that the affairs of men are swayed by large forces whose movement may be studied but cannot be turned, I have ventured to call the Fatalism of the Multitude."

Bryce was correct in distinguishing this fatalism from, and giving it greater appropriateness than, Tocqueville's tyranny of the majority. Tocqueville himself had declared that democratic peoples are both susceptible to faith in ineluctable forces of a massiveness that allows little individual interference and prone to falling into an undifferentiated social mass within which personal ambition and enterprise come to seem unavailing. Still, Bryce's phrase, his direct invocation of fatalism, is the more trenchant.

The question is whether Bryce described accurately the American people of 1880, or whether, as is true so often of Tocqueville's insights into American culture, he extracted a quality or attribute from an ideal type, a theoretical model of democracy in his mind, and declared it a visible characteristic of Americans. It is hard to say for sure. Certainly, few other visitors to this country or native prophets seem to have spied such a fatalism in the American people at that time. What is far more perceptible, through the medium of books, diaries, letters, and speeches of that day, is an ebullience of individual faith in self that borders on hubris.

But Bryce's fatalism does have a striking relevance to the America of a century later, just as so many of Tocqueville's descriptions of Americans in 1830 seem more nearly telescopic previews of the future than accounts of what was around him. There is no mistaking the degree to which Americans today have become fatalistic. In a hundred immediately evident ways, Americans reveal an atrophy of faith in the industrious apprentice, in the Horatio Alger ethic of pluck and perseverance. They reveal too a strong faith in the power of chance, fortune, luck, the random, and the purely fortuitous to affect positively or negatively men's fortunes in life. Rarely in history has so large a proportion of a people become so preoccupied by the occult, the miraculous, and out-and-out gambling. Contrast the savings propensities of Americans of every class a century ago with the virtual antipathy toward savings that is evident today. There is an enormous fund of money potentially savable or investable. The tens of billions of dollars spent monthly by Americans in either domestic or foreign casinos, race tracks, slot machine centers, bingo parlors, lotteries, and numbers games are tribute to that fact. And the whole of this vast orgy of chance bespeaks but one thing: the fatalism of the multitude. The time has passed when gambling was the avocation of the few who were rich, eccentric, or interested in brief recreation. It is the single greatest, though far from only, sign of the true and distinctive temper of this age. The wager is the constant companion in American society today of the occult belief in the stars or other impersonal, unreachable, but decisive forces. Gambling joins a multitude of analogous expressions of disdain for, cynicism about, and superstitious avoidance of Poor Richard's Almanack. What alone matters, in the judgment of tens of millions of Americans young and old, is fate. One may work hard and be very successful; or one may take it easy, and be very successful. In neither case, though, is work or ease the crucial factor. Fate is.

Fatalism is the invariable refuge of the incoherent, distracted, and disenchanted multitude. It is a sign of a failure of nerve—failure of the collective nerve that exists in every true community, local or national, and failure of the individual nerve. There have been many ages of fatalism in world history. The spirit of fatalism waxes and wanes with the health of the social body. It was weak in the Greece of Heraclitus, Protagoras, and Pericles; but fatalism was strong and pervading in the Greece that followed the wars between Athens and

Sparta and particularly in post-Alexandrian Greece, where every conceivable form of occultism, superstition, and worship of chance could be seen. Fatalism was scarcely present in the Rome of the Republic, of Cato and Cincinnatus, but it was pandemic in the Rome of the Caesars. There was much belief in demons in the Middle Ages, as well as saints, but little evidence of fatalism. That was reserved for the Renaissance, another age inundated by faith in fortune, chance, and myriad forms of the occult.

Different explanations are necessary for the fatalisms of different epochs and places. Two explanations are apposite to the present age: the first, oldest, and most entrenched is egalitarianism; the second is inflation. Egalitarianism represents the leveling of all those "inns and resting places" of the human spirit which are found in social hierarchy, tradition, kinship, and institutionalized religion. When a society is leveled, this does not confer equality upon people, only a sense of individual isolation, a traumatic feeling of loss of the social bond, of introduction to the precipice or void. Egalitarianism, far from strengthening the sense of fraternity, greatly diminishes it, leaving what was once a culture a mere mass of disconnected atoms. When family, community, parish, social class, school, and job cease to be evocative, to supply incentive and kindle confidence, nothing else but the irrational, the antisocial, and the occult are left to turn to. Fatalism feeds on the carrion of the social organism.

So does it feed on inflation. Few things are better calculated to induce a permanent social vertigo than the incessant erosion of the values people depend upon for their sense of place and time. When it becomes clear that no amount of energy expended in a job will yield a reward sufficient even to stand still, much less advance, despair quickly becomes disillusionment with the rational and leads increasingly to dependence upon chance, to faith in the stars or in numbers—to, in short, a gigantic, all-consuming fatalism. Bryce's fatalism of the multitude is indeed reality today.

FEUDALISM

THIS HAS BEEN a word of invective, of vehement abuse and vituperation, for the past two centuries. To refer to a practice or institution as feudal is to consign it to perdition. Very little in modern life that displeases the political intellectual goes without the epithet "feudal." Whether it is the business corporation or the totalitarian state, "feudal" is the likeliest choice for its explanation as well as condemnation. From the *philosophes* in the French Enlightenment down to the liberals of today, almost all political and social evil is categorized as a persistence or an eruption of the feudal.

Feudalism became and has remained a word of invective simply because of its association with the Middle Ages in Western history, a period denigrated by all who believe that civilization began in the so-called Renaissance. Only during the past few decades, as a consequence of the immense and fertile burst of medieval studies that began in the nineteenth century, largely in reaction to the hostile and tendentious polemics which had been written by such philosophical radicals as Rousseau, Voltaire, and Bentham for whom anything feudal was, in Rousseau's words, "iniquitous and absurd," has it become possible to put the Middle Ages and feudalism in proper perspective. The realization dawned that any age in which the universities were born and flourished, in which the principles of representation and trial by jury came to the fore, and in which science and invention as systematic pursuits were established cannot be all bad.

Neither is feudalism all bad, despite the contumely that has been poured on it by intellectuals in spiritual service to the modern, absolute state, whether monarchical, republican, or democratic. Feudalism is an extension and adaptation of the kinship tie with a protective affiliation with the war band or knighthood. Wherever feudalism has arisen on earth, it has always been in the context of a deeply rooted kinship system which has suddenly become insufficient or inadequate as the result of dangers of attack and devastation either from the outside or from within. Contrary to the modern political state with its principle of territorial sovereignty, for most of a thousand-year period in the West protection, rights, welfare, authority, and devotion inhered in a personal, not a territorial, tie. To be the "man" of another man, in turn the "man" of still another man, and so on up to the very top of the feudal pyramid, each owing the other either service or protection, is to be in a feudal relationship. The feudal bond has much in it of the relation between warrior and commander, but it has even more of the relation between son and father, kinsman and patriarch. Feudalism in all its manifestations in the Middle Ages is rich in the symbolism and nomenclature of the family. The church's momentous adoption of the central terms of address in the household for its own terms of address was far from unique. In the universities, the guilds, the innumerable mutual aid associations, and even on the manor, the familistic theme was dominant. The seigneur, the rector, the head of a craft guild was a surrogate father, duly recognized as such.

FEUDALISM

The origins of feudalism in the Dark Ages are instructive today. Only when the territorial state, that of the once-respected Roman *imperium*, of the celebrated Pax Romana, collapsed in disorder, its political, military, and police power in shambles, did feudal—that is, private, personal, and contractual—relationships begin to take root and to burgeon in the West. Such relationships had much in common with what is thought of as "protection," licit or illicit, today. So close did these feudal relationships become, so powerful their claims upon people's loyalties, so filled with the symbolism of an entire civilization, that although they succumbed eventually to the fire power of the modern absolute, territorial state so far as ultimate political authority was concerned, they remained strong as social principles, coercing, restraining, and guiding in the social classes, offering, through persistence of feudal-born titles and feudal ways of life, especially on the land, a touchstone of social success, and remaining the essential foundation of the kinds of deference, respect, civility, noblesse oblige, loyalty, and honor which, however battered today, remain vital to any true social order.

A great deal of the present-day disorder of our age that is so commonly blamed upon democracy and capitalism is in fact the result of the decline or displacement of the feudal foundations of these two revolutionary manifestations of modernity. Schumpeter referred to feudal persistences in social class and kinship as "precapitalist strata" and ascribed much of capitalism's malaise to the "crumbling" of these walls. Precisely the same may be said of the problems of democracy. It was conceived by its eighteenth century founders for citizens reared and socialized by fundamentally feudal principles in society. Just as Luther had solidly formed Roman Catholics in mind for the communicants of his antichurch Protestant sects, so the Founding Fathers and their counterparts in Europe had in their minds for democratic citizens men shaped by feudally grounded social and moral disciplines in family, community, and church.

Conventional historiography with its linear treatment of history regards feudalism as falling within a time frame, roughly 500–1500, preceded by the Roman Empire and succeeded by the modern national state organized upon territorial rather than personal principles of organization. But just as elements of Romanism persisted through the Middle Ages, so elements of feudalism lasted into the modern world. For a long time it was largely as a feudal king that the so-called absolute monarch ruled. Down to the sixteenth century basically feudal principles of representation, adjudication, and limited monocratic power continued to exert their influence, and they inspired more than a few of the revolts against autocracy in the seventeenth and eighteenth centuries. To declaim today that "the President must be under the law" is to propose nothing modern at all. The subordination of king to law was one of the most important of principles under feudalism, and it required the alchemy of a very different view of sovereign and law, that inhering in Roman law and its revival in the twelfth century, to commence the gradual destruction of limited sovereignty and the rise of the doctrine of absolute sovereignty. The modern territorial state could scarcely have come into being successfully without the stabilizing continuities of feudalism, but once the modern state was in secure existence, its war with just about everything feudal in its midst was fierce and unrelenting. That war was one more example of the momentous conflict in human history between associations founded on personal principles and associations, such as the state, founded on territory.

Liberal myth notwithstanding, America, in its colonial period and even after, had a distinctly feudal pattern of life. It is simply not correct to say, as is said so often, that America never knew a feudal period. Given the large unknown that was the New World, the absence of central government, the natural deployment of families, villages, and towns, the vital role of the land, and the difficulty of communication, the settlers would have found it only natural to follow conventions and practices that they had been familiar with in their old countries.

By the beginning of the eighteenth century there were some very large manorial estates in the colonies, much like those of England, and most of them were called manors. Despite the existence of colonial executives and legislatures, these manors were virtually closed societies in legal as well as economic matters. There were imposing social classes in the colonies. The great landowning families were the aristocracy, closely bound in marriage and in other respects. Below them came the middle-class merchants, ship builders, large importers, and the smaller landholders. Third down the hierarchy were the skilled laborers, artisans, and small business folk. Below these three classes—each distinct in style of life, manner, and even dress—were two others: the ranks of unskilled laborers, indentured servants, and small dirt farmers in the western regions who would produce what eventually became known as the poor white class; and the slaves. To suppose that such sharply etched classes as these did not matter in society, culture, and government is to suppose fantasy. The old stereotype of America settled exclusively by the middle class and resulting in relative equality throughout the colonies will not serve at all.

Established religion is another feudal institution that flourished in colonial America, indeed in some states until after the Revolutionary

War. Not until the early nineteenth century did it disappear entirely from America. One can imagine the restiveness of, say, Methodists and Presbyterians when forced to contribute regularly to the established Anglican Church or to any other church in the position of establishment.

Primogeniture and entail, both hoary European feudal customs, were found in almost every colony prior to the Revolution. Evidence of the strength and extent of these customs is shown by the speed with which the state governments that came into existence after the Revolution rushed to the abolition of both primogeniture and entail. Tocqueville thought this abolition the most revolutionary of all acts during or after the Revolution. There were in sum no indigenous dukes and earls, no knightly class, little of the pomp and ceremony that characterized Europe, but when one addresses oneself to the substance of feudalism, one can only realize that America was feudal for at least two centuries, and longer in some sections of the country.

How durable the feudal idea of association has been is illustrated by three structures in modern American society: the university, the political machine, and the Cosa Nostra. Until the university began in World War II a politicization that has since continued and enlarged, it richly embodied medieval-feudal themes of hierarchy and corporatism. From its deeply personal system of instruction, with the student in effect an apprentice to a chosen master, to its division into schools and colleges, its virtual immunity from the outside legal world, its hierarchy rising from novice-student through layer after layer of traditional role and status to the rector, chancellor, and president, all the way to the caps and gowns and the ceremonies and feast days, the university was preeminently feudal in structure. The current conflict between the federal government and beleaguered university scientists, whose greed and cupidity after World War II had so much to do with bringing government into the university, is but the latest of what has been a long succession of such conflicts, in a plethora of spheres, since the fifteenth century.

So was the political machine in this country an essentially feudal organization. Although the Founding Fathers contemned parties, which in the words of *The Federalist* would be nothing more than disruptive "factions," parties and then machines quickly became a political way of life in America. Party in some degree and machine in much larger measure were from the outset a kind of mediating demographic and social as well as political structure. They were, irrespective of primary function, the means by which millions of Americans, especially newly arrived immigrants, were enabled to participate in a polity that, apart from the power of the machines, would have continued indefinitely to be governed chiefly by Anglo-Americans. There were no easy, constitutionally anchored ways for the millions of Italians, Irish, and then east Europeans to become full-fledged members of the electorate. Here is where the machine served a democratic function, but it did so by quintessentially feudal means. For the relation between immigrant voter, precinct captain, ward paramount, and ultimately a Boss Tweed or Kelly was nothing if not a feudal, personally structured chain of service and largesse, of unflagging loyalty to organization in voting in return for protection of civil rights and economic assistance in time of need—in all, a relationship in almost direct descent from such late medieval groups as the Guelphs and Ghibellines. The decline of the American political party really began when, as the result of liberal reformism and the spread of a humanitarian Leviathan in American life, the machines were finally reformed out of existence or else atrophied from loss to the state of their social functions. Today political parties do not in any sense reflect the meaning of the term that had currency down through the 1930s; they are rather coalitions of special-interest groups, each seeking to wag the dog.

The Cosa Nostra is far from the only criminal organization rooted in feudal principles, but it would appear to be the largest, most powerful, and most successful. Its essence, symbolized by the blood ritual, is kinship—artificial kinship, one might say, but then all kinship is ultimately not a biological but a social phenomenon. And within a given Mafia "family," governance by the "father" or "godfather" is absolute; devotion and loyalty are expected by solemn oath to be equally absolute. Vast sums of money are dealt with, major decisions pertaining to war and peace among "families" are effected, large corporations and labor unions are infiltrated, high officers of government are bribed, and huge fortunes are amassed, all through a network that operates with an utter minimum of records and of formal organization, its members and retainers locked together tightly by vows, services, devotions, and protections which are feudal to the core. The Mafia is at once economic, political, social, ethnic, and familial in significance, just as were nearly all feudal associations in the Middle Ages.

There is a universalism and eternality about the feudal bond. It waxes in history when the central government over a large territory wanes. When government is no longer able to give its subjects protection through police, justice through law courts and tax agencies, and safety from marauders and enemies through the military, organizations of a basically feudal type begin to proliferate. Such organizations are already numerous, to be seen in the spreading underground economy where word of mouth and unwritten *quid pro quo* govern and where every effort is made to ensure absolute secrecy and autonomy from the state, in the private protective societies where either for money or for exchange of services or commodities citizens may look for the protection in neighborhood and home that the political government can no longer guarantee, and in the fast-burgeoning private community school, conceived as an educational refuge or sanctuary from the marauding, exploitative designs of federal judges and their tyrannous strategies of affirmative action. In this same context, there is special significance in the so-called multinational corporations. They resemble in their way the great merchant guilds of the Middle Ages, organizations like the Rhenish or Hanseatic League, each spread over a large part of the world in its activity, representing an aggregate or conglomerate of smaller organizations, whether medieval cities or modern corporations, each more or less indifferent to the national needs of the hinterland, and caught up in a complex, interdependent, economically motivated internationalism that more and more challenges the once-sovereign national state. Given the manifest feebleness of the contemporary political state in the functions of justice, law and order, and defense around which the state's sole *raison d'être* lies, a resurgence of feudalism, built upon already existent feudalism is to be expected in the West.

FUTUROLOGY

THIS IS ONE OF THE MORE pretentious of the pseudo-sciences of the twentieth century and is fully deserving of the neologism by which it is known, comparable to labeling the study of the past "pastology." The fundamental assumption of futurology is that all the crucial elements of the future—social, intellectual, technological, and so on— are contained embryonically in the present. Such elements include the trends and tendencies, real or imaginary, which the eye discerns leading from past to present and, by easy extrapolation, to the future. Projection and extrapolation of the present are at bottom the unvarying means by which the future is assertedly read by these social scientists.

For this task the most careful study of the present and all its contents is required. Once this study was left to the individual mind, working through observation, intuition, and imagination. Today, sup-

plementing the individual mind are the great memory- and calcula-
tion-banks called computers. So great are the retentive and analytical
powers of modern computers, declare futurologists with stars in their
eyes, that what has immemorially been little more than hunch is now
an exact science. Unconsciously following the Leibnizian "the present
is big with the future," gaggles of futurologists roam the present,
computers behind them, eagerly looking for fertilized eggs or em-
bryos and thus to launch forth into the future.

But the blunt fact is that the present does not contain the future,
and the past did not contain the present. The sciences of the 1930s
did not contain in embryo form the sciences of the 1980s. The flow
of time—itself only a metaphor, a construct—is here confused with
the actual course of events, happenings, and changes. Because the
mode of representing time contrives that seconds become minutes
which then become hours, days, months, and years, it is assumed
without warrant that events and changes do likewise—that events
have, as it were, little events which grow up and have events themselves.

Two metaphors govern the assumptions of futurology. The first is
the metaphor of organic growth. In the history of mankind this metaphor goes very far back. Once the mystery of growth became understood in the plant world, it was irresistible to apply the idea of slow,
sequential, stage-by-stage, inexorable growth to culture and society.
Nowhere in the ancient world was this metaphor more striking and
more implicative than among the Greeks, from at least Homeric
times on. Today it is as customary to use "growth" with reference to
history as to the individual organism. Whether growth is conceived
as linear or cyclical, its power over the human mind is immense. The
futurologist likens the future to the next stage in some process of
growth that has already been discerned, and in the same blithe way
that adulthood is predicted for the child, this stage is predicted as the
iron continuation of the present process of growth.

The second and equally seductive metaphor governing futurology
is that of genealogy. The Old Testament and its numberless begats is
the leading model in Western thought. Generation gives rise to generation in an unbroken chain of births and deaths that has gone on
since the emergence of *Homo sapiens*. From earliest times, mankind
has believed that the idea of a genealogy can also be imposed upon
the events of history. Historians are wedded to genealogy: first this,
and then that. The futurologist believes that by simple extrapolation
the genealogical chain leading up to the present can be continued
into the future.

Metaphors, with their lulling images of growth, development, genealogy, and flow, are probably vital to the human mind in its inevi-

table contemplation of past, present, and future, especially for large entities such as civilizations. But it is perilous to apply the metaphors, consciously or unconsciously, to particulars, economic or political. It is one thing to see, in Spenglerian fashion, the birth, growth, maturation, decline, and death of abstract entities called civilizations; it is something else entirely when metaphor-based reasoning is used to construct forecasts of the stock market, of economic trends, of political conditions, and of all the other practicalities of life. But that is what futurologists do: see past, present, and future in terms of either growth or genealogy, each of which is metaphoric at best, deceptive at worst.

In more pragmatic terms the method of the futurologist is inseparable from the act of projection or extrapolation. The future does not lie in the present, seductive though this organic imagery is. All that lies in the present is the present. Even the past lies in the present and is summoned up with the aid of rituals and records. Manifestly, being without Well's time machine, one cannot take oneself to the past. All one can do is believe in it, seek to reconstruct it, and try to learn from it through the manifold aids at one's disposal. The present was never at any moment embryonically placed in the past; nor is the present the iron consequence of a vast genealogy of events and changes, each succeeding its predecessor in rigorous, unbroken fashion as does a biological generation.

The existence of computers, though more and more complex and capacious in their operations, cannot give to extrapolation any more precision. The computer remains a machine, which can do nothing except respond to human direction. As someone has said, if the day ever comes when a computer beats a world master in chess, it will be necessary to take a fresh look at econometrics and other forms of futurology. But that day has not come nor is it remotely likely.

The computer-futurologist is doing exactly what philosophers, prophets, historians, and the common people have done throughout history: guess, intuit, speculate on the basis of present and past data, with varying degrees of luck and accuracy. Marx looked about him in mid-nineteenth century England and saw, not what was in fact there, to wit the continuing improvement of the life of the working class, but what his revolutionary-philosophical stereotype told him was there, namely the increasing misery of the proletariat which, along with other "contradictions" in capitalism, would lead ineluctably to breakdown, then revolution, and finally the proletarian state and socialism. That Marx has been proved wrong in his own particular form of extrapolation of an imagined trend has in no way diminished him as religious prophet in the twentieth century.

But just as there are false predictions of extrapolations, so there are correct ones. Burckhardt in the nineteenth century correctly predicted *terribles simplificateurs* and "iron commandos masquerading as democrats" ahead in the West. Tocqueville accurately forecast democracy's turn to totalitarianism through the forces of bureaucracy and administrative despotism. These predictions demonstrate that some futurologists can be successful in their efforts. A few people are even on record as having years before the date publicly predicted to the day when a given war would end. The stock market world does not lack its speculators who predict bear and bull markets. Individuals have become rich through successful bets at the race track.

But in no instance have these people looked into the future, much less created a science of the study of the future. There are only good guesses and bad, lucky bets and unlucky. It is all of a piece with stud poker or craps: there are successful "predicters" of the next card or roll of the dice, and there are the less successful. Much the same analysis can be made of Burckhardt's and Tocqueville's predictions. In each case what was being prophesied for the West was already in existence in some degree and was duly noted and projected or extrapolated. Both minds were really only drawing implications from the ideal type of democracy that each had created in his mind and then extending these implications into the future. Moreover, there are many predictions and premonitions in both Burckhardt and Tocqueville which history has proved baseless and wrong.

Futurologists are thus not a concentration of the parapsychologically remarkable but are rather a computer-based pack of trend tenders, tendency herders, and extrapolation charlatans, ultimately less interested in the real future than in their tinker-toy techniques of contriving the future. They recall the story of the mad physiologist who was so struck by the onset and acceleration of growth rates in adolescence that he made these the basis of predicting a twenty-foot tall giant at age twenty-one. The futurologists are innocent of the nature of actual events in history and of the inherent artificiality of trends and "tidal movements," which can never be endowed with the status of laws. They remind one of the hypothetical observer at a craps table who, struck by the high-roller getting three or four naturals in succession, promptly pronounced this a trend or ineluctable sequence. He did not know that no trend can possibly exist, given the actual nature or position of each throw. According to elementary statistics, the probabilities of one more natural are not increased in the slightest, or diminished, if the thrower rolls out five, ten, or twenty successive sevens and elevens.

Historical events and actions, which are and must be the actual stuff of alleged trends, are no different from the throws of the dice.

Inherently, intrinsically, events are not linked to one another, though people are prone to link them in plans and systems, philosophical, economic, or political. Despite Einstein's touching "God doesn't throw dice" in response to the indeterminacy principle which his deeply rationalist-Spinozist mind could not accept, God, or the Muse, does indeed throw dice, and nowhere more regularly than in the vast, infinitely particularized world of human history.

GENIUS

NOT MANY WORDS in the English language have suffered from Romantic puffery and what Fowler calls "slipshod extension" to the degree that the word *genius* has. Prior to the eighteenth century it meant mostly a special talent or skill. But that meaning has for two centuries been buried in large measure by another which the word then took on: a person of greatness who achieves solely through the "genius" that is endowed in him by God or by nature.

Two influences brought about this new meaning of the word: the *philosophes* in France and the Romantics in Germany. The former, in their running warfare with church, university, and other institutions of the old regime, saw themselves as minds of almost unprecedented brilliance, capable of every achievement from running governments to writing encyclopedias. Moreover, in their judgment, history had essentially been made by "geniuses" such as themselves; those of the ancient world, the Renaissance (by definition there were no geniuses in the Middle Ages), the Age of Science, and now in the Enlightenment. Nothing more irritated John Adams across the Atlantic about the French *philosophes* than their incessant posturing about their own inner "genius."

At the same time that the *philosophes* were twisting and puffing the word, the Romantics in Germany seized upon it for special application to themselves and to others of Germanic descent. In the same way that the Romantics found a special genius in their racial ancestry, they found individuals in the past of towering intellect and spiritual being who had helped form and then express the Germanic soul or consciousness. These could be generals or poets, statesmen or painters, religious leaders or dramatists. Each was a "genius" because he had been formed of special clay and from this inner majesty issued forth the great works which characterized his life. What both the French *philosophes* and the German Romantics were doing, at bottom, was reviving the ancient Latin "genius," which meant the tutelary spirit that was believed to accompany each person throughout life and to guide and protect him, except that the French and Germans made the "genius" inherent in the person rather than an accompanying spirit.

The cult of the genius was well formed by the time of Napoleon, and for a long time, in Germany and France alike, he was the focus of hero and genius worship. But he was far from alone. Throughout the nineteenth century in Europe, the Romantic infatuation with genius intensified and spread. Geniuses were believed to have minds of such surpassing creativity or heroism that their rational limits could sometimes give way, leading to an affinity between genius and forms of insanity. Geniuses, above all, were excused from the ordinary conventionalities and could indulge in vices denied ordinary mortals simply because these vices, eccentricities, and unconventionalities sprang ineluctably from the individual's "genius." Given this kind of superstition, individuals, especially in France in literature and the arts, found it useful, irrespective of actual mental powers, to flaunt the attributes of genius, especially those of licentious nature. The *fin de siècle* was rich in poets and painters who were pronounced geniuses, not so much for the true quality of their work as for their highly mannered eccentricities and pathologies.

What proved clinching to the myth of genius was the English biologist Francis Galton, cousin to Darwin, whose best-selling book *Hereditary Genius* was published in 1868. Galton took to himself the question of why the Greeks of the ancient world were so much greater minds than any in Galton's own nineteenth century England. The question is a legitimate one; what is not legitimate is Galton's thesis that the sole and exclusive cause is "hereditary genius," that is, a special intellectual and spiritual power that is inherent in a given person's nature and that transmits itself to succeeding generations through the germ plasm—until or unless, that is, this genealogy becomes corrupted through interbreeding with inferior physical and mental types. Galton's view cast a wide spell, and from it came not only the universal belief in "genius" in the biological and hereditary sense, to the virtual exclusion of historical and cultural influences, but also the pernicious rise of eugenics which threatened to become national policy. Darwin noted that prior to reading *Hereditary Genius*, he had always thought minds were differentiated only by "zeal and hard work." It is a pity that his mind was changed by Galton. So were the minds of countless others, and the physical inheritance of genius became a veritable *idée fixe* in the Western mind. Intelligence tests were rampant in the schools; searches for what were called gifted children went on year after year, culminating in Terman's Thousand Gifted Children of the 1920s, all of whom were confidently expected to become Newtons, Shakespeares, or Einsteins simply by virtue of their I.Q., which early on began to be called genius I.Q. at its highest tested reaches.

That there are individuals born of preternatural intelligence admits no doubt. There are people who from birth are swifter in comprehension, better able to concentrate, quicker to fuse or unite conceptually disparate things, and superior in fashioning with words or numbers or both. These people reach very high scores in intelligence tests, rack up perfect grade averages unless diverted by some alien force, and commonly show extraordinary capacity for solving puzzles.

The question is, however, what forces tend to lead some of them into highly creative work in the arts and sciences but lead others, equally rich in native endowments, to careers of puzzle-solving in its several forms, in as well as outside the sciences and the professions. To make the gigantic assumption that nature endows some of these individuals more than others with great innate mental strengths and only gives issue to these supergifted minds sporadically in time, thus causing those clusters of genius which lie in so-called golden ages, would assuredly be naive. Far more likely is the proposition that the distribution of mental strength in the population remains about the same from one period to another. "Nature uses one paste," observed Pascal, "and she applies it evenly throughout time."

Thus, the nonhereditary, nonbiological forces of history and culture would have to account for that high level of talent in the arts and sciences and for that uneven efflorescence of this level of talent which the historical record makes vivid. As Lowes explained: " 'Creation,' like 'creative' is one of those hypnotic words which are prone to cast a spell upon the understanding and dissolve our thinking into a haze. And out of this nebulous state of the intellect springs a strange but widely prevalent idea. The shaping spirit of Imagination sits aloof, like God, as he is commonly conceived, creating in some thaumaturgic fashion out of nothing its visionary world." This is precisely the myth of genius that the Romantics and Galtonians revered. But, Lowes continued, everyone, whether gifted or not, lives "at the center of a world of images . . . Intensified and sublimated, and controlled though they may be, the ways of the creative faculty are the universal ways of that streaming yet consciously directed something which we know, or think we know, as life. Creative genius, in plainer terms, works through processes which are common to our kind, but these processes are superlatively enhanced."

Working through "processes which are common to our kind" is the first insight into the works of a Michelangelo, a Shakespeare, or an Einstein, and the second is, "processes which are superlatively enhanced." The third and in many ways most important insight, though, is not readily discernible in Lowes's words: the absolutely necessary interaction of individual creators and their milieus in time and space. This is not the simple-minded environmentalism of sociology which implies, if not actually mandates, that all people, geniuses and criminals alike, may be explained by their environment, usually thought of as political and social with heavy emphasis upon social class. In its way, the environmentalism invoked against the Galtonian thesis of hereditary or natural genius is as absurd as what it opposes.

Insight into genius is to be found not in some single and compact hypothesis but rather in the crucial experiences and traits which are common to those of highly creative being. The chief feature in common is milieu, which does not mean quite the same thing as the environment. Symonds clarified the concept: "The intellectual and moral milieu created by multitudes of self-centered, cultivated personalities was necessary for the evolution of that spirit of intelligence . . . that formed the motive power of the Renaissance." The concept of milieu is at once historical, psychological, and also specific. Milieu is that part of the larger environment which is being shaped by the individual and which is also being participated in and swept into the individual's consciousness, so that external environment and individual consciousness are fused into one, into what Whitehead called "mutual immanence," a phrase he owed to William James. James's view of the interaction of mind and environment breaks for once and all the hateful dualism that Descartes gave to the world. For the empiricist James, mind is no mirror, no circuited receiver, but a function, and in this respect it is like breathing, eating, walking—all functions in which the actor and the environment are in mutual immanence.

The special character of milieu is that the only real environment exists in the consciousnesses of the actors—philosophers, artists, scholars, scientists, all—and thereby serves a catalytic function, while the consciousness of the actors is an inalienable part of the surrounding environment. Sovereign time enters the scene at every point. Milieu is nothing if not a point suspended in time. There is temporal as well as spatial interaction, moral institutional, and cultural as well as simple psychological interaction. To cite Lowes again: "Every great imaginative conception is a vortex into which everything under the sun may be swept . . . For the imagination never operates in a vacuum. Its stuff is always fact of some order, somehow experienced; its product is that fact transmuted . . . I am not forgetting that facts may swamp imagination, and remain unassimilated and untransformed."

Every individual above the level of moron is from time to time excited emotionally and intellectually by the people and things around him. It is a fair statement that the highly talented are the most excited in this way, and whether it is a poem or a scientific theory, what we witness is the capacity to internalize a social experience and to make the product socially available. W. H. Auden said that those who possess poetic talent stop writing good poetry when they stop reaching for the world they live in. D. H. Lawrence put the essence of all this admirably: "Everything, even individuality itself, depends upon relationship . . . The light shines only when the circuit is completed . . . In isolation, I doubt if any individual amounts to much; or if any soul is worth saving or even having."

In one of their conversations, Eckermann asked Goethe how he would explain the extraordinary richness and maturity of mind of a young Frenchman still in his twenties who had just astonished them with his learning and agility. Goethe answered: "Imagine a city like Paris where the most excellent minds of a great realm are congregated in a single place and enlighten and strengthen each other in daily association, strife, and competition; where the cream of all the realms of art and nature on earth stands exposed for daily contemplation; imagine this metropolis, where every stroll across a bridge or square brings a great past to mind, and where a piece of history has been made at every street corner. And in addition to all this imagine the Paris not of a dull and unintellectual time but the Paris of the nineteenth century, where for a span of three generations such men as Moliere, Voltaire, Diderot and their like have been circulated, the productive genius in such abundance as cannot be found in a single spot anywhere on earth a second time, and then you will understand how a fine mind like Ampére's can well be something at age twenty-four. If a talent is to develop quickly and joyously, it is essential that there be in circulation throughout the scene an abundance of productive genius and of sound culture . . . We admire the tragedies of the ancient Greeks, but upon proper examination we should admire the period more than the individual author."

In sum, it helps immensely, if one is destined for the arts or sciences, to apprentice in a Paris as described by Goethe, an Athens of the fifth century B.C., a Rome of the first century, or a London of the sixteenth century. No doubt there is the occasional exception, the mind of great creative force that from the beginning buries its light and takes refuge in isolation. But this could not possibly be more than vicinal isolation. It is better to assume that this rare individual through reading, fantasy, and sheer imagination creates his own milieu. Milieu is, however, essential. Great ages in the history of culture are made by their great component individuals, but the reverse is also true, that in large degree great individuals are made by great ages and by all the intellectual circuits which operate at high intensity in such ages. Goethe's adjuration to admire the period more than the individual author is pertinent, since great artist and scientist that he was, he was not likely to be indifferent to individuality. He chose in due time to move permanently to the relatively secluded Weimar, where his greatest works were done or completed. But Goethe never forgot for a moment that his early, formative experiences had put him in continuous contact with minds of superlative powers from whom he learned while they were in turn learning from him; nor did he have to be reminded of the stimulatory effects of the world's light and leading who came to visit him in Weimar. "I sense how it is," Goethe said once, "when men like Alexander von Humboldt visit me and in a single day advance me farther in what I seek and need than on my solitary part I otherwise could have achieved in years."

The past is a very important part of milieu, in the form of tradition, convention, and memory. The great ages of genius, starting with the fifth century B.C. in Athens, have never been calculatedly revolutionary, contemptuous of the past, in avid search for originality. People who seek originality generally wind up with two-headed calves, just as those who use the word *creativity* regularly in conversation are never creative minds. Ages of genius have truth, beauty, and goodness emblazoned on them, not modernism, post-modernism, and futurism. The Impressionists did not, at least in the beginning, consider themselves to be breaking with the past; they believed they had recovered the spirit of the best of the past despite efforts of the establishment in their day merely to freeze or ritualize the past. Planck was a notably conservative, traditionalist mind, and it was only when he had carried classical or conventional theory to its absolute end that he found himself reaching the quantum theory, one of the truly revolutionary theories of the twentieth century. Eliot, Yeats, Pound, Joyce, and other titans of the twenties were one and all reactionaries in politics and profoundly traditionalist in their literary craft.

This suggests another possibly vital element in the formation of genius: emulation. Velleius Paterculus, in his musings on the great Athenian dramatists from Aeschylus to Euripides, thought emulation a crucial desire. Emulation, not imitation. Longinus wrote that selection of a model as early in life as possible was vital to the emergence of great writing. To be as great as the master has surely lifted many

an apprentice quickly through journeyman status to the status of
master and even greater-than-master. Models, like metaphors, are indispensable to the aspiring.

Again it is instructive to quote from Goethe and Eckermann. Eckermann suggested that Shakespeare, magnificent as he was, unique as
he was, would have yielded somewhat different results had he not
been the associate of Marlowe and others of his time, men he was
obliged to respect and learn from, even occasionally steal from. "You
are absolutely right," responded Goethe. Shakespeare without his
contemporaries would have been as it is with the mountains of Switzerland. "Transplant Mont Blanc into the great plain of the Lüfnen-
burg heath and its size will leave you speechless with amazement.
But visit it in its colossal homeland; approach it by way of its neigh-
bors: the Jungfrau, the Finsteraarhorn, the Eiger, the Matterhorn, the
Gotthard, and the Monte Rosa, and, although Mont Blanc will still
remain a giant, it will no longer amaze you . . . Furthermore, whoever
refuses to believe that much of Shakespeare's power reflects the
greatness of his time should ask himself whether he seriously believes this astounding phenomenon we know as Shakespeare would
be possible in the England of 1824, during these bad days of journals
of criticism and dissent."

Emulation, in the full sense, is something that the creative mind
is never very far from no matter how mature and highly developed
such a mind becomes. The emulation may be of those in the past or
of those in the present, or both, but it is emulation—a word, by the
way, that includes in its Latin root and its long English history competitiveness with others, even jealousy. Emulation as a force in the
making of genius includes, in short, a vital negative as well as positive aspect. Geniuses, like the rest of the world, often work with
others looking over their shoulders, as it were, whom they emulate
both positively and negatively.

Accident and chance play their due roles in the formation of high
talent. Dr. Johnson defined "true Genius" as "a mind of large general
powers accidentally determined to some particular directions." It is
doubtful that any of the great creative minds in the arts and sciences—not to mention other spheres of existence—would ever have
discounted the role of chance and the accidental. From Plutarch on,
the biographies of the great are rich in the impact of the purely fortuitous upon human lives. Walpole summed it up with his story of
"The Prince of Serendip," who never found exactly what he was
looking for but who, in the process of incessantly looking for it,
found other things he had not even imagined.

Pasteur went somewhat past mere chance or accident when he

remarked, "Chance favors the prepared mind." Indeed it is not only the unremitting searching for something that creates fertile soil for the benign accident, but also the well-filled mind that is capable of recognizing the entry of Fortuna. This is easy to overlook in those stories of great strokes of insight having come to artists or scientists while they were double-parked or while they were climbing a mountain. Surely the vision came in its crucial form when it was said to, but just as surely long, often agonizing hours must have gone into the search, and without this backdrop, nothing would have happened in the double-parked car or on the mountain slope.

Whitehead remarked on "the monumental one-sidedness" of genius. This is doubtless the case with a great many people of highly developed talent in a field. Although they usually are not lacking in general knowledge up to a point and rarely push their special interest upon one in ordinary casual conversation, their minds and indeed their whole lives are dominated by a single interest. Large minds, but also narrow minds. It was also Whitehead who said that a good education "has got to be narrow; otherwise it won't penetrate." The role recently advertised by a celebrity hostess for the perfect guest, namely a "broad-gauged, wide-ranging, versatile and clever mind," is not likely to be filled by the true genius.

History affects the eruption of genius in various and subtle ways. Turgot, speculating in 1748 on the singular absence of English artists of note for two centuries or more, as compared with the French, German, Dutch, and Italian, noted the desiccating effect of the Puritan Revolution on England. The Puritans, with their hatred of everything in religion that did not proceed directly from faith alone, set themselves to the destruction of works of religious art and, more to the point, of the numerous crafts which fed into religious art, one way or the other. These crafts produced little but cheap medallions, crucifixes, and miniatures, but they were also the places where fathers apprenticed sons who had manifested any interest at all in art. From such apprenticeships often came the greatest painters. To have destroyed the many craft ateliers in England was to have destroyed the roots of the art of painting. No painters of talent were thenceforth even possible, no matter how many boys of potential talent were born.

Turgot's point is well taken. It is said that in the Paris of Cézanne, close to ten thousand painters were at work, the overwhelming majority of whom were mediocre at best, but whose collective presence represented the flood tide upon which the few of signal distinction rode. To change the image, high mountains are almost always surrounded by others nearly as high. A Michelangelo stands out, but only in the company of those who are almost as good. As for the historical development of the scene within which the genius works, Michelangelo simply would not have been possible had it not been for the state of the arts within which he worked—the technological as well as the social and cultural state. Turgot put it nicely: "Not every plowboy can aspire to be a Corneille, but had Corneille been confined absolutely to a village, he would have become only a good plowboy."

Capacity for intense and sustained concentration of mind is also one of the qualities seen oftener in the great than in other people. Johnson's remark on the concentrating effect upon the mind of a man's certain knowledge that he is to be hanged in six weeks has generally been misunderstood. Johnson was specifically answering Boswell's question as to how it was possible for a particular condemned man, a cleric, found guilty of treason, to write the vast amount of sermons he did while awaiting execution.

The final force that figures in the formation of genius is family— perhaps not universally but certainly overwhelmingly. Galton did not err in his linking of geniuses by family and genealogy; where he went wrong was in limiting family to physical genealogy rather than seeing it as the very microcosm of the whole social order, a social, cultural, moral, and intellectual entity as well as a continuity of germ plasm. Heredity, yes, but that word is also properly used when prefaced by the word *social*. Social heredity is the conventions, habits, incentives, coercions, disciplines, and punishments which, once they become ensconced in a household, tend to become traditional, literally "handed down" in the Latin sense of the word. It is astonishing what three generations of exposure to the intellectual and cultural affluence of a family line can accomplish, granted that the family "handing down" also includes the transmission of those innate mental powers which are requisite to all activity of any worth. It is not economic affluence nor material wealth of any kind that is vital here, but rather the closeness of the generations, the intimacy between parent and child, both intellectually and morally, which resembles a close form of apprenticeship, of emulation, and role modeling, allowing for assimilation of the many psychological and social insights, understandings, skills, and techniques which can be done only within the emotion-freighted circle of the kinship group.

It would be a mistake, however, to see family only through rose-tinted glasses. Family and love are by no means linked conditions. Family can house love and respect, but it can also, and frequently does, house hate, resentment, and exploitation. But where there is a deep determination by the father or the mother to teach, to instruct, and to cultivate, and an equally deep determination to accomplish this through whatever means seem necessary, the results can be as extraordinary in the absence of affection and tenderness as in their presence. Beethoven's father was a drunken brute much of the time, and he was not himself an outstanding musician by any means. But he knew music well, he recognized early the sheer physical-mental force contained in his son, and drunk or sober, abusive or laudatory, he knew how to implant the language of music into the young Beethoven's soul. What precise combination of fear, hate, dread, respect, even admiration, lay in Beethoven's lasting response to his father would be difficult to determine. Churchill has written, in partial description of the Duke of Marlborough: "It is said that famous men are usually the product of an unhappy childhood. The stern compression of circumstances, the twinges of adversity, the spur of slights and taunts in early years, are needed to evoke that ruthless fixity of purpose and tenacious mother-wit without which great actions are seldom accomplished." Perhaps so. All that is known about Beethoven's relation to his father is that the same hand that struck his ears punitively, leading to eventual deafness, struck also, in extraordinary ways, chords of a very different kind, chords of devotion, imagination, experimentation, and confidence.

To Beethoven's experience could be added that of the young Mozart, also at the hands of the father who, if he did not drunkenly abuse his talented child, exploited him egregiously. Samuel Butler, one of the most powerful and original minds of the nineteenth century, suffered abominably as a child. But Butler too learned things, experienced states of mind, which could only have been learned and experienced in a context as intimate and dependable as the family. Innumerable instances of the psychic wound as the fertile seed of genius are to be found in biographical accounts of the great, from Plutarch down to Churchill's Marlborough.

But without for a moment disparaging such accounts, the evidence is reasonably clear that love and affection serve far better than hate and pain as the family seeds of distinguished careers. Aristotle's loving relation to his father, the physician-scientist, Bach's relation as a child with his parents and then at their death with his older brother who reared and instructed him in music, and Goethe's relationships of continuing love and happiness with his family undoubtedly are more common in the lives of geniuses than are those of Beethoven.

What is true of individuals is true of peoples. By common assent, the three most talented peoples of the past two and a half millennia have been the Chinese, the Greeks, and the Jews. In all, the role of the family has been distinctively powerful. And in all three the family extended itself into all aspects of the individual mind, becoming the nursery of education, moral precept, citizenship, piety, and craft skill. To repeat, the family is not simply the microcosm, the formative nursery of things loving and good. It can be, as the Jews, Greeks, and Chinese have made clear in their religious and dramatic writings, the setting of greed, fratricide, incest, and other manifestations of evil. The Greeks at least were, on the evidence of some of their greatest works, more interested in the linkage of family and evil than of family and good. But family murder is the price to be paid, along with incest, blood feud, and other linked evils, for the uniquely intimate atmosphere of family, and it is, on the evidence of history, a price that should be paid. Better a society in which these specific evils will always exist as the consequence of the family tie than one in which, in order to abolish the evils, the family itself is abolished. One can somehow live with the evils, but civilization could hardly exist without the primary nurturing ground of its geniuses.

GOLDEN AGES

WHAT FIRST STRIKES the eye when one looks down on the vast panorama formed by the history of the arts and sciences during the past three millennia is the extreme unevenness of line. There appear none of the ordinary marks of growth: slow, continuous variation over long stretches of time. On the contrary, the scene is one of explosive bursts followed by protracted conventionalization, routinization, and fixity. Ages of decay and decline are interspersed with ages of genesis and development. For every Age of Pericles, a dozen, perhaps a hundred, ages of sloth and apathy are to be found in the history of thought and culture in the world. The same pattern of bursts and quick subsidences is to be found in the history of any single art, craft, or science. In philosophy, how rare is the epoch that comes even close to that occupied by Socrates, Plato, and Aristotle. How much oftener and in greater duration come the periods of mere glossing, copying, mimesis, or explication. With much reason Whitehead declared European philosophy to be a series of footnotes on Plato. It is no different in other fields of intellectual imagination and creation. What appears so clearly in the West is equally visible in other parts of the world, as in China, India, and Japan. For every Han or Gupta spasm of creation there are dozens of ages of sheer passivity.

Awareness of golden, silver, bronze, and iron ages in the history of the arts and sciences is quite old. Velleius Paterculus, Roman of the first century, was struck by the rarity and brevity of the great ages in history. He lamented the pitiful shortness of the age in Greece that had produced not just philosophers but Aeschylus, Sophocles, Euripides, Phidias, and Praxiteles. Why, asked Velleius, does such a unique age of creativity have to end so quickly, to be followed by ages of mere imitation? What causes the great ages with their tight clustering of creative talent, and what are the forces involved in their decline and fall?

Many since Velleius have asked the same questions. In the fourteenth century the Islamic scholar Ibn Khaldun addressed the problem. In the eighteenth century Vico in Italy and Turgot in France independently raised the question of rise and fall in the arts and sciences, identifying great peoples and ages, also those of aridity or decadence, and offering speculation on the causes. Both took all mankind as their stage for observation of the contrasting and recurrent ages in history. In the twentieth century major scholars have dealt with the identical problem, including Spengler and Toynbee.

This succession of observers and analysts of the golden and iron ages in cultural history have dismissed categorically explanations based upon race, geographic position, and individual genius. In the absence of knowledge, all races, so-called, are assumed equal in their collective possession of mental powers, large and small. And the same race can manifest over a long period epochs of infertility as well as fertility in culture. Geography fails for much the same reason. The same location reveals itself in the historical record as the setting of cultural stagnation as well as of cultural vitality. The decline of Greek civilization in the ancient world took place in the same areas in which Greek civilization had risen and prospered. As for explanations of biological genius, they assume that nature varies her distribution of human types in such a way as to meet precisely the demands made by the sporadic nature of human progress. It is better to assume that pretty much the same proportion of the bright and the dull exists in all ages.

Equally expendable as explanations of golden ages are Hegelian and Spenglerian fantasies about cultures being biological organisms in effect and thus destined to have their rhythmic patterning of rise and fall, of youth and age. When Spengler wrote, "Each age must be seen to possess the same life-cycle found in individuals: birth, development, maturity, decline and death," this was mere metaphor or analogy, not explanation.

The conditions and circumstances peculiar to great ages of culture must be looked for instead in the actual record of human settlement, migration, invasion, war, economic prosperity, of meetings among peoples and diverse idea systems, of alternations between equality and inequality, wealth and poverty, the sacred and the' secular. Whatever may be teased out of the historical record, not out of any presumed racial, geographic, or biological attributes, will give most understanding of the golden ages.

First and foremost is the mixing of alien ideas and values. The isolated, utterly secluded people is always passive and stationary in culture. The normal tendency of individuals and of peoples is to commit to habit and convention as much as possible in life and to dread thoughts of change and uprootedness. Fixity is as normal in a culture as in an individual. Always, if there is to be significant change, especially progressive change, there must be some kind of stimulus, some form of shock, something that literally forces a people to change. As Whitehead maintained: "It must be admitted that there is a degree of instability which is inconsistent with civilization. But on the whole the great ages have been unstable ages." Indeed they have been made unstable by war, migration, invasion—in sum, movement that begins as physical but shortly becomes social and psychological. What Bagehot called "the cake of custom" is broken only by conflict of some sort, usually military and political in the beginning, but intellectual and moral in due time. It is only when one's own ideas and values have been confronted by ideas and values of others that the processes of awareness, criticism, stimulation, and excitement can be generated.

Historically, war and commerce are the two most common excitations of cultural change. For prior to the present epoch of incessant movement in the world, it was only in the circumstances of war and of trade that diverse cultures came into contact, thus permitting the mind of ferment of ideas that precedes a great age. It is difficult in today's world to imagine that very long time when exposure of one's own sacred values and ideas to others was so dreaded as to make seclusion the highest of aims. Hence, in the past at least, the indispensability of war, for then the commingling and the interbreeding of ideas was inescapable, whether one lost or won. But from early times economic trade has served much the same function. This is why so many civilizations have risen at seaports or in river valleys. The geographic locations almost invited the visitations of other peoples and their values. The great cultural capitals have uniformly been in areas where isolation and seclusion were impossible for very long at a time.

Economic growth and prosperity are requisites to great ages. It is hard to think of any exception to the proposition that prior to any cultural explosion there must be something akin to an economic explosion. In the first place the release from subsistence toil is made possible only by the presence of wealth large enough to provide the leisure of those who paint, sculpt, write, and compose. But much more important is the psychology of growth. Nowhere are growth and retardation more quickly perceived than in the economic sphere. The spirit of growth in the economic realm translates easily into the spirit of growth seen in such a culture as Athens under Pericles. Of all the gospels of defeat and desuetude in world history, the gospel of the virtues of economic inertia, stagnation, and nongrowth is the most virulent. Only where the processes of prosperity are in full swing in the economic order, where wealth, property, and work have become vitally important, does the setting exist in which ideas of freedom flourish. And just as economic growth serves as the indispensable basis of cultural growth, the failure of the one leads commonly to the failure of the other.

A great age in civilization is almost necessarily an age of politics in one form or other. For the state has proved over and over to be the force of allegiance most likely to loosen the binding ties of ethnic and kinship identification and thus in a sense to liberate individuals. The state does demand obedience of its subjects or citizens, but except for the totalitarian state—a twentieth century phenomenon—the authority wielded by the state even under so-called absolute monarchy is never as penetrating, as sealing, as potentially stifling of individuality as is that of the patriarchal family or the religious sect. This is the reason why the dawn of civilization coincides with the appearance five thousand years ago of political empires. Through war and through the special kind of power that inhered in these novel structures, a rising number of individuals were allowed for the first time to experience a climate of power in which in substantial measure individual emancipation was possible. Only under the *imperium* of an emperor, usually a god-emperor believed to be infallible and possessed of the force of his armies, was it possible for otherwise discordant and warring families and religious sects to live together more or less peaceably. The context of political empire alone can explain the rise of the great universal religions, those which, like Confucianism, Buddhism, and Pythagoreanism, took their communicants as individuals seeking perfection and salvation, not as members of tribe, nation, or geographic place. That a golden age of philosophy should have existed over all Eurasia in the sixth century B.C. is at least partially explained by the prior appearance of the requisite political conditions, that is, the great empires.

Nor must one forget the overwhelming importance of the city. In

the city alone can freedom from stunting isolation, from mental and
moral despotism, from mindless orthodoxy, and from the tyranny of
the village—"the idiocy of rural life" in Marx's view—almost predictably be found in history. The etymological affinity between city and
civilization is matched by the actual historical affinity. People who are
entirely nomadic or agrarian can achieve greatness in the domains of
religion and morality, but that is as far as the record allows. If there
are to be citizens, and with them artists, philosophers, dramatists, architects, poets, and scientists, there must first of all be a city, one that
like all of the world's great cities is large in tolerance of diversity and
high in the commingling of minds of all ages.

These, then, are the vital bases of golden ages. They are not,
however, sufficient, for places and ages have existed in which there
was trade, war, empire, and city, but no intellectual-artistic greatness.
Three processes, not easily reduced from generality, appear to be the
final, crucial sparks igniting the blaze of creativity that goes into the
golden ages.

The first of these processes is predicated on the existence of a
strong, widely recognized core of religion, of the sacred, but a core
that is under challenge in some degree or other. Without the sacred
core there can be no true culture of any kind; but without the cata-
lyzing effect of challenge or dissent, there can be only orthodoxy and
passivity of mind. This is a principle of dialectics and also of cultural
dynamics. There must be action but there must also be reaction; sacred tradition but challenge to tradition; conventionality but revolt.
Throughout history powerful currents of religion have been at
work—old religions and new, challenging religions or ethical
creeds—and this holds as true for China and India as for Greece in
the fifth century B.C. and Europe in the twelfth.

Closely related to this conflict between the sacred and the secular
is that between community and individualism. Great ages are invariably strong in the sense of community, be it religious, moral, or political, but strong also in forces which are disruptive in some degree
to community—forces of individualism, libertarianism, and egalitarianism, however restricted and confined such forces may be. If there
is no community to begin with, then, just as with the sacred, there is
nothing to challenge, nothing to fuel the dynamism that is inherent in
such ages. And if there is only challenge and dissent, as in the wasteland of the late twentieth century, then there is nothing to give challenge and dissent purpose, substance, and meaning; there is nothing
but fugitive ideas, each, in Eliot's words, thinking the other is running away. Another way of stating this second principle of dynamics
is to refer to *Gemeinschaft* and *Gesellschaft*, but not as static ideal types,

rather as a kind of single process in which the first is invaded, so to speak, by the second.

The third process of dialectical antinomy that is essential to golden ages is the struggle between hierarchy, or class and caste values, on the one hand and equality on the other. Tocqueville described this process: "If I inquire what state of society is most favorable to the great revolutions of the mind, I find that it occurs somewhere between the complete equality of the whole community and the absolute separation of the ranks." There must be, in sum, a continuation of recognized hierarchy, of noble and base ranks, but there must also be the visible beginnings of the leveling of these ranks, of an emasculation of strict hierarchy. Burke reflected along the same line when he decried the country "which would madly and impiously reject the service of the talents and virtues" to be found in all strata of a society, but added unhesitatingly that "the road to eminence and power, from obscure condition, ought not to be made too easy, nor a thing too much of course." In other words, when the natural struggle between hierarchy and equality is won entirely by equality, then equality will not be the product, but mechanical leveling. What is required is a clear opportunity for vertical movement in the realm of status, but with the milestones of rank still highly visible and, in the intellectual-artistic world at least, the criteria sufficiently stark and elevated to make possible identification of the truly exceptional.

Besides these three processes, another recurrent quality of golden ages is the strong tendency toward the objective, in contrast to the subjective. Goethe stressed this in his conversations with Eckermann, declaring that progressive ages are invariably objective, while ages of decadence and dissolution are heavily subjective: "Our present age is a regressive one, for it is subjective. Not only do you see this in poetry but also in painting and many other things. Every truly excellent endeavor, on the other hand, turns from within toward the world, as you see in all great epochs which were truly in progression and aspiration, and which were all objective in nature."

The final characteristic of golden ages is their shortness of length in time. The creative burst can last just so long, and then everything becomes routine, imitation, convention, and preoccupation with form over substance. To be sure, as the centuries following golden ages often illustrate, the postlude can exhibit very fine work indeed and remain faithful for a long time to the highest standards.

One of the most spectacularly short efflorescences of genius is that of 1850–1855 in America. In that half-decade were published *Representative Men (1850)*, *The Scarlet Letter* (1850), *The House of the Seven Gables* (1851), *Moby Dick* (1851), *Pierre* (1852), *Walden* (1854), and

Leaves of Grass (1855). Nowhere else in the whole of American literature does one find a collection of works to equal that one in sheer
greatness and in lasting impact upon a culture. It would be hard, too,
to find any golden age in world history that offers sharper illustration, well before and during that eruption of genius, of the conditions
and processes essential to greatness.

The present melancholy age in America offers negative verification of the propositions advanced with respect to golden ages. The
stimulating conflict of ideas and values found in those ages is gone
from American culture, succeeded by conventionalities, chiefly from
the left. Economic growth is scarcely even an ideal or hope any
longer. Americans have become estranged from politics in the ancient
and honorable sense; there has been too much leaden bureaucracy
and arbitrary government by judicial activism. Any sense of the sacred has become so vitiated as to make impossible the challenge of
the secular and profane. Everything is secularized. Nor can there possibly be a creative tension between community and individuality.
Community has disintegrated or atrophied in American life, and individuality has sunk into mere egoism. There is no place for conflict
between hierarchy and equality in an egalitarian culture where hierarchy of any kind is spurned as elitism or class oppression. And finally, no age could better exemplify Goethe's dictum on objectivity
and subjectivity than the present. Culturally it is truly an age of iron.

A somewhat different but equally pertinent form of negative
verification is provided by the totalitarian nations of the world. Consider the Soviet Union. Any true exchange of alien ideas and values
is manifestly impossible. The thick hand of the censor sees to that.
Economic growth is as absent, save in the military sphere, as is politics in the vital sense of that word. The sacred-secular antinomy is
made impossible by despotic protection of one form of the sacred:
Marxism-Leninism. The operation of a creative tension between community and individuality is obviated by the lack of any form of true
community whatever and the suffocation of individuality of any kind
or degree. Finally, the hierarchy of the official bureaucracy and of the
military is so granite-like as to make even the thought of a creative
equality laughable. Czarist Russia could yield a golden age of sorts in
the late nineteenth century; but Soviet Russia never.

Heroes

It is often said that the West lost its capacity for belief in heroes in the nineteenth century. The rise of democracy dispersed for good the remnants of feudalism, a form of society virtually dedicated to heroes and hero myths. Critical rationalism and utilitarianism weakened man's capacity for enchantment with God and man alike. Secularism routed old sacred values and scorned introduction of the new.

But high above even these forces in debunking heroes were the influences of Darwin, Marx, and Freud. Darwin toppled man from the semidivine status he had so long known, making him the product of the same evolutionary processes which yielded up apes in the jungle. Marx demonstrated the existence of fixed laws of history actuated by material interests, thereby destroying the myth of man making his own history through volition and faith. And Freud completed the annihilation of man-as-hero through his revelations of the directive power of the unconscious mind and of inherited complexes as opposed to the rational mind. Only with great difficulty if at all could the spirit of heroism breathe in such a rarefied atmosphere.

How extraordinary, then, that the very same individuals whose earth-shaking ideas did so much to obliterate the ancient contexts of heroes and hero worship should themselves have become authentic heroes. That they are heroes in the literal sense is amply attested by the existence of disciples, large eponymous followings, pilgrimages to places of birth and death, texts deemed revelatory and therefore sacred, and recognized apostolic succession. Darwinians, Marxians, and Freudians justify their collective fervor by the towering scientific stature of their respective heroes, and without doubt Darwin, Marx, and Freud were extraordinary minds and dedicated researchers. Even if none of them had a following, and if all three were without the huge cultural impact they have had, they would still merit high respect.

But scientific achievement is not enough to explain the hero status and the hero myths which go with the three. If scientific eminence were alone sufficient, there would be analogous followings for such nineteenth century figures as Mendel, Pasteur, Maxwell, Spencer, and Wundt—all of whom rank as scientists with Darwin, Marx, and Freud. Indeed, neither Marx nor Freud is lauded today in economics and psychology as a masterful creator of their age. Their sheer fame and cultural impact greatly outweigh whatever in these disciplines is directly descended from each. It is different with Darwin. No more lauded name exists in all the sciences, and yet the uniqueness of his position in the pantheon of science still owes more to the ease with which he fits the mold of the hero myth than to the strict annals of scientific achievement.

Certain qualities are necessary to the establishment of heroes, in contrast to mere geniuses and great men. To explain the abundance of legend and the followings about the persons of Jesus and Mohammed, Caesar and Napoleon, Cromwell and Wesley—to name a tiny few—it is necessary to go beyond the unquestioned abilities of these men. Sheer greatness of act or mind is not in itself sufficient. Other qualities are needed, and they are as true of the three heroes of the nineteenth century as they are true of Jesus or of Napoleon.

The first indispensable requirement of heroic status is unshakable belief in one's own charismatic nature—that is, belief that one is on a mission not merely to instruct the world but to liberate it, from dogma and superstition, from torment and tyranny. Darwin explained his objectives in *Origin of Species* as not merely to present a scientific theory but also to destroy the Biblical idea of the separate creation of the species. Marx, too, believed absolutely that he was a liberator of mankind, in this case from tyranny and exploitation. Freud was no different in his conviction that he had found the way to free mankind from the terrible conflict between id and superego through psychoanalytic explorations of the unconscious.

The second attribute of heroes is the heroic deed. It must be vivid, concrete, and lasting. For the scholar-scientist, the deed is the book. A mere collection of research reports and papers, even though as spectacularly original and seminal as Einstein's relativity theories, will not ordinarily do. For Darwin the deed was his *Origin of Species.* For Marx it was *Capital.* And for Freud it was *The Interpretation of Dreams.* No written or oral revelation in religion has ever had more rapt, persisting, and fertile place in the minds of followers than each of these books has had in the minds of its communicants. That the claims made for these sacred books are no longer fully recognized by the secular worlds of biology, economics, and psychology does not affect the matter.

The third attribute, following directly from the first two, is the hero's obsessive sense of coming, as it were, upon a midnight clear, all the world hushed in unconscious anticipation. For the Darwinians, the picture is one in which everyone believed in the literal truth of Genesis until, on a midnight clear, came the *Origin of Species* to bear the Good News. This is pure myth, as Darwin had been preceded by dozens of evolutionary theorists. Butler summed up the situation: "Buffon planted, Erasmus Darwin and Lamarck watered, but it was Mr. Darwin who said 'That fruit is ripe' and shook it into his lap."

Marxians, beginning with Marx himself, are no different. Marx, according to the myth, was the first to break free of a purely static conception of society, to put the present in the context of developmental emergence from the past, and to see the present as a fixed stage in the historical evolution of the human race. The truth is diametrically opposite. From Turgot through Condorcet, Ferguson, Savigny, Saint-Simon, Comte, and Spencer, the perspective of social evolution was deeply ensconced in the Western intellectual mind. Nor was Marx even the first to adduce economic bases for the successive stages of human history. That honor too is claimed by Turgot, who accounted for the development, one from the other, of primitive, pastoral, agricultural, commercial, and industrial stages, in economic terms. All of this was well known to scholars of the time, yet Marx himself was as convinced as any devout Marxian thereafter that he alone had, on a midnight clear, given the liberating truth of social evolution to a world living in darkness.

Freud was thoroughly aware, at least in the beginning, of the well-formed tradition within which physiological psychology was gradually being supplemented by a functional psychology rooted in primal states of mind. The doctrines of the unconscious, the id, the revelatory power of dreams, and the sexual relationship of child to parent were afloat while Freud was a youthful tyro in physiology. But heroic being came to Freud only when he decided that he was first, that all who preceded or accompanied him were charlatans. And in that unconquerable, ineradicable realization, Freud was one with Marx and Darwin.

Fourth in the making of heroes is the all-important exile or ostracism as the direct and immediate consequence of the great deed. It is impossible to become a hero in the world of thought if one's contribution is found either inoffensive or acceptable. Jesus, Buddha, Caesar, Cromwell, Washington, and Joseph Smith all knew, as true heroes must, their respective wildernesses, exiles, castigations by contemporaries, even their Elbas and Golgothas. Darwin, Marx, and Freud too are linked with the ostracism-suffering syndrome.

Darwin, it is said, suffered the incredulity and outrage of a world unprepared for his revelation, for his shattering of their orthodoxies and spiritual comforts. So traumatic was the experience supposed to be that for the rest of his life Darwin suffered almost chronic psychosomatic illness, condemned to virtual isolation at Downs. All of this is nonsense. There was no conspiracy of silence, no glacial indifference, no trauma, no outrage, no visible incomprehension. Reviews were immediate and largely respectful, including one from Wilberforce. Of the hundreds of religious papers and journals in England, few paid any attention to the *Origin*. The august *Church Times* reviewed it favorably, commending Darwin for advancing science without damaging Christianity. There was indeed criticism of Darwin's theory for its limitations, but from contemporaneous scientists, not from the clerical-minded. And the criticism itself was not welcomed, as shown by Butler's account of the reaction when he tried to set the record straight: "I attacked the foundations of morality in *Erewhon*, and noboody cared two straws. I tore open the wounds of my Redeemer as he hung upon the Cross in *The Fair Haven*, and people rather liked it. But when I attacked Mr. Darwin they were up in arms in a moment."

The *Origin* went through a half-dozen editions within a decade. Moreover, again *pace* myth, the book earned respectful mention in footnotes and text references in scores of works in biology within the same decade. When Darwin died in 1882, it was reverently reported in the major newspapers, including the *Times*, and also the *Church Times*. An instant petition from over two dozen members of Parliament led to his immediate interment in Westminister Abbey. Some exile!

It is no different with Marx and Freud. They fit the heroic requirement of ordeal and exile, so far as the myths are concerned, in their mutual ignominy, neglect, ostracism, and loneliness. But in all truth, neither Marx nor Freud ever suffered much in his lifetime, save possibly through self-inflicted mental wounds. Although neither of them had the spectacular success with their publications that Darwin had with his, this was not because of conspiracies among the jealous, opposition from the establishment, or sheer hatred of a suddenly emergent genius, as the myth proclaims.

Within two decades, Marx's whole corpus was making heavy inroads in the German universities, and by the time of his death his name was revered in revolutionary circles all over Europe. As for torment and tribulation, the Marx family lived, with the financial help of the devoted Engels, a comfortable bourgeois existence, with ample time to seek a "good marriage" for each of the daughters into respectable, not revolutionary, circles.

Freud is perhaps best known for having to walk through the wilderness, for being subjected to slights, slurs, and ostracism. "I had no followers. I was completely isolated. In Vienna I was shunned; abroad no notice was taken of me. My *Interpretation of Dreams* . . . was scarcely reviewed in the journals." So Freud wrote of himself, making the myth official. Truth is dull by comparison. His two books on dreams drew dozens of reviews, many of them long and in the best scientific journals, and it was a rare review that was entirely hostile. Favorable reviews predominated. Indubitably Freud's new "science" of psychoanalysis was subjected to sharp criticism from the world of psychology years later, when Freud, through a variety of strategems, asked for it. But to suppose that the original appearance of his major books took place in the hostile or indifferent world, as the hero myth calls for, is to suppose nonsense.

One aspect only of the exile and popular rejection fantasies about Darwin, Marx and Freud is true, and that is the considerable measure of actual isolation experienced by each, which is doubtless vital to the making of the true hero. Hero worshipers do not like the thought of their heroes having been gregarious, hail-fellow types, constantly in association with the light and leading. It is far better to think of them alone or else surrounded only by faithful friends and disciples. And here at least fact accords with myth, for there was, after a certain point in the life of each figure, a near total absence of association with others, apart from the certifiably trustworthy. Darwin in the years following publication of the *Origin* chose to live in near isolation, seeing only those of his own generation, such as Huxley, whom he could trust absolutely and a number of younger biologists who were ready for hero worship. Some brilliant economists were living in the London of Marx, but Marx saw none of them. His life was by choice bounded by the British Museum and his home. Freud too chose isolation or near isolation from the world, living only with family and those who were four-square in their faith in psychoanalysis.

One of the most precious attributes of heroic status is enemies. Without hostile opposition, above all treachery, one cannot possibly become a hero. Alexander had his enemies, ever willing to kill; so did Caesar, Cromwell, and Napoleon; so did Jesus, Mohammed, and Eddy. Enemies are vital to heroic status. And not only are they plentiful in the myths of Darwin, Marx, and Freud, but each had an arch-enemy.

For Darwin, it was Richard Owen, one of the most brilliant comparative anatomists of his time. But Owen had also worked for Darwin prior to the completion of the *Origin*, and much of what Darwin learned about fossils and their correct arrangement came from Owen's teaching. Whatever happened to turn Darwin against Owen is not known, but Darwin hated him to the end of his life. Darwin had his Judas, as shown by a later characterization of Owen by a devoted Darwinian as "this appalling man, with globular eyes like a cod, horribly diseased by professional jealousy"—these words used to describe one of the greatest anatomists of the nineteenth century.

For Marx, the brilliant Moses Hess became the arch-enemy. He came from much the same kind of bourgeois family as Marx and founded the *Rheinische Zeitung* to propagate socialism. The two young men became close friends, and it was Hess primarily who made a socialist of Marx and introduced Engels to communism. Well before Marx, Hess had transformed Hegelianism into a philosophy of history and society that was also a philosophy of will and action, of potential revolution in society. Hess also emphasized economic forces in the history of society and in any calculations of revolutionary change. Hess, himself Jewish, saw Jewry as a potentially decisive force in unifying radical movements and in extending them into the future. But Marx broke bitterly with Hess and for the rest of his life vilified Hess as a traitor, renegade, and secret agent of the capitalists. Thus Marx acquired his nemesis.

Of all Freud's enemies, the brilliant Wilhelm Fliess occupied first place. It was largely through Fliess that Freud was led to abandon his seduction theory and begin his lifelong preoccupation with infantile sexuality, from which other crucial Freudian dogmas flowed. Fliess, though mentally unstable, was noted for his acumen, imagination, and learning, and during the years of their friendship Freud drew a good deal more from Fliess than Fliess did from Freud. But Fliess refused to give that absolute faith to Freud's developing psychoanalysis which was the condition of discipledom, so Freud broke with Fliess and never thereafter let up in his attacks on Fliess.

Although heretics fall under the heading of enemies, they deserve special mention in connection with the heroes Darwin, Marx, and Freud. From the beginning there were Darwinians of less than total commitment to one or other of Darwin's ideas. Butler was perhaps the best known of them. In the beginning an adoring reader of and correspondent with Darwin, Butler became increasingly conscious of the gaps and fallacies in parts of the *Origin*, and it was not long before Butler was dropped hard by Darwin and the Darwinians. But there were others, among them scientists who came to have the very high respect for Lamarck that the younger Darwin had.

There were deviationists and splinter groups whom Marx castigated almost from the time of the writing of the *Manifesto*. Russian, German, and other national groups of self-declared Marxists struggled with each other for supremacy. The orthodox felt a fanatical hatred for those who "softened," "altered," "misunderstood," or "misinterpreted" the holy writ of *Capital*. Heresies abound today. The Marx-Lenin Institute in the Soviet Union arrogates to itself the only true knowledge and interpretation of Marx, which has resulted in a Babel of Marxisms in all parts of the world that for one or other reason fear or hate the Soviet Union.

So were there Freudian heresies which made their appearance almost immediately. Adler and Jung were among the earliest, but the line has been a long and continuous one, nor is it likely to end soon. Where there is dogma, there is heresy; where there is the stuff of hero worship, there is the stuff of excommunication of those imperfectly pious and attentive. Just as Jesus had his Judas and Washington his Benedict Arnold, so Darwin had his Owen, Marx his Hess, and Freud his Fliess. The rest is orthodoxy versus heresy.

Another requisite of heroism, in contrast to the mere state of genius or talent, is the quality of being larger than life. The whole must be greater than the sum of the parts. There must be at least a tinge of what the pious are prone to call divine. A mind may be profoundly original, spectacularly and universally lauded, and still lack this quality. Keynes, a far greater economist than Marx, did yield Keynesians and neo-Keynesians even before he died, but the mentality of the Keynesian can never be confused with that of the Marxist, for a quasi-religious element is missing. The incessant desire of Darwinians, Marxists, and Freudians to prove and reprove their respective hero right, no matter how small the issue, is a sign of the triumph of hero worship over mere veneration. There must, too, be some element of illness and profound physical discomfort in the hero, something akin to the malaise instilled in saints by God. Darwin had his psychosomatic afflictions; so did Marx and Freud. Finally, there must be a kind of mystique in the ideas given up by the hero. No such mystique exists in the works of Newton, Maxwell, Mendel, and Pasteur, great and far-reaching as they are. But there assuredly is mystique in the dialectic, the Oedipus complex, and *Natura non facit saltum.*

HISTORICAL NECESSITY

IT IS A SAFE GUESS that most living historians would reject indignantly an ascription of historical necessity to the narratives they write. They would, in all likelihood, say: "Historical necessity is for philosophers of history, the Hegels, Marxes, and Spenglers who profess to find patterns and fixed rhythms in the past. We see no necessity, only what has happened; and we set this down as accurately as documents and other data permit. We say, with the great Fisher, that the configurations, waves, and undulations which other minds, religious or philosophical, have professed to see escape us entirely. We see only the discrete events, changes, acts, and movements which the record affords us. Ranke's *wie es eigentlich gewesen ist*, 'how it exactly happened,' may be a little grandiose, but at bottom his ideal for the historian is ours."

Granted that professional historians would never make use of such surrogate gods as the dialectic, zeitgeist, or cycle, they are not therefore denuded of pattern or configuration. Pattern lies in the very form that they impose upon historical data for their retailing to the reader. It is the narrative form, the "first this, and then, and then, and then," until a fact or a set of facts fills each open space in the continuity of time that begins with the arbitrarily chosen starting point and ends with the present or with some other arbitrary end-point. The truth is that the distinctive form of narrative history, with its beginning, its sequences of acts and events all within a single time frame, and its ending, which for at least twenty-five hundred years has been the standard approach by historians to the boundless wealth of the past, is as much an exercise in historical necessity as anything described by Hegel, Marx, or Spengler. The narrative historian's mission in life is to select from the infinity of data on the human past a few actors, events, and changes which can be fitted into a single time frame of narration so as to give the reader the unequivocal sense that this is what happened, how it happened, and why it happened.

Behind this narrative form of history, which seems so natural to historians as to be no form at all, no interposition of construction between reader and what actually happened, lies a vital metaphor: genealogy. No one knows when someone in primordial times first thought of applying to events and acts the same kind of relationship that could be seen in the world of nature, that is, the genealogical succession of generations. If animals, birds, and human beings themselves gave birth, in iron succession, to progeny, it could be assumed that acts and events do likewise. Events take place and inexorably lead to other events, and so on *ad infinitum.*

This is at bottom the method of the Old Testament. Action follows action in fixed and unalterable succession. The "begats" apply to events as well as to persons. What happened could have happened in no other way or succession. The necessity in the succession proceeds from God's absolute sovereignty over the whole genealogical pattern.

Narrative genealogy is also Thucydides' way. He above any other Greek is the patron saint of professional historians. He believed that the war with Sparta was the greatest war in the history of mankind and that his duty was to set it all down even while it was happening in order that posterity, in reading about it, might profit, might avoid mistakes, might be impelled to the right course. Thucydides never doubted that the single line of decisions, declarations, speeches, motivations, battles, and personages was a line of genealogical connection and therefore of causality. To his eye, an act that might to the unwary seem only casual became causal. To establish the correct sequence of events and acts, and then to intercalate the causes of these events and acts, was the objective of Thucydides, and it is essentially the objective of most historians today.

Fundamentally the same objective exists in the historical novel, indeed in any novel. Narration, the "first this and then and then," is the novelist's purpose just as much as the historian's. Both *history* and *story* in fact have the same root. However meticulously the historian Mattingly set forth the evidence, and only the evidence, on the Renaissance, he nevertheless presented it in the structure of the story. Oldenbourg, the novelist of the Middle Ages, did the same. True, she was more liberal in ascribing motives and she invented conversation, but this was done within a knowledge of medieval life that was as thorough as any to be found in the professional historian.

It is the method, the structure, the presentation that the novelist and the historian have in common. They both assume that what comes first in time causes or impinges upon what comes second, and third, and fourth. They believe that because time is universally assumed to be a continuous flow, there must also be a continuing flow of events and actions, just as in the genealogy of a family. The task of the historian, as of the novelist, is to arrange the data in strict chronological order—obviously Bismarck cannot be influencing the first Napoleon, or the French Revolution helping generate the American—and then to assign causes for the serially laid out events and actions. This requires penetrating the minds of the actors through the study of letters and memoirs.

A generally odious form of historiography today, called psychohistory, uses psychoanalytic recall at a distance, to discern Oedipal strivings and castration complexes in a Martin Luther or a Woodrow Wilson. Thus, it is said triumphantly, the assignment of cause is now scientific. Another form of history currently vying with psychohistory is quantitative history or cliometrics. The data, the facts all historians work with, are dug out in vast detail and given computer assimilation. The result, it is said solemnly, is the replacement of such vague words as *few* and *many* with *364* and *13,458*, thus giving accuracy and within that accuracy the "true" story.

But however embroidered, however meticulous in documentation, however rigorous the historian's mind, the format is still the

identical format of the storyteller, the novelist or epicist. The format
is a kind of Procrustean bed, for the past is infinitely complex, multi-
ple, plural. There is not one history but a vast multiplicity of histories. This is obvious when considering the whole world from the
beginnings of civilization. But it applies with equal effect to national,
racial, or ethnic histories. The history of France from 1789 to 1914 is
not one history but many thousands of histories—as many, one is
tempted say, as there were individuals. The spectacle of a "world history" such as that of H. G. Wells is comical. It is made possible only
by the fiction of taking one people at a time, usually at their high
point, devoting a chapter to them, then giving a chapter to another
people, also at their apogee, which comes later, and so on. First Egypt
in its zenith, then the glory that was Greece, then the grandeur of
Rome. Nothing is said, though, of what happened to all those Greeks
after they are left for Rome, and under the spell of the genealogical
method, it is possible to forget that Greeks went right on living in
Greece down through the ages to the twentieth century, when the
"world historian" may pick them up again briefly, this time in the
shadow of England or in the context of "the Balkan crisis."

The necessitarianism of even the most objective of histories lies,
then, in the genealogical mode of presentation. The nature of history
is made to conform to the requirement of one linear time flow. Since
at any given minute thousands of things are going on in a nation or
city, there must be selection of what is deemed to be alone crucial for
fitting into that given minute and endowing it with causal power for
what happens in the next minute. Against all logic and evidence,
events are made to give birth to events which in turn yield still other
events down to the selected end point.

In either the historian's or the historical novelist's presentation,
there is always the possibility of a good story, even an important
story, one symbolically nourishing to a people. History is descended
from such tales as Homer's, which will continue to give psychological
satisfaction as long as man lives. At whatever ghastly expense, including the slaughter of millions of competing facts, some facts are
selected, inserted into the narrative time frame, and made to appear
the necessary order of succession in time. Deny though they will the
charge of necessitarianism in their work, historians are incessantly
declaring something "necessary" to something else. They are obliged
to do so in order to meet the genealogical-causal requirements of the
unilinear, narrative method of history. It offends rigorous historians
to admit casualness, accident, the purely fortuitous, the random in
history. When writing the history of World War II, they must somehow account, moment by moment, step by step, for just what caused

a given episode. That there may be no cause in the accepted sense, that it was purely random and fortuitous, leaves historians uneasy. It is their job to show the iron succession of causally linked steps which took Hitler from art school to the making of the Third Reich. Historians who deny any attempt at necessity still speak of the American Civil War as "the irrepressible conflict," a statement utterly beyond proof or demonstration in any full sense. It was necessary and inevitable, in the minds of historians and others, that Franco's defeat of the Loyalists in 1936 would tie him inextricably to the Axis powers; but it did not. Franco's unwillingness to join Hitler and Mussolini was expressed immediately when they asked him, and his sentiment was accepted without demur.

The unilinear, narrative method is obsolete save as entertaining story or as patriotic symbol. Little is to be gained when one more historian writes yet another narrative history of Germany or England. A few facts, perhaps, not heretofore known, or a revisionist hypothesis, or a more felicitous style. But far overriding these small innovations is the fact of the bed of Procrustes on which a complex body of event, act, and thought must be stretched, pushed, chopped, and mutilated in order to fit the requirements of the linear narrative method.

Use of the unilinear, narrative method in history writing inevitably brings forth divisions of the past into usually artificial but not the less enchanting ages—the counterpart to the social evolutionist's stages. Antiquity, Middle Ages, Renaissance, Age of Reason, Enlightenment, and Age of Revolution are some of the labels fixed on bodies of time of highly elastic character. Thus Renaissance alone may mean what its first celebrant, Burckhardt, intended it to mean, that is, the fifteenth century in Italy, or it may mean the period 1200-1600 in all Western Europe. Nominalists from the age of Abelard would have a splendid time with the ages, epochs, and periods which historians so solemnly affix to arbitrary chunks of time.

Another and perhaps more amusing consequence of fixing ages in history is the use of those three cherished words: *crisis, transition,* and *innocence*. Every century since the twelfth has by one historian or another been pronounced a century of crisis. Putting the centuries in line, one can only exclaim: some crisis! Every year there appear titles like "The Crisis of the English Aristocracy," "The Crisis of the Middle Class: 1820-1830," "The Crisis of the Early Renaissance," "The Crisis of the Late Renaissance," "1847: Year of Crisis," and so on. All the befuddled reader can say is, if every century is a crisis, no century can be a crisis. The word *transition* has also been used as label for just about every century, decade, and year in Western history. It

is quite possible that Adam's first words to Eve as they departed the
Garden were, "We are in a period of transition." "Transition from
the Old Order to the New" is one of those titles which can be used
repeatedly and in reference to everything from children's toys to
world empires. And finally there is "the age of innocence," also
drawn from allusion to individual human growth. Again, it is unlikely that a single decade of American history from 1620 on has
escaped labeling in this fashion. Such ages are as subjective and evanescent as those of crisis. If the 1890s, say, are pronounced the age of
innocence in American history, one may be sure that in due time
each succeeding, and preceding, decade will receive the same characterization. From "innocence" to "sophistication" must surely be applied today more often to historical ages than to children growing up.

There are feasible and interesting alternatives to the Thucydidean
method. One approach is that of the *Annales* School in France. It rejects what it calls *histoire événementielle*, literally "history as linked
events," in favor of the intensive examination of contexts, such as
geographical, temporal, and institutional, within which persistences,
slow modifications, and sharp mutational changes may be discerned.
Bloch's study of the Middle Ages, Braudel's of the Mediterranean
during the age of Philip II, and Aries' of death and mourning customs
are excellent examples.

Still another, related way of dealing with the endless multiplicity
of the past and present is called *histoire problème*, which addresses itself to a specific problem and focuses upon what is germane to that
problem. The narrative format is discarded save to the degree that it
may be apposite. The successive religious awakenings in the pre-
twentieth century United States constitute, in their alternations, their
rhythmic periodicities, a problem. It is not necessary to do an *histoire
événementielle* of religion in America to seek answers to such a problem. There is also the problem of accounting for the simultaneous
appearance in the sixth century B.C. of the greatest prophets in all the
history of universal or world religions.

A third alternative to Thucydides' method is comparative history.
Here a problem is studied in comparative focus, while the linear continuity of time is disregarded. To learn the causes of the Great Depression, say, it is necessary to banish the narrative, unilinear, temporal pattern and go comparatively to other, analogous depressions in
history, whether in ancient Egypt or in modern Germany. The problem itself, not the requirements of the narrative time frame, determines the pertinence and appositeness of data.

No doubt there are other possibilities. And they need not replace,
merely accompany, the cherished, age-old genealogical idol.

HOMOGENEITY

MANY OF THE great social critics of the nineteenth century put the future of the West in a dark setting of social and cultural homogeneity. Tocqueville foresaw only the leveled masses, a "countless multitude of beings shaped in each other's likeness, amid whom nothing rises and nothing falls." The thought of "such universal uniformity saddens and chills me," Tocqueville declared.

In England, Mill agreed wholeheartedly. The single greatest contrast he found among nations in the world was that between the "stationary" states and the "progressive" ones. China, with its thralldom of custom, was a very monument to the stationary, the homogeneous, and the passive. The West, especially since the Middle Ages, had been made a dynamic complex of peoples, not by "any superior excellence in them, which, when it exists, exists as the effect not as the cause," but by "their remarkable diversity of character and culture. Individuals, classes, nations, have been extremely unlike one another: they have struck out a great variety of paths, each leading to something valuable."

Mill agreed with von Humboldt that the two decisive causes of human progress are freedom and variety. But, Mill lamented, the second of these was even then diminishing: "The circumstances which surround different classes and individuals, and shape their characters, are daily becoming more assimilated. Formerly, different ranks, different neighborhoods, different trades and professions, lived in what might be called different worlds; at present to a great degree in the same. Comparatively speaking, they now read the same things, listen to the same things, see the same things, go to the same places, have their hopes and fears directed to the same objects, have the same rights and liberties, and the same means of asserting them ... The demand that all other people shall resemble ourselves grows by what it feeds on. If resistance waits till life is reduced *nearly* to one uniform type, all deviations from that type will be considered impious, immoral, even monstrous and contrary to nature. Mankind speedily become unable to conceive diversity, when they have been for some time unaccustomed to see it."

It is impossible to fault the theory, the philosophy of freedom and progress, that lies behind the words of all these prophets of homogeneity and standardization. They are entirely correct in their argument that diversity, heterogeneity, plurality, and multiplicity are vital to the imagination that is requisite to invention and innovation. The only question is how accurate the previsions of these minds have proved to be, indeed how justified in their own day were the premonitions. The answer has to be largely in the negative. For all the power of mind in a Tocqueville or Mill, there was yet a failure equal almost to Marx's in appreciating the sheer profusion of capitalism's contributions to culture and society. Marx's vision of a future in which the overwhelming majority of people had been pushed down into leveled, equal degradation with a relatively tiny class of capitalist masters dominating them is hardly more at odds with reality than the visions of Tocqueville and Mill.

In all truth, there has never been a civilization in the world nor even a period in the history of the West when as much diversity and multiplicity may be found. All societies have, in unequal proportions, universals, specializations, and alternatives. Ethnologists have provided pictures of societies so primitive in culture as to be composed of almost nothing but universals. All men, women, and children engage in the same activities, with a minimal division of labor and a virtual absence of specialization. Choices among alternatives in economy and morality are almost entirely lacking.

In these respects nothing could be more unlike primitive groups than contemporary Western civilization. Nowhere are there the monolithic masses that cultural snobs and dandies of the right and left foresaw a century ago, or the homogeneous citizens foreseen in anguish by Tocqueville and Mill. Western civilization is richer in specializations and alternatives today than even a few decades ago, and it is vastly richer in these respects than were its preindustrial, predemocratic forebears. The disappearance of crafts, skills, and techniques of yesteryear, the manifest decline of the upper levels of art and literature, the spreading egalitarianism of legislation and decree, and the eruption of consumer goods chains where individual enterprise once dominated are justly lamented. But these and many other losses or changes over the past century have not, on the evidence of technology, mores, social differentiation, and cultural alternatives, made the society homogeneous and standardized.

Technology has brought about and continues to bring about an incredible differentiation of occupation. At whatever level this differentiation appears, whether in the profusion of consumer goods or in the burgeoning of scientific elites to conceive and produce those goods, it is vastly greater and richer than at any time in the past. The monotony of mass society, the homogeneity of culture, and the standardization of a single bourgeois morality that intellectuals in the West have accepted as inexorable realities for most of this century are mere fictions. At no time have patterns of living ever been as diverse as today. In just about every sphere, whether work, recreation, reading, music, drama, the media, education, ideology, science, or morality, there is a minimum of the universal and an abundance of specialization, alternative, and sheer eccentricity. In sex alone, that dominance of the bourgeois standardization of morals which was so eloquently predicted only a couple of decades ago has proved a fantasy. Never has sexual diversity or deviance been as widely tolerated and participated in as at present. The kingdom of pornography has never in history flourished as it does today, often in or on the periphery of the very middle class communities which it was once thought would reduce sex to simple procreation.

There are many disagreeable and downright dangerous aspects of society in the West, but advance toward the homogeneity that Tocqueville and Mill feared for the noblest of reasons and that the intellectuals of the new left paraded in the 1960s and 1970s in so farcical a manner is not one of them. On the contrary, for intellectual as well as moral and political reasons, the Western nations could profit from a realization of some of the once-feared homogeneity of life. What has been lost is not specialization and alternative, but universals. Whether it is the plethora of dialects and pidgin-ethnic that are ruining the universality of the English language in America, or the hopeless multiplicity of ideologies in the political realm that are eroding culture, what the West is witnessing is the triumph of the centripetal over the centrifugal.

HUMAN RIGHTS

THE LANGUAGE OF RIGHTS, which goes back to the Middle Ages, is suffering a debauchery at the present time, and in the process the West is being defeated by the Soviet Union and the other Marxist states in the battle of concept and opinion. Until the formation of the Soviet Union and the spread throughout the world of Marxist-Soviet ideologies of so-called rights, there was but one sense of the word *rights* in the civilized world, and that was cast overwhelmingly as rights against the state or government. This sense begins and largely ends with life, liberty, and the pursuit of happiness, or of property. It is the sense found in classical liberalism, in the natural law philosophy of the seventeenth and eighteenth centuries, and in a strong vein of medieval thought. Philosophically, these were not rights given by governments to subjects and citizens; they were rights possessed already by individuals, deriving from God or a presumed state of nature, and not to be infringed upon by the political state. This is what Locke and the Founding Fathers had very much in mind, and the course of English and American history was profoundly affected accordingly.

In the Anglo-American tradition, and to a lesser extent on the Continent, human rights were considered to be deeply implicated in the structure of government. Devoted to natural rights though the Founding Fathers were, they did not feature them and see fit to refer to them in the text of the Constitution. Whether the Constitution would have been ratified if supporters of the document had not yielded and allowed amendments, the Bill of Rights, to be appended is uncertain. But even in yielding, the Federalists saw to it that the language of rights was not inflated or distorted. Nowhere in the Constitution, including the Bill of Rights, is it implied that the newly formed government is granting rights. Far from it. What the Bill of Rights says in effect is that Congress shall not intrude upon rights of individuals. And these rights, it was accepted by all of the Framers, inhere in man, are gifts from God or the prepolitical state of nature. That is the special significance of the Ninth Amendment: "The enumeration in the Constitution of certain rights, shall not be construed to deny or disparage others retained by the people." The genius of the Constitution lies, in sum, in its explicit acceptance of the propositions that rights are human—namely they inhere in the condition of humanness and are not gifts from the state—and that the essential purpose of a bill of rights is to restrain government from transgressing upon these human rights.

This is a far different approach to the problem of rights than was to be taken by the Soviet Constitution. In it, rights of individuals are granted by the Soviet state. There is no recognition whatever of rights anterior to the state. Indeed the whole underlying objective in the Soviet system is to emphasize the fact that rights granted to individuals are granted by the communist Leviathan. The "rights" in the Soviet document are more often those of job, housing, and medical care than of due process before the law. And of rights to free speech, assembly, petition, and religion, there is not a mention. Whereas the American Constitution puts its emphasis upon division of power in the government and upon checks and balances, assuming that rights and freedoms for individuals will automatically flower in the interstices, the Soviet Constitution appends its rights to a main text in which the concentration and centralization of political power are made so mammoth in importance as to reduce to nullity any possible growth of freedom and rights in their historic sense. In the course the Americans took, they were on the side of history as well as moral philosophy. For the prime lesson taught by the history of power is that the only reasonably secure check upon it is, not any documents of guaranteed rights, but the existence of other powers to rival and compete with it in some measure. This is the great lesson also taught by the moral philosophy of the Middle Ages. The constitutionalists of that age saw unity of power only in God; on earth, power was meant to be divided, as between church and state, between church and family, between state and corporation or guild.

But the true origin of such hallowed rights as life, liberty, and property is only secondarily in philosophy. It is primarily in the traditional autonomies and privileges which groups had in the Middle Ages. In medieval law, "a liberty" was something possessed by corporate bodies—guilds, universities, monasteries, village communities. Only later did liberty become rationalized and individualized by the philosophers of natural law. The history of the past several thousand years is rife with assertions of collective or group rights—of families, ethnic communities, religions. The Jews fought and died for their collective identity and their autonomy from pharaohs, Roman governors, and a long succession of other rulers. Thus, long before the idea of rights as such appeared in the literature of Western philosophy, peoples, tribes, and families claimed and often fought successfully for autonomy of ethnic strain, of religious faith, of village. That individuals had, within their community, comparable rights of autonomy and privilege would have seemed preposterous. In ancient and medieval times the individual was important primarily as member, with duties to the larger community.

In short, the idea of individual rights embedded in the natural law is a derivation from the far older and more universal rights which existed by custom, tradition, and convention and were to be seen most often in the privileges, protections, and autonomies granted by emperors, kings, and popes to peoples for their divers faiths and practices. The rights granted such groups necessarily covered the authorities they had over their individual members, which authorities guaranteed the growth of the idea of individual duty. In this light, Burke was able to see rights as merely the other side of duties, unlike the liberal and radical philosophers of his time. Indeed, what made Burke singular in his day was precisely his veneration for the society and his understanding that without "civil bonds" there can be no rights and no liberties.

It is impossible to exaggerate the role of religion in the development of the idea of rights. Nothing mattered more to ancient peoples than preservation of their collective identities, which came only from their prior belief in a deity who had created them, made them in his image, and whose worship was vital. Replace "deity" with totem, spirit, ancestors; the import is the same. Human rights eventually became important only because of religious rights, meaning the rights of gods and spirits to enjoy forever the adulation and attention of the living. Today the nearest to a supra-individual referent for human rights is the vague, amorphous, and basically meaningless "humanity."

The difference between the Soviet Union and the United States, as reflected in their constitutions, consists in the fact that in the American Constitution human rights of life, liberty, property, and due process are not granted by the state but are recognized and even, in the main body of the text, presumed. How very different is the Soviet Constitution, where there are no rights except those specifically granted by the Soviet government. And these have little to do with the classic natural rights of life or liberty and everything to do with social rights which are in effect entitlements, as to housing, jobs, and vacations. Rights in this sense are perfectly compatible with the most despotic of totalitarianisms. Even an Albania bestows such rights upon its thoroughly enslaved subjects; so does North Vietnam, North Korea, and all of the Iron Curtain countries of Eastern Europe.

It is impossible to reconcile the two diametrically opposed conceptions of human rights, for the one aims solely at liberty, at the autonomy of the individual in matters of religious faith, economic existence, and judicial relation to government, whereas the other flouts such rights and insists that true human rights are those which are gifts of the government to its citizens and are inseparable from the development of socialist collectivism.

It was inevitable from the outset, once the idea and strategy of human rights on a worldwide basis had been accepted by the United States and the Western powers, that the struggle between these two broadly different philosophies of human rights would be unending. It was perhaps equally evident to the thoughtful mind that Soviet-style rights would be far more appealing to the great majority of people on earth than would those contained in the American Constitution. For such people have not yet acquired the social and economic institutions, the level of culture and material welfare, and the essentially prepolitical moral values which a liberal democracy requires. If these people, or their self-styled spokesmen at least, see more merit in a constitution that guarantees job, food, medical care, and the like—irrespective of the probability of such guarantees ever being fulfilled— than in one that directs itself to due process, freedom of speech and assembly, they can scarcely be faulted. Too often has the United States, in its well-meant but so often bungled humanitarian work around the globe, forgotten that there are institutional prerequisites to democracy and freedom.

The struggle between the two conceptions of rights on the world scene may well be matched by the same struggle within the United States. Social Security, Medicare, Medicaid, and Aid to Dependent Children are not called rights, in the constitutional sense of the word; these and their hundreds of analogues at the present time are "entitlements," granted by the national government. Thus far, there has been no diminution of constitutional rights as a result of the elevation of these "social rights." But once any people has become accustomed to such "rights" as those contained in the social welfare provisions, it is not likely that they will relinquish them under any circumstances. It is by no means beyond belief that the time could come when the social entitlements will be widely perceived as more important than the constitutional rights. Such a change is comprehensible to any student of history, but if it takes place, it will mean that the essential institutional prerequisites of liberal democracy have eroded away.

HUMANITIES

A FACULTY MEMBER was accosted by a colleague with the words, "I understand you spoke against the humanities the other day at faculty meeting." "No indeed," was the reply, "I love the humanities. I would die for the humanities. All I asked was what the hell are the humanities?"

The question is pertinent at this moment in history when the humanities are lying at death's door. Their condition is known by the fact that they are receiving eulogies throughout the land. University presidents, foundation executives, newspaper editors, corporate spokesmen, Senators, Representatives, movie and television stars, all fill the air with their pious affirmations of civilization's absolute dependence upon the humanities.

Once it was precisely this way with the classical languages. They died, while testimonials to their indispensability lay thick as cherry blossoms on the ground. The official death of Greek and Latin in this country might be put at 1920, the year of publication of a book filled with eulogies to the study of these languages by the same types who today are at work on the humanities. About average in the book is this: "I could never have become President of the First National Bank had I not as a young man applied myself to the classics of Greek and Latin." Or this: "Throughout the great state I am proud to serve in these halls of Congress lie virtues of citizenship which are the heritage of the Greek and Roman Classics. As a republic, we shall perish if the Classics die." Die they did and it is an open question whether the republic has survived.

Greek and Latin began to die at about the time that the word *classics* became popular. In the days when the two languages flourished in America, no one was heard saying, "I study classics." What one studied was Greek or Latin. Granted that, as a wit put it, the students often got just enough Greek and Latin in their systems to have a firm belief in the existence of the two languages, at least they had been exposed to hard things in an unambiguous, uncompromising way. But when one says, "I am majoring in classics," the processes of squish and slush have begun to operate. What happened to Greek and Latin subsequently happened to modern foreign languages in the curriculum, and today the word *humanities* conceals the same processes of squish and slush.

The humanities may be compared in their present manifestation with a midden heap, an archaeological deposit. Farthest down and oldest in time are the courses and works of scholarship which used to be referred to as the liberal arts, always thought of as in close conjunction with the liberal sciences. These, in philosophy, English literature, foreign languages and literatures, history, and certain areas of the social sciences, were almost unvaryingly hard, vertebrate, and worthy of companionship with the sciences. Our classically educated forefathers could have looked with appreciation on what went under the name of the liberal arts down through the 1930s.

Just above this marble-like stratum is a more recent one, which is essentially the detritus of the Great Ooze of the 1940s and 1950s when suddenly hard things became soft, large ones small, and marble and granite were overlaid by the spongy and oleaginous. The Great Ooze was the age of what was called admiringly "cross-fertilization," "synthesis," and "integration." Emphasis was on "breadth," and if anyone then had said, as Whitehead once did, that an education has got to be narrow if it is to penetrate, the remark would have been dismissed instantly as one from a philistine.

Above the Great Ooze lies a still more recent stratum, that of the Age of Vandals, roughly 1960–1975. Here the detritus is different, a bewildering assortment of the mindlessly ethnic, the sexual, the narcissistic and egocentric, the revolutionary, the utopian and futuristic, the profane and obscene, and everywhere, the intellectually boneless and flabby. In the midden heap, this stratum displaces a great deal of atmosphere.

There is one last stratum, not recent but contemporaneous: the detritus of the Age of Political Plunder. The processes of squish and slush have here been stabilized and broadened in effect by politics and bureaucracy. They are not likely to disappear before the next Dark Ages appears with its selective and preservative monasteries of the great and the good.

The word *humanities* is much in vogue today. Although it was always in the vocabulary of the educated, it was rarely used prior to the 1950s save in the ancient contexts of the *Litterae Humaniores*. Much commoner were the terms *liberal arts* and *letters*, both generally linked as "liberal arts and sciences" or "letters and sciences" in the college curricula. Rare indeed were divisions or departments, or even curricula and courses, in "the humanities." All of this began to change during World War II, when councils and committees suddenly appeared to give reverence to and fight for the humanities. Gone now was the slightest pretense of using the word in its ancient and noble meaning of the two great classical languages. There was little sentiment for shoring up these languages in faculties. Even teachers of English literature and philosophy found themselves slipping into references to the "dead languages." As a symbol, the word *humanities* stood essentially for what had long been termed the liberal arts. Increasingly titles appeared such as "The Humanities at Bay" and "The Crisis of the Humanities," and invariably the enemy was science. Gone now was the old curricular companionship of the liberal arts and sciences. The myth was securely in place by 1950: the humanities were under attack, and the villain was the man in the laboratory.

Something else became visible at the dawn of the Great Ooze in the late 1940s: "general education," as it was called, the product of ne'er do-well social scientists and humanists, failed natural scientists, and successful educationists. This curricular blob made all the easier the transmutation of once proud teachers of the liberal arts into "humanists," best defined as those who taught the liberal arts but with all the hard things taken out. By the middle 1950s many self-styled humanists disavowed, in the interest of "integration" and "synthesis," any connection with such fossils as, say, French literature, metaphysics, English history, philology, and logic.

By 1950 keening and wailing at the "plight" of the humanities had become official. Rightly did C. P. Snow refer to the "two cultures" and lay most of the blame for the rift between the sciences and the humanities at the feet of the latter. The humanists saw themselves discriminated against by university administrations in the interests of science, which was anything but true in those lush times. Snobbism increased exponentially in the humanities, and one grew accustomed to hearing nuclear scientists referred to as "plumbers and machinists." How, humanists asked, can scientists be thought educated when they have not read Chaucer and Milton, forgetting that more and more humanists were not reading them either. It never occurred to them, as it certainly would have to Goethe and Dr. Johnson, that they were more egregiously philistine than those they condemned, given their almost total ignorance of the sciences, even the classics of science, such as evolution, thermodynamics, and nuclear energy. Both Johnson and Goethe knew science intimately, becoming as excited over some new chemical or biological discovery as over a new poem or drama.

The humanists themselves were largely responsible for the situation they found themselves in. They were the ones who began the softening of the curriculum, then increasingly its vulgarization, and finally its radicalization. The humanists made a veritable cult out of the humanities, shouting the unique values they purveyed and the unique torments they suffered at the hands of the physical and social scientists. And from cult the humanities quickly became cause, movement, and crusade, ever in quest of preferred status and above all money with which to found institutes and centers.

In order to advance the cause politically and economically, the humanists found it expedient to popularize their wares, to make them more immediately seductive to the businessman and the politician. Less and less was heard about courses in English, French, or philosophy, more and more about courses called "Humanities" which purported to deal with the essential values of literature, foreign language, or philosophy, but without the "walls" and "barriers" which, it was said, militated against the natural unity of knowledge. This amounted to jettisoning the hard and concentrating on the soft. The underlying, component disciplines were cast into the shadows. Introductory, survey, and integrated courses pullulated like laboratory rats, and the withering look became accepted response to the faculty member who wondered if it would be in keeping with the *Zeitgeist* to teach a course in French literature in which knowledge of the language was a prerequisite.

Under the Great Ooze, all pretense of teaching and requiring student work in the foreign languages waned and disappeared. Academic humanists today still put on lugubrious expressions when this scandalous condition is mentioned, subtly conveying the thought that nothing is more important to them than constant reading in the Greek or French, but that they dare not hold courses outside the English vernacular. Humanists love to caterwaul at others—bad schools, permissive parents, hostile administrators, callous trustees, indifferent admissions officers, and above all lack of funds—for the cataclysmic decline and now virtual disappearance of the foreign languages from college. But in point of fact, these languages were casualties of the Great Ooze in the period 1940–1960.

Here is a fair approximation of a typical academic announcement during the Great Ooze, from a college or university that shall be called Muchmore, since that word epitomizes the siren songs of the period from publicity agents for the humanities: "At Muchmore our emphasis from matriculation to graduation is on the Whole Person. The Traditional Walls and Barriers which for so long have Fragmented the Learning Process have been Broken Down at Muchmore, leaving the student in direct contact with Knowledge. The Dichotomy between the Humanities and the Sciences does not exist at Muchmore, and the student in each will receive the full flavor of the other. In keeping with the true Unity of Knowledge, Muchmore has abolished all Artificial Divisions, creating in their place Integrated Courses based upon Values rather than mere words, sentences, and paragraphs. The student at Muchmore is thus spared the Crippling Effects of Narrow Specialization. The essence of teaching at Muchmore lies in the Closeness of Relation between student and teacher. The teacher is more than a teacher at Muchmore; he or she is at once Friend, Father, Mother, Brother, Sister, Depth Psychologist, and Chum. Given this Closeness of Relation, there is no Alienation among Muchmore students." Integration was the magic word in humanities curricula across the land. It should perhaps have been evident then to any reasonably perceptive eye what horrendous problems lay ahead when this pernicious concept was transferred from curricula to races and other ethnic groups in America.

During the Great Ooze still another academic monstrosity came forth: creative writing. Such courses had existed in the college and university before World War II, but they were few in number, not often given place in departments of English literature, and rarely allowed to fulfill academic requirements toward the baccalaureate. During the Great Ooze such courses multiplied, their pullulation aided by the presence of resident writers and numbers of writers' conferences, usually held in the summer, but their residue bound to be present when the academic year began in autumn. No one has ever satisfactorily explained the real mission of resident writers and of writers' conferences. Certainly it is not, on the record of the last three decades, to generate fresh new literary talent, for though this emerges from time to time, in some degree at least, almost never is it a product of creative writing, or of association with the resident writer, or of repeated summers spent at a Breadcrumb Conference of writers.

There is, as a suffering world knows, good writing, bad writing, and creative writing, the last by now more a faith or cult than anything recognizably academic. A student creative writer has little, after all, to write about. The situation calls to mind the cartoon in which a young man is indignantly explaining to a concerned parent, "Father, a writer doesn't write *about things;* he just writes." How true, as the record of the last quarter-century shows. Writers have themselves, of course, and since nothing in their ordinary middle-class lives has given them much in the way of poignance, diversity, and experience, they are inexorably led to explore themselves, centering on school and college experiences liberally laced with the sexual and the scatological. Plot, scenes, and characters are rigorously of this academic mold.

Creative writers, however young and blank, have much in common with academic novelists, those youthful professors who, having acquired tenure, then turn to writing, ever caterwauling about the intrusions of classroom, faculty meetings, and office hours upon their writer mission. Again, those who have spent their entire lives in school, college, graduate work, and then a professorship can have little to write about. Consider a recent short novel, its setting a private room in a faculty club, its characters a half-dozen middle-aged professional men, and its plot an exchange of masturbatory self-revelations, winding up with a collective howling. This product of creative writing became a best-seller, its author a subject for interviews in the leading literary weeklies and television talk shows.

Then came the Age of the Vandals, beginning around 1960 and lasting for a decade and a half. This was the period of the uprising of students across the country in the name of educational reform. Americans watching the evening news became accustomed to scenes involving rock-throwing, window-breaking, unending demonstrations, frequent riots, and calculated spoliation of offices and classrooms. In fact, almost all of these stormings of Bastilles were engendered by the liability of male students to the military draft and thus to being sent to Vietnam. In lesser degree civil rights for blacks played a role. What the riots and demonstrations, led by the new left, were not about was education, either traditional or reformed. Nevertheless Archibald Cox, solicitor general and professor of law, could, in a solemn report commissioned by university trustees, declare the vandals of the 1960s the most idealistic generation in the history of American education.

In one respect, the student vandals were without blame. It was assuredly not their fault that the earlier Age of Ooze had virtually invited their eruptions and incursions through its erosion of ramparts. And the wanderings of the small percentage of all college students who constituted the horde in the 1960s pointed all too clearly to these weaknesses both in the university generally and, almost calamitously, in the humanities. The raids and sorties showed in what tatters lay the fabric of academic and intellectual authority. There is no evidence that the vandals ever improved the curriculum in America, and yet they undeniably provided a certain amount of catalysis. They also helped substantially to bring an American President to his knees, not to mention a score of other presidents in the universities and colleges.

But the most destructive work was done, not by the youthful vandals, but by their mentors. If the depredations had been confined to the campus, they would have been tolerable. Alas, the depredations upon curriculum, by humanitarian humanists on the faculties, were vastly worse. The "vandals," in sum, included those who alone were responsible for the introduction of courses, commonly known as workshops, seminars, and encounters, in which students rather than professors generally took charge, and which served as conduits for entirely new languages—psychobabble, ecobabble, ethnobabble— and entirely new fields: black studies, Chicano studies, women's studies, eco-studies, ego-studies, revolution studies, absurdist studies. For such monstrosities the young vandals on the campuses can scarcely be blamed, and it is a matter of record that students wearied of these courses quickly—but not apparently their teachers, who were fertile in their production and eloquent in their rationalization.

To this moment there appear, at conferences and in publications of the humanists, nostalgic evocations of the founding of these courses. It is said that "their subversive strategies offer an important corrective to the impulse toward premature capitulation to current pressures for 'practical' results," the last a reference to hard courses in the old liberal arts. It is also said that, "as we adapt to a worsening economy, we must take care to include contemporary culture in the curriculum—popular writing, movies, music and television," all of which "have made substantial contributions to the development of student consciousness." The humanities can be defined accurately, but shamefully, as this celebration of ignorance and illiteracy, the elitist brought down to the populist, and the pop culture of television and movies.

In close proximity to this kind of narcissistic hedonism in the

Age of Vandals lay the urge to power—power in the universities, the professional societies, and other avatars of the debased muse. Hence the struggles, always in the name of the student or of the people, for quick command of these groups. If an august association in the humanities had a regularly, democratically elected hierarchy, it must be put down by some kind of coup or putsch, with power transferred to the insurrectionists. Rare was the humanities association of the period in which there was not at least a radical caucus—or black caucus or women's caucus or, *mirabile dictu*, a workers' caucus—standing by waiting for the glorious day when the books of Homer and of Dickens could be cast aside in favor of the works of Cleaver and Malcolm X. No definition of the humanities would be complete without reference to this combination of moral flabbiness and political muscle in the period 1960–1975.

Nor can the true substance of the humanities today be understood without turning to the specters of bureaucracy and politics in the Age of Vandals. Ages of social and cultural debasement are usually prolific in enabling statutes, lofty doles, and intellectual circuses, and that age was no exception. When the humanities were just reaching the height of their debauchment in the 1960s, two National Endowments, one for the humanities, the other for the arts, were created amid cheers from intellectuals and politicians alike. As long as they remained relatively small, they could not do a great deal of harm. Ten million dollars a year is not enough to arouse the lusts of the populace and the power instincts of congressmen. But within a very few years each of the two bureaucracies was much closer to 200 million dollars a year, an amount worth the interest of any politician or special interest group. The Age of Political Plunder had begun.

What had been simplicity in the first years now quickly became Byzantine in complexity and also in opulence. In the name of humanistic piety, receptions became more lavish each year; elegantly catered luncheons were held under royal tents in the Mall and in imposing halls of the Capitol where bureaucrat, intellectual, politician, and socialites could meet under the television lights and be interviewed for the edification of the taxpayers.

Grants to eager, not to say rapacious, applicants became ever more numerous and generous. They ranged from a few thousand dollars for the senior citizen "realizing my potential" by collecting old playbills to several million dollars for the refurbishing of a humanities program over many years and involving paid leaves for all participating refurbishers. Fellowships were available to every demographic cohort in the United States: there were youth fellowships, middle-aged fellowships, and fellowships for those in their dotage. Creative writers were welcomed. In one instance a recipient wrote a pop best-seller for a commercial press, his royalties and film rights soaring into the hundreds of thousands—no part of it returnable to the Endowment for aid to other struggling authors. Many of the grant applications reflected the debauched mores of the humanities at the time, and it could hardly have been otherwise. For if psychobabble, women's rights, ethnic rights, encounter, narcissism, soul, revolutionary strategy, sex, and the like had supplanted a great deal of what had once been the proud liberal arts, an official agency of the people must show itself democratic. With the gentle encouragement of politicians in Congress who had intellectual constituencies, the Endowment complied.

Another contribution of the Endowment was to subject the humanities to the values of populism and egalitarianism. Those in Congress who were so eloquent in behalf of the humanities and who participated in the Age of Political Plunder encouraged these values. No word had harsher connotations by the middle of the 1970s than *elitism*, which almost invariably referred to high scholarship from the few academic monasteries in the country where this tradition remained alive. There must be no elitism, not where the public interest was involved, as it was presumed to be in the Endowment. Every worthy grant to a scholar in the true sense must be balanced, therefore, by a proper number of grants to those in America's towns and villages eager to putter with local history, to revive old and forgotten town festivals, to rummage among records of graduation in the local high school, and to dredge up the sayings of a department store founder half a century earlier. It may be said that all of this is justified by the fact that genuine scholars receive grants too, but this misses the crucial point, which is that bad money drives out good, and that only a few years of such handouts to putterers will be enough to convince the American people that Everyman is a humanist as well as a speaker of prose. It is necessary only to look at the reports of disbursement of funds, especially from the state councils of humanities. There is nothing too trivial, hackneyed, irrelevant, even obscene to get its funding.

The Endowment for the Humanities registered a fascination, as did also its sister endowment in the arts, for certain congressmen once the annual budget went over a hundred million dollars. That is good patronage when the recipients are intellectuals instead of dairy farmers. Hence the predictable fraternizing of politicians and members of the several humanities associations in America. Hence too the predictable invitations by these associations to congressmen to speak at annual meetings. By the time they have reached the speaker's rostrum, they have been wined and dined and fawned upon sufficiently to see themselves as reborn Pericles presiding over the building of a Parthenon. Naturally they flatter their humanist audiences, which flatter back in head noddings of understanding and waves of applause. It all reminds one of the Paris that Tocqueville described in his observations on the Napoleonic age and the Paris limned unforgettably in Balzac's novels: humanists, politicians, and tycoons in affectionate embrace. The day will surely come when a successor to Eisenhower will feel obliged to add humanists to the complex of industrialists, militarists, and scientists against whom Eisenhower warned the nation.

To define the humanities today, a metaphor will do, this time one drawn from the botanical rather than the archaeological realm. The humanities in the United States are an ancient jungle, in which it is necessary to make one's way carefully and slowly, now and then discerning a few tall and stately trees, a few sturdy shrubs, but in vastly greater abundance encountering masses of poison ivy, dwarfed or misshapen trees, and clotted underbrush.

Such a jungle can certainly be thinned out, the poisonous and grotesque removed, the tall and stately nourished, the soil reclaimed. But on the record of what has happened to the classical heritage in America, the prospects for restoring the humanities as they were once known before the Great Ooze, the Age of Vandals, and the Age of Political Plunder are not bright. Perhaps a new Dark Ages is required. In that generally maligned period in Europe, the corrupt and decadent in Roman and Greek culture were left to perish deservedly, while the best was taken by the monks and a few kings or emperors for preservation and, as it happened, for the germination of the great renewal in the twelfth and thirteenth centuries. Whether this will again happen remains to be seen. But for the present, the lamented state of the humanities brings to mind Nietzsche's statement, "When you see something slipping, push it."

IDEOLOGY

THANKS TO FREUD, it has been joked, when a person thinks a thing, the thing he thinks is not the thing he thinks he thinks but only the thing he thinks he thinks he thinks. Fair enough. And thanks to Marx, when a social class thinks a thing, the thing it thinks is not the thing it thinks it thinks but is instead a "false consciousness," in a word, ideology. The influence of Marxism, indeed of modern radicalism generally, on language during the past century is nowhere better illustrated than in the toll it has taken on this once-respectable word, which came initially from the French.

When coined by the French psychologist Destutt de Tracy, the word *ideology* meant no more than the science of ideas and their relation to the brain. In the heavily politicized age of Napoleon, however, changes of meaning were made, even by Napoleon himself, who lamented the ease with which "ideologues" persuaded the people to follow ideas like popular sovereignty, which would ultimately bring them to ruin. It was this Napoleonic sense that captured the minds of intellectuals in Europe. Gradually *ideology* came to mean a more or less coherent body of ideas, an idea system. When Marx and Engels commenced their reduction of all social behavior to class behavior, it was probably inevitable that they would sweep *ideology* into their bag. Marx had a genuine talent for taking old words and phrases and giving them new, tendentious meaning.

Marx and Engels saw to it that the word would be henceforth reflective of social class. Each class—bourgeois, proletarian, or whatever—had, Marx declared, an ideology, one that grew from the class's perception of its economic interest. Generally in history the classes—slave owners, slaves, feudal lords, and serfs included—know their real interest, and their ideologies are therefore reflective. But occasionally a class is deluded by false representations of its interest by another, superior class. This is the origin, Marx wrote, of false consciousness.

Clearly this concept of false consciousness or ideology can have unlimited strategical and tactical use to Marxists or any other masters of the occult with revolutionary aims. Marx's dimly conceived but powerfully catapulted concept of social class proved to be his single most influential bequest to social scientists and other ideologists of the twentieth century. Marx's theory of class is in fact only a half-theory, but half-theories are like half-bricks in that they can be thrown farther. This half-theory was thrown by Marx and Engels so far that German sociology was concerned with little else for decades afterward. The major critic of the Marxian fetish was Weber who, still magnetized by the concept of class, managed nevertheless to bring himself to criticize Marx, finding class an explanatory tool only in the economy, not in the political state or social order. With Marx, class had been an all-purpose weapon in the study of society. To this day, not only in Germany but most recently in England, where Marxism has become a pastime of sociologists comparable in attraction to astrology in the population at large, the cosmic question of Marxian versus Weberian interpretation of class rages, resembling the Arian versus Athanasian battle of definitions in early Christianity.

Nowhere, though, were the social sciences as powerfully ravished by Marx as in the United States in the 1930s, 1940s, and perhaps later. Marxist economists, sociologists, political theorists, psychologists, and even anthropologists prattled, babbled, and gibble-gabbled on Marxian, meaning class-oriented, dialectic-driven paradigms, parameters, and periodicities. Fusing Freud and Marx into a single, double-faceted creed brought joy to the hearts of all but the dourest fundamentalists in each religion. American sociology became two nations: the reactionaries, who thought there still was explanatory value in certain non-Marxist ideas, and others, who had read Marx just well enough to become enchanted by Marx's "bourgeoisie" and "proletariat," each with its ideology, true or false to reality. Much effort was put into demonstrating that when American workers chose to buy automobiles and to work up the ladder of success, they were victimized by a false consciousness of their interest, victims of the capitalist class's wily exploitation of them.

By the late 1940s many of the Marx-oriented social scientists had become bored with Marx's simplistic division of classes and attributions of ideology and began to look elsewhere. This group was fortunate in the arrival in the United States of the so-called Frankfort School. Adorno and Marcuse are perhaps the best-known of the professors in Frankfort, Germany, who had founded the school. They gave ideology and false consciousness a new life through hybridizations of Marxian, Freudian, and even Heideggerian writ. Of a sudden American sociologists and psychologists were happily dazzled by such concepts as "authoritarian personality" and "mass culture," each one a misbegotten and murky effort to show that under capitalist democracy the people do not realize their true debasement of mind and their actual tyrannization under the camouflage of constitutional liberties. But all good fun comes to an end, and within a few years the Frankfort School had collapsed, with only Marcuse left to preach his doctrine of "repressive tolerance," that is, the more tolerant a government is of dissenting opinions or eccentricities, the more repressive it actually is, for it persuades the citizenry that revolution against their masters will be unnecessary.

The next move forward on the ideology escalator was to the French philosopher Althusser. Although he was recently committed to an asylum for the criminally insane for having stabbed his wife, his glory among structuralists and students of ideology will not likely be dimmed. He is the Supreme Pontiff in the succession that began with Marx and Engels.

He is controversial to be sure, but importance in any essentially religious body of thought is gauged by one's capacity for stirring up fascination, not agreement, and it is a rare piece of Marxian theology in the West today that does not go immediately to this shaman either to agree, to trim, to freshen, or to dissent. Althusserianism has be-- come a synonym for the tortuous, the chameleonic, the hollow and pretentious, but only in intellectual circles where syntax, precision of speech, and grammatical discipline are still prized, where above all the sense of empirical reality is still alive. But let Althusser tell it for himself: "In ideology the real relation is inevitably invested in the imaginary relation, a relation that *expresses a will* (conservative, con-formist, reformist, or revolutionary), a hope or a nostalgia, rather than describing a reality."

No age has existed even comparable to the last two centuries in their Babel of ideologies—political, social, and economic. A cre-scendo began in Napoleon's day in Europe that has only rarely been halted, to resume momentarily its screeching climb, an end not yet in sight in the Bedlam that houses ideologies today in America. There is little that does not by now constitute an ideology, that is, a body of ideas the function of which is not to interpret experience or to reveal concrete reality, but to supply the sense of intellectual cohesion, of membership in the columns of the righteous, of liberation from the terror of living one's own life largely alone. Abortion, opposition to abortion, prayer in public school, supply-side economics, mone-tarism, marijuana, child abuse, budget balancing, charity, minimum wage, public education, tuition vouchers, natural environment—a hundred pages could not exhaust the range and diversity of ideology in America today. The present passion to convert every opinion into dogma is boundless.

Ideology is as capable of analysis as is religion. Indeed, ideology is almost exactly that: a religion, or a religious intensity of belief about a cause that has become political. Politics is the nearest to reli-gion as a containing structure. As more and more parts of the social order, more and more cultural traits, become invested with political importance, the greater becomes the desire to transform the intrinsi-cally nonpolitical into the political. If one's wish is to prohibit abor-tion under any circumstances whatever and in process of such a mis-sion to define human life as beginning with the split-second of conception, then by all means organize, create a lobby, inundate all and sundry with pleas, laments, bleatings, scornings, and beggings, in the interest of achieving a congressional statute or a constitutional amendment.

Religious ideologies and their fanaticisms are dangerous enough, but when these or other ideologies become frenzied elements of the political area, the only area of absolute power over human lives, of total bureaucratic regimentation of lives, they become potentially disastrous in their impact upon a free society. The single most revealing and perhaps frightening thing about an ideology is its immunity, once it has begun to grow on its own psychological nutrients, to the voice of experience and concrete reality. The psychologist Festinger touched on this aspect of ideology when he put forth his theory of cognitive dissonance. Belief, he observed in his psychological examinations of religious groups, becomes not weaker but stronger when it is in greatest and most obvious conflict with reality. The nineteenth century Millerites, also known as Seventh-Day Adventists, predicted that the world would come to an end on March 21, 1844. Their number is estimated to have then been 100,000. No such ending occurred, and Miller proclaimed a new date for the conflagration, October 22, 1844. In the interim the number of Millerites went up substantially, and when the second failure of prophecy was made evident, after thousands had sold or given away their material possessions, the number of communicants shot up impressively once more. The religion at the present time is among the fastest-growing in the world.

But cognitive dissonance occurs everywhere that true ideologies abound. An ideology grows on the belief that nuclear energy is uncontrollable and that any nuclear energy producing plant is, in the cherished words of this ideology, a "ticking bomb." Belief hardens and chills into dogma. That there have been no casualties whatever from civilian, peaceful use of nuclear energy has not the slightest impact on the ideology, for that is a fact, and ideologies have nothing to do with facts. A Three Mile Island breakdown occurs in 1979 in Pennsylvania. No one is injured or contaminated, not even those working in the plant, much less outside. At first the residents are calm and matter-of-fact in their reaction, resigned to the fact that all energies have their dangers but not fearful of nuclear energy in any obsessed way. Then the ideologists begin their litanies and dirges—in print, on television and radio, and in visits to Three Mile Island. No casualties, then or since, but the ranks of the nuclear doomsayers have greatly enlarged since the nonevent at Three Mile Island, just as the ranks of the Millerites did during and after 1844.

INDIVIDUALISM

THE DISEASE OF the Western world, Comte called it. Tocqueville said individualism "at first saps only the virtues of public life, but in the long run it attacks and destroys all others and is at length absorbed in downright selfishness." Moreover, Tocqueville continued, it throws man "back forever upon himself alone and threatens in the end to confine him entirely within the solitude of his own heart." Durkheim referred to individualism as a menacing "social current" in the West, manifesting itself in rising rates of suicide, public disorder, and a general weakening of the collective conscience. De Gaulle declared individualism the primary cause of "the moral malaise . . . inherent in modern mechanical and materialist civilization."

Contrast these judgments with those that are much more familiar in the United States. When Tocqueville's *Democracy in America* reached American readers, his remarks on individualism in democracy must have seemed strange to the point of loss of all meaning. From the religious and political tracts which formed the intellectual base of the American Revolution, through the constitutional debates, through virtually the entire literary and philosophical heritage in the nineteenth century, down to the Great Depression in the 1930s, individualism has been praised, celebrated, and honored above all other political values. If there is a single perspective that unites theology, philosophy, and every one of the social sciences which was germinating in the late nineteenth century in the United States, it is individualism. Whether as analytical concept, perspective for understanding society and culture, or program for the good life, individualism governed nearly all American minds. And with this buoyant dedication of every virtue to what Emerson called "the sovereign individual, free, self-reliant and alone in his greatness," there went a corresponding suspicion of all social ties that threatened to become too tight. Emerson's reaction to the failure of Brook Farm was predictable, as were the reactions of most other Americans of the time. Under the massive weight of individualist consciousness in America, at least until toward the end of the nineteenth century, themes of community, of the communal self, of society as *communitas communitatum*, remained inert and fragile.

The immense difference between the French and the American contemplations of individualism are accounted for chiefly through the enormous impact that the French Revolution had upon not merely French but European consciousness. It is unlikely that any other event in history has so quickly and widely become the cynosure of

mass preoccupation. For liberals and radicals it was seen as a fore-
taste of the democratic millennium. The simultaneous exaltation of
individual and of nation (*une et indivisible*) by revolutionary spokesmen made it possible to enshrine *liberté* as well as *fraternité* in liberal
and radical thought. But the special character of the French Revolution, so astonishingly different from the American as Burke was the
first to perceive, produced another reaction that in the long run had
even greater impress on the French mind: the sense of social disorganization. For in many ways the most salient feature of the French
Revolution was the series of drastic or potentially drastic laws which
were passed, commencing in late 1790, at the expense of the hated
ancien régime. In their fervor to create the proper ground for the new
citizen, the leaders of the Revolution, through law and decree, abolished the guilds, the monasteries, the universities, the communes,
the provinces, the patriarchal family and with it entail and primogeniture, and finally, through the de-Christianization laws, the church itself.

The fact that not all of these enactments resulted in a permanent
alteration of the social landscape in France is of less importance than
the fact that for a period of time it looked as though this alteration
was real and would be lasting. And out of the broodings, rumina-
tions, and intimations of the social destruction caused by the Revolution came a state of mind unique to France in the nineteenth century,
one in which individualism connoted, not social health, but sickness,
malaise, anomie, and the social void. The *individualisme* of the Revolution consisted, from this point of view, in the conversion of an organic society into a rabble of disconnected atoms. Individualism came
to be seen as the wretched price that any society must pay when, by
political or other action, its component, constitutive groups—family,
parish, guild, cooperative, neighborhood, church, and social class—
are savaged, as the Jacobins had savaged the groups and associations
which formed the *ancien régime*. This distinctive perception of individualism continued to illuminate French thought down to the present.
Initially found in the writings of the conservatives in France—Bonald,
de Maistre, Chateaubriand—this perception made its way to writers
and activists who were anything but conservative—to Proudhon,
whose aversion to individualism is reflected in his profound emphasis
upon autonomous groups, not individuals; to Lamennais, who long
after his excommunication from the church and his passage from
conservatism to liberal radicalism continued to excoriate individualism and all other forces which weakened the social bond; and to
Durkheim and most other social scientists in France during the nineteenth century. Different as are the ideologies—from Bonald's conser-

vatism to Lamennais and Tocqueville's liberalism, Proudhon's radicalism, Comte's positivism, Durkheim's sociology, and Maurras' Catholic action—they have plainly in common a distaste for individualism, a recognition of it as pathological, a malaise that bespeaks social breakdown.

Western thought as a whole is currently undergoing a transition of the sort that French thinking underwent after the Revolution. Nothing so dramatic as the calculated, planned destruction of a social order by revolution has taken place in America, but the processes of social destruction are only too evidently at work and have been for some time. Whatever the causes—and they are many—the erosion and displacement of family, community, church, neighborhood, and social class, particularly the middle class, are realities in the American mind, and so is the perception of individualism as a form of disease, not health. The Great Depression dampened considerably the traditional individualism of mind in America. There were not many to hail Hoover's call in 1933, for a return to "rugged individualism." Nor have there been many since, though it was not until the 1960s, a decade of near revolutionary upheaval and of sustained preaching of social nihilism, that the American temper was finally and irreversibly transformed with respect to the creed of individualism.

Since World War II the creed of community has won the most converts: community in the local sense of neighborhood, but also community in the diverse sense that includes kinship, religion, commune, guild, and other of man's old attachments. In the nineteenth century, declamations of individualist creed could summon up in the average American's mind images of the lone trapper, hunter, or explorer in the wilderness, of the pioneer on the frontier, or of the small entrepreneur in farm, shop, or office. Today recitation of the bare creed of individualism is more likely to conjure up a vision of alienation from society that has the lonely and fearful old person at one end of the spectrum and the mugger or terrorist at the other. Americans have come to see individualism as Comte, Tocqueville, and Durkheim did, as an atomization of the social order, a conversion of society from *communitas communitatum* into what is at best a sand heap of unattached particles, at worst a jungle occupied by lone but vicious predators.

Americans can accept French teaching on still another dimension of individualism, its natural affinity with centralized political power. Until recently, freedom from power was yet another virtue that Americans insisted upon ascribing to the national creed of individualism. But this simply will not work. If there is a single root meaning of the word *individualism*, it lies in the notion of the discrete being, of I-am-myself-alone-free-of-all-bonds. The ideal type is inevitably a whole nation of largely unconnected, "free" individuals. But this is the best recipe for Leviathan. The genius of the French perspective on individualism is its awareness of the complementary, the reciprocal relation between individualism and collectivism.

It is often said that individualism has declined in America during the twentieth century. It has not. If anything it is more luxuriant, variegated, and insistent than ever before in American history. Nonconformity, a near synonym for individualism, is found widely today in literature, the arts, indeed in the whole of culture, and perhaps most spectacularly in the behavior of people with respect to the old traditions of family, neighborhood, church, and their intrinsic authorities. But all the while this individualism has been advancing, so has the power of the political state over human lives. Political collectivism could scarcely exist were it not for the erosion of the social authorities and the consequent release of masses of individuals.

The Emersonian, all-American individualism of the nineteenth century was destined from the beginning to fail as a creed. In violation of the wisdom of the ages, indeed of simple common sense, it regarded the individual from the "I am myself alone" perspective, thus overlooking the nurturing social contexts in which alone individuality can develop. From Emerson's self-reliant individual needing nothing but his own inner resources to the desocialized, hedonistic, narcissistic free spirit of the late twentieth century is really not a long journey.

INFLATION

OF ALL MODERN pestilences inflation is the most devastating to society and the values upon which it rests. On the evidence, not even war produces the impact upon the social fabric that continuing, ever-escalating inflation does. War indeed, its intrinsic horrors notwithstanding, often leads to a revitalization of economy and society, as the experiences of Germany and Japan after World War II emphasize. It was, after all, the onset of this war in Europe that led to America's escape from the Great Depression; certainly the celebrated New Deal contained nothing that measurably affected America's economic doldrums. It is even possible to see in economic depression influences which are salutary to the social structure, though the awful toll taken by prolonged unemployment should not be minimized, nor should the terrible effects of hunger and poverty.

But there is absolutely no redeeming element in inflation. Everything about it creates distrust and fear, even panic. Bad as are the effects of depression upon culture and its bastions the school, university, church, museum, library, and publishing house, they are far less destructive and minatory than the effects of inflation. It is possible, if one is moderately fortunate, to elude the worst demons of depression. And there is a known solution to depression: prosperity. But almost no one can remain secure of status when inflation reaches epidemic proportions. And worst of all, no one seems to know what the answer is to inflation, except only in the abstract.

If inflation were solely and isolatably economic, the problem would be simpler. There are economists who persist in believing that inflation is analyzable and also curable in strictly financial terms. Reduce the money supply, raise interest rates, initiate massive tax cuts, attend to depreciation schedules and allowances, above all, see to it that too much money is not chasing too few goods. Despite the unquestioned pertinence of these and other measures, to insist upon the validity of the economic alone is to take a singularly narrow view of modern democratic society. It is not unlike a biologist taking a strictly biological approach to the ravages of smallpox, content to describe the virus and its effects, and indifferent to all the contextual circumstances within which the virus is nurtured. In the end inflation may well be a matter of supply and demand and may be terminated only when the economics of supply and demand are stable, but in the meantime supply and demand exist within a social order replete with desires and ambitions, all but a few of which affect the economics of inflation. Inflation simply cannot be understood apart from regnant political, social, and psychological passions.

High among these are the passions unleashed by egalitarianism in the twentieth century, especially its second half. Once social class exerted discipline upon taste and desire. So did family and church. But in the general upheaval that the egalitarian volcano has brought about in the modern age, these ancient disciplines are gone or grievously enfeebled. When Pandora opened the forbidden box, the insects of avarice, envy, pride, hate, jealousy, and other ills flew out into the world. The opening up of the social class system has had comparable effect in modern society. The limits upon desire have been either jettisoned or vastly expanded. Aspiration to worldly goods, that is, consumer goods, is greatly magnified; moreover it is made respectable. Tocqueville was perhaps the first to identify what is today called the revolution of rising expectations. In the long run, no institution, social order, or economy is proof against that revolution. The rage to political entitlements alone is sufficient to explain a great deal of the inflationary engine that lies in the contemporary social system. The wonder is, considering the almost exponential growth of these entitlements since World War II, that economic inflation is not a great deal worse than it is.

Inflation, then, is a monetary, financial, and fiscal phenomenon just as malaria is a viral phenomenon. But such analysis goes only a step or two into the matter. Until the social and political pools in which the rage to inflation breeds are examined, the problem will be as resistant to solution as malaria would be if interest in it ended before identifying the stagnant wells and pools in which the anopheles mosquito thrives. Inflation is indeed a world-wide pestilence, and like smallpox or malaria, it will be eradicated at nothing less than a world-wide level. For the great social revolution of egalitarianism, with its destruction of all the moral disciplines that once held mankind in check and its devastation of the social framework within which these disciplines flourished, is by now world-wide, and this revolution is a long way from the zenith, even in the West.

Affluence of the kind the Western world has known since the ending of the Great Depression in World War II is bound to breed inflationary pressures. For one thing, as every prize fight manager has known since gladitorial Rome, affluence weakens incentive and thereby productivity. The decline in growth of what might charitably be called the educated mind in the United States during the past half-century is a consequence of the affluence that touched teacher as well as pupil, weakening the need to teach and to study. It is no wonder that factory workers have become less and less motivated toward work and the quality of work. After all, university professors and their productivity, teaching and research alike, show a marked decline of incentive year after year. When a corporation executive was asked how many people worked in his great industry, he replied, "About half, I would guess." That figure may be high for the universities in America today.

Inflation is thus both pandemic and inexhaustible. The only way of checking it in the modern world would seem to be for the twin lusts of equality and physical comfort either to subside in the very chaos they create or to be destroyed by a catastrophe of world-wide dimensions. One would like to think that a government may be elected in the United States that is so strong, so courageous, so bent upon doing what is necessary to end inflation that it will resist the raging forces of egalitarianism, the passion for eroding away all social and economic differences, and the insatiable appetite for entitlements from government, but this is doubtful. Moreover, when a pestilence is world-wide, be it smallpox or economic inflation, even the strongest and noblest of American governments remains vulnerable, in a world as interconnected and mobile as today's, to reinfection from abroad.

As long as democracy meant the exclusively political and legal, meant a public sector tiny in functional significance compared to the private, and meant the dispensing of little other than justice and military security, this form of government could not possibly be the generator of inflation. But when the time is reached in which the public outweighs the private, in which the government ceases to limit itself to a few "common welfare" functions, such as interstate commerce and national security, and becomes the citadel for every imaginable form of need and greed, gain and pain, it can hardly fail to be an artesian well of inflation. What Maine, Macaulay, and other seers in the nineteenth century feared would happen, has happened. More and more energy of the poorest 51 percent of the population is going toward a reduction of the wealth of the richest 49 percent. For a century, the sheer power and massiveness of the capitalist engines supplied a fundamental balance as well as growth to the economy; not even the national state was, or chose to be, powerful enough to intrude seriously. But political intrusion is the name of the game today in Washington, for that matter in every city, town, and hamlet in the rest of the United States, and the intrusion of this egalitarian Leviathan cannot help but displace the mechanisms which once made balance in the economy possible.

The political liberalism that is by now the very stuff of American society, having captured both governmental and private sector bureaucracies for the most part, has two overriding goals. First is limitless material abundance in the lives of citizens, accompanied by the generation of ever higher material expectations, and second is limitless political power by which to distribute rationally this material abundance in order to meet these material expectations. The consequence cannot be other than inflation. Americans had better get used to it.

INQUISITIONS

FOR MORE THAN two hundred years one myth has dominated secular and much religious thought on the historical relation between the Roman Catholic Church and science in the West. During the

French Enlightenment Galileo was adopted as the crowning symbol of ecclesiastical despotism over science. Finding Newton, however great, almost fanatically religious, especially in his final years, the Enlightenment chose Galileo as hero martyr. Less was known about his religious commitment, and there was his trial in Rome whereby, the story ran, he had been condemned for his espousal of Copernican cosmology, his development of the telescope, and sundry other views. Cowed by a monolithically hostile church, Galileo was forced to recant, with the result that he was barred from again prosecuting scientific problems for the rest of his life, with a consequent setback to the growth of modern science. From Diderot to Brecht, the myth of Galileo the rationalist-scientist-martyr dominated Western thought, and even today it shows few signs of abating.

This myth reflects the truth as would a badly cracked mirror. As to Galileo's paralyzing intimidation by a single-minded, avenging church, leading to an utter dearth of work afterward, there is not a grain of truth. Probably more scientists have been adversely affected—estopped altogether from a given line of research, guided, shaped, propelled, decelerated, forced into nonpublication secrecy, turned down for funds or promotion, and barred from access to laboratory space or archives—because of defiance of conventional wisdom in America since World War II with its accompanying bureaucratization and politicization of science than existed in the whole of the world in Galileo's day. What Galileo endured is as nothing compared with what bold, intrepid, original young minds face in today's scientific circles, where a given paradigm or program brands all simple difference of viewpoint as "idiosyncratic," "nonsensical," "futile," and "trouble-making"—the modern synonyms for medieval heresy.

The first censorship on Galileo was his own, the result of fear not of ecclesiastical but of scientific-scholarly opinion. In a letter to Kepler in 1597 Galileo confessed his own belief in the Copernican view of the planets, including the earth, moving around the sun, but declared his fear of ridicule from Aristotelian scholars in the universities were he to make his belief public. When in 1609 Galileo first heard of the invention of the telescope, he immediately commenced his own development of this instrument for the express purpose of gazing at the sun and the planets. Honors quickly followed. He was offered a life chair at the University of Padua, but he chose instead to accept a grand duke's offer to become first philosopher and mathematician in the region, thus gaining full time for his research. Acclaimed by all, proud of his accomplishments in astronomy and mathematics, Galileo was persuaded to go to Rome in order to lay before the highest councils of the Vatican the results of his work. He did this in 1611, and the response was overwhelmingly laudatory and encouraging. There seems to have been not a whisper of reproach for the patently Copernican implications of much of what Galileo reported to the Pope and assembled ecclesiastical authorities. While in Rome for a year or two he also published several papers, with unlimited circulation, establishing the superiority—on the basis of his telescopic view of sunspots—of Copernican to Ptolemaic views of the relation of the earth to the sun and universe. There were no protests whatever from the church at that time.

Such protests began after his triumphal visit to Rome, and they were not in the first instance ecclesiastical at all. They came from jealous and apprehensive university professors, the majority Aristotelian and fearful of the effect of Galileo's loud and boastful teachings. Galileo, who was aggressively egoistic from all accounts, was also not above using without acknowledgment works of contemporaries. From professors, in short, came the first attacks on Galileo and with them attempts to silence him lest his destructive effect upon their Aristotelianism should lose them status and even jobs in the long run. Obtaining the cooperation of the Dominican preachers, always in search of some form of heresy or delinquency to thunder about from pulpit and street corner, the assault upon Galileo soon reached the point where he felt it necessary to go again to Rome for reassurance and thus a silencing of academic and Dominican voices.

Galileo had received instant support in Tuscany from high church officials as well as from the grand duke and others of the nobility, all of whom took pride in Galileo's work. Nevertheless Galileo went to Rome, where also he found supporters of highest rank within the Vatican. Galileo argued that for many centuries there had been a canon in the church that made it possible to read any passage in the Bible as allegorical instead of literal, provided a conflict between it and "established scientific truth" were found. This argument was well known to and, in Galileo's case, accepted by a substantial number of churchmen, but not, alas, by the Pope, nor by the chief theologian Cardinal Bellarmine. A decree was issued "suspending" the *De Revolutionibus* "until certain corrections were made," and Galileo was enjoined from teaching the forbidden views. There were rumors that he had been forced to abjure, but Galileo procured from Cardinal Bellarmine himself written assurance that such had not been the case.

This experience in Rome scarcely dampened Galileo's scientific ardor. Along with some striking discoveries by telescope in connection with the sudden appearances of three large comets, he wrote his celebrated *The Assayer* in which, in direct riposte to a Jesuit's sneers at him, Galileo set forth the vital necessity of doubt in all scientific research, taking the opportunity to restate some of his early astronomical views and pointing to works of science all over Europe which were employing Galilean hypotheses and conclusions. Galileo even dedicated this book to his old and devoted friend Cardinal Barberini, who had just succeeded to the papal throne. Galileo's book found great favor with the new pope and the considerable number of other Galilean ecclesiastical supporters who were now in high places in the Vatican.

Galileo was in frequent contact with Pope Urban VIII, and in the course of their private discussions, Galileo not only received permission but was encouraged to commence work on a *magnum opus* that would lay out clearly and decisively all that could be properly said for both the Copernican and the Ptolemaic theories. All that the Pope added was a recommendation that Galileo be as "hypothetical," that is, dispassionate and objective, as possible. There followed his epochal *Dialogue Concerning the Two Chief World Systems*, a remarkable enough accomplishment and publication for someone in fear of his faith and life as the myth solemnly declares. Dissent, tergiversation, catcalling there were indeed, for Galileo had his enemies, lay and clerical. But the blunt fact is that this master treatise was approved by Catholic authorities and given churchly imprimatur.

In Rome, however, academic and clerical assault on Galileo's character, mind, and conclusions began to mount once again, notwithstanding the strenuous efforts made by his friends in the Vatican. Galileo's chief enemy was no churchman at all but a fellow-scientist, deeply jealous of Galileo and convinced that Galileo had stolen from one of his own scientific works. The scientist, Schreiner, and his friends managed an attack, overt and covert, sufficient to bring Galileo once more under suspicion, and a reluctant Pope felt finally obliged to order a trial under the Inquisition. Moreover, an unsigned memorandum was found in the archives stating that its author would never again engage in Copernican discussions. This was attributed to Galileo, despite his protests that he knew nothing of it, and on this dubious and controversial basis, the trial began.

When Galileo had reached Rome, he was treated with greatest courtesy and indulgence, allowed to live where he chose, unsupervised by the church. The head of the Inquisition, a Galileo supporter, sought from the beginning to end the trial with a simple reprimand, allowing Galileo, then an old man, to return to his estate and his work. But the anti-Galileo forces prevailed. He was found "guilty" of Copernican teachings and ordered to recant by a special, long-existent ritual-creed of abjuration, one apparently held in about as much regard by all concerned as are the varied oaths of the courtroom today. He could have been imprisoned, and no doubt his academic and scientific enemies devoutly wished it, but instead he was ordered into "house arrest," which meant that he could return to the villa and estate within which so much of his scientific work had been done.

The trial, far from blighting Galileo's spirit and quenching his science, could arguably be declared a stimulant to work. For during the remaining years of his life he spent much time with his telescopes, until blindness ended that pursuit; he wrote his immensely important and influential *Dialogue Concerning Two New Sciences*, printed in Leyden in 1638; he was in constant communication with the leading scientific lights of Italy and all Europe; he conceived the application of many older principles to new problems or perspectives; and he had as many students as he wished. When he died, indeed, two of his favorite students, Viviani and Torricelli, were with him, each destined to carry on and enlarge Galileo's works.

Such is the skeleton of one of the richest scientific careers in modern history. It needs, however, to be supplemented by additional, somewhat speculative observation. An important question is whether Galileo, through association or correspondence with Bruno, was a member of that heretical underground cult of the Hermetic, Egyptian, Magus orientation which the church understandably sought to extirpate with all possible force, given its deeply anti-ecclesiastical revolutionary aspirations. As yet the answer is not known. All that is known is that Bruno himself was incontestably a member, a very prominent one. Moreover, the Copernican doctrine of heleocentricity was a dogma within this heretical faith, derived presumably from the anti-Christian espousal of sun worship that the humanist Ficino had propagated. Bruno, despite another ascendant myth, was not condemned and burned because he was a scientist. He was burned as a religious heretic of deepest dye, which he was. It is not beyond reason that scholarship will yet show some connection between the death of Bruno and the trial of Galileo.

The one overriding conclusion about Renaissance science, the science of Copernicus, Kepler, Bruno, and Newton, is the enormous role of religion in the minds of these men, whether Catholic, Protestant, or aberrant, as were Copernicus and Bruno in their faith in the Hermetic and the Magus. Newton made plain that the laws he had discovered were the laws of God. Galileo was no less convinced that it was the divine order he was exploring. No church can be blamed for vigilance against true heresy, and Bruno's vision of Copernicanism as an element of a religious reform movement could well have caused the inquisitors to suspect similar objections in Galileo's system of the world.

Whether or not Galileo was in fact being investigated for religious heresy, for linkage with the condemned Bruno, is not known. The fact is, though, that suspicion of heliocentricity had little if anything to do with astronomy as such. After all, heliocentric doctrines had lain in abundance in medieval scientific works. That which in Galileo's day was being searched out in order to destroy it was not, in sum, the proposition that the earth and other planets move about the sun but rather the religiously subversive doctrine of sun worship, of which heliocentricity was only a subordinate dogma.

Galileo was probably cleared of any prior subterranean affiliation with Bruno, Copernicus, or others involved in the black heresy of making science the superstructure of Hermetic belief. It is unlikely that he would have been treated as indulgently as he was, given a sentence so light and undisturbing to his scientific works and communications, and retained so many friends, admirers, and supporters in Rome had there been any real evidence of liaison with the heretical Bruno.

It is hard to know when the old Enlightenment-spawned image of Bruno being put to the stake for his scientific rationalism will disappear. Old rationalist myths die slowly; Christianity still has to be fought and vilified. But one thing is certain: the Bruno myth will die long before the myth of Galileo, the myth of his humiliating, abject reduction to impotence by a united, monolithic, science-hating Christianity.

The principal truth to be drawn from the Galileo story is less dramatic than is the myth, but far more in accord with the emotions and institutional conditions that prevail today much as they did in the sixteenth century. Rivalry, jealousy, and vindictiveness from other scientists and philosophers were Galileo's lot, and they are not infrequently the lot of unorthodox minds in modern times. Anyone who believes that inquisitions went out with the triumph of secularism over religion has not paid attention to the records of foundations, federal research agencies, professional societies, and academic institutes and departments. It is fortunate that in the long run reaction often follows action, allowing a kind of balance of power to exist among the varied agencies and departments. But in matters of priority and of support in the scientific fraternity it is institutional competition and the swing of the pendulum rather than the fabled disinterestedness of the titans in science that generally, though not always, rescues the maverick from the hostile herd. Ideas, theories, paradigms, and values become as ensconced in the scientific as in the theological fraternity. And in the vital areas of financial support, professional recognition, and academic appointment, these idols count heavily. Macromutationists in biology, catastrophists in geology, and cognitive theorists in psychology are among those who have known inquisitions in science. It was twentieth century science, not theology, that sought to prevent by every possible means the publication in the 1950s of Velikovsky's *Worlds in Collision*. The church did not go that far with Galileo.

INTELLECTUAL REVOLUTION

IT IS ALMOST instinctual to think immediately of the political and social when the word *revolution* is mentioned. Far more fundamental in history, though, are revolutions of the mind, those in which major idea-systems are shattered, with new ones succeeding them. Indeed the revolutions of the past that are thought of as political or social turn out upon careful examination to be first of all large-scale movements of thought, usually strongly constituted by religious imperatives. The Puritan Revolution in England began as an essentially religious event, but before it was over, social and political themes were abundant, though always within a religious framework. The Jacobin leaders of the Revolution in France considered themselves direct successors of the Puritans, and although most of the early legislation of the Revolution dealt with political, economic, and social matters, the profoundly moral and ultimately religious aspects of the Revolution were nevertheless prominent. It was by declaration a revolution in the name of moral virtue, and the idea of civil religion, duly equipped with rite, liturgy, and church, was present in the minds of the Rousseau-reading Jacobins from the start.

For at least three thousand years, intellectual-religious forces have been at work in revolutionary fashion. The most seminal of all revolutions took place across the Eurasian continent in the sixth century B.C., reaching from China to southern Italy. The cast of this revolution was nothing short of heroic. In China it included Confucius and Lao-tze; in Persia, Zoroaster; in India, Buddha and Mahavira; in Ionia, Thales; in Israel, Ezekiel and the prophet known as the second Isaiah; and in Italy, Pythagoras. That minds of this luster and world-shaking force should have coexisted within a single century, and on so vast a geographical stage, is one of the most striking occurrences in the whole of world history. Intellectually, all else pales into rela-

tive insignificance, being in some degree a consequence of the powerful doctrines and perspectives associated with these religious-philo-
sophical titans. Their works are usually classified as simply religious
and philosophical, but in truth they commence the great revolutionary tradition that is inseparable from the history of the last
twenty-five hundred years in Asia as well as Europe, a tradition that
includes the Jewish and Christian revolts against Rome, the Islamic
conquests and dominations during and after the seventh century, the
countless uprisings of the late Middle Ages and the Reformation, and
the Puritan, American, French, Russian, and Chinese revolutions of
modern times. One and all these revolutionary outbursts and movements are based upon conceptions of the individual, of social institutions, of community, and of progress toward perfection which go
back to the great prophets of the sixth century B.C.

The revolutionary quality of these men, as of all true revolutionaries, lies in their affirmation of the reality and innate right of the individual, in their nihilistic assault on ancient institutions which were
perceived as fetters upon individual consciousness, and most important, in their declaration of the existence of a form of community, at
once universal and primary, immanent yet supernatural, the great
and real world toward which man should strive constantly for membership, at whatever cost to his worldly possessions. These doctrines
had such shattering implications in the sixth century B.C. in Eurasia
because of the total immersion of human beings in forms of religion
which were inseparable from every part of human existence. Whether
in China, Japan, India, the Middle East, or the West, man was so
deeply subordinated to the collective consciousness of tribe, caste,
village, or primitive monarchy that he was less a human being than a
kind of robot, activated not by self-consciousness or volition but
quite literally by the gods, who were with him constantly, unremit-
tingly, as the result of the iron hold upon him of dogma, rite, and the
whole omnipresent sacred.

For many thousands of years, men lived in a world in which the
individual counted for nothing, in which they were seen and saw
themselves as no more than a node of the sacred-social. Quite possibly this situation existed as far back as the time when *Homo sapiens*
emerged in the evolutionary scale and discovered that his existence
depended utterly upon the social bond—the foraging group, clan, or
tribe which was itself sanctified by union with gods and spirits whose
will could never be contravened. The rise of civilizations such as
Crete and Egypt in the West, China and Japan in the East, did little to
affect the individual's organic connection with the group. In Minoan
civilization, for example, which in art, architecture, and law reached

an impressive level of quality, life was so completely circumscribed by the sacred, by what men told themselves they heard from the gods, that the existence of an active, willing, and self-conscious mind was almost totally impossible. Those paranoiacs in modern times whose contact with reality has dissolved utterly and who are motivated entirely by "voices" that they alone are able to hear give some notion of what an entire society could be like, with the exception that there the "voices" were communal, in concert, heard by all.

Sometime around 2000 B.C. one or more events or spectacles took place which had the effect of throwing shock waves of a sort into the peoples of the whole Eurasian continent, from Japan and China to the Mediterranean. Perhaps it was some vast astronomical spectacle, an immense conflagration that shook up societies everywhere, maybe a sudden, terrifying shifting of the earth accompanied by quakes of unimaginable intensity and destructiveness, or perhaps floods of the scale hinted at in so many of man's earliest legends. But this is only speculation. All that is known is that sometime around the middle of the second millennium B.C., all of Eurasia from the China Sea to the Atlantic Ocean became a scene of almost incessant movement of peoples. By the end of that millennium there was a veritable explosion of migrations and invasions. With innumerable peoples in motion, it was inevitable that they would meet, sometimes peaceably, sometimes in conflict. But however they met, there inevitably followed breaches in custom and tradition, slight relaxations of the absolute power of a people's own gods and dogmas, and the beginnings of an individual consciousness that was made possible precisely because of what was happening to the sacred folds which had once enveloped the human mind. It is not necessary, in short, to predicate, as a physical scientist has, a mutation in the brain about 2000 B.C., one that snapped the chain between the gods and man's mind. Rather, a whole complex of social mutations led to the gradual liberation of the individual from the totalism of previous existence.

These changes followed a pattern all across the continent. The kinds of migrations and invasions associated with the Dorians and Hellenes in the Mediteranean, where they found the long-existent Agean civilization, were paralleled by analogous migrations and invasions in the Middle East, Persia, India, and China. The consequences to society and the individual were also the same: a lessening of the hold of old gods in the presence of new and potentially competing gods; an attenuation of the ties of family, tribe, and city; and a slowly emerging consciousness of one's own separate and distinct self. Behavior was bound to become willed behavior, though the time and the selectivity required for so massive a transformation were considerable. With the dawn of consciousness in the individual were born also the beginnings of doubt, mystery, incomprehension, curiosity, and above all, the sense of estrangement from the world and self that only the human species knows.

It was in this environment that the great prophets of the sixth century arrived almost simultaneously at their revolutionary doctrines. None of them was alone. For every Confucius, Buddha, or Thales, there were doubtless hundreds of others in their time and earlier also preoccupied by the problems of individuality that had been thrust upon the world by the uprooting of peoples and the destruction of ancient verities. This is always the case in history. The Aristotles, Augustines, Michelangelos, Shakespeares, and Newtons are never isolated peaks but rather the highest among whole clusters of high talents. The same holds equally for Confucius, Zoroaster, Buddha, and the others.

The greatest significance of these minds, in both the East and the West, is their establishment of universal religions. What each of the prophets said was: my sacred way is open to any man, irrespective of origin, prior gods, race, family, caste, and village, if he chooses to follow it exclusively. The immensity of this idea is impossible to exaggerate. For countless millennia men had been yoked to intimately personal and local gods by kinship, locality, tribalism, ethnicity, and caste. The idea of being free either to join or to depart a given religion would have been utterly incomprehensible. One was born to one's gods and to the commands which they issued. How remarkable, then, was the proffer of open, universal religion to all people no matter whence they came or why.

In this epochal rise of universal religions, which centuries later would be joined by the equally universal and far more influential religions of Christianity and Islam, political forces were also deeply involved. Where world religions are born, so are world empires, with political rule by king or emperor replacing governance by tribe or caste in the same way that one god, universally accessible, replaces the ancient deities of caste and tribe. Between universal religion and universal empire there is a close and necessary relationship. Whatever reduces the influence upon human minds of the ancient, jealous gods of race, caste, tribe, and place cannot help but make easier the political efforts of rulers to diminish old ethnic identities in the interest of a new and larger empire, one in which, at least in theory, individual subjects, not communal and corporate bodies, are the true elements. Conversely, whatever emphasizes the individuality of subjecthood and citizenship in the political realm aids greatly the effort of the prophet to proselytize in the name of one universal god, with arms open wide to the multitudes without respect to origin or estate. During the first half of the millennium before Christ people all over Eurasia were, through the natural selection of turbulent migrations and interminglings, being prepared for both empire and the kind of religion that goes with the doctrines of the great prophets of the sixth century B.C.

From the new, universal religions certain revolutionary ideas concerning man and society emerged—ideas which would never wholly disappear from Eurasian philosophy and religion, be it Buddhist, Zoroastrian, Isaian, or Pythagorean, and which, in one formulation or another, would underlie innumerable rebellions, revolts, mutinies, and revolutions during the next two and a half millennia. It is impossible to imagine more potentially incendiary concepts than these in the history of humanity. First, the teaching appeared in which the individual, rather than the monolithic tribe or caste and its implacable, soul-destroying gods, was not only the shining reality but also—and here individualism becomes permanent revolution—the *summum bonum*, the goal, the purpose, the unassailable ideal of faith and reason. Whether it is the Confucian jen, with its consecration to individual virtue and self-improvement, or the Isaiahan creed of God's separate anointment of each single individual, or the Pythagorean vision of the heavenly destiny of the individual soul rising to ultimate communion with the divine, all deal with the primacy of the individual, the sovereign reality of individual faith, consciousness, and morality, and the ultimate salvation of the individual in and for him, with all earthly relationships transitory helps at best, rest stations on the sacred way.

From this radical individualism a certain form of nihilism inexorably emerged. It was impossible to sanctify the individual and individual faith and consciousness without at the same time denigrating the social and ritualistic fastnesses within which for so many aeons individuals had been imprisoned. Assault upon social structure may be minor or major in genuine revolutions, but it must always occur in some degree, for otherwise there can be no release of the sanctified individual for higher destiny, no opening up of the way to the sacred kingdom within which no tribe, caste, or race exists, only the universal community of man himself. From Buddha's repudiation of all castes, clans, and kindred, down to the French Revolution's obliteration of guild, commune, patriarchal family, and aristocracy, and on to the Bolshevik extermination of cooperative, labor union, and peasant farm, the whole revolutionary tradition has been that the liberation and purification of the individual calls for the most radical social surgery. If there were no other reason for calling Jesus a revolutionary, his strictures on the patriarchal and fettering family of Jews and Romans alike would suffice.

A third proposition found in the teachings of the great prophets of the sixth century B.C. is directed to the spiritual world within which all liberated souls will ultimately live. Not one of the prophets was without profound faith in a spiritual world to which all men, however humble, might aspire once the authority of the single sovereign spirit was recognized and accepted. Not for these prophets the kind of immortality that was embedded in tribalistic and caste belief, with the hereafter scarcely more than an unending succession of earthly identities and the setting rigorously parochial. Immortality for the prophets escaped all such chains upon the true spirit, as in Buddha's nirvana. The Heavenly City would in time pass easily from sacred thought to the crypto-sacred beliefs of Jacobins and Marxists.

Here a fourth and final vision emerged from the early prophets and became perhaps the most powerful single intellectual force in all subsequent world history. This is the vision of slowly developing perfection. For the first few centuries this idea of perfection had its seat in the individual alone, not in mankind as a whole. But the dimension of perfection was gradually enlarged from the individual to an entire people or body of believers, such as Jews, Zoroastrians, and Buddhists, and then to the whole of humanity. Saint Augustine above all others effected this last expansion by making not simply the individual, nor even all Christians, but all people who ever have existed or ever will exist on earth the collective protagonist of the ever-developing, ever-fulfilling progress toward perfection and salvation.

From the sixth century prophets to the revolutionists of the modern world may at first seem a fragile and unlikely continuity in world history. But it is not. Whether it is the impact of Buddhism on tribe and caste, the influence of Thales and Pythagoras on Greek empire and kingdom, the powerful upsurge of Judaic-Christian forces in Rome, or the Puritan, American, French, Russian, and Chinese revolutions of the past three centuries, all manifest in unvarying fashion a complex of ideas that are at once religious and revolutionary: the free individual, liberated from the tyrannies and torments of the material world; a universal community capable of containing all men, irrespective of birth, creed, race, nation, or caste; and an ethic that contemplates the individual and all mankind as subjects of progress toward perfection, whether in the next world or this. From Confucius to Lenin and Mao runs a golden avenue, a *via sacra*, that is formed of these ideas and values.

INTIMACY

OF A CERTAIN Cardinal de Retz it was said that he had "the terrible gift of intimacy." Misused, it is a terrible gift indeed, for it can break down the ordinary carapaces of our minds and spirits more easily than can humiliation or torment. There are two natural abodes of intimacy: friendship and marriage. Probably the first has been more often the seat of deep psychological intimacy, at least until the present age in which friendship has become rare, too difficult for most people to sustain. The burden of intimacy is thus put upon the marital tie which is often too fragile to bear up under it.

From the classical world came the ideal of friendship—between men, of course. Cicero's *De Amicitia* is perhaps the finest testament to friendship ever written, and it served as touchstone for almost two thousand years in Europe. In the classical sense, which survived through the nineteenth century, one had very few friends, often no more than one. The contemporary use of the word *friend* is pure debauchery against the canons of the old order. Our ancestors would not have known what we are talking about when we say, "I made dozens of friends in the army" or "We're having a few dozen friends over for drinks." A friend was usually a man whom one had known from at least youth and with whom the closest of relationships persisted through all the years, untouched by marriage, vocation, or any of life's ordinary vicissitudes. To a friend went confidences in all matters, confidences returned in the intimacy of complete trust. Friendship in the classical sense made for a higher degree of intimacy of mind than marriage, if only because such intimacy was the whole purpose of friendship, whereas in marriage the sexual relationship—a form of intimacy to be sure—cannot help but impinge upon the tie of friendship. The very nature of sex is to create occasional turbulence of relationship. Moreover, until the present century, it was rare for the man to confide in a woman, including his wife, any of the confidences, indeed any of the details, of his business life. A true friendship survived everything but the act of betrayal.

Betrayal of friend was for many centuries regarded as the blackest of sins, worse even than betrayal of kinsman, for the tie of blood was, so to speak, forced upon one, whereas friendship was voluntary and formed of absolute trust. The statesman Dean Acheson drew much contumely and derision when he said of Alger Hiss, indicted in effect for treason against his government, "I do not turn my back on a friend." Most Americans could not understand that, but their forebears could have, as could more than a few Europeans. Forster wrote that if he had to choose between betrayal of a friend and betrayal of country, it would be the latter.

Despite the inundation of me-ness in modern times, the quest for intimacy has become pandemic in American society, as shown by the classifieds in many journals and newspapers. A recent book proposes celibacy within marriage on the ground that a far richer intimacy will develop without the accompaniment of sexual intercourse. Yet sex has nothing to do with greater or less intimacy. What keeps intimacy of mind going is, quite simply, richness of mind, and very few are blessed with the depths, recesses, and caverns of consciousness which make possible prolonged indulgence in intimacy. In most people, intellectual capital is quickly expended when drawn upon by the spirit of intimacy. This is one reason marriages so often founder in America today. Belief that the intimacy of the marriage bed must be accompanied by an intimacy of minds cannot help but, by reason of quick and ample withdrawals of sense and sensibility, leave each mate barren, empty, and sterile. What our grandmothers failed to learn in a lifetime about our grandfathers, try as they might, is now learned within weeks, and usually before marriage. And what is exchanged is usually of such exiguous character that disillusionment and boredom, as well as the specter of scarce resources, are the consequence.

In a message to soldiers in the British Expeditionary Force in 1914, Lord Kitchener counseled, along with patience, energy, courage, and honor, "while treating all women with perfect courtesy, you should avoid any intimacy." If Kitchener's wisdom could just be extended from the special meaning that is manifest in the words and made to include all but the rarest of encounters in society, it could properly be emblazoned upon the doors of all schools, colleges, universities, personnel offices, psychoanalysts' retreats, institutes for self-enrichment, studios of role abandonment and sex mutilation, radio talk shows, and not least, each and every newly-wed household.

Once entered into with another person, intimacy poses the terrible danger of entrapment. There is a tyranny in intimacy, once one of the individuals has wearied of or become estranged from it. Some individuals, both male and female, possess a kind of lust for intellectual intimacy with another. Typically, they work patiently and subtly, waiting for the day when the other person realizes he has divulged so much of himself, lost so many of his carapaces, that he is trapped. There is only one solution for this entrapment, one form of liberation from the tyranny of intimacy: *Ecrasez l'infame.*

I SMS

THE RAGE TO REIFY during the past two centuries in the West has no better illustration than the companionate rage to ismatize. English is far from alone in the disease. German and French would be nowhere without their *ismuses* and *ismes*. Our forefathers used the suffix occasionally, as in *baptism* and *Machiavellianism*. But meaning was precise and quickly grasped, and one can read hundreds of pages out of the seventeenth and eighteenth centuries without encountering an ism. The nineteenth century, the century of Hegel and Marx, is the real starting point of modern ismatizing. Think only of *industrialism, agrarianism, capitalism, Owenism, Hegelianism, Marxism, Comtism, feudalism, romanticism, socialism, mechanism, scientism, humanitarianism, utilitarianism, vitalism, individualism, liberalism, radicalism,* and *atomism*—all products of the nineteenth century's effort to encapsulate the *Zeitgeist*, to take the burden of responsibility off the individual and lay it on abstractions. Prior to the modern age, Tocqueville noted ruefully, writers did not make abstractions such as individualism do what he made it do, that is, cause, influence, and modify just as if it were an animate being.

Two broad patterns of ismatizing are to be found in the nineteenth and twentieth centuries. The first is eponymous, or rather, eponismatic. Here the name of an individual receives the suffix, as in Millerism, named after the founder of the apocalyptic sect, Marxism, after a German philosopher no less apocalytic in inspiration, and in the twentieth century, Couéism, after the vulgarizer of the idea of progress.

The other pattern is anonymous, or better, anonismatic. Here there may well be in the beginning an eponism, but for one reason or other it is succeeded by the ismatizing of a doctrine or sacred noun. Millerism came to be Seventh-Day Adventism. The early effort to name after Mary Baker Eddy the sect founded by her quickly ended, no doubt to the advantage of all, though detractors of Christian Science for long made use of Eddyism. Anonisms greatly outnumber eponisms, in philosophy, the social sciences, political science, and for that matter in common speech. The nineteenth century was prodigious in the coining of isms based on a single word or a Greek or Latin root. *Socialism, capitalism, nationalism, radicalism, conservatism,* and *liberalism* are but a few of these coinages, without which the nineteenth century would be unrecognizable, so accustomed have they become. There was no better way to dignify an individual or a simple word than to ismatize it.

The student of isms, the ismologist, is aware of a process that may properly be called ismosis. This is most succinctly defined as the absorption of a meaning or obscurantism by one ism from another in direct proximity. Ismosis occurs often in political and social philosophies or ideologies. The greatest artists of political ismatics come from the left. Beyond count are the isms which have been generated by energetically polemical radicals, sweeping all dissent and difference away ismatically. Marx is without question the god or prime mover of ismatics in modern thought. To be sure, by comparison with later acolytes, Marx was sparing in his use of isms. But history saw to it that his would become the premier ism of the twentieth century. The radicalism of the past century and a half has been a stage on which ism after ism has postured. Some degree of sophistication is required if one wishes to become an ismaticist, for as with most abstractions of the spongier kind, any given ism may be employed as a term of accolade or of denigration. An ism may be used to canonize or to anathematize. Marxism, Leninism, and for a long time Stalinism were largely honored isms in the left, until the convulsive civil wars that raged a half-century ago between true communismatics and the heretical, devil-inspired Trotskyismatics—with little guerrilla wars between Lovestoneismatics and Schachtmanismatics in New York.

Ismology—the science of isms, their formation and uses—is without doubt the destined science of the future. The language is by this time so decimated of the rich abundance of the concrete and individual which it had through the eighteenth century and so clogged by isms, all so much alike as to be more and more difficult to identify, that only those who become masters of ism—ismasters—can be relied upon to lead the language into the next century. One wonders, though, how archaeologists a thousand years hence will deal with the shards of isms.

JUDICIAL ACTIVISM

THE GREATEST PROBLEM for contemporary American democracy, reaching crisis proportions, is that whereas the society is democratic, manifest in egalitarianism and permissiveness throughout the social order and the cultural sphere, the government is not democratic, that is, genuinely responsive to the *considered* will of the people. It does not matter that elections are held every two and four years which produce presidents and congressmen, governors and legislators, mayors and city councils, school boards and other local bodies, all more or less the choices of the people, or that a diminishing sector of the whole population still finds the will power and sense of duty to go to the polls. It does not matter for this reason: whatever the firm desire of a majority of citizens may be, the chances of this desire becoming manifest in law or executive decree are rapidly decreasing. Before the chance approaches zero, it is safe to assume, democracy, even in its current hollow form, will have ended.

The reason that democratic government is less and less evident in contemporary history lies in two mammoth institutional realities, neither of which was foreseen for a second by the Founding Fathers. The first institution is the constricting, penetrating, often suffocating jungle of regulatory agencies, the bureaucracy. The second is in many ways more powerful, simply because it has what the bureaucracy does not have: status in the Constitution on the same level as the legislative and executive branches of government. This is the Supreme Court and the whole burgeoning judiciary, especially the federal echelon, which shows increasing evidence of being the real ruler of the American social and political scene.

The federal judge has in a rising number of instances come to resemble the creation of the mad but brilliant Bentham: the omnipotent magistrate. Bentham detested democracy or any other form of popular government. That any matter at all should ever be resolved by majority vote struck him as just as irrational as would be the case if the laws of mathematics and science went to popular referendum. In his later years he saw nothing good in government that did not become subject to the mind of one person, the omnipotent magistrate, motivated solely by pure reason.

With Bentham's centralization of government and law went a crusading hatred of all the historic immunities and privacies of the common law. His hatred extended to the lawyer-client relationship, the doctor-patient, the priest-communicant, even the husband-wife. Bentham considered the historic immunity of one spouse to testimony by the other in a law court to be against reason and contrary to effective government. The idea of the secret ballot struck him as absurd, as also the jury system. If truth is what one seeks, its attainment should not be trusted to the mere counting of votes. The sovereignty of reason must be made manifest by the sovereignty of the single judge, alone omnipotent, alone capable of the independence of mind and vision of the whole that Bentham thought requisite to a scientifically constructed government.

A whole universe yawns between Benthamite thought and the ideas which governed the minds of the framers of the Constitution of the United States. Instead of centralization, they sought decentralization; instead of legal monism, pluralism; instead of a monolith of power, a system of divided power through checks and balances. Executive, legislative, and judicial must be sharply separated, with every effort made to prevent encroachment by one branch upon the rights and duties of the other branches. The two essential functions of the Supreme Court would be interpretation of the Constitution and adjudication of conflicts arising between branches of the national government and between the national government and the governments of the states.

But behold how the country has fallen. More and more the Supreme Court and the puissant federal judiciary which that Court ultimately dominates enter into the lives of the people, into the autonomies and privacies of the major institutions, into decision-making that takes the judiciary into every nook and corner of American life. The immunity of wife to husband and of husband to wife in the law courts has already been breached by the judiciary with the approval of the Supreme Court. Bentham would be overjoyed. The privacy of the newspaper office, historically sacrosanct under the First Amendment, has been violated. A professor has been jailed and fined by a federal judge for refusing to divulge publicly his personal vote on a confidential review committee involving a colleague's tenure, one of the oldest and most honored confidences in the history of the university. Still another judge has granted, by direct order, tenure to a faculty member to whom it had been denied by the college after thorough investigation and assessment.

But there is more. Whatever else the Framers may have had in mind for the conduct and deportment of judges, administering with absolute power school districts was assuredly not a part. The right of communities at the local level to create and administer, through elections of school boards, schools for their children was until recently as widely accepted as any right in the history of American government. No longer. City after city provides the disagreeable, actually absurd spectacle of judges, not one of them responsible by the elective process to the people concerned, administering school districts and forcing upon them affirmative action programs involving hundreds of millions of dollars which near-bankrupt school systems can afford if at all only by diminishing what is taught and learned. It does not matter how intimate the privacy, how hoary the immunity, how cherished the democratic practice: the omnipotent magistrate will strike with the combination of legal passion and indifference to democracy that was dear to Bentham—though only in his fantasy.

Abortion, household discipline, sexual relations between marriage partners, cohabitation of the unmarried, are but a few of the privacies into which the judiciary so recklessly enters, and with total irresponsibility to anything but the next higher level of courts. The admissions policy of a great university, the confidential records of faculty government in colleges and universities, training programs for workers in industry, management of housing, private as well as public, these are but a few more of the historically autonomous ways of life in America which the judiciary boldly abrogates in the interest of Benthamite rationalism.

It is no wonder that voter alienation increases annually in the United States, with fewer and fewer citizens going to the polls. Why should they go? If the majority will in a school district is unavailing, if local majorities, duly recorded, cannot prevail against federal legal decisions in such vital matters as obscenity and pornography in their neighborhoods, if the expressed majority will of Congress on financing of abortion is declared unconstitutional by a federal judge, if after being overwhelmingly elected to the White House, the President finds himself stopped by either bureaucratic or judicial opposition from fulfilling the very policies which helped get him elected, if in sum there is a higher will than the people's constitutionally expressed one, a will that is by its nature unilateral and supervening, why, it may be asked, should the people bother with expressing their will?

Among the flaws in the Constitution brought out by historical experience is the role given the Supreme Court, and thus derivatively all federal courts, with respect to the other two branches of government, executive and legislative. The Constitution was properly declared by the Framers to be the "supreme law of the land." But the genius of the constitutional separation of powers lies in the fundamental equality of these powers. Within its own appointed sphere each is sovereign. There is no inherent reason why Congress should not be qualified to decide on the constitutionality of its legislative acts. Nine human beings who have been appointed for life by the President, who may or may not even have legal experience, whose consensus has so often been demonstrated to be ridiculously out of harmony with popular consensus, have no reason to be regarded as superior in constitutional wisdom to several hundred duly elected servants of the people. Nothing in the Constitution confers superiority upon the Supreme Court. Mr. Justice Holmes put it this way: "I do not think the United States would come to an end if we lost our power to declare an Act of Congress void"—even though he himself thought more highly of the Court's function with respect to the constitutionality of the laws of the several states.

The Court's dubious constitutional-interpretive role notwithstanding, some kind of check upon even popular majority will, quite
apart from congressional will, is valuable to the stability of a republic, a possible guardian of vital traditions. But again, the question is
whether the Court of nine appointed people—so pathetically few of
whom in history have resembled Solomon or have even measured up
to the average of the Senate—are better at this function than the
Congress. Repeatedly the Supreme Court has shown itself to be mis-
interpreting when it claimed to be interpreting tradition or the real
will of the people. The Dred Scott decision is the most historic in this
respect, but there is no dearth of more recent illustrations. The
Court's ruling in 1934 on the unconstitutionality of the National Re-
covery Act was flagrantly, arrogantly counter to congressional and
popular, as well as presidential will. A few years ago the Court,
claiming as usual to be speaking for the real will of the people, declared capital punishment to be no longer in accord with current
community ethical values. How wrong the Court was in this assessment became quickly evident as state legislatures, under the heat of
popular sentiment, rushed to enact new laws mandating capital punishment, laws which could be considered constitutional under the
Court's most recent language on the matter. And by no constitutional
or moral standard is the Court authorized to enter such delicate, fragile, deeply personal areas as abortion and the artificial sustainment of
a dying life. One of the tragedies of American history is that an arti-
cle in the Constitution designed to divide further the powers which in
England were vested in but one body, Parliament, has proved to be
the basis over the past century and a half of a centralization of power
in Washington that cannot even claim plebiscitary democracy as its
foundation, that has in fact all of the arbitrariness and unchecked
force that the framers were eager to prevent. This is one more melancholy illustration of the principle that man proposes; history disposes.

Perhaps the single most devastating and desolating outcome of
judicial activism is its impact upon the whole web of authority that
naturally exists in any society, a web spun by family, locality, voluntary association, business enterprise, profession, and civil law. Until
quite recently the authority of the school went unquestioned. Textbooks were selected by the local school board; discipline was enforced by administration and faculty of the school and reinforced by
parents who felt not outrage but a sense of social contract when their
children were punished, often physically, for infractions; and no one
would have dreamed of going to court to ask for an injunction or judicial intervention in the operations of the school system. It had its
own "law," one duly respected by all involved. But today that natural

authority of the school, which once made it possible to educate children, has been reduced to chaos in large and spreading sectors of public education. Egalitarianism has been the main pulverizing influence upon this as upon all other natural authorities, but judicial activism, in its pillaging by litigation of the school's historic authority, has been the cutting edge.

The crusading and coercing roles of the Supreme Court and the federal judiciary, which have been increasing in size almost exponentially in this century, have created a new and important model for all those whose primary aim is the wholesale reconstruction of American society. In the beginning, just as the authors of *The Federalist* foresaw, Congress presented the greater hope for those of revolutionary inspiration. But by the time of first Theodore Roosevelt, then Woodrow Wilson, and above all Franklin Roosevelt, the Presidency loomed up as the power to capture for purposes of reform and revolution. A whole generation of intellectuals wrote of the possibilities inherent in a single office, indeed a single individual, for replacing private interests by public and sections or regions by the nation as a whole. But at the present time it is the Supreme Court, indeed the whole federal judiciary, that has captured the minds of the seekers of power for social and political change. How much better and easier, the argument runs, to work directly with individuals who have never been tainted by the demands of the electoral process, who are appointed for life, whose powers have evolved over the years to the point of absolutism, and whose inbred preference for action by injunction or mandate can so inexorably reduce the role of both Congress and President. There are more and more judges, more and more lawyers, and more and more law students and professors who have entered easily into a state of mind that sees in the Supreme Court precisely what Rousseau saw in his archetypical legislator and Bentham in his omnipotent magistrate: sovereign forces for permanent revolution.

L IBERALISM

THE QUESTION IS how liberalism has come to represent, after two centuries, so blatantly schizoid a condition. There are two easily predictable penchants in the contemporary liberal mind. One has to do with power, the other with freedom reaching the boundary of license.

Liberals are first and most important the ardent advocates of the kind of power that is resident in the national state. They are never so happy as when something in the private economic or social sector is being brought within the purview of the federal bureaucracy. When they see something big and private, they lust for its nationalization.

But at the same time contemporary liberals are perversely the friends, if not the ardent advocates, of certain types of freedom in the moral and legal realms. They sympathize with the mugger and the rapist in contrast to the victim. Indeed the only victim with whom liberals identify is what they call the victim of society, of a social order not yet fully politicized in the name of equality. There is no extreme of obscenity and pornography that liberals will not justify in the name of the First Amendment. Fully liberated women, homosexuals, lesbians, sniffers of cocaine, members of the Weatherman underground, and thrice-convicted felons who can write letters are all objects of liberal adoration. The lover of political power, a liberal is the knee-jerk adversary of all moral authority.

To explain this mentality requires going back to the origins of liberalism in the eighteenth and nineteenth centuries, primarily in England and France. The origins are significantly dual in nature. On the one hand is the liberalism that became best known in the writings of Adam Smith, the Founding Fathers in America, and perhaps most memorably Mill. Spencer was a later exponent. The solid emphasis of this school of liberals was on the individual's freedom from the state, from other types of tyranny or potential tyranny as well when necessary, including patriarchalism, public opinion, schools, and business enterprises, but overridingly from the political government, especially in matters of economic enterprise. This is what is commonly called classical liberalism, and *laissez-faire* or *laissez-aller*, drawn from the liberal physiocrats in France, comes close to being its motto.

But across the Channel, reaching its height in the second half of the eighteenth century in France, was the liberalism of the Enlightenment. What caught the eye of the French liberal was somewhat less the state than the assemblage of historically evolved authorities which made up the social order. Social authority was what evoked the hostile glance of the *philosophe:* the authority of the traditional patriarchal family, the guild, the aristocracy, the ancient commune, above all the church in its many divisions and parts. This was the sphere that the *philosophes* detested and sought by every possible means to destroy. They did not necessarily like what they saw in the French government, or at least all that they saw. But they were able to make a pregnant distinction between the trappings of monarchy, which they disliked, and the intrinsic power of the political state, which they very much liked. Even the physiocrats, committed though they were to the ideal of an economic natural order, saw the power of the state as indispensable in the rooting out of all the social impediments to this natural order, of which there were many in the *ancien régime*, starting with such "feudal" institutions as primogeniture and entail, the *levées*, the guilds, and chartered companies. The essence of this school of liberalism was, in a word, *étatisme*, or statism, and it was fully recognized as such by the major political voices of the Enlightenment and then of the Revolution.

France, *une et indivisible*, dedicated to the goddess Virtue that the Jacobins tirelessly worshiped, and freed of all the hateful detritus of feudalism, could be made reality only through the most extensive powers of the state. That is why the successive assemblies and committees of the Revolution, starting in 1790, continuously engaged in the passage of laws which, on the one hand, wiped out so many of the social authorities and, on the other, created new political authorities, all centralized in Paris. Thus a bifurcated ideology existed among the French liberals, supporting a powerful, nationalized, and centralized state, but with it a substantial degree of laissez-faire, of atomistic individualism in the moral and social realms. The result was seen most vividly in the Napoleonic society that emerged directly from the Revolution and its works. All of the centralization planned by the Jacobins reached fruition in the bureaucratized, militarized government of Napoleon; power lay everywhere. But side by side with political authoritarianism existed a generalized license, corruption, libertinism, and moral decay which equaled anything known in the courts of the Bourbons.

A small group of thinkers in France recognized this combination for what it was, the most celebrated of whom was Tocqueville, but who also included Lamennais, Montalembert, and Lacordaire. They recognized, just as had the traditionalists during the Revolution, that what was being created was an omnipotent state of the masses. Tocqueville was by far the most eloquent interpreter of this state. Liberty in a democracy can exist only on the basis of a strong moral, religious, and social order, an order replete with its natural authorities. Precisely the same holds for a true intellectual and artistic culture. Only if predemocratic, preliberal standards and canons survive will the culture and society of democracy remain healthy. But as Tocqueville also repeatedly stressed, the very nature of democratic political power is to become ever more centralized and bureaucratized and, in so becoming, to erode away the predemocratic social and cultural strata, leaving in consequence the plebiscitary, absolute, infinitely penetrating state and below its government a vast horde of atomized individuals rendered egocentric, selfish, grasping, and hedonistic. There is every reason for calling Tocqueville a liberal—freedom was his obsession—but there is a vast difference between the liberalism of Tocqueville and either of the liberalisms epitomized by *laissez-faire* and statism.

Those two types of liberalism were to be seen in uneasy juxtaposition in the West throughout the nineteenth and early twentieth centuries. In the United States and England the libertarian ethos was largely dominant, the ethos that Mill had made famous in his "one very simple principle": to wit, the government is justified in interfering with an individual's thought and behavior only when that thought and behavior can be shown to jeopardize the existence of others in society. Such interference cannot be justified merely in the ethical, educational, esthetic, or self-preservative interests of the individual himself. Here was *laissez-faire* liberalism in full panoply, and there were millions in the Western world to make it a veritable theology. That the eminently cultured and self-disciplined Mill, significantly qualified his "simple principle" by ruling out from it the retarded and demented, the indigent and needy, those who had not yet attained the age of citizenship, all "backward" peoples of the world (who, Mill said, would require enlightened despotism for long periods ahead), and even those whose exposition of philosophy or creed caused public commotion was not noticed nearly as often as the bell-ringing principle itself.

The great deficiency of this classical liberalism was its inability to recognize the indispensable importance of the social contexts of individual freedom, *laissez-faire*, and the noninterventionist state. So consuming was the emphasis upon the individual that the social sources of individuality tended to get neglected. Classical liberalism sees only the political state, its functions limited to those described by Smith and the American Constitution, and a vast sand heap of individuals. There is little if any recognition, as there was in Tocqueville, of the network of social relationships which lie intermediate to the individual and the state, relationships which serve not only as buffers to the state but as nurturing beds of moral and social character, of the disciplines and incentives which manifest themselves in human conduct.

Into the twentieth century flowed two powerful currents of nineteenth century ideas, one the product of Mill's radical individualism, the other a legacy of the French Enlightenment and Revolution. Together they make up contemporary liberalism. The first current is manifest in America in such early twentieth century movements as sexual liberation, the revolt against the village and small town, progressive education, liberal theology, the elective system in college, and modernism and futurism in the arts. The literature of the period—that of Dreiser, Cabell, Fitzgerald, O'Neill, Masters, and Mencken, among many others—was strong in the theme of individual liberation, not from the ties of the political state but from those of family, village, small town, and church. The culture of the Roaring Twenties was in fact well formed by the outbreak of World War I on both sides of the Atlantic. Greenwich Village will long remain the perfect symbol of this drive toward individual liberation from the traditional moral and social authorities. From the Greenwich Village of the early twentieth century to the contemporary chaos of cultural anarchy, hedonism, narcissism, and generalized flouting of idols there is a straight line best defined as Mill's one very simple principle.

In almost perfect complementarity the second stream of ideas out of the nineteenth century also swelled and spread its waters over the landscape. The ideal of the state consecrated to improvement of man's moral and social life, which had emerged from the French Enlightenment and been brought to luster during the French Revolution, was the perfect companion in the early twentieth century to the moral individualism that dominated art and life. For it was not any assemblage of social authorities, any hierarchy of cultural imperatives, that this vision of the political state demanded, but rather a generally atomized population, one in which institutional competitors to the state's power were either eliminated or enfeebled. Thus the writings of Veblen, Dewey, Ward, Ely, and many others express a rising demand for the interventionist state, the provider state in American life. Herbert Croly electrified American intellectuals by offering a new "promise" of American life, one in which a new nationalism would replace traditional pluralism and a new and democratic collectivism would stand in contrast to the individualistic values which Croly believed to be obsolete in industrial society. However the new liberalism was conceived by its apostles, one aspect was unvarying in its centrality: the political state. There was much stress on social justice, social responsibility, social control, social rights, and social welfare, but what each of these came down to in concrete terms was ineradicably political, inseparable from political government.

Philosophers, sociologists, and political scientists provided the raw material of the new liberalism, but the rapid transformation of old to new cannot be understood without reference to two extraordinary political leaders in America: Woodrow Wilson and Franklin D. Roosevelt. Of the two, Wilson is seminal. Long before he went into politics, he had come to revere the state as his forefathers had the

Calvinist Church. Service to the nation and the nation's service to its citizens obsessed Wilson, and his famous "Princeton in the nation's service" during his presidency there sprang less from love of Princeton than of state. Himself a scholar and teacher, it was perhaps inevitable that he would exert a fascination on intellectuals beyond anything known for at least a century. An eloquent and powerful speaker, his travels across America, beginning with his tenure at Princeton, brought him in touch with scores of influential teachers, scholars, and other intellectuals.

Only Wilson could have attracted, as he did, the great majority of teachers, scholars, and other intellectuals to support, in 1917, America's entry into the war in Europe. Above any other American President up to his time, Wilson politicized the academic profession. He did this by bringing it into almost every corner and crevice of the war state he created in the interests of victory abroad. It was as war measure, not socialist gospel, that worker councils appeared overnight in industry, that mills and factories, communications, and transportation systems were put under direct, central control of government, that minimum wage decrees were announced, that health and safety measures were taken in the factories and offices, and that a plethora of emergency laws were passed at Wilson's behest by which food was distributed to all Americans. That along with such actions, Wilson instigated rigid censorship, partially suspended habeas corpus, revived the once-hated sedition laws, and ordered full prosecution of Eugene Debs, Max Eastman, and others who protested entry into the war, was understood no doubt by the liberals who followed Wilson, but without lasting effect.

When the war ended, almost all of the bureaucratic machinery that had given effect to the war-sprung political humanitarianism was soon dismantled. But a permanent change had been effected in both the American social order and American liberalism. The sheer power and intensity of the war effort under Wilson took a great deal away from the historic values of localism, regionalism, and decentralization. These would never again shine as they had prior to World War I. By the same token, an irreversible change took place in the liberal mind, especially the acdemic mind. For the first time in many decades this mind became largely Democratic and, within that, increasingly social democratic. The old liberalism did not die overnight, but in retrospect one can see the new liberalism, with the provider state as its pivot, taking command by the end of the 1920s.

Franklin D. Roosevelt, who had served in high office under Wilson and was a profound admirer of his, may not have had more on his mind than the promised 25 percent cut in federal budget and bu-

reaucracy when he took office in 1933 with the Great Depression raging around him. But he was a master improviser, and within a year
many of the agencies which, under whatever name, had existed in
World War I were revived and in the aggregate became known as the
New Deal. Burke had written in 1790 of "the new dealers" who incessantly speculated with the fortunes and lives of citizens in France,
but no liberal was likely to be reading Burke in 1933. By 1936, liberalism in America stood for little else but support of agencies such as
the NRA, AAA, PWA, WPA, and CCC, one and all instruments of
bureaucratic invasion of the social and economic orders. Wilson's
mesmeric personality had begun the change in American liberalism;
Roosevelt's possibly more mesmeric personality brought it to lasting
fruition.

Roosevelt was fond of military imagery, and he never lost an opportunity to remind the citizenry that the President was also Com-
mander-in-Chief. In his inaugural speech in 1933 he urged the
American people "to move as a trained and loyal army, willing to
sacrifice for the goal of a common discipline." He expressed unhesi-
tating willingness to assume "the leadership of this great army of the
people dedicated to a disciplined attack." In the sheer abundance of
centralized, collectivizing bureaus and agencies and, not least, of academic intellectuals who had gone to Washington to wage war against
the depression through decree and order, the infrastructure for
World War II could have been seen forming several years in advance
of when the war actually struck. The liaison of the liberal and bureaucracy was thoroughly formed by the middle 1930s, and all that
was required to make statism the very religion of the liberal was
World War II. To this day the briefcase veterans of that war remember with fond pride their supervision from Washington of almost
every aspect of American life. Power rather than liberty had become
the sustaining value of liberals. In this they were one with their Jacobin predecessors. The fateful complex of intellectual-industrialist-mil-
itary general was cemented for once and all in World War II, and by
the time John Kennedy took office in 1960, prominent liberals in the
universities, foundations, government, and even the corporate world
were only too eager to assume once again an identity that was as military in essence as it was intellectual. Predictably, the Pentagon was
by far the greatest magnet for the liberal, as that was where action
could be confidently expected sooner or later.

The future of liberalism is very bright, at least in the short run.
Now, to be sure, a conservative reaction is going on. But this reaction
is not likely to survive long, unless some kind of seismic change
takes place in America, and if such a change is to happen, it must

come, as seismic changes in society almost always do, from the ranks of the religious. The nearest the country has come to a real counterforce to the liberalism of statism and of cultural license is the so-called Moral Majority. Whether it will succeed in the long run is impossible to foresee. Such "majorities" have in the past, from time to time, ever since the Reformation, but that is all one can say. To an astonishing and hilarious degree the Moral Majority has already succeeded in worrying American liberalism in its twin aspects as it has not been worried before, perhaps in its entire history. When the presidents of great universities, when editors of noted newspapers and magazines, when prominent politicians in both political parties, and when the vastly wealthy foundations all issue statements of alarm at the sight of the Moral Majority, one may safely assume that a few tremors at least of some seismic disturbance, however small, have been felt. It is well to remember that the Reformation began in very humble circumstances indeed.

METAPHOR

FAR MORE THAN simple adornment of language, metaphor is in fact a profound and indispensable way of knowing. It is not only a key element in the formation of language but also one of the fundamental mechanisms of the evolution of human thought. Metaphor is the means of effecting instantaneous fusion of two or more separated realms of experience into one illuminating, encapsulating, iconic image. As Herbert Read observed, metaphor is "the expression of a complex idea, not by analysis, nor by direct statement, but by sudden perception of an objective relation." Wallace Stevens wrote of the "symbolic language of metamorphosis," thus indicating that the relationship between metaphor and metamorphosis in the world of meaning is much more than etymological.

Fowler distinguished instructively between "live" and "dead" metaphors. The first are obvious when heard or seen. "A mighty fortress is our God"; a sunset is "the hemorrhaging of God"; "our bodies are our gardens"; "his ideas reached their critical mass"; "the speaker saved his long bomb for the end." In each a familiar image in one sphere of life is used to identify or illuminate something in another sphere. But "dead" metaphors are far more reflective of the

lasting power of this form of knowing. They have become so intimately a part of language that they are no longer seen for what they
are. Fowler explained that dead metaphors "have been so often used
that speaker and hearer have ceased to be aware that the words used
are not literal."

Consider: *wintry, glacial, icy, cold, frozen, chilly,* and their close synonyms. Consider also *warm, heated, hot, boiling, burning, flaming,* and
their close synonyms. All have their primitive origins as words in the
contexts of weather and climate. But no one is likely today to think
of weather when describing a look or verbal expression as "icy" or as
"heated." It is not a simple verbal phenomenon taking place here,
but a conceptual phenomenon. One conceptual system—climate—is
transfused into another conceptual system—human emotion.
Through metaphor it is possible to move from one universe into another, the act of metaphor making the transition acceptable if not always agreeable.

The history of great ages of thought—Periclesian Athens, Augus-
tan Rome, Elizabethan England—turns out to be also the history of
great metaphoric creation. Plato's metaphors were alone enough to
form the whole powerful and penetrating Platonic tradition in Western thought. Strip the metaphoric images from Elizabethan drama or
poetry, and one has torn away large pieces of flesh—of thought.

By all odds the most powerful and seminal of metaphors are
drawn from the biological world of plants, micro-organisms, animals,
trees, and human beings. The acts of birth, growth, maturity, senescence, and death were unavoidable observations and experiences for
primitive man. They could be seen everywhere in nature, and even if
the conception role of the male was for long unsuspected, the sex act
itself was a very ordinary fact of experience, as was birth and also
the relation of the generations. Few things could have been more
prominent in primitive life than birth, growth, death, and genealogy.
It was inevitable that anything known as thoroughly as these organic
processes and relationships would be transferred metaphorically, be
made the basis of myths, rites, and eventually whole conceptual systems, philosophies, and religions.

Without number are the expressions, the ideas and concepts, the
systems of thought in the West which are founded basically upon the
assumption that what is so literal and obvious in the organic realm
may be reckoned true and illuminating in all other domains. Hence
the enormous use of copulation, parturition, senescence, and death in
the early myths, not least in those pertaining to the gods. Hesiod's
Theogony, filled with the couplings, writhings, and orgasmic convul-
sions of the gods and goddesses, takes its place in what today might

be called sacred pornography. But metaphoric imagery drawn from the organic world is far from limited to ancient myth and rite. How natural to explain, as the earliest Greeks seem to have, the unknown of history and society by use of the biologically known. Hence the appearance as early as Homer in literature of the idea of the growth and development of civilizations. A great deal of Greek thought is inseparable from the component metaphor of organic genesis and decay. And a great deal of all thought by this time has to be seen, however dimly and subtly, as no more than an extension of what were in the beginning live metaphors and which in the process of becoming dead—that is, no longer recognizable—have in effect created the very means by which people think, by which they convert vague, primal feeling into what they believe to be knowledge.

The organism serves not only as a model of growth for contemplating the world, but also as a model of structure, of the articulation of separate entities, such as the heart and lungs. To emphasize the harmonious interaction of parts in an organization, it is customary to use "organic" as highest praise. Hegel gave impetus to the philosophy of "the social organism" in his assault upon English atomism and utilitarianism. Burke's rage against the Jacobin dismantlement of so many traditional institutions was based upon his conviction that society is an organism and can no more be an object of large reconstruction than can the human body.

And then there is the vital biological connection known as genealogy. That one generation produces another and another, *ad infinitum*, was obviously not long in the knowing by primitive man, and here was still another metaphor to use toward the conquering of the unknown. If human generations form a lineal thread in time, so may the gods, the mountains, the seas and plains, and the very acts, events, and changes by which all of these came into their present existence. From Hesiodic and Hecatean genealogies of the gods was but a short step in thought to the narrative genealogies of events which have been the stuff of history writing since Thucydides at least. It is unforgivable by all ordinary standards of logic to endow historical events with genealogical connection, with events giving birth to events and then other events, but the power of metaphor is limitless when there is nothing to check it. And the result is a vast area of not only language but thought itself that may be seen as the issue of biological metaphor—birth, development, decline, and death. Teleology and anthropomorphism are at root no more than enlargements and subtilizations of the prepotency found first in the seed and then in the mature offspring.

But while the organic world provides the most puissant of meta-

phors in the history of human thought, there has been no want of
other sectors of the world from which to draw. Warfare, inseparable
from the human if not the entire organic condition, is a bounteous
source of metaphor. Not only is argument "war," with the dialectic a
"grand strategy," but the whole history of thought is composed of
the "defensible," the "indefensible," the "assault," the "defense," the
"victory," the "defeat," and their innumerable analogues. Such is the
antiquity and universality of war in human history that it may well
be second only to the organic as the most fertile source of metaphors,
live and dead. From earliest times games also furnished their full
share of productive metaphors, and games continue to do so in modern society. One could fill a small volume with words and phrases
which are no more than live metaphors drawn from the variety of
sports known to Western man. In America at present "the bomb" is
much more likely to refer to the long pass in football than to the falling, lethal explosives which the air age brought about. From military
to football, and now to thought generally, "bomb" as noun or verb
not only fills the vocabulary but shapes the very thought behind the
vocabulary.

It has been argued that the ultimate test of science, in contrast to
popular or literary ways of thinking, lies in its complete liberation
from metaphor. The scientist's mission is thus to discover or determine the literal truth or reality, not what reality is merely like or
analogous to. Just so. But everyone knows that science today works
in terms of models—of light, of the origin of the universe, of the
economy—and a model is really a metaphor. To speak of waves and
particles of light is to speak in metaphors. That thought can ever dis-
pense with metaphor is unlikely, for this would imply that there is
no longer an unknown to be approached with the aid of the known.

MILITARISM

MORE PEOPLE ARE LIVING at this moment under military government, in what can only properly be called garrison states, than at any
other time in world history. These governments include not just the
transparently military regimes where the highest officials are military
officers in rank and uniform but especially such countries as the Soviet Union, the People's Republic of China, and Cuba where, under

the name of socialism or communism, society, economy, and polity have been intensively militarized, with every possible aspect of life brought within military command. The faces of Marx, Lenin, Stalin, and Mao may be emblazoned on banners in these states, but to uncover their true roots, it is necessary to go back to Clausewitz's *On War*. The official rhetoric is drawn from nineteenth century socialism as revamped by Marx, Engels, and then Lenin, but underneath the thin veneer of appeals to the working classes of the world lies the monolithic reality of a despotism shot through with military ends, values, and strategies. Such despotisms, whether nominally socialist or capitalist in their economies, can be expected to proliferate during the rest of the century, possibly even coming to include the Western democracies.

That the twentieth century would prove to be, in unprecendented degree, the Age of Militarism was foretold by prophets in the nineteenth century, Tocqueville and Taine among them, who saw the future in terms of what Burckhardt called "military despotisms masquerading as republics, led by military commandos." But overwhelmingly the seers and prophets of the century concurred with Bagehot and Spencer in seeing militarism rather as a necessary early stage of social evolution and thus a form of society from which all active forces were irreversibly disengaging Western man. All over the West, on both sides of the Atlantic, the dominant spirit was one of confidence in this respect. To both radicals and conservatives in politics, the advent of industry, commerce, science, technology, and popular government suggested the utter extinction of war and the obsolescence of the military class. There were some who actually "proved" that Western economies had reached the stage in evolution where war was as wildly inappropriate, and so recognized by the captains of industry, as reversion to oxen carts for transportation.

All such euphoria notwithstanding, the whole world, commencing in 1914, moved relentlessly toward ever larger wars and ever increasing hegemony of the military class, defined in its widest possible sense to include technologists, purveyors of weapons, scientists, and intelligence. For a time in the 1920s and 1930s, it could still seem highly probable to many otherwise perceptive minds that the recent world war was the last one, that men of good will and reason would never again allow themselves to become the wretched fodder for guns, gas, and trench rats. The literature of pacifism, much of it of high quality, predominated in poetry, novel, and drama as well as in tract as it never had before in the West. Movies such as *All Quiet on the Western Front*, *A Farewell to Arms*, and *Grand Illusion* flourished at box offices. Students at Oxford took an oath never to go to war for king and country. The munitions industry, under heavy congressional investigation, became a byword for the corrupt, the malevolent—and the obsolete.

What was unthinkable through about 1935 became of a sudden only too thinkable, and by 1938 the fever of war, though not yet its substance save in the Far East where Japan was ravishing China, was markedly apparent in Europe and the United States. True, there were passionate opponents of a European war in England and France, and in America by 1939 isolationists presented a formidable political force. But all this notwithstanding, the possibility of war, once again total war, became stark to a degree that would have been unimaginable a decade earlier.

The reason, it may be said with much truth, is Hitler and the rearmament of Nazi Germany, followed by the invasion of first the Ruhr and then Czechoslovakia. Had there been no bellicose Hitler, there would have been no need for the answering military buildup in France and England. The last, however, is hypothetical, for no one can foretell the specific guise in which the agents of war will appear. What can be said with high probability of truth is that, whether Hitler or someone else, the seeds of war will be ideological in the extreme, whether from the political right or left. For that is the distinctive mark of wars since the French Revolution. With ever rising intensity, especially in the twentieth century, war and ideological crusade have become virtually inseparable.

The origins of mass warfare lie in the French Revolutionary armies, committed to carrying the Revolution to every part of Europe. The *levée en masse*, passed by the National Convention in 1793, put all Frenchmen in permanent requisition until the last of France's enemies had been defeated. It was the first mass conscription in Western, possibly world, history. War upon foreign enemies was only an extension of the Revolution, which had been purely domestic until the end of 1792. The emphasis upon the people, the nation as a whole, one and indivisible, which was a fertile one from the Declaration of the Rights of Man onward, was simply passed over to the military. The same leveling of conventional rank that had taken place in civil society now took place in the military. Gone was the hereditary acquisition by nobles of commissioned rank in the French army. Henceforth the egalitarian principle of "careers open to talents" would prevail in the military as well as in civil society. With every reason Napoleon could later say that a marshal's baton lay in the knapsack of every soldier. All of his marshals had come up from the ranks.

No greater change in Western history has ever taken place than this democratization of the military and, at the same time, militarization of democracy that took place in France during the Revolution. The "nation in arms" was for the first time a reality. Distinction between revolutionists as such and soldiers in the French army no longer existed after 1793. Just as the original revolutionists had sought to root out all evidences of the *ancien régime* in France, now the soldiers, numbering first in the hundreds of thousands, then in the millions, were engaged in destroying iniquitous rank and privilege in other parts of Europe. Wherever they went, the army's banners were emblazoned with the familiar *liberté, egalité,* and *fraternité.* And at home those who worked in the munitions factories, in the fields, indeed everywhere in the war economy, were praised as soldiers on the home front.

The great and lasting effect of the French Revolutionary and Napoleonic wars was the uniting for the first time of war and moral crusade. There had been feudal wars for hundreds of years in which the values of chivalry could occasionally shine, but such wars, save only for the religious crusades to destroy the infidel, were highly limited: limited in number of fighting men, in technology available, and in goal, usually no more than acquiring or shoring up territory. So were the wars of the eighteenth century—prior to the French Revolution—limited. Little more than dynastic ambition brought wars into existence; soldiers were professional and their numbers were small. It was a rare war that involved armies of more than twenty to thirty thousand men, and there was never any pretence that anything but territory or dynastic succession was the mission. The American Revolutionary War was an exception, at least from the point of view of the American militia, but at no time did the frenzied spirit of crusade take over Washington and his generals or their troops. To find precedent for the French Revolutionary Wars, one is obliged to go back to the religious wars of the sixteenth and seventeenth centuries in Europe. What had formerly been unthinkable to professional soldiers fighting each other for purely political reasons then became wholly acceptable: the slaughter of civilians, women and children included, the poisoning of wells, the burning of villages, and the widespread use of torture and terror. For when Catholic fought Protestant, total good and total evil were in the minds of the combatants, and to give quarter, to show mercy, was tantamount to trafficking with the Devil. No longer, in short, was war limited by purpose. It became apocalyptic and therefore boundless in ferocity.

The religious wars came to an end, but their special crusading, avenging, and millennialist passions were transfused to the French armies at the end of the eighteenth century. These passions would appear only fitfully in the nineteenth century. They showed up in some degree in the American Civil War, also a war of mass armies, one in which for reasons of ideological passion, little quarter was given on either side. And they showed up again in the Paris Commune in the Franco-Prussian War.

Not until World War I did the legacy of the French Revolutionary Wars bear full fruit. Rarely has any war in history been in fact more nakedly concerned with old familiar issues such as alliances, treaties, territorial lusts, and dynasties. But this fundamental reality became shortly covered over by spiritual and moral rhetoric, especially after America entered the war under Wilson. Of a sudden that war became a crusade to make the world—the whole world— safe for democracy. As in the religious and French Revolutionary wars, this war became one of boundless moral zeal, of fanatic ideologies. From the Allies' point of view, thanks to ever-working propaganda machines, it was not a German king, related closely to the royal family in England, they were fighting, but the "Beast of Berlin," the arch-rapist of Belgian girls, the prophet of slaughter extended to babies. Of a sudden it was discovered by the Allies, especially the Americans, that the Germany of rich culture, science, art, music, and learning which had been so universally admired into the twentieth century was in fact a horde of Huns bent only upon conquest of the world. From the Allies' point of view, especially after Wilson brought America into the war, far more than war was being fought; it was revolution, that is, the overthrow of every possible element and attribute of the wicked old order of nations. Liberation of the subject nationalities of Europe, indeed of the world, became a sovereign purpose.

But as war became at bottom revolution for the Allied enthusiasts, so revolution became for the newly formed Soviet state in Russia a form of war, civil in the beginning, national in the end. Lenin saw with extraordinary clarity how national wars could be converted into civil wars and then into revolutions. For Lenin and Trotsky alike, war and revolution were but two points on a common spectrum. Both saw the appointed role of the Soviet Republic to be the military destruction of bourgeois governments surrounding it by "a series of the most terrible conflicts." But equally important was that the "proletariat, if it wishes to rule, must demonstrate this also with its military organization." Of a sudden the army in Russia—that is, the parts willing to swear fealty to the new Bolshevik government—became the Red Army, largely designed in structure and strategy by the brilliant Trotsky, and from the moment that the Red Army became a fact, the whole of Russian society began to be brought under its control, subject to its needs, in short, militarized totally.

War is revolution, revolution is war: this apothegm epitomizes what has made the world so different a place since 1918. Permanent revolution is hardly too strong a phrase with which to label what has gone on with increasing ferocity in Africa, Asia, and Latin America. Whether the revolutionaries choose Leninist or Wilsonian rhetoric, now seeking "liberation of the working class" or instead seeking "freedom from colonialism," the results have been the same. The world has been little less than a seething cauldron for over half a century, with racism joining revolution and nationalism as the third element in the unholy brew, with age-old institutions such as village, caste, kindred, and guild destroyed or badly eroded, with most forms of traditional authority atomized in the name of worker, nationalist, or both, and everywhere, irrespective of precise cause or objective, the military class brought to the fore. Whether war is revolution or revolution is war, it has to be fought successfully, and this means that there is no substitute for the soldier, who has become increasingly professional. Moreover, if the "gains" of revolution or national war of liberation are to be consolidated, protected from counter-revolution, and then built upon, a wall of military steel is necessary, an army consecrated to "revolutionary" or "nationalist" ends, and thus a form of government that will sacrifice everything to the military, that will be the war state, the garrison state. Such clearly is the Soviet Union, the People's Republic of China, and each of the so-called socialist or people's states which have been fashioned in the image of those two. Behind the facade of a Politburo is the reality of military government; with every reason, Stalin, Mao, and Castro chose the military tunic as their invariable public dress. And from these revolutionary-militarist states, large and small, issue forth terrorist squads, guerrilla units, and spies enough to keep the other half of the world in ferment and apprehension.

Action invites reaction, and among the consequences of this kind of ideological militarism are such states as Argentina, Chile, Bolivia, Turkey, and occasionally Greece, which by no stretch of the imagination can be called revolutionary in nature but are assuredly military in government. These states, however, show no sign thus far of seeking the degree of militarization that is present in most of the revolutionary states. The private sector in these states remains vigorous generally, and in Chile the military government actually seeks to keep the free market alive in the economy. But they are no less military in nature of government and add significantly to the number of military states in the twentieth century.

This number is likely to be further increased, with some of the Western democracies themselves becoming increasingly militarized as the century winds to an end. One indication of this trend is the permanent danger represented by Russia and doubtless before long China once again, together with their respective minions. When war or threat of war is sporadic, a democracy may face it without more than temporary loss of its fundamental values and institutions. But garrison states of the size and aggressiveness of the Soviet Union cannot be long dealt with appropriately by governments whose democratic institutions and legal freedoms for all make the exportation of terrorists and guerrillas almost irresistible to the revolutionary-military states. The United States has a huge military structure itself, and for one reason alone: the Soviet Union. One of the burning questions for America in the rest of the century will be the degree of limits which are to be placed upon the American military Leviathan, limits of economy but also of civil liberties. The Soviet Union's military machine suffers from no such burning question, and it is to be expected that a rising body of opinion in the United States, profoundly apprehensive of the threat of the Soviet and its minions, will question the moral, constitutional, and economic limits now placed upon the military, within which must be included the CIA and much of the FBI.

There is also the ominous fact that a special kind of domestic as well as foreign security can seem to attend the militarization of society. Hobbes saw the absolute, monolithic state as the sole protection of human beings from the eruptions of the state of nature where life had been nasty, poor, brutish, and short. So does a rising number of Americans see the necessity of far greater police, or better, military, power as the means of keeping the domestic peace. America is unique in the number and the solidity of its civil rights, and their strength should not be underestimated. But in the Civil War and in both World Wars, some of these rights were jettisoned for the duration, without great outcry. When the streets and neighborhoods of America come to seem sufficiently like combat zones, one may be certain that the cry for something approximating martial law will grow loud.

All evidence suggests that the military government of a Chile or an Argentina is popular with the majority of the citizens of these countries, and the reason is not far to seek: for the average citizen, life is safer and property is more secure. Such a citizen is not likely to brood over the summary disappearance from society of a few thousand individuals known or strongly suspected to be terroristic in character. If in a Chile inflation can be reduced drastically, economic life can remain largely private in nature, and revolutionary violence can be rendered negligible, all for the suspension or abolition of a few legal safeguards that the ordinary citizen rarely if ever needs, there is reason to vote strongly for continuation of the military, as the citizens of Chile recently did by more than two to one.

Nothing can reduce a community to social rubble more quickly than blind fear for life and property, the kind of fear generated by the fanatical revolutionary-terrorist working with near impunity within that community. It does not much matter whether the terrorist is an import or is native grown; the consequences are the same. Democracy became possible in the West only when a solid foundation of morality and appropriate social structure had been achieved. Because of this foundation, the Hobbesian state was not needed or wanted. The French Revolution reached, within a year or two, the point of Terror, secret police, and despotic centralization of power; the reason lay in the Revolution's remorseless assault upon moral and social traditions which had given society its cohesion. Between the rabble and the omnipotent state no middle ground existed. No such destruction of foundations took place in America after 1776 because the object of the revolutionary soldiers was simply and solely liberation from the British Crown. Social reconstruction was not an end, and the result was that society could take care of itself without a strong central state, without much in the way of police, and without a standing army. What is explicit in democracy, such as its stated liberties or voting rights, is less important than what is tacit: the predemocratic resolve of people to live their lives generally in accord with the Judeo-Christian precepts.

It is the loss of so much of the tacit that has led to modern democracy's plunge into the explicit—the innumerable laws, regulations, and decrees which make citizens feel like Gulliver in the hands of the Lilliputians. But as government in the democratic states becomes more and more intrusive and suffocating, its actual power, its police power, becomes smaller and smaller. The primary purpose of all government, to provide protection and justice for its citizens, becomes invisible and largely impotent as the result of the jungle-like overgrowth of secondary and tertiary functions.

Even if there were not a constantly accelerating danger from abroad, from the permanent war waged through revolution and terror by the great military despotisms, commencing with the Soviet, there would be a strong tendency toward the militarization of society in the Western democracies. There is all too manifestly a spirit of rebellion, insurrection, and social nihilism in all parts of the world save only those occupied by the centralized military collectivisms. As the Soviet example makes clear, they too have their problems in this respect, from rising rates of crime and delinquency to dissidence and loss of the work ethic, but as the Soviet history makes even clearer, ways are instantly available to take care of most of these problems—ways so well known to Stalin and his lieutenants. Moreover, in none of the military despotisms do there exist to any significant degree the kinds of problems of survival that today torment millions of citizens in the democracies with fear for their lives and property. One does not have to speculate long on what the decision would be by average Americans if they were presented with the certain prospect of physical safety at all hours and in all places in return for giving up a few legal rights which in their minds are in any event the joys of criminals alone.

The spirit of nihilism, which devours equally culture and public order, has its roots in the compost of the social order left by decaying institutions and values. Now that the family, to use but one example, has been subjected to depredations by the state through its bureaucratic penetration of every family privacy and through lethal tax laws, it is not surprising that the number of youthful predators in society steadily increases. One does not have to premise original sin in man to understand that, apart from the whole complex process of socialization with its innumerable forms of discipline, coercion, incentive, and persuasion, human beings would be brutish.

More than 90 percent of the violent, brutal, sadistic type of crime that now infests so many sectors of society, that drives fear into the hearts of citizens everywhere, comes from the young, mostly male, but increasingly joined by the female. If life becomes more and more of a nightmare, increasingly dominated by the dedicatedly or compulsively violent, people will turn gratefully to the military for protection and will, with equal gratitude, jettison the present legal and judicial rights that make existence relatively easy for the new savages in Western society.

The future almost certainly belongs to the military. Even if there were not the dangers posed by the thick, brutalitarian governments of the kind Stalin and Hitler designed, the present rampant, endemic spirit of nihilism that runs through the social orders of the Western democracies would ensure a turning away from the social rubble to the military. One may hope that, among Burckhardt's military republics led by commandos in the twentieth century and after, there will be a few states, still buoyed by the memory of a democracy that worked, in which martial law will take on a more benign cast than can be found in a Soviet Union or North Vietnam.

Nostalgia

Living with the past is vital to individual and society alike. Prevention of what Eliot called "disowning the past" and what Plumb called "the death of the past" is a responsibility of scientist and humanist alike. Man is a time-binding creature, and commitment to the past is but the other side of devotion to the present.

Nostalgia is, however, a special and far from salutary approach to the past. It is even at best a rust of memory, often a disease. Nostalgia breaks the telescopic relation of past and present that is the essence of ritual. It makes of the past a cornucopia of anodynes and fancies to draw from at will. It seizes upon some period, decade, or century and bathes it in solutions of sentimentality. The past, so necessary to replenishment of the present when properly understood, takes the form of memorabilia, golden-oldies such as records, books, and movies which should not be wrenched from their ages. Rarely does any effusion of nostalgia last long, but on the evidence of modern times, one effusion will shortly be followed by another, however different. Now it is the 1890s, then the 1920s or 1930s, even, *mirabile dictu*, the 1950s.

One form of nostalgia invites special attention; it is what the French call *nostalgie de la boue*, literally, nostalgia for the mud. Individuals reach a point in their lives when they become preoccupied by warped memories of childhoods spent in poverty, squalor, the gutter. In recapturing this "mud," the imagination filters it, driving out the evil and converting it into something that, although crude and coarse by one's mature standards, nevertheless presents a picture of straightforward honesty, of rugged health, in contrast to the present. Much of the current fascination with "roots," with genealogical origins, has *nostalgie de la boue* mixed with it. One recreates an early Brownsville, Hell's Kitchen, or Salt Flats, in part to remind oneself of how far one has come in the world, but in equal part simply to return to the "mud" of childhood and youth.

Such nostalgia is to be found in those who have served in war. No matter how appalling and seemingly unbearable the actual experience of war may have been at the time, the passage of a few years is usually enough to transfigure the experience, to purge it of all that was terrifying or horrible. The mind goes back with appreciation to battle episodes, to the inanition of garrison life, to the special hardships and deprivations. Sometimes this nostalgia comes very quickly once war is over. The contrast between the communalism one had known in a military unit and the more impersonal civil life just returned to can be sharp. Most war memoirs have this element of *nostalgie de la boue* in them.

Spreading nostalgia for the Great Depression is a glittering example of *nostalgie de la boue* at the present time. Doubtless some of it is the consequence of living in an age of inflation and soaring interest rates. But a larger part of the Depression nostalgia is occupied by filtered memory of a simpler form of life, of hardships met, suffered from, and overcome, of a higher standard of morality, of closer cohesion of family, and of a smaller generation gap. There is a special bond today among those old enough to have gone through the Depression, and also a certain sense of snobbery toward those who were not then born.

Nostalgia can overtake whole nations. One of Hitler's great talents was his capacity for arousing sentimental memory of the times when *Deutschland über Alles* was recognized by the whole world, until, as he tirelessly proclaimed, Germany had been stabbed in the back in 1918. Germany is by no means alone in its penchant for national nostalgia. One need think only of post-Napeleonic France. In America at the present time there is a growing nostalgia for the Presidency of Franklin D. Roosevelt, even, somewhat more strangely, that of John F. Kennedy. The image of Camelot has proved to be a successful one. The politics of nostalgia is real in most elections and mass movements.

Nostalgia, like boredom, is difficult to measure, but that it is a force in history is hardly to be doubted. It is a reasonable guess that nostalgia of all types will play a larger role in the future. The greatest barrier to nostalgia, in contrast to simple respect for the past, is a social structure in which the forces of stable growth outweigh those of instability and perceived formlessness. Ritual—religious, political, and other—is a strong force against nostalgia. But, as is evident enough, both the stable and the ritualized are diminishing in this century. And there is nothing to suggest a reversal of this trend.

OLD AGE

AMONG THE NOVEL problems faced by modern, especially American, civilization is that of old age and its cultural and psychological impact upon the rest of the social order. The nuclear bomb is a new

problem also in mankind's history, but everyone knows what to do
about it: not use it. There is no such clarity of vision about old age.
Its sheer burgeoning mass in society presents difficulties which are
not going to be easily resolved.

That a single age-cohort can affect, even shake, the social structure was made evident in the 1960s, one of the most tumultuous decades known in American history. That was the decade in which the
baby boom of World War II came of age, reaching adolescence and
early maturity. Never before had there been anything to compare
with the demographic mass of this cohort in its relation to all other
age strata, and never before had society been subjected to the tremors, shocks, and quakes registered upon American culture by the distinctive styles, tastes, and patterns of this age mass. In countless
ways, ranging from sexual mores to art, music, and literature, this
immense group left permanent imprint on America. It has passed by
now into a higher, older, and quieter range on its inexorable way to
the ranks of old age, but what it did as an age group will remain for
a long time.

Its impact, great though it was, does not equal what may be foreseen from the old-aged in American society starting early in the next
century. There are at present more than 35 million Americans sixty-
five and older. This proportion of the total population presents its
full share of problems, but these problems are for the most part economic and medical. Much more difficult, even baffling, will be the
cultural, social, and psychological problems posed by the vastly
greater number and proportion of the old aged a mere half-century
from now. By the year 2035 the number sixty-five and older will have
shot up 119 percent, while society as a whole will have increased by
only 34 percent. The percentage of those eighty-five and over will go
up 206 percent. If breakthroughs occur in the diagnosis and treatment
of heart disease and cancer, all of these percentages must be revised
upward, magnifying many-fold the impact of the aged.

The nature of the special difficulty posed by the presence of so
many elderly will not be economic. Unless births drop sharply in the
years ahead, the economic aspects of the aged can doubtless be
worked out, though not without social and political strains. The generations have already been separated by the fragmentation of the
family, and youth and age will become like two great social classes in
potential conflict of interests, the one mindful chiefly of taxes, the
other of benefits. Except in a utopian economy, there cannot help but
be a sharpening tension between these classes for the essentially finite social budget.

The more baffling problems, however, will be the psychological and cultural effects on the young and middle-aged of a constantly expanding army of the elderly. The work incentive may become still further diminished in youth as a result of the heavy taxes required for the support of the old. The culture of the elderly is manifestly different from the culture of the working young. Different cultures, especially when arrayed in potentially competitive positions within the same society, cannot help but develop ideologies that are increasingly antagonistic. It will be like two nations within one state. The ties between the generations, historically among the most important in the whole social fabric, are already loosening quickly, as a predictable result of the fragmentation of the traditional family which, despite its tensions and animosities, did manage to offer some kind of social contract in this respect.

The effect upon the buoyancy and creativity that lie naturally in youth in far greater degree than in age may well be damaging. The overwhelming amount of inventiveness, using the word in its full sense, has come from youth. It is youth that has repeatedly broken the cake of custom, solved old enigmas, broken through to higher plateaus, pioneered in all realms, and in general advanced civilization. Exceptions certainly exist. Moreover, there is a special kind of leadership, in state, church, and other realms, that comes uniquely from the gifted aged. Think of Churchill's age when he assumed the prime ministership of Great Britain at the beginning of World War II, or of Adenauer's and de Gaulle's ages when, after the war, they remade their respective nations. A quality of wisdom and of spiritual strength comes in age that is not often found in the young and middle-aged. Nor is the record of the aged in the arts and sciences entirely bleak. Goethe was in his eighties when he wrote Part II of *Faust*. Haydn composed some of his finest works while in his seventies.

But all of these men had been brilliant and creative in their youth; the excellence found in their old age was thus in substantial degree excellence born in youth, manifested in youth, and then set deeply in habits and rhythms which could stand the test of time. In any event, great as Goethe was in his eighties, he was the first to admit that his creative energies had been vastly greater in his extraordinary youth. The same holds true for others in the arts and sciences.

The record is clear. In the history of invention, innovation, creative fashion, and discovery, youth is overwhelmingly the superior. What is notoriously true in mathematics, theoretical physics, and music—that unless high talent is achieved very early in life, it never will be—is at bottom almost as true of other areas of the arts and sciences. The individual who has not begun his creating and achieving in his twenties at the latest is unlikely ever to commence anything of consequence. Age may refine, add luster, mellow, and lend leadership to the arts and sciences, but it does not have, on the record, the capacity for great and novel attainments.

There should be no mystery in this. We commence aging from the time we are born. Physically we reach our highest powers in our twenties, and thereafter these powers begin to diminish quickly. Athletes are old and needing replacement by forty at the outside. Creativeness in the arts and sciences requires physical as well as mental strengths. Given the continuum of body and mind, it seems natural that the manifest decline in physical powers should be accompanied in some form and degree by decline in the powers which go into intellectual achievement. Age has knowledge and, sometimes, unique wisdom, but that is about all that can be said.

There always has been a kind of ecological relation between youth and age in society, a balance and proportionateness. But this balance threatens to vanish in the vast increase of the aged in the decades ahead, unaccompanied by any like phenomenon in youth, given the constantly lowering birth rates. From the point of view of youth and middle age, the presence of large numbers of the elderly, with their increasing sense of collective identity, their foisting of different styles and patterns upon the culture, and their expanding organization and political action, will surely seem like a giant pall. The aged will inevitably become a minority group possessed, on present indications, of all the lust for recognition and status that is seen in some of the ethnic minorities. Age will be at least as effective a unifier of ambitions and aspirations as color or religion.

It is not likely, or at least cannot be taken for granted, that the historic volume and intensity of the work ethic, the creativity drive, and the rage to innovation will hold up in youths who find themselves confronted for the first time in history with so vast an aggregate which must be supported economically by those in the diminished work force and which will inevitably leave the impression of a gerontocracy rather than a republic or democracy. Throughout the human past, the aged have been tolerated at best when their usefulness seemed ended or significantly decreased. Even within the ancient family system with its telescoping of the generations, conflicts could reach tragic proportions. Conflicts in the future can hardly be fewer when, in the absence of the old extended family, youth and age are arrayed against each other as two great classes, each with distinctive interests, needs, aspirations, and ideologies. The class conflict Marx saw and foresaw between labor and capital may well prove to be a class conflict between the working and the nonworking. At this mo-

ment the single most resented tax in American society is the constantly rising Social Security tax. At the end of 1981, 27.5 percent of
the federal budget went to the old-aged, a doubling of what was contained in the 1961 budget. Given the growth rates of the elderly and
the growth rates too of political acumen and economic demand, the
relationship between the two great classes cannot do other than grow
ever more bitter.

It is exceedingly unlikely that we shall revert to the practices of
our primitive and ancient forefathers, that is, deliberate depletion of
numbers when the aged threatened to become too numerous. Neither
are we likely to invoke a moratorium upon all scientific research that
leads to higher longevity. But there are indirect ways of accomplish-
ing results which were accomplished directly by the ancients, and if
the current, still largely potential conflict of interest between youth
and age, between the working and the nonworking, becomes significantly heightened as the ecological imbalance grows, there is a strong
possibility of overt war between the classes. It may well be that the
horrifying increase in assaults of the young upon the aged in modern
cities, assaults once virtually unknown, has in it some dreadful hint
of things to come.

ORIGINALITY

THIS IS AN AMBIGUOUS, if not treacherous, virtue. How fatuous the
writer, painter, designer, or inventor whose overriding aim is that of
being original, nothing more. Almost invariably this indicates a failure of objective, and if anything is salvageable, it is the aspect of the
work that is not original. The Ph.D. degree in America reaches the
peak of absurdity in its requirement that a dissertation be "an original work of scholarship." The results, with rare exception, have been
dismal since this degree became a *sine qua non* of academic life about
a century ago, just as William James and a few others warned at the
beginning. The candidates' frantic need to be original drives them
ever deeper into the recesses of the trivial or out to the margins of
the insignificant. What candidates should be set at, from the beginning of their study to the end, is cultivation of what already exists,
original or not, so long as it is important.

In the history of culture as well as in nature, the original is by no means always salutary. The two-headed calf at the county fair, the grossly fat child, the furless cat, are all originals which fortunately are usually unfertile or otherwise nonreproductive. Precisely the same has been true in the history of culture. The truly, conspicuously original painting, novel, musical composition, drama, or poem has failed of survival far oftener than it has succeeded. And this merits gratitude. It as though there operates in culture over time a process of selection analogous to that in nature which so carefully rejects the monstrous or condemns it to infertility.

The great works of art have never been original in the sense that a two-headed calf or a paint-splattering expressionist's canvas or a wildly atonal and dissonant sonata is original. Those who designed and brought to completion the Parthenon were certainly not seeking originality, only perfection under the laws of esthetics as then understood and piety in the eyes of the gods. The Impressionists of the late nineteenth and early twentieth century in France have repeatedly been hailed as revolutionary in their originality. They were one and all accomplished painters in the classical tradition, and their objective was to build upon or modify this tradition, bringing it to a different richness, rather than repudiating or disowning it. The great creators in all of the disciplines from art to physics have respected the past, learned all they possibly could of the past, and set themselves to fulfilling the past as Jesus did the law he had been born under. Admittedly, the results of such efforts can prove—as the Impressionists' canvases did, as Jesus's teachings did—revolutionary in impact. But this does not gainsay the truth that such revolutionary impact comes from seeking perfection or truth, not seeking originality in and for itself.

An invention is a novel rearrangement of existing ideas, substances, and techniques. Rarely is the completely new idea or substance the key to success, assuming such idea or substance has played any part at all. Planck "invented" the quantum theory, often described as the single most revolutionary development in modern physics, solely through a different reading of, and then fusion of, ideas which lay for all to see in the published literature in 1900. Nor was he for a moment seeking originality, only the solution of a classical problem that had eluded the efforts of others.

Neither he nor Einstein dismissed the past, radical though the results of each proved to be. Nor did Phidias and Praxiteles in their Greek sculpture, the Impressionists in their epochal canvases, or the Wright brothers in their final mastery of the flying machine. All of them possessed extraordinary knowledge of and insight into what others before had done, and all sought the solution to a recognized problem that had itself emerged from the past. It is always pleasant to think of something beautiful, brilliant, or ingenious as original, and in a valuable sense it is. But woe to the misguided who set out to be original, for verily they will produce a two-headed calf.

PERMISSIVENESS

THIS WORD IS an inelegant variation of a simple failure of will. Much of what is called permissiveness in modern times is no more than the quailing of the parent before the child, the ingratiation of the teacher into the brittle affections of the pupils, the referral to committee of what should be decided instantly by the executive, or the hand wringing of the judge who cannot bear to impose proper sentence upon the mugger or rapist. Western society is shot through with permissiveness, starting with the family, the natural authority of which has been preempted in large part by the bureaucratic state, thus leaving members of the family in uncertain roles. Permissiveness is not the cause, but the result, of the breakdown of authority. This is as true of the school, the university, the law court, and the local community as it is of the family. The dislocation of the historic authority of the school board by the federal bureaucracy and by activist federal judges leads inexorably to the failure of will of school board members, and of principals and teachers, even in the few areas that are left open to the exercise of such will.

Dislocation or preemption of authority by the state is the primary cause of permissiveness, but this malady has been stimulated by a generally loose morality which is itself the result of the insidious apothegm, "To understand all is to pardon all." That counsel might safely be left to God, but not to any living human being, nor to any institution. Freudian psychology, the virtual whole of sociology, and progressive education of the past few decades have all aided in the weakening of will in matters of authority. Each of these forces has laid heavy emphasis upon the nonresponsibility of the individual and the full responsibility of either an unmanageable id or a harsh and exploitative society. The result is the appalling failure of nerve in such institutions as school, local community, and university. The permissiveness of the parent and the teacher leads inevitably to an escalating permissiveness in other spheres of society—to judges setting low bail or dealing out light sentences, to university professors and deans passing inferior work, and to legislative bodies tolerating illicit behavior, however egregious, from one of its members.

Nor is the economy spared. Permissiveness on the part of plant foremen and general managers, as well as of chief executives, is to be seen in the astounding failures of quality in American manufacture, as compared with, say, Japan. Japan, happily for its productive efficiency, has enough remnants of feudalism left in its social order to undergird admirably the needs of the assembly line and the office.

Permissiveness is a recurrent phenomenon in history. Plato described and diagnosed it, though he labeled it democracy. When a state has degenerated from aristocracy to democracy, Plato observed, there is seen a breakdown of roles and of the authorities set in these roles. Lacking the protection or reassurance of traditional roles, individuals, largely through either fear or effrontery, make strange liaisons or indulge in bizarre behavior. Thus "the father habitually tries to resemble the child and is afraid of his sons, and the son likens himself to the father and feels no awe or fear of his parents so that he may be forsooth a free man. And the resident alien feels himself equal to the citizen and the citizen to him, and the foreigner likewise . . . The teacher in such case fears and fawns upon the pupils, and the pupils pay no heed to the teacher or to their overseers either. And in general the young ape their elders and vie with them in speech and action, while the old, accommodating themselves to the young, are full of pleasantry and graciousness, imitating the young for fear that they may be thought disagreeable and authoritative."

"Disagreeable and authoritative"—no imagining of one's public self is more horrid to contemplate than that in the present day as in Plato's. To be authoritative in one's job is to run the dread risk of being thought an "authoritarian personality," and that, it may be remembered by those familiar with the now defunct Frankfort School in the social sciences, could easily lead to fascism. Such nonsense seems not to have been part of American thought prior to half a century ago. It is doubtful that Presidents of the United States and heads of great business and professional organizations were haunted by the specter of authoritarianism. Far better, it was believed, to be thought too authoritative than too indulgent or too lax in standards of others' performance. Whether as schoolteacher, foreman, or military commander, the reputation of being hard or tough was generally a good reputation.

For the cause of this fear of and flight from anything resembling exercise of authority in government, industry, the schools, and the family, one must again go to Plato. The cause is, in a word, equality.

True liberty, he explained, turns into license or permissiveness when liberty is obliged to fuse with equality. The craving for equality and the hatred or resentment of difference in rank lead to generalized envy and distrust of authority in any form. Those who obey the governors of the state out of a sense of patriotism are, Plato observed, "reviled as willing slaves and men of nought, but opinion commends and honors in public and private rulers who resemble subjects and subjects who are like rulers."

From Plato comes also prevision of the fate reserved for the permissive and their charges: tyranny. For under egalitarian democracy, people learn to "pay no heed even to the laws, written or unwritten, so that forsooth they may have no master anywhere over them." And this, Plato concluded, "is the fine and vigorous root from which tyranny grows."

Permissiveness is eventually swallowed up by some form of tyranny because the time comes when it has nothing left to feed upon. As, one after another, the constituted authorities erode away under the acids of egalitarianism, the time is reached when there is nothing any longer to be permissive about. Permissiveness is like secularism in this respect, tonic only as long as there is still a solid wall of the sacred against which to tilt. It is not the crumbling of individual freedoms so much as of social authorities that leads finally to despots.

PROGRESS

THERE ARE AT LEAST two misconceptions about this historic idea: first, that it is a uniquely modern idea, and second, that its rise is the consequence of secularism, of Western thought's liberation from Christian theology. But the truth is that the idea originated in classical Greece and subsequently achieved its fullest expression in Christian philosophy of history. It is in fact the general weakening of the Christian foundations of Western culture that explains much of the parlous state in which this once-grand idea now lies.

The origins of the idea lie among Greek recreations of their own past. A strong intimation of the belief in progress is found in Homer, specifically in Odysseus' contemplation of the dread Cyclopes, their own primitivism appearing to him much like what the Greeks themselves had known long ago. At the end of the sixth century B.C., Xenophanes wrote, "The gods did not reveal to men all things from the beginning, but men through their own search find in the course of time that which is better." Growth, slow, gradual, and continuous, is the essence of that statement. In Athens' golden age, the fifth century B.C., philosophy, history, literature, and art are rich in their evocations of a very long past in which man ascended from the cultural void to present grandeur. Aeschylus, Sophocles, Protagoras, Thucydides, and Socrates are among the many lustrous minds which lauded human advancement through the ages. Plato referred to progress that took place "little by little" over "an immense and incredible time."

What the Greeks first set forth the Romans, particularly Lucretius and Seneca, expanded upon and made systematic. Not until the eighteenth century does there appear again such a richly anthropological statement of human progress over the ages as provided by Lucretius, who indeed first used the word *progress*, in the phrase *pedetemtim progredientes*, literally, "step-by-step progression." For Seneca, progress in past, present, and future is the subject of numerous discourses and random reflections.

What the pagan classical philosophers began, the Christians continued and substantially added to. Not only was the Greco-Roman emphasis upon the progress of knowledge through past and present incorporated in key works of the Church Fathers—Tertullian, Eusebius, and most puissantly Saint Augustine—forming what Augustine called "the education of the human race" ever since Creation and the Fall, but it was set alongside another and potentially far grander envisagement of spiritual and moral progress, culminating in, not simply an eternal and blissful heaven, but before that a millennium of paradise on earth, under the governance of a returned Christ. Christianity united the Greek belief in natural growth through time with the Jewish conception of sacred history, that is, history that could not have been other than it actually was. From this union came the Christian, largely Augustinian, belief in historical necessity. Another momentous Christian perspective is that of the unity of all mankind, the ecumenical ideal. In this case the protagonist is not just a single chosen or destined people, Jews or Romans, but all mankind, made one by the single creation of Adam.

All of the essential ideas involved in the philosophy of progress—slow, gradual, and continuous advance through time of all mankind, in a pattern of successively higher stages of development, the whole process revealing necessity, direction, and purpose—are to be found in the Christian philosophy of history. From Augustine down to the modern world, with the exception of the Renaissance, when cyclical conceptions of history crowded out the linear scheme inherent in the idea of progress, these ideas have been powerful in impact, adhered to by some of the greatest minds in Western history. At no time was the vision of progress and of a glorious millennium on earth, with all mankind rich in both knowledge and spiritual joy, more resplendent than in the Puritan mind of the seventeenth century on both sides of the Atlantic. The Puritans joined together, as they had never been joined before, the two ideas of advancing knowledge, meaning the arts and sciences, and advancing morality and spirituality. To a Newton or a Boyle, the cultivation of scientific knowledge was vital as the means of hastening the onset of the millennium, which they and their contemporaries chose to see in strikingly secular terms.

The move from the Christian to the "modern" conception of progress was short and uncomplicated. Providence retreated farther and farther into the background, but what is really vital in the idea of human advancement—past, present, and future seen as a long, continuous unfolding, an intellectual, cultural, social, and moral ascent to the ever better—was stated not much differently by a nonbelieving Condorcet in the late eighteenth century than by his distinctly religious predecessors Bodin, Vico, and Leibniz. Moreover, even in the Enlightenment, Christianity and with it the Christian epic of progress could flourish, as in Lessing, Herder, and Kant. Turgot provided insight into the whole process. His own personal intellectual history was, so to speak, ontogeny to the phylogeny of the larger history of the idea of progress. After he entered the Sorbonne to train for the Catholic clergy, his first notable address, in July 1750, dealt with the progress of Christianity and the causal effect of this progress upon the whole progress of man. Everything he said suggested a still-dedicated Christian. But by December of that year, when he presented his second public address, on the "successive advances of the human mind," often declared the first statement of the "modern" idea of progress, there was much less stress upon Christianity and much more on natural causes, though even here religion, specifically Christianity, received tribute.

The nineteenth century is without question the preeminent epoch in the long history of the idea of progress. Not only was the idea the cornerstone of the new social sciences—sociology, anthropology, political science, economics, and psychology—each seeking the crucial causes and stages of a progress that none of them questioned, but it became a popular faith on the scale of a religion. "Laws" of progress were seen everywhere: by Comte in his "social dynamics," by Saint-Simon in his new Christianity, by political economists in the notion of economic liberty based on private property and competition as the purpose of the laws of human progress, and at the opposite pole, by Marx and Engels in the gradual, stage-by-stage ascent of human history, through class conflict, to an eventual classless communism with private property and profit gone forever. Spencer summed up the prevailing view of progress among social philosophers: "Progress . . . is not an accident but a necessity." In or out of Christian context, faith in mankind's advance to an ever better future assumed the same kind of evangelical zeal, especially among the American masses, that is associated with religion.

The idea, again *pace* conventional wisdom, did not "die with the nineteenth century" nor was it "killed by World War I." Belief in the certainty and inexorability of progress was never more compelling than during the first four or five decades of the twentieth century. Whether presented in the rhetoric of classical liberalism with its stress on the free market, in the rhetoric of the new liberalism with its emphasis upon the state and political planning, or in the jargon of the ever-enlarging socialist and communist spheres, the idea of the progress of mankind remained luminous through World War I and even the Great Depression. Powerful minds in a diversity of intellectual areas, including Hayek, Julian Huxley, Charles Darwin, and Chardin, argued with all the eloquence and conviction of their forebears in the eighteenth and nineteenth centuries on human progress. The idea is currently moribund, but by no means yet dead.

Its current fragile and faded condition in Western thought cannot be accounted for by war, economic depression, or comparable ills and torments. Through twenty-five centuries the idea was rugged enough to survive such conditions, including famine, plague, and appalling poverty. More fundamental causes are necessary to explain the debility of an idea possessed of the antiquity and ubiquity of the idea of progress. These causes are found in the crucial loss of belief in the second half of the twentieth century in the premises of the idea of progress. No major idea, whether salvation, revolution, equality, or freedom, can survive the erosion and disappearance of the assumptions or axioms on which the idea rests.

The idea of progress, from the time of the Greeks down to the beginning of the twentieth century, was closely associated with myth, ritual, religion, or concepts such as the *Zeitgeist* and the dialectic in the nineteenth century which are surrogates for religious creed. The idea was, in short, born of religion in the classical world, sustained by religion from the third century on, and now threatens to die from the loss of religious sustenance. For no century in Western history has proved to be as nonreligious, irreligious, and antireligious in its major currents of philosophy, art, literature, and science as is the twentieth. Faith in progress cannot long last when its historical foundations have weakened or dissolved.

But the idea of progress has suffered other vital losses of premise in this age. First is the effective loss of the past as an integral, remembered part of the present. Through loss of ritual, ceremony, public commemoration, respect for or even interest in ancestors and their ways of life, and history in the classic, traditional sense of the story of past and present, the contemporary world has been deprived of one of the vital dimensions of the idea of progress: a respected past from which a more illustrious present has emerged, thus making possible real hope for an ever more illustrious future.

Another loss is the displacement of the West in the current scene. Western civilization cannot for a moment be thought to have the kind of eminence and dominance in the world that it knew from roughly the fifteenth century on. And from the very beginning in the history of the idea of progress, from the Greeks through the Romans, the Church Fathers, and all their successors, the supremacy of Greece, Rome, and then Europe under Christianity was taken for granted. Such supremacy can no longer be taken for granted or indeed entertained seriously. A powerful "second world," led by the Soviet Union, and an increasingly prominent and aggressive "third world" make thought of the West's automatic and assured preeminence mere nonsense.

Still another loss is the changed attitude, especially among intellectuals, toward economic development throughout the world. An increasing number of intellectuals, inspired by environmentalism, by unalloyed hatred of economic prosperity and its cultural and intellectual byproducts, or by other values and causes, have adopted a position of hostility to further economic growth. Such a hostility is bound to extend to the perspective of progress, one of whose foundations has from the beginning been economic and social improvement.

And the last loss relates to an intellectual mood which could not possibly have been foreseen even three decades ago, the mood of disenchantment and disillusionment with technology and science. More and more these two great forces, no matter how fruitful to human comfort, decency, health, and happiness they may once have been, are seen today as far more lethal in consequence than life-giving, bringing nuclear radiation, toxic chemicals in air, ground, and water, industrial waste, spoliation of the earth's mantle by technological depredations that destroy vital ecosystems, and most horrifying in prospect, earthly catastrophe resulting from science-spawned atomic weapons of almost indescribable destructiveness.

These fundamental losses largely explain the current malaise of the belief in progress. The question now is whether the idea of progress, once a powerful intellectual force behind Western civilization's spectacular achievements, once a very dogma in Western life and a popular faith rivaling Christianity itself, is likely to pass from moribundity to death, or whether there is ground to hope for its renewal and wide reaffirmation. The answer can be short and quick. The idea is dead as long as its vital premises are dead. But if these become somehow revived, then there is the very high probability of the rediscovery of one of the West's oldest and most fertile ideas.

PSYCHOBABBLE

THERE ARE THOSE, wrote the ancient sage, who know and know that they know; those who know and know not that they know; those who know not and know not that they know not; and those who know not and know that they know not. That adage has to be rewritten for the modern day. The more conventional wording would now be: there are those who feel and feel that they feel; those who feel and feel not that they feel; those who feel not and feel not that they feel not; and saddest of all on the scene today, those who feel not and feel that they feel not.

For these last unfortunates there is by now a vast culture in America that ministers. In lectures, encounters, retreats, clinics, meditation groups, and psychobabble best-sellers, these forlorn souls are addressed. Psychobabble is the pidgin formed over the last few decades from scraps and morsels of clinical psychology, sociology, and liberal theology, the test of acceptance in this pidgin being wholehearted concern with feelings, emotions, awarenesses, and awarenesses of awarenesses of self, the me, the ego. Subjectivism is the politest word to give to this culture of the self and to the pidgin spoken.

"Epochs which are regressive," said Goethe to Eckermann, "and in process of dissolution, are always subjective, whereas the trend in all progressive epochs is objective." The word *subjectivism* only barely gives the flavor, however, of the modern age of self-spelunking, ego diving, and awareness intoxication. Novelists and playwrights have made small fortunes out of public exposure of their psychogenitalia. The compulsion to expose such parts is particularly fierce in the breed known as creative writers, indigenous largely to college and university campuses of America. Most of them, knowing little else but a lifetime in the closet of academia, have nothing else to write about but themselves—their early toilet training, coatroom sex experimentation, and the rest of the *Sturm und Drang* of the typical academic's biography.

But the culture of psychobabble is everywhere in the modern age, not least in some of the social sciences. The ultimate goal of sociology, intoned a leading mandarin, is "the deepening of the sociologist's own awareness of who and what he is in a specific society at a given time." As a goal, that one would not have interested Marx, Weber, and Durkheim, to be sure, but it is about par for what is today delicately referred to as "humanistic sociology." That prince of psychobabbling caretakers of the unconscious, R. D. Laing, won wide renown among intellectuals for his praise of states of consciousness which derive from "our looking at ourselves, but also by our looking at others looking at us and our reconstitution and alteration of these views of others looking at us." That is not one of Laing's famous schizophrenics talking; that is Laing himself, in pristine psychobabble. The greatest single difference between the old left and the new left of the 1960s lay in the latter's ineradicable fondness for the pre- and nonrational states of mind, ogled by no one better than by Reich and Roszak. Any members of the old left worth their salt would have used economics as the base of their several stages denoting the progress of society toward socialism; but not the psychobabblers of the 1960s and 1970s, for whom it was Consciousness I, Consciousness II, and so forth.

It is no wonder, given the culture that produced these gems of psychobabble, that special forms of wisdom are found in the minds of schizophrenics and others similarly set apart from reality. If the truest experience is direct experience of self, unmediated, untrammeled by use of the conscious rational mind, then it follows that there is much to learn from those in asylums whose renunciation of the external world of reality is almost total.

A friendly symbiosis has been reached today between the schools and the cultivation of psychobabble by teenagers. Very little is now taught about the external world, its history, its geography and place in the universe, for this would tax the minds of pupils accustomed from infancy to being asked in loving detail by their parents about their views on all that comes up in the household and the outer world. Expose them to a course in which it does not matter an iota what their feelings are about the subject, and their eyes glaze over. Desperate at the thought of losing them, the teacher quickly adapts the course to intimate discussion rather than serious learning. Thus the riot of courses in schools and colleges on self-development, realization of potential, sexual and psychosexual fulfillment, meditation awareness, with advanced courses ahead on awareness of awareness, all calculated to anesthetize the individual pupil from the pain of recognition of self or anything else. At one illustrious university campus an entire program exists on the nature and history of consciousness, the proudest claim for the program being that only a minimum of reading is involved. And at another university something called ethnomethodology is taught, or rather transmitted through feeling, in which, through long silences, nocturnal retreats, and a special psychobabble that requires months to learn, reality is finally perceived for what it is: a psychosocial ocean formed of wave upon wave of personal and interpersonal awarenesses.

An affecting story epitomizes the natural affinity between certain babbles. A young woman majored in something called eco-feminism at a university and graduated with honors. She betook herself to Washington, D.C., knowing that the city is alive with lobbies for ecology and feminism alike, and assuming that a well-paying job would be waiting for anyone, armed as she was with such duality of being. But even ecological and feminist lobbies require people who can read, write, count, and in general ratiocinate; she thus became one of the large number of genteel unemployables.

The conditioning supplied by psychobabble was what made it easy for educators to commence lauding black English a few years back, the barbaric syntax and impoverished vocabulary of this alleged language notwithstanding—or actually held up in some quarters as a model of linguistic directness. After all, if language and culture have been breached by the celebration of affective states in which reason, logic, and grammar play no roles, little further harm is done by pretending that black English is a language.

There is every reason to believe that psychobabble is, or will shortly become, the *lingua franca* of the age. Someone of a perverse turn of mind once made a color movie that consisted of nothing but the sight of food being chewed in an individual's mouth, the camera sensitive to every shape, sound, and color of what was being masticated and swallowed. Revolting? Not nearly so revolting as the lecture, column, tract, novel, and drama in which every conceivable opportunity is seized for exploration and dramatization of the most intimate parts of the author's or his audience's mind.

Socrates is sometimes blasphemously invoked as the founder of the cult of me. He said, "Know thyself." But the founder of Socratic rationalism had mind and reason foremost in his thinking when he said this. Were Socrates alive today and obliged to teach in any ordinary school, to fill out report cards long on traits of self, short on those of mind, and to adjust himself generally to the age of psychobabble, he would surely say, "Explore thyself." And this his pupils would be willing to do and to continue doing, the while they sought out forest and seashore where, uniting psychobabble and ecobabble, they could meditate as druids clothed in Calvin Klein.

PSYCHOHISTORY

THIS OFFENSIVE WORD serves as label for an even more offensive practice in the contemporary writing of history. That is the use of concepts drawn overwhelmingly from clinical study of the mentally ill to explain the public acts and decisions of major individuals in history and, even worse, the condition or behavior of whole social classes and even nations.

That historians should be interested in the motives and other springs of action in the great and illustrious is hardly matter for wonder. From ancient times, in ritual and tragedy, in commentary and chronicle, in written and unwritten literature, the lives of kings and emperors inevitably invited speculation on what would today be referred to variously as their unconscious, underlying, instinctual cravings or patterns of behavior, ranging from the eccentric to the pathological. Plutarch marveled at such patterns, fascinated both by Alexander's relation to his mother and by Julius Caesar's bizarre dressing habits. Much of the early Herodotus is taken up with musings over character defects or peculiarities and their effect upon great events or decisions.

To this day historians continue to relish explorations of a biographical-psychological kind. The greatest historians are generally the most successful in making their subjects' minds and characters harmonious with their deeds, thus bringing the *dramatis personae* alive. May this quest for understanding continue forever; may there be an unbroken succession of new Lincolns to add to those portrayed by Charnwood, Sandburg, and Thomas; may the contradictions, inconsistencies, and conflicts which exist in all powerful minds be studied and written about to the end of time.

But in their own terms, not in terms which have been dragged in from the psychiatric clinic. The psychoanalyst requires many hours of continuing, direct, personal analysis in order to reach the depths of the patient's conscious and unconscious mind. It is therefore shocking to assume, on the basis of writings, paintings, letters, diaries, memoirs, and biographies of the great, who often lived hundreds of years ago, that complex concepts from the sick room can be made to serve as solemn explanations of their acts and decisions or, worse, as explanations of whole movements and epochs.

Consider Eriksen's presumptuous study of not just Luther but the Protestant Reformation. This tumultuous and traumatic set of events has defied the efforts of the greatest historians, not one of whom has thought of reducing the age to the thoughts and seizures of one man, not even a man of Luther's genius. Even less would a true historian consider making a single alleged state of personality, a psychological complex, the root of the great religious, political, and economic transformation. But where historians fear to tread, clinical psychologists break into a run. Thus Eriksen, psychoanalyst of sorts, employs the concept of identity crisis to throw light on first Luther and then the Reformation.

This concept came into Eriksen's mind when he was working with psychiatric cases in veterans' hospitals just after World War II. He thought that at the bottom of many of the nervous diseases which had been precipitated by war's trauma there lay a stubborn incapacity on the part of the ill veteran to recognize his own real identity— who he was and what he was. From this asserted discovery, Eriksen made his way to the conviction that some degree of identity crisis is suffered by everyone, and that in some individuals this form of crisis can be devouring. The most extraneous of acts and decisions can be put into the pigeonhole of identity crisis. This is the pigeonhole where Eriksen put the young Luther. Like all young men, Luther suffered a crisis of identity, except that his, Eriksen claimed, was so wracking, so convulsive, and so imperious that nothing less than revolt against Rome would resolve the crisis. Hence the multifold and spectacular events of Luther's life; hence the Protestant Reformation.

Given the fascination of the psychological, this interpretation provides the satisfaction, brief though it is, of reducing a towering complexity to something as simple, often banal, and as immediately recognizable as an identity crisis. More than a few readers will go through life convinced that a young man's identity crisis in the sixteenth century resulted in nothing less than the Protestant Reformation. Carlyle's vision of history as governed by heroes has at least the merit of recognizing the great for what they are. Not as much can be said for visions which seek to bring heroes down to the level of clinical patients.

But far worse than pseudo-explanations of individuals in history through the long-distance use of concepts born in the mental clinic are pseudo-explanations of such social aggregates as classes, ethnic groups, even whole nations. This practice did not begin with Freud, who confined his long-distance lines to Leonardo and Wilson and a few other individuals, biographically and biologically oriented as he was. Perhaps the practice began in the 1930s when Marxists sought to give a veneer of the psychological to their rough social and economic determinism by transferring Freudian concepts from individuals to the same social categories from which Marx had rigorously excluded individuals. Thus Oedipal hatreds and strivings were seen in the proletarian, jealous of distribution of commodities, and ready to attack his capitalist father. Since, it was argued, Freud had placed what were in fact social complexes in the unconscious mind of the individual, thus making them consequences of biological inheritance, the proper strategy was to apply to social groups concepts which Freud had buried in the id. Explanations of Nazism ranged all the way from the "castration complex" suffered by the German nation when it was separated by the Polish Corridor from East Prussia, to the "repressed conflicts" long buried in the German people's collective id going back to the time when the Germanic barbarians had entered the Roman Empire. Explanations of Nazism as the emergence of elements of a Teutonic "dark unconscious" were almost as common in the 1930s as were explanations of Nazism as an atavistic reversion to medievalism.

These are extreme instances and would only embarrass a Marxist-Freudian or Freudian-Marxist of the 1980s. But ever since the spirits of Marx and Freud were brought together in the 1930s, the temptation to arrange for final consummation has been present. Thus when a historian argues that during the *fin de siécle* in Vienna the Jewish bourgeoisie had Oedipal strivings toward the Austro-Hungarian fatherland, it is evidence that psychohistory flourishes. To be sure, the question remains what kind of Freudian strivings lay in the Jewish proletariat. All such treatments, monstrous or banal, are perfect illustrations of Fowler's "slipshod extension," monuments to the kind of credulity that is excited whenever catch phrases like "class struggle" or "Oedipus complex" begin circulating among intellectuals in the modern West.

But one should not end on a negative note. Authentic psychohistory can be found. It appears in autobiographies, especially those of the genius of Saint Augustine and Rousseau, and in biographies of the excellence found in Boswell on Johnson, Lockhart on Scott, and Freeman on Lee. Add to these such studies of a given creative work as that of Lowes on Coleridge's *Kubla Khan*. What they all have in common, apart from the authors' genius, is a willingness to accept what Bacon called "the multitude of particulars" and to withstand the seductive appeal of boneless, puncture-proof, self-sealing abstractions—especially those drawn from the clinic.

PUBLIC OPINION

SIR HENRY MAINE wrote, "*Vox Populi* may be *Vox Dei*, but very little attention shows that there never has been any agreement as to what *Vox* means or as to what *Populus* means." So it is today with public opinion. Thousands of polls are taken in America every year in the efforts of politicians, manufacturers, media executives, and social scientists to ascertain what people think about issues, goods, and personalities. What is elicited by the polls and processed by computers is gravely referred to as public opinion. It is rarely that, however, and far oftener not public but popular opinion. The difference is great and, in the long run, crucial to democracy.

A true public is at bottom a community, constructed, as are all genuine communities, around certain ends held in common and supported by traditions, myths, and rituals which are the yield of a common history. The people as such do not form a public. Neither does any majority or any minority form a public if the individuals involved do not participate in what Burke called a "constitutional spirit," that is, a consensus fashioned by consciously held ends, purposes, and rules of procedure and, equally important, by unconsciously held values which are the products of a respected past. It is impossible to exaggerate the importance of the past, not as a temporal abstraction, but as something cherished, respected, and depended upon in the present. More than anything else, it is America's separation from the past, through the erosion and atomization of rituals once celebrated, through the displacement of history as a discipline in school, and through futile and vaporous flirtations with the future, that makes true public opinion almost impossible to find.

What America has in abundance is popular opinion, which is by nature shallow of root, a creature of the crowd or mass, anchored in the fashions and follies of the marketplace. Popular opinion necessarily lacks the cement that time and convention alone can provide; it is in constant flux, appearing and disappearing like the froth on an ocean wave. Its ease of ascertainment by pollsters is in direct proportion to its superficiality. Merely name the subject, and an instant opinion will be had, an opinion no doubt forgotten before the day is out, but an opinion that, when joined by the computer to many others on the same subject, can be presented solemnly as "public" opinion, which of course it is not.

Public and popular opinion are not totally unconnected. What proves to be public opinion on a given matter is generated initially by opinions popularly held, but it is only through processes of adaptation and assimilation, involving the sturdy filter of long-shared values and traditions, that true collective, or public, opinion comes into being. What Justice Holmes said of sound judgment may be said with equal force about public opinion: it comes "out of experience and under the spur of responsibility." When the feelings, passions, and perceptions of the crowd become transmuted into the convictions, however dimly articulated, of the public, of the political community, public opinion may be said to exist.

The distinction between popular and public opinion is more easily discerned in retrospect, when Hegel's owl of Minerva flies, than when the distinction is a matter of immediate necessity. But there is no surer sign of the great leader, especially in politics and statecraft, than a capacity to identify true public opinion and avoid the snares of popular opinion. To call the roll of the great leaders in the history of Western civilization—Pericles, Augustus, Cromwell, Washington, Lincoln, Churchill—is to single out men not only of superlative inner resources but also of uncanny ability to distinguish between public and popular opinion.

From the time of the Constitution's creation in America, the mainstream of political thought in this country has recognized the crucial importance of knowing the one from the other. There is no want of deference to the will and wisdom of the people in the Constitution, but there is deep distrust of popular opinion. Hence it protects the true public from the multitude through such devices as the electoral college for the selection of President and Vice-President, the indirect election of senators, and the mode of amending the Constitution. Madison firmly dissented from Jefferson's proposal for a quicker and simpler means of calling a constitutional convention, arguing that revision of the Constitution should be possible, but not easy. If such a convention could be quickly brought into existence, it doubtless would be, and the ease of the operation would in time become tempting in its own right, thus diminishing respect for the Constitution, for the branches of government it established, and not least for the amending process itself. At such easily called constitutional conventions, Madison observed, "the *passions* . . . not the *reason* of the public would sit in judgment."

Tocqueville may have exaggerated the "tyranny of the majority" in the American governmental process, but he did not exaggerate the dangers of rule by the majority unchecked by either institutions or constitutional safeguards. And where he saw the "omnipotence of the majority" at work was not in the federal government but in the states: "The authors of the Federal Constitution worked . . . to hobble the march of the majority. In the individual states, on the contrary, men strove to render it more rapid and more irresistible." Tocqueville's fear was not of public opinion as expressed through constituted legal and political channels. The danger lay not in a majority forming around a given political issue or personage, which is the essence of the democratic process, but rather in those seizures of collective opinion which by their suddenness, irrationality, and ultimate fragility bespeak the mass and the crowd. The Constitution would, through its prescribed channels, receive for the most part the judgments of the public, not the multitude or mass. It was in the areas of life outside the constitutional-political-legal sphere, areas of mind and morality, that the mass of people were most likely, Tocqueville thought, to "glide with the stream of the crowd and find it hard to maintain alone an opinion abandoned by the rest."

Because of the incessant pressure today of an increasingly hedonistic and materialistic society upon a political structure that was designed to rest upon a very different set of moral and social values, ascertainment of public opinion has become fraught with difficulties and uncertainties. As the multitude presses on the historic national community, as the crowd assaults the public, fissures appear in the body politic which rapidly become abysses. The rupture of the social contract, seen in family, church, and locality, has been leading for more than half a century to a rupture of the political contract that was signed in 1787.

The pathetic decline since Theodore Roosevelt of political leadership in the United States is no doubt due in part to defects of nurture in those who have sought to lead. But this decline has to be attributed in part to the social and political maelstrom that even a Washington or Lincoln would have found difficult to cope with. That both of these Presidents read correctly public opinion in their respective ages permits no doubt. Popular opinion was opposed to a war for independence in 1776; and popular opinion was equally opposed to a war in behalf of the Union and of emancipation of the slaves in 1860. The genius of each President was to make his way through these currents and cross-currents of popular opinion to the opinion that flowed from the true public, from those who lived and knew that they lived in a political community.

But the task of making one's way to public opinion today is an almost impossible one, and not the puniest of inhabitants of the Presidency can be wholly faulted. Huge though the problems faced by Washington and Lincoln were, they existed in the context of a real public whose real opinion could be read and acted upon. That is scarcely the case now in America. In the first place the actual public itself has shrunk. Second, between what is left of the public and the eye of the would-be leader is a vast cloud of popular opinions, ranging from the narcissistic and hedonistic to the fanatically idealistic. The country has lost its great political parties, gaining in their stead a chartless jungle of deadly single-interest groups for each of which the public and the republic alike are important chiefly for their instrumental value. As Lippmann observed: "It is often assumed, but without warrant, that the opinions of The People as voters can be treated as the expression of The People as a historic community. The crucial problem of modern democracy arises from the fact that this assumption is false. The voters cannot be relied upon to represent The People ... Because of the discrepancy between The People as voters and The People as corporate nation, the voters have no title to consider themselves as proprietors of the commonwealth and to claim that their interests are identical with the public interest. Prevailing plurality of the voters are not The People."

Lippmann's words bring to mind the concept of "stake in society" that is properly associated with the American Revolution in contrast to the French. Those who led the American war of liberation were without exception planters, shippers, businessmen, and lawyers, all with solid economic and social interest in their revolutionary actions. They could lead American public opinion because they were and had been among the shapers of this opinion, less by virtue of any specific political action than by virtue of their regular economic, social, and political roles in the social order. Very different was the position of the French leaders with respect to the nation. They had little stake in the society they sought to lead so far afield from its roots. They were for the most part, in Burke's words, "new dealers," interested not in what the people in the corporate, historical sense wanted, only in what they themselves wanted, whether actuated by pure reason, by humanitarianism, or by eagerness to convert paper wealth into land.

The reason both *vox* and *populus* are difficult to read today, even by the most astute political leaders, lies in the fact that too many of those who participate in the political process are without genuine stake in society. In this they are like those who governed the course of the French Revolution, either rootless and easily swayed or else seeking to impose, under the guise of public interest lobby, their own wills upon the nation. The American Constitution is still fundamentally what it was at the time of its ratification. What has changed is the nation, moving from a national community to a mere aggregate of particles occasionally magnetized into short-lived crusade, but for the most part passive and inert.

R ACISM

THIS AFFLICTION OF THE MIND, in both its malign and benign forms, is a product of modernity, the spawn of the Reformation and the Enlightenment. The ancient world assuredly knew its divisions of mankind based upon ethnic descent. But such divisions were more nearly religious than racial. It was distrust or fear of alien gods that drove the Israelites to their numerous wars. Skin color seems not to have mattered, save as possible indicator of something far more important. The same was true of the Greeks and the Romans, in each of whom there were "barbarians" who as slaves looked scarcely different from their masters and in both of whom there were honored citizens whose forebears had been captured and dealt with as barbarian slaves. Language, culture, and submission to the mores were far more important than color or physiognomy. Saint Augustine was insistent upon the unity of mankind. There was but one genesis. God created only one man, "not certainly that he might be a solitary, bereft of all society, but that by this means the unity of society and the bond of concord might be more effectually commended to him, men being bound together not only by similarity of nature but by family affection." Moreover, God took care to avoid creating woman separately and directly but "created her out of the man, that the human race might derive from one man." Whatever the divisions of the ancient and medieval worlds, they were not based upon belief in some phylogenetic odium that resisted all spiritual and cultural influence.

It was in the Reformation that things began to change significantly. Doctrines of polygenesis mushroomed, and the Augustinian dream of the unity of the human race was finally defeated. In their reading of the Old Testament, the followers of Zwingli, Luther, and Calvin matched the enemies of God's chosen people with accounts of strange and distant peoples on earth they had heard of or read about for generations. It was almost inevitable that those of black skin would be singled out as special bearers of odium, for with the collapse of the idea of monogenesis along with the unity of Christendom, there was little left but racial and ethnic identities with which to be concerned, and of these the ones most different in appearance were bound to bear the brunt of Western exploitation. Such peoples were beyond the pale, and entitled to, at most, protective servitude. The rise of the slave trade came from many forces, but the spreading belief in the genetic inequality between black and white could cite Scripture for confirmation of a sort.

With the Enlightenment came first ideas of evolution and of unequal development of the several races on earth. Again, it was inevitable that the black would be placed lower in the evolutionary hierarchy, given the profound cultural differences between Africa and Europe. Moreover, at about this time the great apes of Africa were discovered by Europeans. The European mind, already fevered by evolutionary imaginings, saw these animals as the proximate ancestors of what were deemed to be the lower orders of the human race. One member of the Scottish Enlightenment, the vastly learned Monboddo, specifically linked the orangutan of Africa and the Negro.

Adding to the tendency to place blacks very low in the human chain of being and evolutionary scale was the cult of Greco-Roman art with its fixed criterion of all that was good and beautiful. Those most unlike the figures revealed in white marble statuary were deemed the ugliest and least likely to be of good descent. Paralleling this fixation on Greek and Roman beauty was the rise of "scientific" interest in measurements of both body and mind. The rise of malign racism was made inevitable, in sum, by the polygenetic theories of evolution, the cult admiration of Greek and Roman bodies in marble, and the belief that science through measurement and calculation could fix upon true superiority and inferiority.

There is thus nothing novel about the spread in the nineteenth century of racist philosophies, the most notorious of which was Gobineau's. Tocqueville, who admired and liked Gobineau in many ways and corresponded with him for years, could not stomach Gobineau's doctrines and wrote with fervor against all such "determinisms," asking Gobineau what he thought would be the condition of the French if early Roman thoughts of the inferiority of the peoples of Gaul had hardened into insurmountable bonds of servitude. Gobineau, Chamberlain, and their numerous disciples, chiefly but by no means exclusively in Germany, were most responsible for racist conceptions which spread all over the world with the expansion of Western influence and power. Invariably in these conceptions, those most different in measurable attributes of body or manner were placed lower in the scale of races. The white, blond, and tall were usually at the very top, their physical features made symbolic of inherent cultural and political virtues, and in descending order came the darker, shorter, and squarer-visaged peoples, with those of Africa, sometimes also parts of Oceana, at the bottom. These "scientific" rankings of the races encouraged slave owners in America and elsewhere to feel comforted in their domination of the black, so evidently at the bottom of the evolutionary scale.

The fascination with race and its measurement grew rapidly in the latter part of the nineteenth century. In France, Germany, and the United States, tests were abundant by which to place the innumerable peoples on earth into different main stocks or races—Caucasian, Asiatic, Negroid, and so forth. The old doctrine of separate species in biology was given new life, so to speak, in the doctrine of the separateness of races on earth. Rare indeed was the school or college in the West by the early twentieth century that did not have in it a multicolored chart of the races of mankind, each limned as distinctly as were animals and birds. The intelligence test craze reached its height in the same era, basically a product of French preoccupation with races but quick to surge in both England and the United States. Once again the IQs of peoples most unlike the Europeans, especially the sainted Nordics, Anglo-Saxons, and their nearest relatives, were found almost invariably far below the IQs of the chosen. Belief in the heritability of the IQ reached almost fanatic intensity in the United States, where fear of miscegenation with the blacks also reached psychotic proportions. Just as children were segregated by color, so now were they segregated in many schools, irrespective of color, by IQ, deemed to be permanent and inescapable.

Malign racism is the conviction that separation of one kind or other, whether in schools, theaters, streetcars, or residential zones, is not only expedient but justified by the science of race and racial intelligence. Malign racism has not yet disappeared; perhaps it never will. As Tocqueville observed, if many centuries were required in Europe to erase the social and legal discriminations against serfs and their progeny, all of whom were of the same racial stock as their lords, many millennia will doubtless be necessary to erase discriminations when directed against peoples of different physical stock.

What has taken place, unhappily, is not the erasure but the reversal of discrimination. This is benign racism. It too has its roots in the Enlightenment and then in the Benthamite creed of total social reconstruction by omnipotent magistrates expressing the real will of the people, the will that antiquated legislatures, elections, and other representative mechanisms could never, in Bentham's imagination, come close to. It is largely through magistrates, specifically federal judges, in the United States that benign racism has come into existence. This kind of racism is best exemplified in affirmative action, based upon judicially assigned quotas in the schools, colleges, factories, and offices of the nation, quotas of blacks, Hispanics, and women of all ethnic groups.

No one but a malign racist could have found fault with the judgment rendered by the Supreme Court in *Brown* vs. *Topeka* in 1954, for what that unanimous decision did was to activate the Fourteenth Amendment. It did not seek to impose integration; it sought only to make unconstitutional and illegal all arbitrary segregations of races in public schools—schools supported by the taxes of those forbidden to enter them. From this it was only a short step to the outlawry of arbitrary acts of discrimination and segregation in other public areas of life and eventually to a voting act in 1964 that accomplished for the first time what the Fifteenth Amendment had authorized for nearly a century—the right to vote of groups and classes long barred by local and state laws.

In sum, malign racism was in substantial measure on its way to extermination in the United States by the middle of the 1960s. The aim in each instance, whether by judicial decree or by enacted law, was to make more real the constitutional ethic of equal opportunity under law. That aim, expressed so eloquently both in the Federalist papers and in the amendments to the Constitution, was to make certain that no legislative body or executive could deny individuals their basic, natural, or human rights, such as freedom of speech, of assembly, and of religious worship. The Founding Fathers were aware, as are all people of common sense today, that there is no known way to make full equality of opportunity available to human beings, for there are too many variables to manage, starting with those of heredity. But there was a way of seeing to it that irrespective of the inequalities imposed by nature upon individuals, all would be equal in access to the law and equal under the law in their pursuits.

But affirmative action and other expressions of benign racism make such equality of opportunity impossible. Acting in the name of social equality—an impossible ideal—federal judges, encouraged by Congress and the Executive, applied quotas and other mechanisms of benign racism to just about every sphere of the public order. Those who had fought malign racism under the banner of the color blindness of the Constitution now discovered awareness of color, of sex, and of physical attributes to be the constitutional law of the land.

Whereas in *Brown* vs. *Topeka* the Supreme Court had rendered void laws of segregation, thus giving at least constitutional base to equal opportunity, now through the federal courts something very different took place—the mandating of integration. Under the tyranny of malign racism, substantial groups had been denied exercise of rights by all the machinery of inegalitarianism, nowhere so manifest as in the preposterous intelligence tests that had hypnotized American education. But now, under the tyranny of benign racism, equally substantial groups are denied exercise of their rights of equal opportunity. And all groups, whether "favored" or "unfavored" by the spirit of affirmative action, suffer the loss of equality of opportunity under constitutional law. Never can the talented among a race, sex, or ethnic group know for sure that they are talented in life and achievement if they must be forever haunted by the thought that they are products not of individual ability but of benign racism. A plantation mentality is not made the better for being benign in intent. Malign or benign, such a mentality is opposed to everything that is essential to the exercise of liberty and to the realization of individual opportunity.

All arbitrary authority is crippling to those under it, but by far the most crippling is that arbitrary authority exerted in the name of kindness, redemption, and love of its subjects. The will to resist such authority is quickly deadened by the sense of privilege gained over others. In the long run the human race will be just as wounded by benign racism as ever it was by malign racism.

REIFICATION

BE FRUITLESS AND REIFY. That is an appropriate adaptation of the Book of Genesis to the modern age. Snuff out the lives of particulars through suffocation by structures, isms, and systems. Agree with Blake: "I must Create a System or be enslav'd by another Man's." Regard events and individuals as so many masterless dogs needing impoundment in a theory. *Grau ist alle Theorie,* wrote Goethe, but no one today would realize this from all the colored ribbons which bedizen pet principles, laws, and axioms in the human sciences. The rage to reify, to pretend that life and meaning exist in boneless abstractions, is a special mark of ages such as our own.

The Oxford English Dictionary lists the word *reif* (or *rieff*) just before *reification*, defining it as the act of robbery or as the one who commits robbery. Reification is in its own way robbery: the stealing of life from the individual and the concrete in order to secrete it in some ontological invertebrate. Considering the combination of robbery and violence, the act of reifying may be likened to mugging.

The Age of Reification began in the nineteenth century, chiefly in Germany and France. In Germany, the language of Goethe and Lessing suddenly gave way to the language of Hegel, which William James declared could be understood only under the influence of laughing gas or nitrous oxide. It was Marx, though, who canonized reification for the social sciences when he declared that "individuals are dealt with only insofar as they are personifications of categories." For the revolution-minded, there is great advantage in reifying, for one cannot lead a revolution against a host of individuals or a cloud of particulars. It is one thing to mutiny against Captain Bligh, but for an honest-to-god revolution, a blob like capitalism is necessary. There is not the slightest paradox in Marx's simultaneous status as revolutionist and reifyer.

Matters were little better in France, home of a language that by the end of the seventeenth century was unrivaled in Europe, possibly in the world, for its sharpness, precision, and concreteness. But these virtues began to diminish during the Enlightenment. The passion to generalize, to convert the concrete into the abstract, took over much of the French literary mind. Tocqueville described the process among the *philosophes:* "Their very way of living led these writers to indulge in abstract theories and generalizations regarding the nature of government, and to place blind confidence in these. For . . . quite out of touch with practical politics, they lacked the experience which might have tempered their enthusiams . . . As a result our literary men became much bolder in their speculations, more addicted to general ideas and systems, more contemptuous of the wisdom of the ages." Rousseau is known for his style, but no political mind of the preceding century would ever have concocted something so alien to experience as "the General Will." The Jacobins, masters of reification, for a single abstraction gladly sent tens of thousands to their deaths. In the nineteenth century the number of French words ending in *isme* soared to the same heights which were reached in Germany. Such masters of the language as Sainte-Beuve, Flaubert, and Balzac criticized and condemned to no avail. More and more French thought lived under the narcotic clouds of abstraction and generalization. No one was more sensitive to this change in language than Tocqueville, who observed: "Democratic writers are perpetually coining abstract words . . . in which they sublimate into further abstraction the abstract terms of the language. Moreover, to render their mode of speech more succinct, they personify the object of these abstract terms and make it act like a real person." The practice is common, Tocqueville continued, to people living in democracies, who "are apt to entertain unsettled ideas, and they require loose expression to convey them. As they never know whether the idea they express today will be appropriate to the new position they may occupy tomorrow, they naturally acquire a liking for abstract terms. An abstract term is like a box with a false bottom; you may put in it what ideas you please and take them out without being observed."

If the social sciences had not existed, they would have had to be invented in order to satiate the lust to reify in the present day. Economics is not the dismal but the pathetic science, using that word in Ruskin's sense of "the pathetic fallacy," endowing abstractions with animate being. The science is riddled with such phrases as "the market decides," or "thinks," or "is frightened" or "is confused." But sociology, anthropology, and political science have hardly been dilatory about reification. Lives of individuals in these disciplines are slaughtered genocidally, leaving only interconnecting banks of system, structure, function, and the like. Once upon a time, anthropologists were known as "fact-worshiping and theory-dreading," but in the modern age that epithet requires reversing. The densest thickets of reification are to be found in such bizarre fabrications as semiotics and hermeneutics, not to forget something known to its inmates as ethnomethodology.

Structuralism is without question the opiate of the reifying masses. Whether a literary text, an act of murder, a job, a marriage, a birth or death, each must be buried in a "structure." Seemingly structures multiply sexually and asexually in the social sciences and humanities. One of the most amusing, if ultimately futile, examples of sexual multiplication was the valiant effort of the Frankfort School to mate Marxism and Freudianism. The awe in which this preposterous group and its descendants are still held in American sociology and some branches of psychology and anthropology is a monument to the gullibility of man. If it is a counterpart to Phineas T. Barnum one seeks, Max Horkheimer does very well. It is doubtful, though, that even Horkheimer can quite equal, in reification play, the master of the art, Herbert Marcuse.

Structuralism is in fact the modern Slough of Respond. How one structuralist responds, and responds and responds, to another structuralist is the very stuff of the more sophisticated in the social sciences and humanities. An awesome event any month is the response of an Althusserian to a letter published by Godelier, itself a response

to a Freudian structuralist's fierce attack on Lévi-Strauss or one of his
disciples. Lévi-Strauss is by any reckoning a superstar of structuralism and a world class grand-master of reification.

It is an interesting question whether Marxism or Freudianism has
done the most to spread the epidemic of reification during the past
century. At first sight dialectical materialism, alienation, and class
consciousness appear formidable and undefeatable. But one has only
to gaze a few moments at the libido, the death wish, and the Oedipus
complex to feel less certain.

The rise of democracy and the system of mechanized division of
labor in industry also provided fertile soil for the spread of reification
in the nineteenth and twentieth centuries, according to Ostrogorski.
A leveling process occurred in which concrete human identities were
succeeded more and more by generalized classes and things. Instead
of the familiar figures of Jim or Tom, regular recipients of charity in
the village, it was now the poor, or the poor class. The equally familiar figure of Squire Bridges was replaced by landlordism. Ostrogorski
wrote: "In the eyes of the manufacturer the mass of human beings
who toiled in the factory were only *workmen*, and the working man
associated the factory only with the idea of *capitalist* or *master*. Not
being brought into immediate contact, they formed a conception of
each other by mentally eliminating the special characteristics of the
individual and retaining only what he had in common with the other
members of his class."

There is some truth in Ostrogorski's characterizations, but they
omit the powerful role of intellectuals in effecting this transformation
of consciousness. The ideas of poverty, class conflict, the unemployed, workers, and capitalists—each an abstraction—would in all
likelihood not have come into existence but for the economists of
every ideological persuasion who, uncomfortable with the individual
and concrete, buried each in a category. Democracy and industrialism
are indeed soil for the age of reification, but without the catalysis
provided by the intellectuals, especially those of the political left, not
nearly as much would have happened as has been the case.

Another aspect of reification that deserves comment is its integra-
tive role in the intellectual's mind. After the gods have retreated and
the sacred has been sterilized by rationalism, there is a yearning for
new gods and for a new sacred. The human mind cannot tolerate a
vacuum. If it is no longer possible to feel kinship with God, then
commit oneself to Marxism, Freudianism, structuralism, functional-
ism, or social evolution.

And finally, an age of reification flourishes under the spirit of
egalitarianism. This spirit tends to dissolve differences of individu-

ality into a paste of abstraction known affectionately to all central-
izers and egalitarians as "community," that is, national community.
The only possible way that modern governments, committed as they
are to humanitarianism and populism, can ever give any semblance
of succeeding is to reify, and then, through powerful propaganda, to
convince the multitude that what is reified—Gross National Product,
Consumer Commodity Index, War Against Poverty—is real.

R ENAISSANCISM

THE ITALIAN RENAISSANCE of the fifteenth century is unique
among ages of claimed cultural efflorescence, or so-called golden
ages, in that it is almost entirely the product of egocentric illusion.
The century was barely under way when the Italian humanists began
to celebrate what they called, with consummate impudence, the *età
moderna*, the modern age, the age of renewal of civilization, after the
long dark night of the church-dominated millennium, the *medium
aevum*, that separated them from classical civilization. They were destined, the humanists believed, to terminate the murk of scholasticism
by calculated revival of Greek and Roman ideas, style, dress, and
ceremonies. On the basis of this revival, they would bury medieval
culture and at the same time build imperishably to the future. They
and they only were the true heirs of Plato and Aristotle and also the
architects of the future of Europe.

Their preposterous reading of history and themselves notwithstanding, the humanists deserve admiration for one thing at least:
they made their humbug work. Such was the effect of their self-
publicity that by the beginning of the nineteenth century, almost all
Europe had come to believe them. Ask Everyman even today what is
the greatest age in history, and he is almost certain to say: the Renaissance. *The* Renaissance, for it is unlikely that Everyman has been
introduced by his Europocentric teachers to other claimed efflorescences of culture in world history. If asked, Everyman would gladly
adapt Pope on Newton:

Europe and Europe's mind lay hid in night;
God said, "Renascence be!" and all was light.

For how many people even today must those lines not seem obvious. To this moment the highest accolade that can be given to anyone is simply: "Renaissance man."

That the Italian fifteenth century was one of often impressive art admits no doubt. One can overlook the rapacity of the Renaissance architects who, being well paid and protected by their patrons, the new men of power and wealth, saw nothing obscene in ripping acres of marble away from ancient and medieval structures. Nor is it necessary to cavil at length about the crass imitativeness of so much Renaissance art, not least its sculpture and architectural design. One can simply accept the fact that Renaissance art enchants to this day, especially when seen in its setting.

But the philosophical thought of the age requires objective scrutiny, which it seldom receives, except from specialists. Somehow the humanists managed to insinuate themselves and their imitative rhetoric into the mainstream of Western philosophy and science, at least to the satisfaction of their successors in the French Enlightenment. They must be given credit too for the image of the three preceding centuries, the high Middle ages, that has persisted in European consciousness until recently: an image of torpor, superstition, monolithic attention to the supernatural, and obstinate resistance to reason, logic, and other attributes of human beings in this world. This was the image of the Middle Ages that the leading Reformation figures loved, for it confirmed them in their hatred of Rome. So did the *philosophes* in the French Enlightenment cherish the image, as also did the humanists whom Condorcet and others elevated to virtually divine status for their assaults upon church, monastery, and university, and they bequeathed it to the rationalists and revolutionists of the nineteenth century. The scholarship of the past century has shown how absurd this image of the Middle Ages is, but the message has not yet penetrated Everyman's mind. For after all, as long as the myth of the Renaissance survives, there must survive also the Renaissance humanists' myth of the Middle Ages. How otherwise could those thrilling phrases be justified: "The Discovery of the World and Man" and "The Development of the Individual."

Myths to one side, historians of science, philosophy, and culture have shown that it was in the twelfth century that consciousness of individual and cosmos began to flourish, that serious exploration of the rest of the world all the way to China commenced, and that the ideas of individualism, secularism, progress, experimental science, and technology were once again to be seen across the landscape. By comparison, the fourteenth century in Italy was, as Spengler, Toynbee, Petrie, Kroeber, and other comparative historians emphasized, a minor eddy at best in the stream of Western culture. Butterfield noted that in the history of science, neither the Renaissance nor the Reformation exists as a significant moment, and nearly all historians of philosophy have affirmed this judgment for their own field. Kristeller, himself a Renaissancist, labeled the humanists as rhetoricians, no more.

How, then, does one account for the tenacity of the myth of the Renaissance as the seedbed of modern philosophy, science, and civic humanism, as the vital link between ancient and modern culture, as the slayer of medieval obscurantism? The question is made all the more poignant by realization of the high incidence in the Renaissance of the occult, of the kabbala, or worship of the Magus and the goddess Fortuna. And it was in the fifteenth and sixteenth centuries that the craze of witchcraft reached mammoth proportions among educated and uneducated alike, the church no longer capable of repressing this craze as it had throughout the Middle Ages. The Renaissance was also an age of personal despotism in government, of despot worship indeed, a lamentable interruption of the conciliar and parliamentary trends which had come out of medieval pluralism and decentralization.

There are two explanations of how such an age could have reached the sacred place it has in the popular mind today. First and solidest is a single book published in 1860, *The Civilization of the Renaissance in Italy*, by Burckhardt, Swiss historian. Burckhardt was far from being a lover of the period; indeed he steadfastly refused to write another book on the Renaissance despite entreaties from publishers, and he particularly despised the humanists, whom he saw correctly as forerunners to the coffee house intellectuals, the *revolutionistes*, of his own day. But Burckhardt believed, as did nearly all historians of his time, that if the rise of modernity, with its individualism, secularism, rationalism, and liberalism, was to be explained against the background of what was then so widely perceived as medieval supernaturalism and corporatism, a formative transitional period must be introduced in which medievalism withered and modernism germinated.

The result illustrated once again in history the power of a single book. A book does not have to be entirely or even mostly correct in its thesis to become a major cultural event. *Origin of Species, Capital, The Interpretation of Dreams*—not one of these is without serious faults in the judgment of biologists, economists, and psychologists, but that has not prevented each book from becoming deeply influential in shaping modern culture. The same is true of Burckhardt's classic. His very concept of a Renaissance in Italy in the fifteenth century is deeply flawed, and much of the development of his argument is rejected today even by Renaissancists. But faults and flaws notwithstanding, Burckhardt's book was a cultural event, recognized as such even in his day. And it remains one. Thousands of copies of his book sell each year in America, and although historians of the period may utter ritual disclaimers in their prefaces, Burckhardt's influence upon them persists. This book more than anything else was what brought the guild of Renaissancists into being in academia. No matter the book's sins of omission and commission, its opulent imagery, its sweeping and exciting style, and its memorable phrases such as "the discovery of the world and man" continue to charm its readers and lull them into belief in the reality of the Renaissance.

The second reason for the survival of the concept of a Renaissance in the fifteenth century is the spell that is cast on the Western mind by the very word. The idea of rebirth and renewal has held much fascination from at least the time of the classical Greeks. Demeter was Athens' cherished goddess, and the idea of her daughter Persephone "dying" each year and then being "reborn" was of endless appeal to even the most rationalistic of Athenian minds. It remains appealing, and will doubtless acquire even greater appeal the longer the present decadent culture and disintegrating social order persist into the future. It is in the nature of man's concern with time to look to the future for relief since nothing at hand promises it. "Humanists" are still around today, in direct line from the Italian humanists and the *philosophes* of France. These modern humanists are also characteristically arrogant, opinionated, rootless, cynical, willing to sell themselves for power and affluence, ever eager to assault the public order and disturb the moral peace, and only too happy to sacrifice profundity, wisdom, and learning upon the altar of brilliance. Their presence, their incessant posturing, feuding, and caterwauling, should convince Everyman that any relief, any rebirth and renewal of society, is not immediately in view. But the myth survived the Italian humanists, and it will no doubt survive these too.

R ITUAL

MAN, it is said, is alone among animals in that he drinks when he is not thirsty, eats when he is not hungry, makes love at all seasons, and ritualizes his behavior. The word *ritual* comes, appropriately, from the Latin *ritualis*, which meant rite or ceremony in connection with human life and all that sustains it. No civilization has exceeded

Rome, especially during the long history of the Republic, in its consecration to ritualized behavior. There was almost nothing that could
not be converted into an occasion for ritual attention. Not just birth,
marriage, and death but also the tilling of fields, the building of
houses and temples, the conduct of war, all of these and much else in
Roman society was given ritual significance. That Rome achieved its
historical greatness in the realm of action and structures rather than,
as had the Greeks, in pure thought is understandable in view of the
degree to which almost every aspect of life and thought was literally
enclosed in a structure, to wit, a ritual of some kind, a measured, regular pattern of behavior designed to commemorate the sacred.

Ritual is the dramatization of thought and faith. It converts ordinary, utilitarian behavior into sequential acts which are given a
meaning that is far beyond anything deducible from the mere existence of the behavior. Consider birth, biological coupling, and death,
for instance. It is entirely conceivable that human beings might have
their babies just as they would acquire another acre of land or one
more machine; that they might be treated after death as rubbish subject to quick disposal of biological remains. Yet the act of boy meeting girl, boy proposing cohabitation to girl, and boy taking up residence with girl, though a very simple, natural, and irrepressible
function, is surrounded in every culture or civilization on record with
the infinity of rites and ceremonies that attend what are called be-
trothal, marriage, and family life. The reason, in a word, is man. It is
seemingly inconceivable to man that some part of his life not be
roped off, as it were, and given sacred, ritual significance. On the historical record, nothing is free of at least the possibility of becoming
sacred, the occasion of ritual.

Ritual probably began as representation and then prerepresentation, according to Jane Harrison. To act out birth, sexual union, the
hunt, the planting of seeds, and death is to recognize the importance
of these to the community and to reinforce individual memory. That
is representation. But once a relation is seen between the acts and the
representations, there is a temptation to use more or less the same
dramatizations as helpful, possibly success-assuring anticipations of
those acts. That is prerepresentation. Ritual, in essence, is drama, art,
relief from the strictly utilitarian or profane, the humdrum and the
monotonous. Use and wont may be the raw material of ritual, as of
drama, but ritual ranges all the way from comedy to tragedy, with
human beings—dead, living, and unborn—as actors. There is nothing
strange in the fact that drama in the modern sense emerged from
myth and ritual so memorably at the beginning of the fifth
century B.C. in Athens. Only the inherent drama of ritual, with

its profoundly sacred themes, could have prepared human minds for the suspension of disbelief and the thrill of the vicarious that must attend the enjoyment of actors speaking lines in a *mise en scène*.

Ritual served primitive and ancient man as art does modern man. Relief is granted from what a poet has called "the long literalness of life." It is impossible to exaggerate the importance of ritual and art to man, given his highly developed nervous system, as prone to depression and boredom as to exhaltation, and his capacity for abstract and therefore rootless thought. Once the elementary, basal needs for sheer preservation are satisfied, the human mind is capable of experiencing a higher set of needs: social, spiritual, and intellectual. Among these are the needs for community, for identity, and above all, for meaning—of the cosmos, of existence, and of the human estate. No matter how dimly felt these higher needs were in the beginning when the struggle for mere survival was almost monopolistic of attention, they were there, to be satisfied by myth reinforced by ritual, and in the process to be given surcease from boredom.

No less important is ritual's function in protecting man from the uncertainties of life which, if left unguarded against, would overwhelm by their abundance and unpredictability. One may, after a time, deal well enough with the certain through simple reason or utilitarian action: one can prepare for birth and death, for planting and harvesting, for dealing with marauders. But nothing is ever absolutely certain in life. The role of accident, beneficent or malign, becomes only too familiar. The utilitarian means which work successfully within the realm of the known and the certain cannot work against the purely fortuitous, the utterly unpredictable—the physical catastrophe, secret subversion, unforseen attack. Here is the seed ground of ritual which, though based upon sacred belief and myth, is capable of acquiring a power over and significance in human life that goes well beyond its ostensible purpose, that becomes the means of drama in an otherwise psychologically empty, stale, and barren world.

Ritual has the additional function of enabling man to deal with time, indeed of giving an ordered sense of time. Past, present, and future become, as it were, bound together in the human mind. Memory is not only made possible but also given vital importance in human life when embodied in tradition and custom. Durkheim argued that not only time but other categories of the mind, such as space, mass, and force, evolved with the help of ritual and its representations of reality.

One other function of ritual is to reinforce thought, particularly faith and belief. By itself, existing only in an individual's mind, belief can become faltering, fragile, easily subject to dislodgement. No greater mistake could have been made by the Protestant reformers of the sixteenth century than to suppose that simple, unadorned, direct faith in God is sufficient and that all externalities, including church rituals, are thus expendable. They are not, as Luther's followers came early to realize, which allowed modern Lutheran Christianity a degree of sacramentalism and ritual character scarcely different from most Catholic worship. Even the Calvinists, after a century or more of denunciation of everything in religion that is not strictly contained in individual faith and belief, found it necessary to readmit in different guise ritual elements that Calvin had scorned. Religions which jettison completely rite, ceremony, and other external representations of belief, such as the Quakers and Unitarians, are unlikely to claim more than a few followers, as compared with the religions that are rich in ritualism, the Roman Catholic foremost among them. No matter how intense the belief in God may be in an individual mind, that belief can be made both securer and above all more likely to survive intact when transmitted from generation to generation if it is ensconced in ritual act.

What is true of religious belief and its relation to ritual is scarcely less true in the political realm. The bonds of patriotism, of devotion to king or nation, are inevitably closer when they are ornamented by rites and ceremonies in which individuals can act as well as believe. However much Americans today scorn the kinds of popular enthusiam which once attended the Fourth of July, the decline of ritualism in the body politic has been accompanied by a decline of patriotism. Rousseau recognized the importance of this connection when he prescribed a "Civil Religion." So also did the leaders of the French Revolution understand what was involved when they designed a religion of civic virtue, complete with sacraments and rites, which would fill the emptiness left by their de-Christianization decrees and would give intensity to the popular devotion to France.

American society is fast becoming sterilized of traditional ritual, ceremony, and form. Such legacies from the past are not easily reconciled with an ever-more egoistic individualism, on the one hand, and on the other, an ever-more dominant state whose apparent determination is that of replacing them as widely as possible with formal law and judicial decision. There is a price to be paid for their loss. What Tocqueville wrote on forms applies to all rituals and ceremonies as well: "Men living in democratic ages do not readily comprehend the utility of forms: they feel an instinctive contempt for them . . . Yet this objection which the men of democracies make to forms is the very thing which renders forms so useful to freedom; for their chief merit is to serve as a barrier between the strong and the weak, the ruler and the people, to retard the one and give the other time to look about him. Forms become more necessary in proportion as the government becomes more active and more powerful, while private persons are becoming more indolent and more feeble."

And more jaded—a consequence of the loss of still another form or ritual in American society, that of the game or play. Just as sacred ritual builds symbolically upon the crises of individual existence—birth, marriage, and death—so play ritual builds upon the elements of conflict, chance, and uncertainty in life. Whether in representational or prerepresentational form, play ritual reenacts the battle, the hunt, the chase, or the search. In its traditional form it is like sacred ritual in demanding participation within a community. But play ritual has today suffered the same fate that has befallen sacred ritual: bureaucratization and industrialization. The evolution of play has been from the game to the spectator sport to the huge industry known as the National Football League.

There are only two things which, on the historical evidence, have ever given man repose, surcease from attacks of disabling or barbarizing ennui: fulfilling work and religion. In the first, man is able to enjoy this world and its challenges to strength and mind; in the second, man is provided escape, to both past and future and also to the vicarious and the suprarational, but without loosening his hold on terrestrial reality and his own dignity. But alas, *homo faber* has been replaced all too often by automated technology, with consequent diminution in the worker's self-importance; and *homo socialis* has been virtually destroyed by a centralizing bureaucracy seemingly intent upon exorcising all that is volitional and spontaneous in society. Many changes must lie ahead if ritual is again to serve its ancient religious and psychological functions. For the present and foreseeable future, millions more of Western populations will doubtless seek release from malaise through one or another type of "liberation," sexual, narcotic, or political, only to discover what their predecessors have: what is required is not liberation, but legitimate moral authority, reinforced by the soothing disciplines of ritual.

SNOBBISM

THACKERAY OBSERVED, "He who meanly admires mean things is a Snob." To which he added, "It is impossible, in our condition of Society, not to be sometimes a Snob."

And in our own. The writing of a book on contemporary snobs
in America, similar to the one Thackeray wrote, might be recom-
mended, were it not for the certainty that it would be largely read,
not for simple interest or amusement, but for guidance in becoming a
better and more successful snob. Snobbism is to be seen in many
areas of American life, and it is idle to think of giving them identity;
they are too well-known and experienced.

One current expression of snobbery, though, unlike most other
expressions, is confused with virtue, with guarding the ramparts of
the republic of letters. High among snobs in America are the word
sniffers and routers of the colloquial whose special form of the affliction has proved suprisingly contagious. A best-selling dictionary
proudly lists a "Usage Panel" of several dozen appointed experts in
the English language, some of whom are notable in their own right as
composers of graceful and effective prose. The panel is presided over
by a television news reader who moonlights solemnly as, indeed is
widely accepted as, a usage expert, a word sniffer. Periodically the
editors of the dictionary conduct votes in the panel as to the accept-
ability of a given word or phrase. Most Americans in the past, including our most illustrious writers, would doubtless have been
amused at the idea of trusting a ballot more than one's own reading
and judgment in such matters, but then, today Americans live in a
more democratic age, one in which to vote is to be virtuous. The editors of the dictionary polled their panel on *hopefully,* used objectively
rather than subjectively, and 56 percent of the word sniffers were
duly offended. "Abandon 'hopefully' all ye who enter" was emblazoned on their office doors with Rabelaisian mirth. To say, "The
food, hopefully, will be good," is to say in effect, intoned the panel
snobs, that food can hope. "Hopefully, I'll get there by dusk," is to
say, whether one means to or not, that the individual will arrive with
hope in his mind.

But this is absurd. If the word *curious,* to name but one of many,
can have an objective as well as subjective sense, duly honored by
the Oxford English Dictionary, *hopeful* is assuredly not ruled out.
When one says, "Curiously, the frog just sat there," no normal lis-
tener is likely to conclude that the frog was in a mental state of curiosity. If that is what the speaker meant, he would have to mend his
syntax.

Someone has sagely suggested that the widespread colloquial use
of *hopefully* in the objective sense is simply an easy substitute for
"God willing," a bit of theism that few intellectual and literary snobs
are likely to be heard expressing. Manifestly, the word *hopefully* in the
colloquial sense has utility, a reason sufficient for the Shakespeares,

Dickens, and Mark Twains of the world to accept it. "Hopefully, the weather will be good when you arrive," is to be preferred to the prissy "it is to be hoped." To say "I hope" puts an entirely different construction upon meaning. "Let us hope" is prayerful and almost invites a lowering of heads. "We shall hope" is arrogant unless a poll has been taken. Moreover, the speaker may not care a fig whether the weather will be good when the other person arrives, may even hope maliciously that the weather will be dreadful. *Hopefully* takes care of all states of mind.

Usage snobs too often leave the impression that the English they are interested in imposing upon the masses is the King's English, whereas it usually turns out to be the King's butler's English, that spoken by Hudson downstairs, not the Bellamys upstairs. There is the stuff of the pedant in word snobs, an insistence upon writ instead of an honoring of the processes through which language grows and prospers, such as use and wont, children's mispronunciations that find their way into the mainstream, coinages by the Spensers, Shakespeares, and Miltons, and the formation of idioms. The thought of a panel of word sniffers voting on some new mutant in language is almost as funny as the thought of a panel of biologists passing on each new variation in the species.

If there are nonsnobs who feel insecure about their knowledge of English, let them go to Shakespeare, who did not disdain for a moment to write "between you and I" and "like I said" or even to coin "infamonize." Or to Dickens and his "nobody will miss her like I do" and "he don't seem well"—both of these taken from his correspondence, not from one of his fictional pickpockets. Dr. Johnson, who had full appreciation of his language, said nevertheless, "The pen must comply with the tongue." That is much better than the pen complying with the latest majority on a panel of word snobs.

SOCIAL CHANGE

"WHEN IT IS NOT NECESSARY to change, it is necessary not to change." That declaration was made in Parliament before Pym and Hampden by Viscount Falkland, who struggled so hard and so futilely to avert the Civil War in seventeenth century England. As an apothegm, it fits English conservatism perfectly. But it may also be con-

sidered a principle in the study of social and cultural change, for neither the individual nor the group is likely to deviate in habit or
folkway from Falkland's observation. If people are not obliged by
discomfort or exigency to alter their behavior, they are almost certain
to preserve it, and with conscious satisfaction. For whether it is a
habit in the individual or a convention in the group, each serves, in
William James's phrase, as "the flywheel of society."

The historian Elting E. Morison told a story that in the early days
of World War II when armaments were in short supply in England,
an old field piece from the light artillery was resurrected along with a
crew of five experienced in its use, which went back to the Boer War.
A time and motion expert was brought in to observe the crew in action and grew puzzled by one act of the crew: during the firing operation, two members, exactly three seconds before the firing, stopped
all movement and stood rigidly at attention until all sound had sub-
sided. No one could explain this patently superfluous act, and finally
the expert summoned an old, retired colonel of the artillery to inquire what it was that led to this strange behavior on the part of the
two men. For a moment or two the colonel too was baffled. Then his
face suddenly cleared: "I have it. They are holding the horses."

When it comes to human behavior and to the power of habit,
role, and tradition, utilitarian facts have little to do with the matter.
There always had been five men to a crew, there were five now, and
if there were no longer horses for two men actually to hold and quiet
while the burst went off, let the two merely stand at attention for
three seconds. Under no circumstances alter behavior that had stood
the artillery in good stead for many decades.

That principle is by no means confined to the military or to great
repositories of ritual, such as religion. Persistence, fixity, and the
clutching gratefully for habit and convention lie in all areas of
thought and action. That is why, to understand change, it is necessary
to begin with an understanding of fixity, of the stationary and immobile. The first law of change, so to speak, is: Everything is in a state
of rest until exigency disturbs it. Not even exigency is a guarantee of
disturbance becoming a force of change, for the world is filled with
peoples who will suffer pain and death before they will yield belief
and custom to exigency. Nevertheless, nothing cultural in man's history ever has changed, or ever will change, until the privilege of habit
is dislocated by the exigencies of life, ranging from the merely uncomfortable to the catastrophic.

Habit and convention are so native to human beings, as to every
other organism, because all behavior is purposive and adaptive. It is
aimed at the solution of problems which beset the person or orga-

nism from the environment or from within. Once a solution has been found, it becomes instinctive, over a long period of time, in organisms, and it becomes institutionalized in human society. Every institution is basically the solution to some problem. Moreover, institutions in a given culture have a functional relationship with one another, as is the case with kinship, local community, religion, economy, and so on. Each is dependent in some degree upon the other. The desire to achieve or to sustain interdependence, that is, to gain relief from conflict and disharmony, is so great as to be called a rage. The rage to persistence is powerful simply because what persists is viewed by almost everyone as security from the uncertain, the unknown. With good reason the ancient Romans made the same word, *hostis*, mean "stranger" and also "enemy." For the stranger by very viture of his alien cast, his ignorance of the true gods and verities, had to be an enemy, *in potentia* at least.

Even in philosophy and science, areas of consecrated search for the truth, or at least knowledge, and where the principals are thought to be tireless in search of the new, persistence and conventionalization are legion. Once a new idea does come into existence, it normally becomes a paradigm for not only a continuity of thought but also a whole intellectual community, one that takes no more readily to fragmentation by new and potentially warring ideas than does a religious community. Changes of paradigm, Thomas Kuhn stressed, in both philosophy and science have a strong resemblance to political revolution. Many years ago the literary scholar Livingston Lowes demonstrated how even poets, individual inspiration notwithstanding, strongly reflect conventionalization for long periods, in thought, language, and meter.

It is true that people yearn occasionally for change, if only of scene. But that judgment applies with more accuracy to people in the world today, and especially to the peoples of the West, than to mankind at large in history. For them, as for most people even today, change is, in Eric Hoffer's word, an ordeal. They dread almost any change—of political or religious faith, of locale, of personal habit such as smoking, of work, leisure, or recreation. The move from one house to another is properly declared third only to divorce and death in trauma aroused. The thought that things might well be improved tends to trail far behind the gigantic conviction that they could well be a great deal worse.

Morison described the astounding difficulties experienced at the beginning of the twentieth century by a British and an American naval officer, each of whom had come up with a technological solution to the ancient and exasperating problem of holding a gun fixed to the deck in accurate aim on the target while the ship rolled. To both of these officers almost simultaneously came the liberating thought of allowing the gun pointer to keep his sight and gun barrel on the target throughout the roll of the ship by altering the gear ratio in the elevating gear to permit the pointer to compensate for the roll of the vessel by rapidly elevating and depressing the gun. The advantages were obvious, as was the additional advantage now made possible of using a telescopic sight also held firm on the target instead of going inexorably up and down with the gun. But there was resistance at every level, cold, harsh, hostile resistance by captain after captain, admiral after admiral. This went on for years, until the American naval officer, fortified by knowledge that his British friend was seeking the same objective, in desperation wrote directly to the President, Theodore Roosevelt. No President has ever prided himself more on his knowledge of the navy, and as Assistant Secretary of the Navy Department, Roosevelt had seen his full share of the results of inertia compounded with tradition. He ordered the naval officer from duty in the Far Pacific to a naval yard near Washington, giving specific instructions to the Bureau of Ships that full attention was to be given to demonstrations of the new technique, with reports directly to himself. Within a few months all ships, American and British, could avail themselves of the luxury and efficiency of continuous-aim firing of heavy guns.

Another story was told by Tylor about the Sea Dyaks of Borneo. When Europeans first settled among them, they were struck by the natives' insistence upon cutting down trees with a straight transverse cut by their ax instead of the vastly quicker and more efficient V-cut that Europeans used. No amount of effort could persuade the Sea Dyaks to change their communal habit, but after a year or two Europeans became aware that when they chanced to come upon a single Dyak out in the jungle, well separated from his village, he would invariably use the European method, there being nobody to witness it.

People are so resistant to a simple technical change because there is in fact no such thing as a "simple" technical change. For the American naval command and the Sea Dyaks the overriding issue was not the technical improvement, which was obvious enough to the eye, but the preservation of the community, within which old conventions, mores, and habits formed a seamless web of the secure and comfortable. Similarly, acceptance in America after World War I of the combat plane was rendered glacial in speed by the fear haunting every captain and would-be captain that whatever good might come from the new air forces would be greatly outweighed by the harm it would surely do to the capital ship, whose command was every officer's dream, and service on which was the essence of every sailor's professional delight. In sum, more than a ship was being threatened by the plane; it was a powerful, tight, cohesive, and proud community.

Despite the mass of evidence for fixity, conventionalization, and habit being the natural state of man, the litanies of change litter the social sciences, the philosophical systems in the West, and for that matter the marketplace itself. "All is flux," "change alone is real," "motion," "movement," "development," "evolution," "revolution"— these are the commonest signs and symbols of man's estate in Western thought. The reason lies in the extraordinary fascination that organic growth has held for Western thought since at least pre-Socratic Greece as the model of social and cultural change. What a Heraclitus could see happening to plants and other organisms served perfectly in his imagination as explanations for the changes of communities and states. They too could be seen as naturally in growth, from small seeds, as it were, to the full-blown Greek civilization. Change is thus as natural to society as it is to the organism. In each case dynamics and statics are fused: change is the natural property of any social structure; the structure itself, like the organism, arrives at what it is only through patterned change.

From this early observation and metaphoric use of organic change came a host of Western theories and philosophies, with high among them the ideas of progress, recurrent cycles, and social and biological evolution. What all these ideas have in common is the premise of the inexorability of change. All that is necessary is simply accounting for the direction of the change through analysis of the efficient causes, whether divine, secular, political, or economic. There has never been a time in Western thought when the image of social change has not been predominantly biological in nature.

Certainly that is the case today in the social sciences and the humanities. The attributes of growth are made willy-nilly the attributes of change, social or cultural, although a monumental assumption is being made when social behavior is likened to something as unique in nature as growth with its intrinsically teleological character, that is, with its entire pattern of change coded in advance in the seed, from birth to death and then recurrence through fresh seed of the entire pattern.

The great objective of current theory in the social sciences, with sociology and ethnology in the vanguard, is to deduce change from structure. Indeed this objective has been sovereign in Western thought since Aristotle, crowning Christian as well as pagan and secular theories of society for well over two thousand years. When the

functionalist or structuralist in sociology tries to solve the great paradox of order and change, it is with the image of biological growth in
his head. All structures in society are said to be dynamic, not static;
in their functioning, deviations from norm are as common as strict
conformities to norm; these deviations are essentially of social roles
held by individuals; deviations are minute changes, comparable to the
minute variations in nature hypothesized as explanation for evolution; the deviations accumulate, just as do the infinitesimally small
variations in the growth of the plant; and when these deviations from
role accumulate to a certain, not easily specifiable point, change takes
place in the social structure, just as birth ensues in the organic realm
when embryonic changes have reached a given point. In sum, all social change is natural, inherent in social behavior, and whether evolutionary or revolutionary, the product of immanent, potentially explosive, tiny deviations, tensions, or other aberrations from the norm.

The whole picture is so felicitous that it tests one's skepticism. In
fact, with all respect to its hoary ancestry, the picture is a hoax. There
is not the slightest warrant for considering social and cultural change
identical with or analogous to biological growth. Social change, unlike biological, is not the product of immanent, endogenous forces. It
is not natural, not native to social institutions and other structures, as
growth so plainly is to organisms. If anything is natural or native to
the social, it is rather fixity.

The simple but powerful truth is that social change can no more
be deduced from social structure than social structure can be deduced from physiological structure. To seek to find in the human
body or in the human mind elements from which it becomes possible
to predict the actual variety and diversity of social behavior in the
world, past and present, is, the instinctualists and sociobiologists to
the contrary, fatuous. All that the human brain gives in this wise is
its inexhaustible capacity for generating and assimilating an endless,
infinite variety of behavior. From that point on, only history can explain the social. Precisely the same is true of structure and change.
Structure by its very existence limits, channels, restrains change,
serves as a kind of filter for change. But the dynamic elements of
change are not found in the composition of the social. For those elements too it is necessary to turn to history.

Much of the current confusion with respect to change comes
from lumping under the one word a great many phenomena which
may reflect adjustment, readjustment, bustle, alternation of techniques and habits, and other instances of mere movement or motion
but which do not reflect outright change or transformation, as, say, in
change from the extended family to the conjugal, from capitalism to

socialism, from faith in Christianity to faith in the Marxian dialectic, from agrarianism to industrialism, from village culture to town and city culture, from horse-drawn transportation to automotive, from noncomputer to computer world, and from closet pornography to un-fettered, high-visibility smut. When two people decide to be married, change of a sort is represented: from separate residence there is now joint, and a new legal relationship has been added to the social order. The appearance of children also represents a change. But such changes are really nothing more than the choice to enter into a thoroughly conventionalized and ritualized mode of behavior in so-ciety. Entry into matrimony is a vastly different kind of change from that made evident when the structure of matrimony is changed, when as the result of the disarray caused by great events such as war, revo-lution, migrations, and invasions, vital roles are suddenly altered, an-cient authorities are supplanted, and the very function of the struc-ture is transformed.

True social change is inseparable from crisis of one kind or other. For that matter, true thought, in contrast to mere musing, rev-erie, and idle association, is stimulated in humans only when they perceive some kind of problem, which is a form of crisis. They turn their thinking upon the accustomed ways only when some kind of interruption occurs, some crisis, however tiny it might seem. The more deeply planted in their allegiance is some pattern of thought or behavior, such as religion, kinship ties, ethnic affiliation, and social class or caste, the greater the shock and crisis must be for any signifi-cant change to take place in that pattern. It is thus impossible to un-derstand the nature of change apart from the impact of events upon people's lives. Only changes of the most trivial kind, mere modifica-tions, take place in the absence of some precipitating event that leads to a new relationship between the individual and the pattern of be-havior in question. So long as kinship, village, clan, tribe, and caste in the world were untouched by invasion or other kind of interrup-tion of the old and traditional, these unities remained almost identical with what they had been for thousands of years. The world revolu-tion that is now moving in hurricane ferocity across the planet is the result of a continuing battery of events—invasions, migrations, inter-ruptions of every kind—precipitated by the West about three cen-turies ago. Hindu caste, Chinese clan, Middle Eastern village, African tribe—all of these, when come upon by Western soldiers, administra-tors, missionaries, and other invaders, were no different from what they had been thousands of years earlier. Thereafter, though not without resistance that could at times be formidable indeed, these an-cient bastions of morality and security were fragmented, atomized, and devastated, in every instance by the insistent pressure upon them of external, largely Western values, disciplines, and incentives. The twentieth century has been the greatest century of social change in all history, and the reason is bound up inextricably with this tidal wave of events which has washed over even the most remote and isolated areas of the earth. The present century is the grand climax of the cosmic hurricane.

A look back in macroscopic focus on human history cannot help but reveal the spasmodic and undulatory patterns of change. There are large areas on the human historical map which reveal no change at all for considerable periods of time but then, of a sudden, are charged with dislocation and disorganization, followed by fresh patterns of thought and conduct. It is the very nature of these eruptions to be infrequent and brief in manifestation. The reason is simply that they too are forms of social change and hence are as dependent in their efflorescence upon the random event, the fortuitous interruption, and the purely accidental in history as is any other change or innovation, small, medium, or large. In their infrequency and brevity may be seen also the weight of the adage: "When it is not necessary to change, it is necessary not to change."

SOCIAL REVOLUTION

THE CONVENTIONAL and by now congealed view of social and political revolution is that it springs directly and more or less spontaneously from such material conditions as poverty, imperfect land distribution, unemployment, and exploitation, real or imagined, by an upper class in possession of the government. So much is pure litany for the columnist and newspaper editor, not to mention varieties of social scientists and the clergy. A whole phantasmagoria about Latin America, Africa, Southeast Asia, and other areas has come into being on the basis of the conventional wisdom of revolution.

This literary-ideological tradition holds, in effect, that revolutions are very much like volcanoes. Deep subterranean forces of poverty and exploitation must exist; they become steadily more galling and also widespread in the lives of the people. Finally, the conditions become so intolerable and the social structures around them so unable to contain any longer the pent-up forces of revolt that what has been subterranean now becomes actively volcanic. London, Paris, Saint Petersburg, Peking, and Havana must be seen as release points of the fearful pressures which have been built up below in the peasantry and working class. Through perfectly natural, inexorable, and unswervable forces in the lives of the people, revolution bursts forth to liberate the masses from their heritage of torment and deprivation. A "smoldering cauldron" has "erupted" or "exploded."

All that needs adding to this stereotyped vision of revolution is the fable of "long-overdue reforms." If only the ruling government had been willing to make reforms in the conditions of the oppressed masses—reforms commonly meaning redistribution of wealth and the proffer of myriad entitlements from the government—revolution could have been staved off. The deep subterranean tensions would have been brought to an end or else greatly moderated. A final note in the litany of conventional wisdom is to label governments, unless they are already communist or socialist, as "corrupt," "reactionary," "feudal," and naturally, "hated by the people."

There are several major flaws in this almost universally accepted analysis of revolution. First, poverty does not incite to revolution; it incites to nothing except continued poverty. That is a very depressing reflection upon the human mind, but the unvarnished truth, attested to repeatedly in world history. The exploited, degraded, and impoverished worker-peasant does not revolt, save perhaps in an occasional short-lived mutiny or revolt, usually triggered by religious causes, as with the Sepoys in India and the Boxers in China. The great revolutions of the modern world—and revolution, in contrast to simple uprisings and revolts, is peculiarly modern—are not rooted in the poverty of the masses, except now and then in the official rhetoric of the revolutionary leaders. The list is unbroken: of the Puritan, the American, the French, the Bolshevik, the Chinese, and the Cuban revolutions, not one boiled up from below, the result of mass deprivations suffered too long and become uncontrollable. In each instance the real causes were leaders, ranging from middle to upper class men, who had no personal experience of or usually sympathy with the poverty in the country in question, but who found no difficulty in making the condition of the workers and peasants the stuff of rhetorical enlargement. So far were the impoverished from being principals in the revolution in any significant degree that they commonly had to be dragooned by the Robespierres, Lenins, Maos, and Castros—dragooned and not seldom imprisoned, tortured, and executed as counter-revolutionaries.

A second major fallacy about revolutions concerns the relationship of reforms to revolution. The stock lore has it that if only reforms in the conditions of the people were made, and quickly, all possibility of revolution and its aftermath would be obviated. There is no question that a great many reforms are needed in this world, starting with the affluent United States and reaching the meanest, most squalid and impoverished of third world countries. Reforms are good or bad in themselves, without reference to what they may or may not be able to avert. But each of the major revolutions of the past two centuries was preceded by a series of reforms that had been pressed for by leaders or representatives of the oppressed or discontented. Not only did such reforms fail to head off revolution, but they actually paved the way. The point is that reforms and capitulations to demands of noisy minorities much more often hasten revolution than avert it. Such reforms stimulate the appetite for the main dish, which is revolution, capture of power.

Consider that the position of the American colonists of all classes was much better in 1770 than it had been several decades earlier. But such improvement only quickened the desires of the pamphleteers which for a combination of religious and secular reasons had reached apocalyptic intensity by the 1760s, with millennium-by-revolution the increasingly ecstatic dream of those who, for reasons almost wholly unrelated to actual social, economic, and cultural conditions, wanted war and revolution.

Consider that in Russia between 1860 and 1914 a large number of political, economic, and social reforms took place. The condition of serfdom more than anything else tormented revolutionists and reformers within Russia and offended Western visitors. But the emancipation of the serfs in 1861 only widened and intensified agitation among the freed serfs, a fact that haunted Dostoevsky and helped shape his profound understanding and also hatred of revolution and revolutionary fanatics. But liberation of the serfs was only the beginning. A series of major reforms occurred during the next fifty years: inauguration of trial by jury, reshaping and expanding of the Duma and of voting rights, instituting of free or nearly free universities for the economically poor, and opening of Russia to industry and commerce and to Western culture. All of these and many other reforms took place. So did a veritable efflorescence in the arts and sciences, largely as a result of the social and political reforms. But all the while, the number, the skills, and the devotions of revolutionists were also undergoing unprecedented prosperity. The sad truth is that reforms only quicken and inflame desire for revolution when such reforms are set in an already revolutionary situation.

There are several components to a revolutionary situation, none of which is poverty, unemployment, and poor housing. The first factor is a government grown flaccid and weak, and perceived widely as such. If there is one single cause of revolution, it is this. Even if the conditions of the people are on the whole reasonably good, the mere fact that the government has come to resemble increasingly an animal *in extremis* causes hunters, revolutionists, to spring into existence. The oppressed, deprived state of the peasantry, working class, or bourgeoisie may be seized upon by the voices of revolution, may be shouted for all the world to hear, but the only crucial cause of the revolutionary outburst, its Boston Massacre, its Bastille, its Winter Palace, is widespread recognition that the government has become a weak reed. By this point it is too late for reforms even to decelerate and dampen revolutionary passions. Such reforms are seen correctly as merely further symptoms of the desperate state of the government; far from helping to subdue, mollify, and ameliorate, they are like buckets of gasoline thrown in a bonfire.

The ruling order may give up many things in the interest of its citizens, but when, in the interests of benignity, or guilt, it dismembers and jettisons its authority in the lives of its citizens, it is ripe for revolution, a seductive prey for revolutionists, an irresistible opportunity for political rape. Nothing so brings out the aggressive, rapist disposition as does perception of some inviting weakness. This holds true fairly widely in direct human relationships; it holds true almost absolutely in the relationships between political orders and their opponents. The conventional wisdom says that revolutionary ferment, rising inexorably from below in the population, destroys a government's authority. As usual, such wisdom is in error. The prior destruction, the erosion or attrition, of authority in the state creates the revolution.

At no recent time was the validity of this principle more evident than in the 1960s with reference to the student revolution on many of the nation's campuses. During the preceding decades of affluence, expansion, and freebooting at colleges and universities, the traditional structures of authority had been badly weakened: the authority of trustees, of administrations, of faculties, and of student governments. They had been weakened by the spirit of hedonistic materialism that took fire under the financial encouragement of the federal government and the foundations; they had been weakened by the intrusion of institutes, bureaus, and centers, one and all consecrated to large-scale research, one and all essentially hostile to the accustomed lines of authority on the campus—those of department chairmen, deans of colleges, and academic vice presidents. The heads of the institutes and bureaus had little responsibility for students, only for the management of prestigious research and consultation with government and industry. Generally, they had even less interest in students. Old claims of departments and colleges upon the loyalties of their faculty and students paled before the challenge of the new, generally wealthy, and always autonomous institutes. It was inevitable that the students would acquire some of the contempt for presidents, deans, and chairmen that was all too implicit in the new class of administrators and researchers on the campus. Given this contempt, it was almost equally inevitable that the students would revolt and that the revolt would be contagious across the United States.

If lack of authority or visible waning of authority is the first cause of revolution, the second is growth in the number of theories of revolution. Studies of crime show that poverty does not itself lead to crime. But the popular theory that crime is caused by poverty exerts a good deal of causal effect. As long as society accepts the theory, that theory is almost certain to become self-fulfilling through the actions of those for whom the theory becomes at once stimulant and justification. So it is with revolution. In every major revolution, from the Puritan to the Cuban, Vietnamese, and Cambodian, theorists of revolution have been in the forefront of agitation. These political intellectuals are equipped with a rhetorical arsenal on the one hand of evil governors, corrupt landowners, shoddy businessmen, rotting morality, and decay of law, and on the other, of promises of peace, justice, food, equality, and liberty. That each and every revolution during the last three centuries, the American alone excepted, has led to a magnification of power over the citizen and indeed to a degree of despotism, linked with a deprivation never before seen in the society, is seemingly not noticed.

Robespierre and Saint-Just, Garibaldi, Lenin and Trotsky, Mao, Castro, and Pol Pot—all were intellectuals fired up with a passion for revolution from the earliest years of their lives. They were never interested in peace and reform, in stability and justice. Lenin left Russia at one point in the belief that too many reforms had taken place there, so that the authority of the government was still unassailable, and he went to, of all places, Switzerland. There he found racial balance and harmony, wide enfranchisement, and a striking picture of political and economic equality. Class hatred simply did not exist. But none of this meant a thing to Lenin, for he saw, not what lay around him—no true revolutionist ever does—but pictures in his head of a utopia that he and other committed Marxists would bring into being by force, all the force necessary. And for some time Lenin, never thinking for a moment of the security of person he enjoyed or of the widespread contentment of Swiss citizens, persisted fanatically and fatuously in the effort to bring down the Swiss government.

Ideas rule the world. That is an old and obvious truth. Revolutionary ideas rule revolutions. That is less obvious but no less true. Tocqueville showed how revolutionary ideas work and become effective in the hands of "literary politicians" or intellectuals grasping for power. First, a government must become, through internal or external forces, weak, unable any longer to govern; second, there must be a sufficiently rising standard of living among the people to create aspirations for a still higher standard; third, there must be a significant degree of decay and rot in the police and military, brought about by unanswered requests for higher wages or better working conditions; and fourth there must be veritable hordes of intellectuals meeting in small groups, joined in endless epithet- or slogan-composition and in endless competition for supremacy among themselves while they try to stir up the people. And the best possible way of stirring the people into action—amorphous, inchoate, and mindless though such action may be—is through promulgation and dissemination of theories of revolution. The Russian Revolution at the end of 1917 had nothing to do with a long-suffering proletariat rising from the deeps to overthrow a long-ruling capitalist or landowning class, but in the skilled and prehensile hands of Lenin, Trotsky, Bukharin, and other Bolshevik intellectuals, the revolution had a great deal to do with Marxian slogans and catchwords on the proletariat and capitalist class. Lenin knew well how vital the intellectuals were. As he repeatedly observed, peasants left to themselves will seek only such land as they can till; workers left to themselves will wind up in trade unions, mere mechanisms of capitalism. And so on. Only the revolutionist, with what Dostoevsky called a "fire in the mind," can bring about a revolution, for he is carrying that most combustible of messages, the promise of a millennium.

There is an ineradicably religious component in revolution. It is not strange, therefore, that the nearest Europe came to actual revolutions prior to the seventeenth century were the religiously intoxicated bands of peasants in the late Middle Ages and Reformation putting to torch, to knife, and to ax all that lay before them until, in a final act of heavenly ecstasy, they in effect destroyed themselves. Tocqueville recognized the French Revolution as different from any political event in all history by virtue of the deeply religious strains of millennialism, redemption, salvation, Armageddon, and heaven-on-earth which ran through the minds of its makers, the Jacobins foremost. Such strains, in varying degrees, have been present in all modern revolutions, the American included.

Here is the proper formula to mount a revolution in order to relieve a psychological itch. First, find a country that has a feeble, fal-

tering government virtually asking to be captured in coup. Introduce
theories of revolution, say on the revolt of workers, the rise of the
landless, the rebellion of the impoverished, the historic destiny of the
proletariat, or the inevitable conflict of the classes. Such theories will
ignite the minds of a few of those in each category who will then
themselves strut as revolutionists and guerrillas. Capture the government and immediately introduce terror. The terror must in a short
time come to include even the hardest working of revolutionary
allies, the most indulgent of bureaucrats, the most loyal and effective
of soldiers, and the most innocent of subjects and citizens, for it is
terror alone that can, through torture, imprisonment, and execution,
with the help of spies and secret police, so terrify and demoralize the
populace that their minds are open to any and all propaganda and
bovinely grateful for any boon whatever, be it stale bread, stale slo-
gan, or stale confinement.

The relation between war and revolution is very close in history.
In the first place, many wars, such as that between the American colonies and the British government, take on a revolutionary flavor even
when, as in America, social and economic objectives are few and far
between, the Englishmen in America wanting only what the
Englishmen in England had in the way of traditions. From many
points of view the real French Revolution, the one with lasting effects, was that carried by Napoleon and his troops throughout Europe. Every conquest was followed by the seeding into foreign soil of
French Revolutionary ordinances and laws through French-backed
governments.

War and revolution are related in another sense that is equally
important. Weakness of the incumbent government is the first cause
of revolutions, and nothing can so quickly bring a government to its
knees, make it ripe for internal subversion and capture, and render
the people into a helpless mass or mob as war, especially futile,
failed, politically disintegrating war. There would have been no Russian or Chinese revolutions had there been no World War I and
World War II. Only governments battered, devastated, and bled
deeply of their white cells by war—war that in Russia's case resulted
in the slaughter of close to twenty million soldiers, unprecedented
famine, and almost total disorganization of government at all levels—
could have been so easily toppled by a relative handful of insurrectionists. Lenin, brought back to Russia from Switzerland by order of
the German High Command in order to lead the Bolshevik weakening action against the Russian government, had little difficulty in
working his arts of duplicity and chicanery, among his own followers
as well as the government in power, or in instituting terror and heavy

political imprisonment once the Kerensky mockery of government was brought down. If ever a country was ripe for revolution it was the Russia of the last of the czars and of his impotent successor Kerensky. But the war alone made Russia ripe to the point of rotting.

Precisely the same is true of the Maoist revolutionary forces in their prolonged opposition to the government of Chiang Kai-shek and his Nationalist Party. Of the loyalty and strength of the Communists there can be no question, as the Long March made clear. The same holds true for the tactical and strategic brilliance of Mao and his lieutenants. But had the Nationalist government not been enfeebled by the terrible successes of the Japanese, successes made relatively easy by the gross stupidities of Chiang, the Maoist capture of China after the war would not have been possible.

The idea of revolution is by now an ineffaceable attribute of the modern mind. In no other respect do intellectuals today differ so radically from their ancestors, at least those prior to the eighteenth century, for whom the very thought of rising against government was abhorrent. Despite the hideous toll taken by twentieth century revolutions in life, freedom, and security, the luster of revolution from the left only grows in the intellectual's mind—one more instance of the principle of cognitive dissonance.

SOCIAL SCIENCES

THE SOCIAL SCIENCES in America are currently in what appears to be the final act of a drama that has been going on since World War II. Whether it is tragedy or farce is still unclear, but that it is the final act is made clear by the suddenly grievous condition of economics, for long the queen of the social sciences, now reduced to ignominy and welcome company to its until recently envious sister-disciplines.

Keynes lifted economics to near-aristocratic level in the late 1930s. No other social science could claim any living representative who came close to Keynes in brilliance, erudition, influence upon the world's policy makers, and charisma. He has just barely missed hero status of the kind known to Darwinians, Marxists, and Freudians. Keynesians lack that proper sense of religious awe, willingness to suspend all judgment, and disposition to regard as sacred every text and utterance to qualify Keynes as hero or demigod.

The rise of economists to peerage came around 1950. That was when the discipline came into its own as a reputedly mathematical and exact science, when economists began to be sought out by Presidents and Congressmen, and when observations on the state of nation and world by economists were deemed of front-page significance by newspaper publishers. Further kudos came at the end of the 1960s when economics was admitted to the select circle of sciences whose members were eligible for the Nobel Prize. Diffidence in individual economists became increasingly rare. More than a few of them believed between 1950 and about 1980 that they had acquired the knowledge to forestall inflation and deflation, recession and depression. Laws and principles abounded, each the key to some previously arcane sector of the economy. All that was required for permanent economic growth and prosperity was that White House and Congress pay attention.

By the end of 1981, however, all of this had changed calamitously. It became humiliatingly evident that economists not only had failed throughout the 1970s in forecasting from one year to the next but were even wanting in explanations after the unforeseen rises or falls in the economy had taken place. One Nobel laureate in economics was candid enough to state then that in every crucial respect the economic behavior of the 1970s had eluded him and all other economists in the United States. Such candor is not common even yet, but realization of the situation is. The consensus wisdom is gone, succeeded by sheer Babel: monetarists, Keynesians, neo-Keynesians, supply-siders, and many others, each group speaking to itself, not to others. Economics is by now in much the same situation each of the other social sciences has been in for varying lengths of time since World War II: bankruptcy, intellectual capital gone and credibility exhausted.

By 1950 most of the social sciences enjoyed a status they had never had before World War II. They were taken seriously by physical scientists and general public alike in their frequent opinionations and predictions. The Ford Foundation, with assets in the billions, was established for the express purpose of providing ample funds for the social—or increasingly the behavioral—sciences. Other foundations rallied, and by the middle of the 1950s, it was a rare social scientist of quality who did not have the perquisites of status that physical scientists had known from the beginning of World War II. Research institutes mushroomed in the social sciences; offices became ever more luxurious, their occupants ever more engaged in research, consultation, government advising, travel from conference to conference all over the world—in just about everything but the teaching of undergraduates, a responsibility increasingly turned over to graduate students and technicians. Although sociologists and political scientists may not have made the peerage, their status and affluence were higher than they had ever been before.

The fall of the social sciences began in the early 1960s and was well along by the end of that decade, the sole exception being, for another decade, economics. By 1970, what a sociologist, political scientist, social psychologist, or anthropologist said on any subject whatever was, for the American people generally, a matter of no consequence. The credibility they had enjoyed for nearly two decades after World War II was in tatters, their numbers depleted, and their capital assets nearly gone. Now that economics has joined them, the drama is over, the rise and fall of the social sciences complete.

When the social scientists themselves are asked about the forces which broke their disciplines, leaving them objects of pity and wonder in the 1980s, three answers are almost tropistic: first, insufficient money for research; second, youth, meaning that the social sciences unlike the physical sciences are still in their youth; and third, complexity of data. All three answers are as false as they are self-serving. Abundant funds have never been a condition of success in the history of the sciences. First scientists become successful, then they become affluent. Nuclear physics evolved in the 1920s and 1930s on bare pittances. Nor are the social sciences in their youth. Their history goes back to the Greeks, just as do the histories of the physical sciences. And as to complexity of data, there is nothing in the universe as it has come to be known in the twentieth century that is not complex. Even if all three of these tropistic responses were correct, they would explain only the secondary position of the social sciences, not their collapse.

So much for self-pity. The real reasons for this collapse are fourfold. There is first the ostentatious scientism that came over the several disciplines in the 1950s. It was apparently assumed that if their practitioners walked like scientists and quacked like scientists, the world would believe they were scientists. More and more writing in the social sciences came to look as though it had been done by a mediocre chemist or geologist. Much was made of theory, general and special. Much more was made of what was called methodology, which made it easy for inept individuals to check their minds, so to speak, and to live off formulas. The air was filled with "hypothesis," "verification," "replication," "law," "paradigm," and worse. The penalty imposed by history upon this pretentious and unconvincing scientism was the replacement of hard-nosed behavioral social science by the soft-nosed, mind-blowing subjectivism of the 1960s.

The second reason for the current disrepair of the social sciences is the megalomania that came over them in conjunction with their scientific posturing. As early as the 1950s, only a few years after the social studies had begun dressing up like sciences, there was the cry for such monstrosities as a national academy of social science, a national endowment for social science, and a national social science foundation. Further cries went up for such positions as "Social Science Adviser to the President" in Washington. The land overflowed with the complacency of the social scientists. All that was needed for the instantaneous eradication of poverty, crime, racism, bad housing, and war was a political government duly advised by resident social scientists. Hubris; pride virtually demanding the fall.

Third is the rank politicization of the social sciences. The very concept of the social is a coinage of the early nineteenth century, in which an old word was given new meaning. When Comte, Haller, and others called for a social science, they did so with the specters of political government and political or legal science in their minds. They were seeking a knowledge and then a policy that would make it possible for the social order to be largely autonomous, free of the constricting bureaucratic control of the kind of state the French Revolution had yielded. *Social*, as a word, meant family, village, parish, town, voluntary association, and class, not the political state. But the corruption in the twentieth century of the word *social* has been a symbol of the politicization of the social sciences. Today, given the extent to which all of the social sciences have become monopolized by political values and aspirations, it would be much more correct if they were called the political sciences.

Fourth is the monolithic liberalism of the social sciences since World War II—liberalism in the sense of the new liberalism, the ideology of the provider-state. It would be hard to find in all history a more flagrant scene of hypocrisy than that which was presented by social scientists, pretending to be scientists, assuring the world that objectivity was quite as possible in the study of human beings as of atoms, but all the while making certain that their assorted hypotheses, principles, and conclusions emerged in a fashion that would make them presentable at any liberal caucus. The litany of liberalism was the litany of social science, with the possible exception of a small but growing sector in economics. The litany begins, "Crime is caused by poverty; poverty is caused by racism," and proceeds predictably from there. Any social scientist's conclusion that did not end with an appeal to the national government to take immediate action, properly funded, was purely accidental. In consequence, social science associations led all the others in stamping out "chairmen" and replacing them with "chairpersons" and "chairs," in passing petitions demanding governmental action on all social problems, in waving the banner of affirmative action, with imprisonment and heavy fines for the guilty, or in protesting police brutality in cases of murder and robbery. Those who attended meetings of the various associations during the 1960s and 1970s could have been forgiven for not being sure whether it was a professional meeting or a monster rally in behalf of all the liberal and radical icons.

Happily, a small minority in each of the social sciences during the past four decades consisted and still consists of highly talented individuals doing their very best to achieve a true science or, if not science, an equally high level of scholarship. As is true in the humanities, there are tall trees to be seen, but also great expanses of dwarfed shrubs, porous soil, poison ivy, and pure weeds.

SOCIOBIOLOGY

IT IS A NEW NAME for a hoary belief that the proper explanation of anything social or cultural lies in the realm of biology. Nothing seems to give sociobiologists more delight than drawing conceptual lines from turf-guarding geese and gazelles all the way to armed soldiers on a border. That fish, fowl, and animal observe boundaries and can be both altruistic and aggressive is for the sociobiologist enough to awaken dreams of someday having students take their political science and sociology in biology departments. The possibility that human culture may be a realm as distinctive as the biological and thus is no more susceptible to being reduced to the biological than biology is to being reduced to the chemical or physical is ignored by the sociobiologist. And the idea that law, morals, religion, and family can be sufficiently analyzed and explained in the terms of the norms of culture, a domain unique to man, awakens only negative response to the sociobiologist.

Although this discipline traces its ancestry back to Darwin, particularly to his *Descent of Man*, its roots go much farther back in time. Aristotle was being sociobiological when he concluded that slaves are what they are because of their own nature and that families, communities, and states exist because man is by nature social. The moral philosophy of the eighteenth century was richly sociobiological, especially that in Scotland, where Adam Smith, Ferguson, Millar, and Kames, among others, located the source of every significant pattern of behavior in some passion, drive, or instinct. Altruism, Smith thought, was the innate drive in man that made society possible, just as the "instinct" to truck and barter, to buy and sell, was the true source of the economic system.

Turgot was almost alone in the eighteenth century in his realization of the great power of culture, in contrast to the biological realm. Man is unique, he concluded, in the whole biological kingdom in being able to accumulate generation by generation an ever-growing stock of knowledge that makes it unnecessary for each generation to repeat in exact detail the ways of the generation before and makes it possible to lift the capacities of man in a constant course upward through time.

The modern theory of culture is the work largely of Tylor, whose *Primitive Culture* was published in 1871, the year in which Darwin's *Descent of Man* appeared. Tylor's is much the more original and significant of the two works. Tylor demonstrated at length and in detail, through comparison of dozens of societies, how very large a number of traits of human behavior are entirely dependent upon the culture one is born in. Culture, he wrote, is the sum total of those ideas, values, norms, artifacts, processes, and symbols which are inherited by individuals socially, through one or other form of postnatal training, education, and socialization. Once the idea of culture had been assimilated, it became possible to raise the level of interpretation in the study of human behavior from animistic, prepotent drives or tendencies supposedly inherited through the germ plasm to the historically transmitted incentives and imperatives which are at the heart of man's unique social behavior.

The idea of culture is, however, a difficult one, especially for biogists, to assimilate. When man engages in economic or political behavior, the sociobiologist therefore concludes that it must have some genetic cause. Sociobiologists grant that much in human behavior is the result of culture, but their referent is usually language, dress, ornament, or technology, not ideas and values which drive human beings to heights or depths of behavior unknown to subhuman species. For the sociobiologist, an explanation of economic activity that goes beyond the hunting and foraging proclivity that man shares with all animal species is somehow superficial.

Sociobiologists have a hard time accepting the fact that social scientists are generally quite aware of the patterns of animal behavior which are dear to their hearts, such as communal feeding, mate protection, care of the young, altruism, aggression, and turf guarding. Indeed one would have to go back a long time in history to find a period when people were not so aware. But most humanists and social scientists question the value of dwelling on these patterns *ad infinitum* to the exclusion of important work that can be done only by economists, sociologists, and political scientists. It may be nice to know that all animal life, man included, possesses something analogous to an acquisitive instinct, but such knowledge does not carry one far when the object is understanding of the business cycle. It must be known to every child that man shares with other forms of life the biological urge of sex and also of care of the young. But again, that knowledge, while salutary, does not carry one more than a few inches in the long course of learning about and explaining the incredibly complicated systems of kinship which have existed on earth, systems which are as far from sex or maternal instinct as higher mathematics is from the multiplication tables.

One sociobiologist, Ghiselin, asked why social scientists do not scrap their present interests and techniques and simply apply Darwinian principles to the study of society. There are two answers to that question: first, as is becoming amusingly evident, Darwinian principles are now being found inadequate for even biological questions; and second, the essential Darwinian principles are as irrelevant to the nature and history of human culture as Newtonian principles are to the study of the genetic code. Utterly different areas of reality are involved.

Sociobiologists are incessantly pressing Darwin's *Descent of Man* upon humanists and social scientists, declaring with Darwinian mandarin Simpson that everything written earlier on morals and social behavior is automatically obsolete. But this book and Darwin's separate study of the emotions in man and animals leave one with mixed reactions. Indubitably they fall among the classics of nineteenth century biology. Yet Darwin was also the perfect Victorian in his convictions that race is the true source of man's differential abilities, that behind all nationalities lie races, and that the epic of human evolution is little more than the survival of the fittest races. Darwin maintained that Anglo-Saxon superiority over the French was racial at bottom and that the French male's greater expressiveness with his hands and his quicker tendency to tears were race-linked characteristics. Moreover, women were said to be inferior to men in capacity for profound thought, for imagination, and even for sensory stimulus. All of this is nonsense, and it is therefore difficult to know what Darwin has to teach humanists and social scientists, except perhaps superlative English style.

Sociobiologists often recommend scrapping the study of human history as now known and replacing it with the Darwinian evolutionary approach, but using gene pools instead of races which have fallen on conceptually hard times. Darlington in fact wrote a history of human civilization in which genetics crowds out history save as illustration of what gene pools and genetic transmission have accomplished during the past five thousand years. He argued that the fundamental gene pools—master and slave, mechanic and philosopher, priest and communicant, prophet and soldier—all came into fixed existence many thousands of years ago, and that the history of civilization is at bottom no more than encounters of these gene pools. Christianity is simply a matter of gene flow, to which may be traced "the intellectual leaders of the Christians for all later times." The Huguenots were a genetically homogeneous group, from whose genes their special qualities of business and political leadership derived. The Renaissance, which Darlington misread as the breeding ground of the "Scientific and Industrial Revolutions," was the outcome of the genetic crossing of "the mechanic" and "the philosopher," a thought that would have shaken the arrogant humanists with fury. According to Darlington, "the inborn character of the dissenters . . . created their industries, their religion, and their politics."

The tension in American history between equality and the achievement ethic was also described by Darlington as genetic. "This was a problem which Alexis de Tocqueville, who looked at American society . . . could never understand. For he was concerned with the *ideas* of democracy and aristocracy; the possibility of their having a genetic basis was entirely withheld from him." Poor Tocqueville. In truth, Tocqueville was fully cognizant of genetic interpretations, and his eloquently critical letters to his friend Gobineau, arch-exponent of the racial-genetic view of human history, are models of the kind of devastating refutation that racist doctrines always deserve. In one letter, Tocqueville noted that "Julius Caesar would willingly have written a book to prove that the savages he had met in Britain did not belong to the same race as the Romans." Even the cherished Hollywood Westerns were in for a jolt from Darlington, who argued that in America "the mixture in settling has everywhere separated and assorted in level and in locality according to the inborn and genetic inclinations of its component individuals and families. It is assorted into communities in such a way as to preserve that culture, as well as that genetic character which each would lose by coalescence." Thus, a genetic community had been drawn to the Far West to become gunmen, killing "some 20,000 men in the western states between 1870 and 1895." That historical studies have failed to come up with anything even close that figure is of less importance than that the killers formed a gene pool. But there is more: "All governing classes and all slave classes evidently arose in the beginning from the coming together of different races to form stratified societies which always competed favorably with unstratified societies. They were more competent because their genetically different classes cooperated . . . They were also more adaptable because hybridization between classes could . . . release new variability in the stratified society."

It could have been bees and ants that Darlington was writing about in those words, and that was presumably his intent. The case of the sociobiologists would be stronger, in fact irrefutable, if they could only by some leap of experimental genius show the gene pools and their claimed social and cultural prepotency *before* showing the events and changes in culture which are assertedly reflections of these same gene pools. Sociobiological demonstrations have a circular, self-sealing character, indeed a *post hoc, propter hoc* quality. For the sociobiologist it is axiomatic that genetic mechanisms not only underly but generate and govern social behavior. Therefore just about anything human, ranging from a child care center to a summit conference among the powers, is *ipso facto* another illustration, comparable to any coming from geese and gazelles, of man's iron genetic heritage.

The achievements of biologists in genetics and microbiology in the twentieth century have been spectacular, ranking with the best in any science. Biology is many leagues ahead of what it was in Darwin's day. But if its scientific achievements were greater by a hundred or thousandfold, they would still be no closer to a valid and useful explanation of man's culture and social behavior. The reason lies in the type of reductionism that is favored by the sociobiologist. Edward O. Wilson wrote in connection with the recent great achievement in biology: "I suggest that we are about to repeat this cycle in the blending of biology and the social sciences and that as a consequence the two cultures of Western intellectual life will be joined at last." Lest the social scientist react with joy to this announcement of *Anschluss*, take heed of Wilson's further remark: "The heart of scientific method is reduction of perceived phenomena to fundamental testable principles. The elegance, we can fairly say the beauty of any particular scientific generalization is measured by its simplicity relative to the number of phenomena it can explain."

Very well, but there is an old warning to beware of reductions not effected by oneself. It recalls the Baptist clergyman who orated to a large interdenominational audience: "Why don't we end our differences and controversies and simply unite in one great Baptist church." Wilson should be reminded, when it comes to reduction and to elegant and beautiful theories, that a few physicists, unimpressed by the principle of natural selection, have proposed that physics take over biology, with that principle becoming a corollary of the second law of thermodynamics. Whatever the present state of disrepair in the social sciences, in short, it is in no way related to a lack of attention to charts and graphs on altruism and aggression among the primates.

TECHNOLOGY

FROM THE BEGINNING of the Industrial Revolution in England in the late eighteenth century, technology has had bad odor in the minds of artists, writers, and intellectuals generally, in one more instance of the deep gulf between popular and intellectual culture in the modern West. Few things seem to have delighted the people of England more than the machine-driven factories which Blake and his genus found satanic. Such delight was only enhanced and broadened by the railroads, the telegraph, the telephone, the automobile, and the innumerable other inventions which in the aggregate give the nineteenth century unique importance in the history of man.

But where the people saw wonders of the world, a long and continuous line of intellectuals saw alienation of the human spirit, a despotism greater than any wielded by man directly. Where the people rejoiced in liberation or promised liberation from the back-breaking toil and drudgery of yore, minds as diversely constituted as Carlyle, Tocqueville, and Nietzsche could only lament the mechanization of the world and the degradation of the human body and mind that went with it. With their characteristic and cheerless joy in *Weltschmerz* the Germans led all the rest in the writing of litanies of despair. Though the country was prodigal in the mounting of its own industrial revolution in the late nineteenth century, threatening England and America in world commerce, a succession of German philosophers, historians, and journalists saw in the new technology only a never-ending source of *angst*, accidie, anomie, and other sicknesses of the soul. Technology, with its transfer to machine of native strengths of the human body and mind, bespoke for these metaphysicians of alienation an enslavement of the body and a crippling of the spirit and, worst of all, a production of the modern masses—inchoate, void of will, as dangerous as any slumbering monster of the Silurian Age.

But Germany was far from alone in this *Weltschmerz*. Poets, artists, and essayists vied with one another in France in contrasting the beauties of nature with the desolating yield of the machine. Writers of the *fin de siècle* in France and England alike thought of technology and its culture almost uniformly in terms of a wasteland, a conception to which T. S. Eliot in perhaps the most famous and influential poem of the twentieth century gave world importance. J. L. and Barbara Hammond, Fabian historians of the industrial era, contrasted the factories of their day and their iron disciplines with the freedoms man had once known within "the rhythms of nature, the spell of the seasons, and the mystic bond of man and earth." That for the vast majority of people reality in the pretechnological, preindustrial had far more to do with the bone weariness and mind starvation of what Marx correctly referred to as "the idiocy of rural life" was of no visible importance to the Hammonds or many others of their time. For them, between the authentic nature of man and the whole assemblage of machines that is called technology, there is a deadly conflict that must end eventually in the complete degradation of man, creator of his own destruction.

This all too familiar litany has not much substance. The flaw of all such lucubrations is that the abstract quickly numbs any sense of the concrete. People do not commonly think of actual implements and machines, ranging from an electric appliance in their kitchen all the way to computer-driven rockets to the moon, when the word *technology* is thrust before them. Captured, as the human mind so easily is, by an abstraction, they find themselves forgetting the particulars—and Blake was right that only the particulars matter—and becoming addicts to the general and abstract. Instead of the automobiles they drive, the electricity that lights and warms, the computers which free their minds and lighten their load, and the planes and trains which carry man to all parts of the earth, instead of these and other actual manifestations of technology, they choose to think of technology as a metaphor for all that is oppressive and dominating. It is hard to think of any given part of technology, any particular device, that does not by its very nature serve man. And this is as true of nuclear reactors as of electric lamps. But in the large literature on technology, the protagonist is almost invariably a master, not a servant.

That technology, in the abstract or the concrete, alienates man from others and from self has been said so often by poets, artists, and other intellectuals as to be a part of the conventional wisdom. But if there were in fact something alienating about technology of the modern kind, a great many alienated people would have existed in the last two hundred years, the period of the technological revolution. In the hundred years after the spread of the railroad in England human beings were exposed in quick succession to the steam ship, the telegraph, the telephone, the automobile, the radio, and the airplane, among other striking innovations. More than a few individuals by dint of longevity lived through the advent of most of those, but there are no records of any deep estrangement of the human spirit, of lament at the loss of the immediacy of man and nature, or of belief that man had transferred vital parts of body and mind to the impersonal machine.

Even when long-isolated primitive peoples have been brought into sudden contact with Western technology, there has been no sign of technology shock. Such peoples have indeed been decimated and devastated by diseases brought to them by Western man, and their cultures and social organizations have been severely dislocated by Western systems of administration which either bypass or actually root out cherished groups and symbols. But while technology may well accompany the social and psychological alienation of a people from sacred values, it is not the machine that is responsible; it is the indifference or ruthlessness of mind that bears the machine.

That small, isolated people discovered a decade or so ago in the Philippines, a people living in Stone Age simplicity and innocence, as devoid of implement or weapon as had been their ancestors of a hundred thousand years ago, might have been expected to cower in fear and terror when the helicopters hovered overhead and then landed, disgorging creatures whose dress and manner could not have been more bizarre had they come from Mars. What in fact happened was the natives' courteous, dignified acceptance not only of these novel beings from another world but even of the helicopters, which they immediately reduced by playful mimicry to the level of the comic.

It has been said by artists since the beginning of the technological-industrial revolution that the effect of technology is to take away from man his native strength, then his skills, and finally his mind, all of these God-given human capacities transferred to the machine. Tocqueville declared that the inescapable effect of technologically based specialization was the degradation, the brutalization, and the enslavement of the worker: "The art advances, the artisan recedes." Well before Marx, Tocqueville saw forming two classes of men, the one debased by enchainment to machine and division of labor, rendered almost totally dependent, the other composed of masters and owners, a new aristocracy, its power constantly increasing in proportion to the technologically based dependency of the working class. But Tocqueville has been proved by history to be as wrong in this analysis as Marx was in his theory of the progressive immiserization of the proletariat. Neither was able to see clearly what was already beginning to happen in their lifetimes: the slow but inexorable rise in the fortunes and the comforts of people, and above all, in their bases and contexts of dignity.

Of all the boons and benefits resulting from the development of technology, the greatest is surely the release of human beings from the kind of labor, whether agricultural or industrial, that can only degrade the human mind and dull its edges. To live in a world as filled with wonders and attractions as this one is, but to be condemned to work of paralyzing monotony or repetitiveness or of a complexity that would place no real demands upon the clinical moron, is to know a special form of misery that was not known to man's earliest ancestors, whose world was a simpler one uncomplicated by expectations generated by forces beyond his control. It is fallacious to say that technology has created all these menial, mind-eroding jobs. One need think only of the peasant, his brutish, immobile, heaviness of face, his shambling gait, his animal coarseness of manner, his vacant stare. Millet painted and Markham wrote of "the man with the hoe" whose numbers were once vast in Europe but are now virtually gone. It was once thought that so physically as well as psychologically different was the peasant from the rest of humanity, from middle and upper classes, that Europe was forever condemned to two distinct races. But today one has to look carefully and hard to find survivals of the once-vast peasantry. What seemed, to minds as humane as Dr. Johnson's and Burke's, to be ineradicably set in physical heredity proved to be evanescent once the peasant "race" was liberated by technology from its degradation and soul-shattering drudgery.

Sociologists have written for nearly a century that technology has led to a disintegration of the family, of the local community, of church, and of the greater part of traditional morality. All of these, it is said, are products of the pretechnological era going back many thousands of years, and the machine has served to displace them from their ancient contexts and functions. This view is a product of the same mentality that characterized poets and artists in the early nineteenth century. Technology has had no disintegrative impact upon traditional institutions. What has had such impact is the state and a system of power that has usurped the natural authorities of the institutions, thus separating individuals from their historic means of identification and bringing them ever closer to political government. Those who indict the automobile for disruption of settled family life or the pill for corruption of traditional sexual morality would do better to indict the state and its bureaucratic invasions of, and thus in time its spoliations of, the fabric of family authority.

The final ground for fear of technology is that in its currently fast-advancing computerized and automated forms it will eventually take from human thought the sovereignty it has had in the world, thus reducing human beings to the level of mere appendages of the machine. But this fear too is baseless. The one thing that cannot be transferred to the machine is human imagination. Electronic machines perform wonders galore, but they are and will always be limited to the wonders implanted in them by man's unique and untransferable imagination. It is undetachable, untransferable imagination in union with the technological imperative that is likely to produce the great symbols of this age, symbols that lift the mind in the same way that the cathedrals of the Middle Ages and the Parthenon of Athens lifted generations of minds. Those in the West who scoffed at the few billions of dollars the United States put into the moon landing are descendants of those who in the fifteenth century scoffed at the navigators' search for a passage to India. But just as in that day a large and eager public existed for such exploits, evidenced by the enormous circulations such works as Purchas and Hakylut enjoyed, so is there today a vast public for moon landings, for unmanned spacecraft traveling millions of miles into the universe, and for the most recent marvel, the *Colombia*. Just as high technology in its awe-inspiring ways is the present-day cathedral, so the rocketed vehicles in outer space are the modern *Pinta, Santa Maria*, and *Nina*.

Henry Adams was right in his selection and contrasting of the Virgin and the dynamo. Each in its way epitomizes admirably the medieval and the modern age. But Adams was wrong in his morose and self-pitying disparagement of the dynamo. The history of science and technology has shown clearly that, however different the two symbols are, there is not the slightest necessity of any incompatibility.

TYRANNY

IT IS A PITY that this word has largely disappeared from textbooks in government, for the indications are that future historians will refer to the present age as one of the resurgence of tyranny. The word has been made into an archaic label for excessive authority of any kind, but this misses not only the true meaning, dating back to the Greeks, but the special character of the dominant forms of political power in the twentieth century, which is not only monocratic but charismatic in some degree at least. *Tyranny* was reserved by the Greeks for one-man rule, whether enlightened or not. Both Plato and Aristotle spent time advising tyrants, seeking to instill some of their political philosophy into the minds of individuals who had absolute power. It is a great convenience to the philosopher or political intellectual to be able to deal with monocrats instead of assemblies and oligarchies. What Plato and Aristotle learned, the Italian humanists relearned in the fifteenth century and the *philosophes* in the eighteenth. This surely explains the popularity with certain types of political scientist and historian today of Presidents such as Franklin D. Roosevelt. It was in large degree to help develop the power of the Presidency that John F. Kennedy attracted the large number of political intellectuals he did.

It was hardly envisaged at the turn of the century that this century, coming hard on the heels of the century of great hope, of classical liberalism, of burgeoning republics and democracies, would become best known for its multitudinous dictators. Yet by anyone armed sufficiently with Platonist and Aristotelian perceptions, this turn of history might have been foreseen during World War I. For the condition of tyranny, the Greek philosophers stated, is the kind of internecine war, class conflict, and general political anarchy which that war was so plainly germinating, at least from 1917 on. Aristotle would have foreseen a tyrant emerging in both Russia and Italy once the war was finished, and it would not have mattered to him what particular ideology was espoused by either. He would no doubt have foreseen, looking at the dismembered body of Europe in 1918, ancient empires and monarchies toppled, nationalities struggling to become independent states, the old social contract exploding from class strife in almost every country, and the rise of even more tyrants in the future, in all parts of the world where the traditional social and political bonds were coming asunder. There has been a steady increase in the number of tyrants in the twentieth century. Empires and imperialistic regimes were overthrown often in the name of democracy or socialism, but what the great majority of the liberated peoples have gotten, on most continents of the world, is dictatorship, military or civil.

Lenin, Stalin, Hitler, Franco, and Tito, all fit the type of tyranny. China, after millennia in which emperors ruled with supposedly absolute authority, saw genuinely absolute authority when Mao, speaking the language of democratic socialism, reached power. It would be hard to find in all history a monocracy more centralized, more sweeping, more penetrating, and also more charismatic than that of Mao, Hitler, or Stalin. The divine-right monarchs of the sixteenth and seventeenth centuries in Europe were absolute largely in theory, not practice. Whatever the intent or hope in the mind of Louis XIV when he said *L'état c'est moi*, fulfillment was out of the question. Old authorities of town, aristocracy, church, and guild were still too great, and in any event both the sociological and the technological prerequisites to absoluteness of rule were lacking.

Not only were the twentieth century's tyrants unforeseen at the beginning, but so also was the remarkable popular acceptance of the tyrants. Social democracy, far from conditioning the masses against one-man rule, encouraged them to accept if not seek it. The horrifying record of torture, imprisonment, and mass execution that the dictators of this century, especially those on the political left, have left to posterity may easily obscure the fact that it was always minorities, not majorities, whom the Stalins and Hitlers imprisoned or exterminated. Everything is done by the tyrant in the modern world, as in the ancient, to keep the majority of the people fed and protected; there thus develops the kind of bond between the people and the ruler that is commonly denoted by the words *Caesarian* or *Bonapartist*. In 1932 that bond was an attractive one to large numbers of Germans whose image of democracy was one of decadence combined with class conflict and gross inefficiency. It was equally attractive to people in Italy after World War I, and there is no reason to suppose that, if World War II had not destroyed Hitler and Mussolini, the great majorities of their peoples would have become disenchanted in time.

Popular rule, whether in a republic or in a democracy, is not as popular, in the full sense, as the dogma of democracy would suggest. Especially in the more successful democracies, such as that of the United States, most people are loath to give their time to management of the state, to do much more than vote occasionally. The rhetoric of democracy is full of attestations of the citizens' desire to participate, with their life's blood if necessary, but this is simply not true. Both Learned Hand and Joseph Schumpeter commented on this fact, Schumpeter observing that most citizens put in much more thought on their bridge games than on the problems of democracy. True, there is an advantage to free government in this fact. After all, the nations which boast of their 98 percent turnouts for elections are tyrannies in which the facade and luster of democracy are sought by rulers. The peoples of democracies are the freer to pursue their moral and social ends and thus to move toward the civilized life when they are not largely occupied by political duties. That is the inherent paradox of democracy. There have been approximations of totalitarian democracy, as during the French Revolution when, in the major cities at least, large numbers of citizens were constantly occupied by their civic duties. What makes a government totalitarian is less the structure of government than the relation between state, irrespective of government, and society. If the Politburo were abolished and nothing else changed, the Soviet Union would be just as totalitarian under its party rule or the rule of its large legislative assembly as it is now. The greatest single foundation of liberal democracy is not its constitution, which can always be changed or given novel interpretation, but a reasonably secure and stable social order.

But the number of other types of tyranny, in the strict sense of the word, is growing in democratic countries, including the United States, and those living under them appear to enjoy the experience. The absolute, unqualified personal rule of the gang leader is a grim reality today in ghettoes all across America and the West. There is not only a willingness but a positive desire, a craving, for the lash. All manner of rites exist, some violent and sadistic, by which followers prove their total devotion to the leader. The Manson family in southern California is one example. The desire to serve Manson rather than any relish for criminality as such was what drove the family members to their ghastly acts of mutilation and murder. Everyone in the family belonged only to Manson, and there were various ways, sexual and other, by which they could demonstrate their willing, happy abasement before him, could ritualistically reaffirm the power of the tyrant and the subjection of the individual.

The Jonestown episode is instructive here. Granted the ultimate loyalty of Jones not to any religion, cult, or obsession but to the Soviet Union, there remains to be explained the passion of the people, young and old, black and white, male and female, for the person of Jones himself. There was seemingly no limit to his powers over followers. He could take their property, confiscate their money, dissolve a marriage, call to his bed any member, deny exodus however temporary from the group, and as the world learned, successfully order them to destroy their lives with poison by the tubful. And the horrifying reality is that during the several years that this group existed, in California and then in Guyana, the bond between tyrant and the tyrannized became constantly closer. Newspaper exposures of the true venality, terror, and exploitation of Jones over his members had very little effect on the cult; some deviated, but even among these a fealty to Jones remained in some degree.

There are the Moonies, Hare Krishna, and dozens of other less wealthy, less influential religious groups of the same basic order, all so deeply magnetized by those who lead and command that few of their members are ever separated from the group save by parental or

other force from the outside, accompanied usually by psychiatric attempt to free the mind. It would be inaccurate for the most part to
assume that these followers, mostly young, were psychiatric cases to
begin with. Apart only from the iron devotion to their orthodoxy and
their prophet, the majority are reasonably normal. "Clean, well-
scrubbed, literate, and polite" is the well-worn description of most of
them.

The prospect of continued tyranny in the world is very real,
whether it be the kind symbolized by dictators of left and right or
the kind represented by the Manson family, Jonestown, and the
Moonies. The institutional buttresses of genuine democracy either
have never existed, do not now exist, or are in process of erosion and
disintegration. The result is a failure of nerve on the part of majorities that makes the advent of the tyrant welcome.

UNCERTAINTY

SO NUMEROUS AND DIVERSE are the traits of culture oriented exclusively toward the uncertainties of life that the humanities and social
sciences would be justified in creating an "uncertainty principle" of
their own. Starting with the major dogmas and rituals of religions
and continuing all the way down to the simplest and most elemental
of superstitions, there is a vast sphere of culture that has no other
reason for being except to cope with the unforeseeable, the unex-
pected, and all those aspects of life, real or imaginary, which cannot
be brought under the grip of the utilitarian or rational. A great deal
of what is called *politesse*, manners, decorum, and protocol falls within
this sphere and may be traced back historically to the need for some
means of neutralizing possible assault or invasion. But most of these
traits and patterns of culture are aimed at protection from the purely
fortuitous, the irregular, the adventitious, and the random.

Man has a terror of the chaos of uncertainty. He is as driven
therefore to the construction of rites and beliefs to combat this terror
as a spider is to the weaving of webs. Such rites and beliefs are never
oriented toward what man has full control over, only to what, with
the best of preparation, remains hazardous or capricious. However
carefully one proceeds in life, there is always the possibility of accident. For many thousands of years people have sown, tilled, and har-
vested their crops, invariably applying to their work the best available skills. Everything certain can be taken care of through the purely

utilitarian without recourse to propitiation or ritual. But there is the dread possibility of hailstones at harvest time crushing and destroying the crop despite all that has been done in its care or of a plague of life-destroying insects, or of human predators bent upon their own engorgement without pity to others. These are the strokes of chance and fortune; they are all instances of uncertainty and must be guarded against. Hence the existence in every part of the world of rites designed solely to ward off the uncertain. No sphere of life is altogether free of such rites, no matter how much utilitarian knowledge may have been accumulated. For, as the poet says, "The best-laid plans of mice and men . . ."

It used to be thought that magic is a fixed stage in the evolution of culture, followed in due course by science; that the latter is the replacement of the former; and that whereas early man in his ignorance turned to magic, modern and future man may be expected to rely solely on science. But this is a gross distortion of reality. The most primitive of peoples never turn to magic when the situation calls for the application of technological skill, however rudimentary it may be. Magic is never a substitute for the technological or scientific. It is used only where ordinary knowledge must be unavailing, where, in sum, uncertainty reigns. Ordinary common sense and experience teach everyone how to build a shelter, but not how to cope with the evil demons and malign circumstances which, if not guarded against, would destroy what has been built. Fear of the uncertain is what leads people today to take out insurance on their houses; and insurance is indeed one way of acquiring security of mind through an offering, in this instance financial offering. But there are still large numbers of people in the world who achieve equal security of mind through ritual practice, ranging from the killing of the sacrificial lamb to the hanging of talismans at the front door. What is now called a house-warming is only the end product of what used to be called a house-blessing.

Wherever danger to life or property or pride is constant, irrespective of one's skills, a turn to the ritualistic is almost universal. The most careful and proficient of soldiers is never averse, upon going into battle, to turning to some cherished form of ritual even if it is no more than crossing his fingers or reciting a line or two that has been found "effective" in the past. Gamblers are also prone to this kind of behavior. The expert poker player habitually does something or, equally important, avoids something that has no rational or logical connection with the game. Professional athletes, ever apprehensive of injury or humiliation on the field, are notoriously given to the wearing of talismans even when it is nothing more than a particular, never-washed pair of socks; and at the beginning of a game when the second baseman or the safety crosses himself, he is almost certainly not making a signal, only guarding against overconfidence and bad luck.

The progress of knowledge does not necessarily lead to the retreat of uncertainty in the world and thus of the traditional uncertainty rites. There is little doubt that these rites have become much fewer in number, but it also appears that visits to fortune tellers, astrologers, and the like have vastly increased. For with all respect to what science and technology have been able to supply in the way of tested knowledge to those who grow crops and search for water and oil, it does not follow that the larger world of uncertainty has diminished much, if at all. It is at least possible that the uncertainties of life and fortune actually increase in a world such as today's, with high culture and advanced technology on the one side and, on the other, rising death rates in both war and peace as the result of violence on the battlefield and crime in the streets. More and more people find themselves echoing Montaigne's "Each second that I am alive I count as an escape from death." There is a case to be made for the proposition that the more certainties, near certainties, and apparent certainties science has rained upon man, the larger the number, paradoxically, of uncertainties. For the seven deadly sins continue to prevail, undiminished by science and education, and modern life gives them more, not less, leeway within which to act. It is one thing for gluttony, envy, and covetousness to operate in a simple village; it is something very different in the modern city. There was a strict limit to what the berserker could accomplish in the South Asia of a century ago; there is almost no limit to what the mad bomber, if sufficiently sophisticated, can do to cities today. The thought of water supplies alone is enough to make one cross one's fingers when going to the tap. Lord Harden's words have more appositeness today than in his time: "The hazards surrounding human life today are so great that we *live* by accident rather than die by it."

VICTIMOLOGY

THIS WORD WILL not be found as yet in most dictionaries and doubtless will strike the sensitive ear harshly. But so far as meanings go, this word has as much prima facie right to existence as *criminology*, the study of criminals and what they have in common. It only later occurred to students of crime that victims in the aggregate might also be shown to have a good deal in common.

There are those who victimize—dominating parents, older brothers and sisters, employers, police, asylum tenders, and physicians as well as common ordinary felons. Victimizing comes more easily and naturally to some than to others in the population. But so does victimhood come more easily to some than to others. Clinical psychologists assert that some people need and subconsciously enjoy being victimized, being exploited, browbeaten, tightly ruled. It is as natural for them to be victims as for others, of different temperament, to be victimizers.

Although interest in the class characteristics of victims of crimes goes back to the founders of criminology in the nineteenth century, it was not until the middle of the twentieth century that victimology became a specialty within sociology and social psychology. The scientific research conducted so far leaves no doubt that the study of victims of thefts, robberies, rapes, assaults, murders, and other crimes is almost as rewarding and illuminating as is the study of criminals. The inescapable fact is that just as there are murderers, so there are murderees. Without victims there can be no victimizers, and temperaments of certain individuals have been shown to lead to ways of behavior which come close to inviting victimization, such as theft, rape, or assault. This does not mean that people conspicuously lacking in the stigmata of victimhood do not also suffer victimization of every kind. It is simply a matter of statistical probability. The majority of those who are mugged on the city streets have in common certain attributes which are less likely to be found among those never or rarely mugged. In sum, precisely as one cannot learn all there is to be learned about leadership without attending also to fellowership, so with peccadilloes, cruelties, sins of man against man, and crimes: the victim is as important to a knowledge of crime as is the perpetrator.

But there is very different and wholly political meaning today to the words *victim* and thereby *victimology*. This meaning is inseparable from the welfare Leviathans that have been built up in the West during the last century or two. The source of this meaning is the do-gooder and uplifter that became widespread in the nineteenth century. Those who were poor, unemployed, chronically drunk, and even criminal in tendency were, by some sociological legerdemain, decreed to be victims—of society. This form of thinking allows two victims for any given crime and no victimizer or criminal. The individual robbed, raped, or slain is certainly a victim, but so is the robber, rapist, and murderer a victim—of circumstances, of poverty, of broken family, in sum, of society. Few things please the liberal heart more than a victim, especially that of society, and when a choice has to be made between the rights of the victim who was robbed and the victim of society who did the robbing, the right-thinking humanitarian almost tropistically sides with the latter.

In this special, very modern social sense of victimhood, there can be no end to the process of creating victims. At this moment, at least 75 percent of the American people are victims. From the point of view of the ardent women's liberationist, all women, or some 51 percent of the population, are victims. Add the blacks, Hispanics, Indians, farmers exposed to drought, unemployed, mentally disturbed, pupils in the public schools, and many other groups in the population, and even an estimate of 85 percent might seem absurdly low. Wealth and high status are no protectors. A new species of victimhood has just been publicized with excellent market results: children of celebrities. They too must be seen as victims. In wife beating there is manifestly a female victim, but the subtlety of the victimological mind should never be underestimated. The husband administering the beating is also a victim—of childhood, say, in a wife-beating home atmosphere—and cannot properly be held accountable.

Accountable! Human society is ultimately possible only when people are accountable for their actions, that is, responsible. The moron who murders, the poverty-stricken who steals, the clinical sadist who tortures and mutilates, the psychologically disturbed who rapes, the insane who slaughters boys by the dozen after sodomizing them, assassins and would-be assassins of Presidents and other high officials of state—all of these are manifestly the causal agents of their various crimes and are recognized as such. Once they would also have been declared responsible and accountable for their crimes. They would have been duly punished by execution, sometimes in a manner as painful or nearly as painful as that inflicted upon their victims. Punishment would have been swift and public, for punishment can exert its cathartic effect upon a community that has been grievously violated only if the punishment is observable by all.

Correctly did Maistre maintain after the Revolution in France that the executioner is the necessary symbol of the social order. If everyone is a victim of some sort, even a Gacy in Chicago who sodomized, strangled, and buried under his house some three dozen boys and men, then there are no criminals. If there are no criminals, there cannot logically be any punishment. Nor can rehabilitation be the goal, since most students of the rehabilitation process, even at its most expert and humane, pronounce it a failure.

There is no substitute for punishment in a social order, and that means holding human beings accountable, treating them as human and therefore responsible. Concern for human rights is rampant these days, but a right is possible in the strict sense only for beings who can be rationally regarded as responsible. The celebrated dignity of man oozes away in an atmosphere where man is so little prized for his unique mental and moral qualities as to be classified from the start a victim. Rights, duties, responsibilities, restraints, consciences, moral codes, all of these are visibly softening and decaying under the influence of victimology—no longer a specialty of criminology but a gigantic malaise of Western society.

More victims, of a different order, have appeared during the last year or two on the American scene: college students, writers, artists, and musicians. They are all victims, it is said, of the federal government's effort to reach a balanced budget without placing punitive taxes on other citizens. For many years government loans were available to nearly all students who requested them; often these loans were not paid back, with government agencies reluctant to prosecute lest they seem to make victims of the delinquent. Now when something of a cut is made in the funds for loan use, or at least a slight deceleration in the rate of increase of these funds, thousands of new victims, the middle-class students, suddenly appear.

Similarly, although the budgets of the National Endowments of the Arts and Humanities rose in the fifteen years between 1965 and 1980 from 10 million to around 170 million each, the result has been only to create more victims, among artists, writers, and musicians. Testimony before Congress by a best-selling novelist, himself acquainted with grants by taxpayers, tells the story: "The truth is, if you are going to take away the lunches of school children, payment to miners with black lung, store front legal assistance, you might as well cut the budget of poets, artists and musicians. You cannot rip up the texture of our national life and expect it to survive . . . What does it matter if our theaters go dark or if the libraries close their doors . . . I recognize a simple undeniable eviction procedure in which most of us are the widows and orphans . . . As a writer of fiction, I could not relate or tell of this. I could not get away with a portrayal of such sanctimonious cruelties." The entire reason for this bleat was simply that a few million dollars were to be lopped from the proposed increases in the budgets of the two endowments. One wonders how Dreiser, Cather, Hemingway, Faulkner, and Cozzens were able to do their writing in an era when there was no endowment, or how the scholarship of McIlwain, Kittredge, and their many peers across the country came about without such endowment. The truth is that they were victims, and egregious ones for they did not even know they were victims.

But Americans do now. By the year 2000, the whole of American society will be composed of victims, or so perceived by the prophets of liberal cant, and perceived no doubt the same way by those aggressive enemies abroad who in their own Soviet-communist garrison states do not recognize victims.

War

FROM THE eighteenth century on, war has had a bad press in Western society. This was the century in which the modern form of the ancient idea of progress became shaped by such men as the Abbé de Saint Pierre, Turgot, Condorcet, and others. In brief, the argument of these intellectuals was: there is an appointed course of progress for humanity, one that will take mankind to ever higher levels of the arts and sciences and thereby ever higher states of learning and philosophical reasoning for the common man. But, the argument continued, there have been in the past and there still are various hindrances, blocks, and barriers to man's progress from ignorance and superstition; chief among these is war. Once war has been eradicated, the flow of human advancement will move in unchecked fashion.

It is an attractive thesis to any Westerner. No one can reasonably doubt the horrors of war, the slaughter, devastation, and production of what Ruskin called illth. General Sherman had a point when he remarked that "it is a good thing war is as hellish on the battlefield as it is; otherwise men would grow to love it too much." That war is or can be hellish is known to anyone who has participated in one or other of this century's numerous wars in all parts of the world. But Sherman's more important words are "otherwise men would grow to love it too much." They contain vast psychological and historical implications.

Psychologically, war tends to fulfill powerful needs in human nature. The first is the need for new experience, for release from the often constricting, stupefying pressure of the mundane. Thoreau's observation to the effect that most of us lead lives of "quiet desperation" is pertinent here. The whole tendency of any stable social order—and until the present century most social orders were stable—is to enmire human beings in habit, custom, use and wont. So strongly are these involved in even the most vital aspects of exis-

tence—work, family life, neighborhood, birth, marriage, and death—
that very few individuals have the psychological resources to rescue
themselves by their own energies from the boredom which can en-
velop human life. This is why in the hearts of most of us, reaction to
a catastrophe, natural or man-made, is mixed: horror, pity, anxiety, to
be sure, but also a sudden alertness, a welling-up of energy, a thrill
and excitement coming from disruption of the accustomed. War is
the oldest and most universal of such catastrophes. Until the modern
era war, with all its frequent cruelties and devastations, was the only
release afforded the vast majority of human beings, the only opportunity for at least temporary surcease from the boredom produced by
the unremitting tyranny of custom.

Even in this war-ridden century, as I can attest from direct experience, war can offer this surcease. I had an excellent academic post
in a major university, was ambitious as teacher and scholar, was possessed of family and comfortable home, enjoyed colleagues and
friends, in sum, lived the good life. But when, as became true in
1942, I saw all around me the fevered activity of Americans as we became overnight a nation in arms, became caught up in whatever ideology governed American entry into World War II, began to see the
uniform, female as well as male, everywhere and read daily of Allied
operations in distant parts of the world, even the comforts and normal stimulation of career became more and more disquieting. An occupation that only a year or two earlier had seemed inexhaustible in
its psychological benefits now seemed routine, exasperating at times,
and produced a sense of ennui that no amount of service on war-re-
lated academic committees, no amount of patrolling of blocks at
night as an air-raid warden, could lighten. Hence, despite draft-defer-
ment, the decision to volunteer as an enlisted man; hence the ever
growing excitement at the prospect of enlistment, the sense of fulfillment upon being sworn in, and the fierce competitiveness of field
training—so welcome after the cloistered, secure life in academe.
And in my young and perforce frugal life, in no other way could the
incessant itch to travel, to see for the first time places only read and
heard about, have been satisfied, this side of middle age at best.
Thus, although I was horrified at times by what I saw overseas, in
fear at other times, and frequently anguished by homesickness, I
through war satisfied a desire for new experience, felt the exhilaration of serving directly in a noble cause, enjoyed the sense of superiority to all those who had chosen other ways of enduring the war,
and in the process acquired new stimuli, new sources of psychic energy which served me well for many years. My experience can be
multiplied by a large factor in the history of World War II. If war

meant what it did in this respect to me who was well favored, think what it meant to hundreds of thousands of young men and women to whom service meant liberation from squalor, drudgery, meniality, and suffocating monotony.

The second, equally imperious, need that war can satisfy is the need for community, the kind of community that is brought into existence by emergency and then reinforced by shared values and emotions which reach to the depths of human nature. The sense of community experienced in modern wars by the millions of soldiers in their squads, platoons, companies, even regiments and whole armies, was for a huge number of men and women wholly novel. Now for the first time in their lives they were separated from the economic exploitations, from egoistic calculations, from competition so often unrelieved by love and friendship, and from the long literalness of civil society. Any veteran knows well the closeness, the intimacy, the sense of bond and attachment that could spring up in a newly formed outfit almost overnight. So powerful and indestructible could this communal bond be that stories are legion of men separated from their units by injury and hospitalization and promised honorable release from future action who literally fought their way out of the rear echelon in order to rejoin their unit no matter where or in what exposure to hazard. And when the war ended, millions of men and women found return to civil life—for all the fact that this return had been passionately dreamed of—unsettling, disquieting, not seldom disorienting to neurotic degree. It was not the hell of a beachhead landing that was missed and subconsciously mourned; it was, in a word, community, the almost monastic closeness of personal life that went with the occasional hazardous operation. Studies have shown the extremely high positive correlation between the valor and fortitude of soldiers, their seeming immunity to combat fatigue, and their membership in a well-led, well-organized division within which a plurality of concentric communities existed.

There are equally pressing historical-institutional forces which add to the appeal, conscious or subconscious, or war. Those well-meaning *philosophes* in the French Enlightenment who thought war an enemy of intellectual and cultural progress were simply ignorant or blind. The unassailable truth is that, apart from war, there would be a great deal less of what is known as progress in the West, social as well as technological. This remains true even today when trade, commerce, and other forms of communication give man a degree of interaction with other peoples, cultures, and societies which was unknown until a century ago. War was especially important in primitive and ancient times. Everything in peacetime tended toward mere conservation of what was already possessed, not toward discovery of new worlds and horizons. Man is by nature a creature of habit. Some perceived block to normal existence, some crisis, is required to galvanize most people into activities other than their regular ones. This is true equally of groups. Primitive and ancient communities were compounded of ritual, routine, and rote. Initiative, boldness, and inventiveness were discouraged, even punished severely, for any departure from convention threatened to alienate the gods. War almost alone in the distant past made it possible for peoples to meet, and even in combat some degree of cultural intermixture was often reached, resulting in the liberation of the individual mind, however briefly, from accustomed idols.

The parts of the earth where civilization flowered earliest are the seaports, river valleys, and natural land routes where alien peoples in migration were most likely to be brought into contact with each other, and although in due time trade would provide the same opportunity for cultural mixture, it was in war alone that peoples of different gods first met. The building of empires came directly from military success, from the capturing and often enslavement of the defeated. The very essence of the ancient empire was military rule over large numbers of naturally unlike peoples, each with its own gods, sacred conventions, and fierce desire to protect these. Such imperial rule had the effect in time of melting many of the cultural differences and of yielding new ideas and values.

War has long been the nourisher of science and invention. Its stimulus to bravery is stimulus also to the inventive mind. For a long time engineering meant military engineering alone, which is the reason that at the beginning of the nineteenth century the word was prefaced with "civil" to distinguish it as a peacetime activity. The reception of gun powder in the West at the end of the Middle Ages and its immediate conversion to war use presented problems of casting, forging, and rifling guns and also of ballistics, which in a short time were transmuted into the problems of science. Tartaglia, often said to be the founder of dynamics in modern physics, took as his starting point the problems involved in the firing of cannon and in calculation of the trajectory of the balls fired. The great majority of mechanical inventions prior to the eighteenth century were within the military realm. When Leonardo once drew up a list of his accomplishments for a potential patron, nearly half of them were military weapons or fortification reinforcements. He listed painting and sculpture jointly as one accomplishment. The modern age has not appreciably changed the relation of war to technological inventions. With each major war in the twentieth century knowledge in science and engineering has spurted. Particularly important is the immense step forward medicine takes in war. Techniques of surgery can be experimented with in wartime hospitals in a measure that is lacking in peacetime. The same holds true for medicines, drugs, antibiotics, techniques of nursing, and anesthesia. Truly, as Roger Burlingame observed, if war were to be abolished, some substitute for it would have to be found so far as technological invention is concerned.

War has an impressive record with regard to the development of business. The first predictable large-scale demand for goods in early modern Europe was military, made in behalf of the enlarging standing armies. A great deal of the economically important coal industry was stimulated by military need; much the same was true of iron, its mining and processing. Standardized parts were military in the first· instance, used for weapons. The sewing machine was invented in France specifically for quicker processing of orders for uniforms. More important perhaps is the tonic effect wars usually have on the economies of the nations involved. World War I was followed by a great boom in the economy, as a consequence of the heightened productive capacity during the war and of the amount of consumer capital suddenly released when controls were taken off. The development of commercial radio and of air transportation was entirely a byproduct of the war and of the great amounts of development money the military could provide. The relation between both of these industries and military departments was very close until about 1924. Hollywood, a modest if promising industry before 1917, was given a tremendous boost by the use of hundreds of films for propaganda purposes in World War I. The same happened in World War II on a still larger scale. Hundreds of war movies were made by Hollywood in that war; television was brought forward chiefly through military use and experiment; so was the electronics industry. Another outcome of the war was the nuclear industry.

But war is salutary in another respect. It generally brings prosperity both during and afterward. Economists did not know how to bring the United States out of the Great Depression. Nothing tried by President Roosevelt worked to that end. The chief value of the New Deal was psychological. Unemployment totals were as high in 1937 as they had been four years earlier, and productivity was as low. The approach of war in Europe and the very evident intention in Roosevelt's mind of bringing America close to it if not actually into it began to give faint but evident stimulation to the economy by late 1938. By 1940 the business cycle was beginning to turn significantly, and from Pearl Harbor the story is of nothing but immense economic prosperity. Recession was predicted by many economists for the immediate postwar period, but there was none. On the home front during 1941–1946 there was an intoxication of economic growth with all its dividends to the masses. Economics has not yet learned the secrets of depression and prosperity, but war has.

Democracy, in all its variants, is the child of war. The first-known democracy in the world was that of Athens, and it was brought into being through the Cleisthenean reforms at the end of the sixth century B.C., which were stimulated largely by the need for drastic military reform. The first break with the time-honored solidarity of the Roman family took place when Augustus, in the interest of increasing the size of the legions, allowed the individual legionaries to keep for themselves all they earned in war instead of turning it over, as hoary custom demanded, to their families of birth. Most of the social character of imperial Rome—its greater moral and intellectual freedom, its closer and closer relation between the emperor and the masses, and its large number of entitlements to citizens—were products of what had been in the first instance limited to legionaries and to veterans of war. Condorcet, no friend of war, declared the rise of the infantry in the late Middle Ages the true beginning of democracy. The command of the socially leveled infantry might be severe, but it could not compete in authority with the hierarchical form of warfare fought in the feudal system. Garrisons were hatching places of first military and then, increasingly, civil democracy. Burke feared almost above anything else the "military democracy" that the French revolutionists had created in the interest of raising their mass armies. The universal conscription introduced as both a revolutionary and a war measure represented the consummation of this military democracy. No longer was the nobility the sole source of commissioned officers. Henceforth they rose from the ranks.

In both world wars in the twentieth century, long steps toward further democratization of society took place. The enfranchisement of women owed almost everything to the war record of women in the first war. Not from the ideology of socialism or social democracy came the numerous laws, decrees, and groups which greatly lightened the burdens of workers in the factories, but from the needs of war in 1917–1919. It was World War II that shook up ancient racial and ethnic taboos, the Fair Employment Practices Commission in that war serving as the serious start of legislation which in unending line would change the ethnic character of the American electorate. For good or ill, the Great Society legislation pushed through Congress by President Johnson was inspired by Johnson's desire to make more acceptable to the American people the war in Vietnam in which he was enmired. It was also the start of the greatest period of inflation in the twentieth century, but that is another issue.

The special kind of intellectual who loves to sit at the right hand of power cannot help but love war. The Italian humanists of the fifteenth century gave freely of themselves in advice and counsel to the dukes and others who were engaged in the innumerable city-state wars of that century. Humanists could reach hysterical heights of war fever on occasion. Consider these words from one of the most notable humanists, Salutati: "Thou knowest not how sweet is the *amor patriae:* if such would be expedient for the fatherland's protection or enlargement, it would seem neither burdensome and difficult nor a crime to thrust the axe into one's father's head, to crush one's brothers, to deliver from the womb of one's wife the premature child with the sword." Rare patriots, the humanists of the Renaissance. The *philosophes* in the eighteenth century also loved to mix war, or advice on war, with their enlightenment of the world. The so-called benevolent despots of the century were liked by the *philosophes* and never more so than when one or other of them were at war. Intellectuals flocked to participate in World War I under their beloved fellow-intellectual, President Wilson, in a way that was not shared by the great middle class of America. The opportunity to do great things on a large scale, to draw up in secret at the President's request the Fourteen Points, to dream up a league of nations, to help spread American democracy over all the world, such an opportunity was not to be missed by political intellectuals.

Intellectuals more than any other group in American life pushed the United States into full political and military intervention in South Vietnam under President Kennedy. Kennedy, it appears, was indecisive and apprehensive for a long time. But not McNamara, Rusk, Rostow, Bundy, Galbraith, and Schlesinger, nor a Pentagon intellectual named Daniel Ellsberg. All of them favored the fullest possible political intervention, even to the extent of deposing of President Diem, and most of them were equally in favor of military intervention. When Kennedy went into office, there were around nine hundred military advisers from the United States in South Vietnam; in 1963, at the time of Kennedy's assassination, there were sixteen thousand uniformed troops under a four-star general, along with tanks, helicopters, and other weapons of war. Moreover, virtually all of the intellectuals of the media were in favor of full political and if necessary military entry into Vietnam. The newspaper correspondents in Saigon—Halberstam, Browne, and Sheehan foremost among them—kept up a continuous din of hatred for Diem, and they had as much to do as any other political intellectuals with Diem's calculated fateful deposing by Washington and then his murder by the generals involved in the American-planned coup.

The great liability of political intellectuals, though, is the ease with which they can turn coats. Those involved in the Vietnam venture were happy about it until the new left in the United States stirred up American opposition to that war. Increasingly, the Hilsmans and McNamaras acquired the capacity to walk down both sides of the street at the same time—to be hawks by day, doves by night. But even that was not enough, and by 1966 most of them—Rostow and Rusk conspicuous exceptions—had walked out of the war party and into the antiwar party, with everybody blaming the war on Johnson the man who as Vice President had counseled against deposing Diem and sending more than modest increases in number of advisers to South Vietnam.

Entirely characteristic of the political intellectual at war was the preposterous Project Camelot that came into existence in 1962 under Kennedy's administration. It was a secret agency for the training of covert anti-insurgent operators to be sent to all parts of the world. The project was based in a university, manned by university professors, and had an all-academic advisory committee. Most of its members were liberal to radical in political convictions, but that only added spice to the work of remaking the world through the instrument of the army. Only when one of them became disaffected and told all to the press was the existence of Project Camelot made known to Congress and the media. Needless to say, most of the eager intellectuals fled immediately to the hills.

Whether war's historic contributions to the social bond, to science and technology, to the business cycle and the political state, will continue into the future is difficult to foresee. For some time after Hiroshima and Nagasaki it was said that the awful destructiveness of nuclear weapons had made war obsolete. But that had been said before, as when gunpowder was introduced into European war, or when the automatic machine gun, the Big Bertha, and the bomber made their successive appearances. During the decade before World War I the pacifist movement hoisted itself on the proposition that advances in weaponry had made war unthinkable. Between the end of World War I and the beginning of World War II a strong pacifist assault on the idea of national wars was mounted, evidenced in best-selling novels, movies, testaments, investigations of the munitions industry, and resolutions by college students on both sides of the Atlantic never to go to war again.

The Middle East, Latin America, and parts of Africa are three areas where wars show little sign of decreasing, the nuclear age notwithstanding. What America's response to them will be is far from clear. Vietnam, the most unpopular war in American history, has left deep scars on the American consciousness, and it will be a long time before they disappear. There is also the strong possibility of the will to war disappearing in the Western nations and also Japan. It would not have seemed possible a half-century ago that the world's two most militaristic nations, Germany and Japan, would be among the least militaristic and the most commerce-minded within a decade after World War II. Pacifism is not the word to describe the sentiments of apparent majorities in the Western countries, for it is too positive in thrust; passivity, a sense of futility, and dogged fear of becoming enmired in another Vietnam are more nearly the sentiments of the majority.

World War II may be the final European national war. Should the Soviet Union strike the West, it will not be a traditional national war but one of collectivist aggression in the name of the people of the world, as defined by the Politburo. Guerrilla wars and terrorist activities are bound to increase in the future, as these forms of war are very difficult for a great nation to cope with. Declarations of war are already close to obsolete. The specter of nuclear war among the superpowers, the United States and the Soviet Union, has to be felt for as long as there are nuclear weapons, and these will assuredly increase steadily, not only in the two great powers, but in other, smaller, less predictable nations and peoples.

On the whole, though, so far as war's impact upon culture and society is concerned, the presence of nuclear weapons is less responsible for the unpredictability of the future than is the general fragmentation of war: from conflict among ancient empires and nation-states in the West to a devil's potpourri of ethnic, racial, mini-state, border, and guerrilla wars. War was for a long time in man's history an empire-building, state-strengthening, and society-galvanizing phenomenon within which there could be exhilaration, patriotic fervor, a marked tightening of community, a freedom from passivity and boredom, and a general sense of participation in something great if not moral. Those luxuries appear to be gone from the present world of war.

WIT

THE NINETEENTH CENTURY English wit Sidney Smith once observed in melancholy that while he had sunk by his own levity, his theologian-brother had risen by his gravity. A good case can be made for the proposition that those who live by the quip are more likely to be themselves slain than to slay others with it. One brief eruption of Oscar Wilde's wit in the courtroom when he was on trial for sodomy did more than the evidence to bring in a judgment of guilt and two years of confinement in Reading Gaol. When Alger Hiss was under Senate Committee investigation in August 1948 after he had been charged by Chambers with having been a Communist and traitor, he had a generally compliant and genial committee before him until his efforts at wit, combined with a certain arrogance, changed the temper of the committee, the result being two trials, imprisonment in the federal penitentiary, and disgrace.

A single bit of caustic wit by Thomas E. Dewey in his 1948 campaign against President Truman, made at the expense of the locomotive engineer who had inadvertently backed up Dewey's train too far at a speaking spot, almost certainly cost him that very close election. Locomotive engineers were still heroic figures in America, and Dewey was not. Adlai Stevenson is the candidate *par excellence* in the lists of politicians who sank by their levity. The relatively dour Eisenhower kept looking more and more responsible to the American people. Very probably the fatal burst of wit for Stevenson occurred after Norman Vincent Peale, a clergyman nationally revered for his radio and television sermons and his best-selling books, had indicated his own preference for Eisenhower. Stevenson, in Saint Paul and with a vast radio audience before him, could not resist saying: "Saint Paul is appealing and Saint Peale is appalling." Amusing, without question, but costly.

Wit cast in polemical form and made into a genuine weapon of attack might occasionally succeed, provided it is cast in proper rhetoric, the kind that can bring an audience quickly and enthusiastically into the spirit. There was a degree of wit, or at least high humor, in Franklin Roosevelt's famous refrain "Martin, Barton, and Fish" in a campaign speech for reelection in 1940, but far more important than whatever wit might lie in this attack upon three Republican Congressmen was the opportunity skillfully given a large audience to pick it up as a refrain in tumultuous answer to Roosevelt's astute rhetorical questions. The same holds with the Falla story: political merriment, not wit. Nor was it wit in the true sense when Churchill, though concededly one of the great wits of the century, aroused his Canadian Parliament and large radio audience with the words "Some chicken; some *neck*" as he paid his respects to the Hitler who had promised to wring England's neck as he would a chicken's. Suppose Churchill had in a campaign, before a large audience, used another celebrated piece of his wit, "An empty car drove up, and out stepped Clement Attlee." Or tried to regale an audience with his reply to a cockney member of Parliament who, having told Churchill that he had an 'ell of an 'eadache, received the reassuring words, "Nothing that a couple of aspirates won't take care of." It is a good guess that many of Churchill's hearers would think that a reincarnation of the playboy Churchill of the 1920s and early 1930s had occurred, and they would not like it. Lincoln saved his wit and humor for Cabinet meetings and other small occasions. There is classic oratory in his Second Inaugural, phrase after memorable phrase, but no wit.

One thinks of Mencken. He will be known forever as the wit who chose to lacerate the booboisie of America and to deliver daily thwacks to the Bible Belt. And his wit could indeed be coruscating, well worth preservation in miscellanies. But in the body of the wit was lost the body of Mencken the literary critic and philologist. For at least fifteen years Mencken was writing the best, truest, and most creative literary criticism in this country, and it was through his labors alone that several novelists, American and foreign, received the laurels due them. There have been few editors of Mencken's equal during his great years on *The American Mercury*; his cultivation of new writing talent is legendary. Finally, his study of the American language, reaching some three volumes before he turned his hand elsewhere, falls among the classics of philology. There is little doubt that had Mencken restrained his Rabelaisian sense of humor, disregarded the denizens of the Bible Belt and the nation's Rotary Clubs, and confined himself solely to literary criticism and his study of the American language, he would be now known as one of the most original, learned, and forceful scholar-critics of the first half of this century. Happily, there is no evidence at present, as there was in the past, of a loss of interest in Mencken. But so much said, he did pay a heavy price for his wit.

I have known academic minds of genuine if never outstanding wit, minds able to animate a lunch table or cocktail party regularly, to become famous on the campus for their wit, but I have never known one of these to reach the highest level of regard as scholar or teacher even when it seemed to me that many of them were fully equal in the substance of their scholarship to those who had arrived at the top level of regard by contemporaries. Wit can be as risky in academic as political career. Too much of it, or any of it at the wrong time, will offset the serious theme of a lecture no matter how distinguished that theme may be. Too much wit, and listeners will go away half forgetting the profound substance of the lecture with only the wit in mind, and soon the reputation of the academic has been securely established: a very witty mind, but thin in scholarship. If I list in my mind the ten greatest, most influential and admired men and women I have been privileged to know in forty years on university campuses, I think of only one who had some degree of wit, and he confined it to office or home; never did it enter a lecture or published research. These figures, one and all, humanist and scientist, rose by their *gravitas*, perhaps the most honored of Roman virtues.